Gratian the Theologian

Studies in Medieval and Early Modern Canon Law

Kenneth Pennington, General Editor

Studies in Medieval and Early Modern Canon Law

VOLUME 13

Gratian the Theologian

John C. Wei

The Catholic University of America Press
Washington, D.C.

Library of Congress Cataloging-in-Publication Data
Wei, John C.
Gratian the theologian / John C. Wei.
pages cm. — (Studies in medieval and early modern canon law ; Volume 13)
Includes bibliographical references and index.
ISBN 978-0-8132-3635-3 (pbk : alk. paper) 1. Gratian, active 12th century. 2. Theology—History—Middle Ages, 600–1500.
3. Penance—History of doctrines—Middle Ages, 600–1500. I. Title.
BX4705.G61835W45 2016
262.9'22—dc23 2015032939

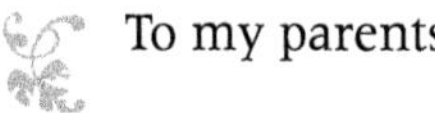

To my parents

Contents

Tables

Preface

Numerous friends and colleagues have contributed to this book and the ideas contained therein. My deepest thanks go to Anders Winroth, who provided me with advice and encouragement throughout the entire process. I have also benefited greatly from the input of Marcia Colish, Tatsushi Genka, Cédric Giraud, Joseph Goering, Eric Knibbs, Atria Larson, Titus Lenherr, Russell Osgood, Pablo Silva, Mary Stroll, and CUA Press's reviewers. I would like to thank Peter Clarke and Kate Cushing for organizing annual sessions at Leeds, where I presented the paper that became the core of chapter 6. Peter Landau and Jörg Müller of the Stephan Kuttner Institute of Medieval Canon Law (at that time in Munich, since then transferred to New Haven) kindly provided me with hospitality and resources the many times I visited, as did first Harald Siems and then Susanne Lepsius of the Leopold-Wenger Institut für Rechtsgeschichte. The staff members at both the Bayerische Staatsbibliothek and the Monumenta Germaniae Historica were immensely patient and generous with my requests.

Without funding, of course, I never would have had the time or resources necessary for completing this project. My thanks go to the Fulbright Program, which provided me with a research fellowship for the academic year 2006–7; the National Endowment for the Humanities for a summer stipend in 2010 for the study of a work closely related to Gratian's theological sources, the early scholastic sentence collection *Deus non habet initium uel terminum;* and the Alexander von Humboldt-Stiftung for a research fellowship in Munich for the academic year 2011–12.

It goes without saying that I alone am responsible for the various oversights, misinterpretations, and errors that undoubtedly still remain.

A Note on the Sources

I generally give the material sources of Gratian's canons and, where relevant, the formal sources as well. For papal letters, I usually provide only the number in Jaffé's *Regesta*. But I always provide more exact references for forged papal letters, for example, the *False Decretals*. For other material sources, such as conciliar canons or patristic texts, I always provide citations to specific editions. For canonical collections, I provide citations to specific pages in the relevant edition only where I actually quote from the edition. Where I rely on manuscripts, I always provide a citation.

Some of the secondary literature cited in this book has been collected and reprinted in volumes with continuous pagination. When citing such literature, I give both the original pagination and the new pagination from the reprint, which is sometimes distinguished in the volumes by an appended asterisk.

Abbreviations

3L	*Collection in Three Books*
ac	ante correctionem
add.	addidit
AKKR	*Archiv für katholisches Kirchenrecht*
App.	Appendix
BAV	Biblioteca Apostolica Vaticana
BGPM	Beiträge zur Geschichte der Philosophie des Mittelalters
BGPTM	Beiträge zur Geschichte der Philosophie und Theologie des Mittelalters
BMCL	*Bulletin of Medieval Canon Law*, new series
BNF	Bibliothèque nationale de France
C.	Causa
c.	canon/capitulum
Capit.	Capitularia
Capit. episc.	Capitula episcoporum
CCCM	Corpus Christianorum Continuatio Mediaevalis
CCSL	Corpus Christianorum Series Latina
Cod.	Code of Justinian
Conc.	Concilia
CSEL	Corpus Scriptorum Ecclesiasticorum Latinorum
D.	Distinction
De cons.	*De consecratione*
De pen.	*De penitentia*
del.	delevit
Dig.	*Digest of Justinian*

d.a.c.	dictum ante canonem/capitulum
d.p.c.	dictum post canonem/capitulum
Epp.	Epistolae
fol./fols.	folio/folios
Fontes iuris	*Fontes iuris Germanici antiqui in usum scholarum separatim editi*
Friedb.	*Corpus iuris canonici* 1: *Decretum magistri Gratiani* (ed. Friedberg)
inscr.	inscription
JE, JK, JL	Philip Jaffé, *Regesta pontificum romanorum* [Samuel Löwenfeld, Ferdinand Kaltenbrunner, and Paul Ewald assisted with the preparation of the work. Hence JK is used for letters to the year 590, JE for letters dating to 590–882, and JL for letters dating to 883–1198]
LdL	*Libelli de lite imperatorum et pontificum*
MGH	*Monumenta Germaniae Historica*
MIC.A	*Monumenta Iuris Canonici, series A: Corpus Glossatorum*
MIC.B	*Monumenta Iuris Canonici, series B: Corpus Collectionum*
MIC.C	*Monumenta Iuris Canonici, series C: Subsidia*
om.	omisit
pc	post correctionem
PG	*Patrologiae Cursus Completus, Series Graeca* (ed. Migne)
PL	*Patrologiae Cursus Completus, Series Latina* (ed. Migne)
pr.	principium
praem.	praemisit
q.	quaestio
r	recto
RDC	*Revue de droit canonique*
RTAM	*Recherches de théologie ancienne et médiévale*
SS	Scriptores
sup. lin.	supra lineam
tit.	titulus
tr.	transposuit
v	verso
v.	verbum
Werck.	*Décret de Gratien: Causes 27 à 36* (ed. Werckmeister)
ZRG KA	*Zeitschrift der Savigny-Stiftung für Rechtsgeschichte, Kanonistische Abteilung*

Gratian the Theologian

Introduction

Few, if any, medieval jurists have achieved as prominent a place in the Western legal tradition as Gratian, the "father of the science of canon law."[1] His *Concordia discordantium canonum* or *Decretum*, as the book later became known, was the medieval equivalent of a modern bestseller, but even more successful and influential.[2] Almost immediately after its publication, the *Decretum* became the foundational textbook for a new academic discipline of canon law and a valid law book in Catholic ecclesiastical courts.[3] As the first volume of what would eventually become the *Corpus iuris canonici*, the *Decretum* for centuries provided the starting point for the analysis and elaboration of canon law issues.[4] Teachers developed and refined new le-

1. Stephan Kuttner, "The Father of the Science of Canon Law," *The Jurist* 1 (1941): 2–19.

2. The more than six hundred extant medieval manuscripts that we currently know of testify to the *Decretum*'s success. For lists and descriptions, see Stephan Kuttner, *Repertorium der Kanonistik (1140–1234): Prodromus corporis glossarum*, Studi e testi 71 (Vatican City: Biblioteca Apostolica Vaticana [hereafter "BAV"], 1937), 1–122; Anthony Melnikas, *The Corpus of the Miniatures in the Manuscripts of Decretum Gratiani*, 3 vols., Studia Gratiana 16–18 (Vatican City: Studia Gratiana, 1973–75); Rudolf Weigand, *Die Glossen zum Dekret Gratians: Studien zu den frühen Glossen und Glossenkompositionen*, Studia Gratiana 25–26 (Rome: Libreria Ateneo Salesiano, 1991), 661–1004.

3. The best English-language introductions to medieval canon law are James A. Brundage, *Medieval Canon Law* (London: Longman, 1995) and Richard H. Helmholz, *The Spirit of Classical Canon Law* (Athens: University of Georgia Press, 1996). But see also the Catholic University of America Press's History of Medieval Canon Law series and Anders Winroth and John C. Wei, eds., *The Cambridge History of Medieval Canon Law* (forthcoming).

4. That is why modern monographs on medieval canon law doctrines typi-

gal doctrines by lecturing on and engaging with the ideas set forth in the book.[5] In turn, the body of jurisprudence that resulted from the learned commentary of the schools influenced the legislative decisions of contemporary popes and councils, particularly the new decretals and canons that came to form the *ius novum*.[6] Together with medieval Roman law, these canonical sources and their learned commentary comprised a pan-European legal system, the *ius commune*.[7]

On account of these later developments, modern scholars have generally focused on Gratian as a jurist. They have looked at his treatment of legal and jurisprudential subjects, explored his connection to earlier canonical and Roman law works, and examined how later legislators and jurists developed or modified his teachings. However, the *Decretum* treats a far wider range of issues than what we today would consider either "law" (rules, standards, or principles for ordering human activities and relations that are enforceable in court) or "jurisprudence" (reflection on law), and Gratian's treat-

cally begin with an examination of the *Decretum* before moving on to a study of the decretists, papal decretals, and decretalists. See, e.g., Patrick Hersperger, *Kirche, Magie und "Aberglaube": Superstitio in der Kanonistik des 12. und 13. Jahrhunderts* (Cologne: Böhlau, 2009).

5. This development can be traced in the abundant glosses written for the *Decretum*. On the evolution of the glosses and gloss apparatuses to the *Decretum*, see Rudolf Weigand, "The Development of the *Glossa ordinaria* to the *Decretum*," in *The History of Medieval Canon Law in the Classical Period, 1140–1234: From Gratian to the Decretals of Pope Gregory IX*, ed. Wilfried Hartmann and Kenneth Pennington (Washington, D.C.: The Catholic University of America Press, 2008), 55–97, which summarizes the results of Weigand, *Glossen zum Dekret Gratians*.

6. See, e.g., Walther Holtzmann, "Die Benutzung Gratians in der päpstlichen Kanzlei im 12. Jahrhundert," *Studia Gratiana* 1 (1953): 323–49; André Artonne, "L'influence du Décret de Gratien sur les statuts synodaux," *Studia Gratiana* 2 (1954): 643–56. See also Antonio García y García, "The Fourth Lateran Council and the Canonists," in *The History of Medieval Canon Law in the Classical Period*, ed. Hartmann and Pennington, 367–78, at 368: "The major sources used by Innocent [III] in these constitutions [of the Fourth Lateran Council of 1215] are the *Decretum* of Gratian. . . ." On the development of decretal law, see Kenneth Pennington, "The Decretalists 1190–1234," in ibid., 211–45; Charles Duggan, "Decretal Collections from Gratian's *Decretum* to the *Compilationes antiquae*: The Making of the New Case Law," in ibid., 246–92; Kenneth Pennington, "Decretal Collections 1190–1234," in ibid., 293–317.

7. On the *ius commune*, see Manlio Bellomo, *The Common Legal Past of Europe, 1000–1800*, trans. Lydia G. Cochrane (Washington, D.C.: The Catholic University of America Press, 1995).

ment of these other issues is often bound up with his treatment of legal and jurisprudential ones.

The topic of this book, what I shall call Gratian's "theology," provides a notable example. In the narrow, etymological sense prevalent in the early twelfth century, theology referred simply to "discourse about God," that is, the study of the divine nature.[8] During the course of the twelfth century, however, the term acquired a broader meaning, one that eventually came to encompass almost anything related to God's activity in creation and salvation, but which most later writers agreed did not include canon law.[9] Because Gratian worked at a time when the narrow definition of theology was still prevalent, he almost certainly would not have thought of himself as a theologian, and this book will not argue that he did. However, as Gratian also worked prior to the development of theology and canon law into distinct academic disciplines, he produced much that we would today consider theology rather than—or perhaps in addition to—law and jurisprudence. It is in the later medieval and modern sense that this book shall speak of and try to shed light on Gratian the theologian.

Modern assessments of Gratian the theologian have varied widely. In a posthumous work published in 1918, the famous German jurist Rudolph Sohm argued that the *Decretum* treats nothing but the sacraments and, consequently, that Gratian was exclusively a theologian and not a jurist.[10] Most scholars in the immediately following decades rejected Sohm's thesis, espousing instead the view that Gra-

8. That is why Peter Abelard's various *Theologiae,* which date to the 1120s and 1130s, are not proto-*summae,* but instead deal merely with the doctrine of the Trinity.

9. For an overview, see Yves Congar, *A History of Theology,* trans. Hunter Guthrie (New York: Doubleday, 1968), 25–36. A few prominent writers, most notably the decretist Rufinus (fl. 1160s) and the decretalist Hostiensis (ca. 1200–1271), defended the view that canon law was a form of theology. Heinrich Singer, "Einleitung" to *Die Summa decretorum des Rufinus* (Paderborn: Schöningh, 1902), lxvi n5; Arturo Rivera Damas, *Pensamiento político de Hostiensis: Estudio jurídico—histórico sobre las relaciones entre el Sacerdocio y el Imperio en los escritos de Enrique de Susa* (Zurich: Pas-Verlag, 1964), 39–42. But most other theologians and canonists took the opposite view and tried to distinguish canon law from theology based on subject matter or method (see below).

10. Rudolph Sohm, *Das altkatholische Kirchenrecht und das Dekret Gratians* (Munich: Duncker and Humblot, 1918).

tian was both a theologian and a jurist.[11] In the 1950s, a new picture of Gratian began to dominate: one that claimed he was mostly a jurist and only incidentally a theologian, if at all. Various scholars argued that the theological sections of the *Decretum* were later additions.[12] Other scholars proposed interpretations of Gratian and his work that minimized the significance of theology. Stanley Chodorow, for instance, argued that the *Decretum* was a work of political theory and contained only a minimal amount of theology, at least in its original conception.[13] Similarly, R. W. Southern maintained that Gratian was a practicing jurist rather than a master of theology, as older biographies sometimes asserted.[14]

For the most part, these differing interpretations of Gratian the theologian have been due to the number and nature of the extant sources. Aside from the *Decretum*, we have little to no reliable sources of information concerning who Gratian was or what he was trying to accomplish with his textbook. In addition, the *Decretum* itself makes no explicit statement about Gratian's biography and only one explicit statement about the *Decretum*'s purpose. The original title, *Concordia discordantium canonum* (*Concord of Discordant Canons*), indicates that the *Decretum*'s methodological goal was to bring "harmony from dissonance," to use Stephan Kuttner's classic phrase: that is, to reconcile the numerous contradictory authorities in the church's legal and disciplinary tradition.[15] But what other information there is

11. E.g., Stephan Kuttner, "Zur Frage der theologischen Vorlagen Gratians," *Zeitschrift der Savigny-Stiftung für Rechtsgeschichte, Kanonistische Abteilung* [hereafter "*ZRG KA*"] 23 (1934): 243–68, reprinted in his *Gratian and the Schools of Law, 1140–1234*, Variorum Collected Studies Series CS185, 2nd ed. (London: Variorum, 1994), no. III.

12. E.g., Karol Wojtyła, "Le traité 'De penitencia' de Gratien dans l'abrégé de Gdansk," *Studia Gratiana* 7 (1959): 357–90.

13. Stanley Chodorow, *Christian Political Theory and Church Politics in the Mid-Twelfth Century: The Ecclesiology of Gratian's Decretum* (Berkeley: University of California Press, 1972).

14. R. W. Southern, *Scholastic Humanism and the Unification of Europe*, 2 vols. (Oxford: Blackwell, 1995–2001), 1:285–86 and 301–4.

15. Stephan Kuttner, *Harmony from Dissonance: An Interpretation of Medieval Canon Law* (Latrobe, Pa.: Archabbey Press, 1960), reprinted in his *History of Ideas and Doctrines of Canon Law*, Variorum Collected Studies Series CS113, 2nd ed. (London: Variorum, 1993), no. I.

to be gleaned about the *Decretum* must be inferred, and inferences based on the work's text and structure have until recently rested on a shaky textual foundation.

For almost a millennium, scholars were able to approach the author of the *Decretum* only through the longer form of the text found in most medieval manuscripts and modern printed editions, including the standard edition edited by Emil Friedberg.[16] As printed by Friedberg, the *Decretum* consists of three main parts: a series of 101 distinctions on the sources of law and the ecclesiastical hierarchy; thirty-six *causae*, each of which begins with a hypothetical legal scenario known as a case statement, followed by two or more *quaestiones*; and a tract on liturgical and sacramental matters known as *De consecratione*, which is subdivided into five distinctions. The third question of the thirty-third *causa* corresponds to a tract on penance known as *De penitentia*, which, like *De consecratione*, is divided into distinctions. Each distinction and question consists of a combination of the compiler's own words ("dicta") and "canons" or "chapters," that is, texts of or excerpts from authoritative sources of law or doctrine, such as the Bible, papal decretals, conciliar canons, Roman law, secular law, and the writings of ecclesiastical authors (such as the Church Fathers). Some sections of the *Decretum* have a high proportion of dicta to canons, whereas canons far outnumber dicta in other sections.[17]

In the early twentieth century, scholars began to realize that the long form of the *Decretum* contains many interpolations and additions that probably do not stem from the original author himself. The *paleae*—canons found in only some complete manuscripts of the *Decretum*, generally labeled *paleae*, whose origins date to the second half of the twelfth century—present the most well-known example.[18] But scholars also found indications that other sections of

16. Emil Friedberg, ed., *Corpus iuris canonici* 1: *Decretum magistri Gratiani* (Leipzig: Veit, 1879; reprinted Graz: Akademische Druck- u. Verlagsanstalt, 1959).

17. On these points, see Peter Landau, "Gratian and the *Decretum Gratiani*," in *The History of Medieval Canon Law in the Classical Period*, ed. Hartmann and Pennington, 22–54, at 25–42.

18. On the *paleae* and their history, see Rudolf Weigand, "Versuch einer neuen, differenzierten Liste der Paleae und Dubletten im Dekret Gratians," *Bulletin of*

the *Decretum* were later additions. Writing shortly after World War II, Adam Vetulani presented convincing arguments that most of the Roman law texts in the long form of the *Decretum* were added at only a late stage in the composition.[19] And beginning in the 1950s Jacqueline Rambaud drew attention to evidence that *De consecratione* was also a later addition.[20]

In the decades that followed, scholars developed increasingly sophisticated methods to determine how the *Decretum* was constructed. Three scholars were particularly important. The first, Peter Landau, showed that while the canons in the *Decretum* ultimately derive from a large number of "material" sources (original sources), Gratian took most of the *Decretum*'s canons from just a small number of "formal" sources (intermediate collections).[21] A second scholar, Titus Lenherr, showed how identification of the *Decretum*'s formal sources could be used to reconstruct the way in which various sections of the *Decretum* were stitched together.[22] Building on the findings and meth-

---

Medieval Canon Law, new series [hereafter "*BMCL*"] 23 (1999): 114–28; Jürgen Buchner, *Die Paleae im Dekret Gratians: Untersuchung ihrer Echtheit* (Rome: Pontificium Athenaeum Antonianum, 2000).

19. Adam Vetulani, "Gratien et le droit romain," *Revue historique de droit français et étranger*, ser. 4, 24/25 (1946/1947): 11–48, reprinted in his *Sur Gratien et les décrétales*, ed. Wacław Uruszczak, Variorum Collected Studies Series CS308 (Aldershot: Variorum, 1990), no. III; Adam Vetulani, "Encore un mot sur le droit romain dans le *Décret* de Gratien," *Apollinarius* 21 (1948): 129–34, reprinted in ibid., no. IV.

20. Jacqueline Rambaud, "L'étude des manuscrits du Décret de Gratien conservés en France," *Studia Gratiana* 1 (1953): 119–45, at 129–30; Jacqueline Rambaud, "Le legs de l'ancien droit: Gratien," in *L'âge classique, 1140–1378: Sources et théories du droit*, ed. Gabriel le Bras, Charles Lefebvre, and Jacqueline Rambaud, Histoire du Droit et des Institutions de l'Église en Occident 7 (Paris: Sirey, 1965), 3–129, at 90–99.

21. Peter Landau, "Neue Forschungen zu vorgratianischen Kanonessammlungen und den Quellen des gratianischen Dekrets," *Ius Commune* 11 (1984): 1–29, reprinted in his *Kanones und Dekretalen: Beiträge zur Geschichte der Quellen des kanonischen Rechts* (Goldbach: Keip, 1997), 177*–205*, with retractations at 475*–77*; Landau, "Quellen und Bedeutung des gratianischen Dekrets," *Studia et Documenta Historiae et Iuris* 52 (1986): 218–35, reprinted in his *Kanones und Dekretalen*, 207*–24*, with retractations at 477*–79*.

22. Titus Lenherr, *Die Exkommunikations- und Depositionsgewalt der Häretiker bei Gratian und den Dekretisten bis zur Glossa ordinaria des Johannes Teutonicus* (St. Ottilien: EOS Verlag, 1987).

ods of Landau and Lenherr, a third scholar, Anders Winroth, made a groundbreaking discovery in the 1990s. Winroth demonstrated that manuscripts previously believed to contain abbreviations of the *Decretum* in fact contain an earlier version, now generally referred to as the "first recension."[23] Subsequent studies confirmed his findings.[24] The first recension contains a shorter and more coherent text of the *Decretum* than the long form found in other medieval manuscripts and printed editions. Canons that source analysis reveals to belong to later redactional layers are missing in the first recension, as are texts long suspected of being later additions, such as most of the *paleae*, Roman law excerpts, and *De consecratione*.

Today, virtually all scholars accept the correctness of Winroth's primary claim, that the first recension contains an earlier form of the *Decretum* than the long form. But other arguments by Winroth have met with less acceptance. In Winroth's view, the first recension constitutes a true recension of the *Decretum*—that is, a distinct published work—and its author, whom he calls "Gratian 1," differs from "Gratian 2," the person responsible for the longer, vulgate form of the *Decretum*, which he dubs the "second recension."[25] However, some scholars contend to the contrary that the same person was responsible for both the first and the second recensions and that the manu-

23. Anders Winroth, "The Making of Gratian's *Decretum*" (PhD diss., Columbia University, 1996).

24. The bibliography is vast. Among the most important studies are: Anders Winroth, *The Making of Gratian's Decretum* (Cambridge: Cambridge University Press, 2000); Rudolf Weigand, "Causa 25 des Dekrets und die Arbeitsweise Gratians," in *Grundlagen des Rechts: Festschrift für Peter Landau zum 65. Geburtstag*, ed. Richard H. Helmholz et al. (Paderborn: Schöningh, 2000), 277–90; Mary E. Sommar, "Gratian's Causa VII and the Multiple Recension Theories," *BMCL* 24 (2000–2001): 78–96; Tatsushi Genka, "Zur textlichen Grundlage der Imputationslehre Gratians," *BMCL* 25 (2002–3): 40–81; Kenneth Pennington, "La Causa 19, Graziano, e lo Ius commune," in *La cultura giuridico-canonica medioevale: Premesse per un dialogo ecumenico*, ed. Enrique de León and Nicolás Álvarez de las Asturias (Milan: Giuffrè, 2003), 211–32; Frederick S. Paxton, "Gratian's Thirteenth Case and the Composition of the *Decretum*," in *Proceedings of the Eleventh International Congress of Medieval Canon Law*, ed. Manlio Bellomo and Orazio Condorelli, *Monumenta Iuris Canonici, series C: Subsidia* [hereafter "MIC.C"] 12 (Vatican City: BAV, 2006), 119–30; John C. Wei, "Law and Religion in Gratian's *Decretum*" (PhD diss., Yale University, 2008).

25. Winroth, *Making*, esp. 122–96.

scripts present us with snapshots of different, largely haphazard stages of the *Decretum*'s development rather than being true recensions of the work.[26] Various proponents of this latter position furthermore claim that a manuscript from St. Gall, not originally studied by Winroth, contains an even earlier stage of the *Decretum* than the one attested to by the "first" recension.[27] While highly technical, these textual disputes are of great interpretive significance. One's picture of the origins and development of law and jurisprudence in the early to mid-twelfth century will look very different depending on whether one follows Winroth or instead the various theses of his main critics, particularly if one accepts the priority of the St. Gall form of the *Decretum*.

The present book contributes to and sheds light on these debates and issues by reconsidering and reevaluating an under-studied aspect of Gratian's work, his theology. Since Winroth's discovery of the first recension, more and more scholars have come to pay attention to Gratian's theology, both in its own right and as it contributes to his analysis of legal and jurisprudential issues. Titus Lenherr has done groundbreaking research into Gratian's use of the *Glossa ordinaria* to the Bible, the role of biblical texts in the *Decretum*, and Gratian's direct use of patristic texts.[28] Tatsushi Genka has investigated Gratian's possible use of Peter Abelard's *Sic et non* and the role of patristic texts in Gratian's doctrine of culpability.[29] Anders Winroth has studied the relationship between certain aspects of Gratian's doctrine

26. E.g., Carlos Larrainzar, "La formación del Decreto de Graciano por etapas," *ZRG KA* 87 (2001): 67–83; Larrainzar, "Métodos para el análisis de la formación literaria del Decretum Gratiani: 'Etapas' y 'esquemas' de redacción," in *Proceedings of the Thirteenth International Congress of Medieval Canon Law*, ed. Peter Erdö and Sz. Anzelm Szuromi, MIC.C 14 (Vatican City: BAV, 2010), 85–116.

27. See chapter 1.

28. Titus Lenherr, "Die 'Glossa ordinaria' zur Bibel als Quelle von Gratians Dekret: Ein (neuer) Anfang," *BMCL* 24 (2000): 97–129; Lenherr, "Zur Redaktionsgeschichte von C.23 q.5 in der '1. Rezension' von Gratians Dekret: The Making of a Quaestio," *BMCL* 26 (2004–6): 31–58; Lenherr, "Langsame Annäherung an Gratians Exemplar der 'Moralia in Iob,'" in *Proceedings of the Thirteenth International Congress of Medieval Canon Law*, ed. Erdö and Szuromi, 311–26.

29. Genka, "Zur textlichen Grundlage"; Genka, "Gratians Umgang mit seinen Quellen in der C.15 q.1," in *"Panta rei": Studi dedicati a Manlio Bellomo*, ed. Orazio Condorelli, 5 vols. (Rome: Il Cigno Edizioni, 2004), 2:421–44.

of marriage and contemporary theological writings.[30] Finally, both Atria Larson and I have written on Gratian's penitential theology.[31]

Building on and going beyond these narrower, more specialized studies, this book attempts to understand at a broader level and more comprehensively how "Gratian"—the name I will use to refer to Winroth's Gratian 1—approached theology, what Gratian believed, and the way that theology shaped both the first recension and Gratian's treatment of legal and jurisprudential issues. This book will look at the second recension only occasionally, and when it does, it will always signal that it is turning to the "redactor of the second recension," which is the name I will use for Winroth's Gratian 2. My book treats three topics: Gratian's handling of the Bible, his penitential theology, and his treatment of the sacraments and the liturgy.

All three of these topics concern, at least in part, what later medievals and we moderns would consider to be theology. As theology and canon law developed into distinct academic disciplines over the course of the twelfth and thirteenth centuries, theologians and canonists began to draw boundaries between their respective subjects and in the process allocated the Bible, penitential theology, and certain sacramental and liturgical questions to the theologians.

Writing around 1180, Peter of Blois the Younger differentiated the types of law studied by theologians and canonists and assigned the Bible to the former. Theologians, he writes, concern themselves with natural law and Mosaic, prophetic, evangelical, and apostol-

30. Anders Winroth, "Neither Slave Nor Free: Theology and Law in Gratian's Thoughts on the Definition of Marriage," in *Medieval Church Law and the Origins of the Western Legal Tradition: A Tribute to Kenneth Pennington*, ed. Wolfgang P. Müller and Mary E. Sommar (Washington, D.C.: The Catholic University of America Press, 2006), 153–71.

31. Atria A. Larson, *Master of Penance: Gratian and the Development of Penitential Thought and Law in the Twelfth Century* (Washington, D.C.: The Catholic University of America Press, 2014); John C. Wei, "Gratian and the School of Laon," *Traditio* 64 (2009): 279–322; Wei, "Penitential Theology in Gratian's *Decretum*: Critique and Criticism of the Treatise *Baptizato homine*," *ZRG KA* 95 (2008): 78–100. See also Wei, "The Sentence Collection *Deus non habet initium uel terminum* and Its Reworking, *Deus itaque summe atque ineffabiliter bonus*," *Mediaeval Studies* 73 (2011): 1–118; Wei, "A Twelfth-Century Treatise on Charity: The Tract 'Vt autem hoc euidenter' of the Sentence Collection *Deus itaque summe atque ineffabiliter bonus*," *Mediaeval Studies* 74 (2012): 1–50.

ic law (that is, the law found in the Bible), whereas canonists concern themselves with canon law in the narrow sense of the term.[32] Around a decade later, the decretist *summa "Reverentia sacrorum canonum"* repeated these ideas.[33]

In the thirteenth century, however, thinkers began to differentiate theology and canon law based on method and the type of questions investigated rather than just subject matter. Bonaventure of Bagnoregio, for instance, located the distinction between theology and canon law in their formal objects. Canon law, he states, concerns itself with *quia* (how things are), whereas theology concerns itself with *propter quid* (why things are the way they are).[34] Augustinus Triumphus agreed with Bonaventure's analysis, but in his *Summa de potestate ecclesiastica* from 1320 listed additional ways in which theology and canon law differ from each other, several of which are relevant for understanding how theologians and canonists came to divide penance between them. Theology, Augustinus Triumphus wrote, is geared principally toward contemplation, canon law to action and practical solutions. Theology concerns primarily the worship of God and the integrity of the faith, while canon law treats the ecclesiastical hierarchy and business (*negotia*). And theology pertains more to uni-

32. Peter of Blois, *Speculum iuris canonici*, ed. Theophilus Augustus Reimarus, *Petri Blesensis opusculum de distinctionibus in canonum interpretatione adhibendis sive, ut auctor voluit, speculum iuris canonici* (Berlin: Sumtibus G. Reimeri, 1887), 6: "Secundum diuersos hominum status et tempora, diuersa institutionum genera prodierunt. Prima quidem fuit lex naturalis, secunda lex Mosaica, tertia prophetica, quarta euangelica, quinta apostolica, sexta canonica. Sed quia theologice considerationis est de quinque primis disserere, solius sexte et ultime originalem causam et occasionem breviter enodemus."

33. *Reverentia sacrorum canonum* ad D.1 pr. (Erfurt, Wissenschaftliche Allgemein-Bibliothek, Ampl. q.117, fol. 116rb): "lex scripture, que distinguitur in legem Mosaicam, in legem propheticam, in legem euangelicam, in legem apostolicam, de quibus non est disserere presentis propositi set theologice inquisitionis." On this *summa*, see John C. Wei, "The 'Extravagantes' in the Decretist *Summa 'Reverentia sacrorum canonum,'" BMCL* 29 (2011–12): 169–82, and my forthcoming critical edition of the *summa* in *Monumenta Iuris Canonici, series B: Corpus Collectionum* [hereafter "MIC.B"].

34. Bonaventure, *Commentarium in quattuor libros Sententiarum*, lib.4, dist.18, p.2, a.1, q.3, ed. Collegium S. Bonaventurae, S. Bonaventurae Opera omnia, 11 vols. (Ad Claras Aquas [Quarracchi]: Ex typographia Collegii S. Bonaventurae, 1882–1902), 4:488: "Sed licet in hac quaestione canonum sit dicere *quia*, tamen theologiae est dicere *propter quid*, tanquam scientiae superioris."

versal matters and the internal forum of penance, canon law more to particulars and the external forum of penance.[35] Based on the criteria set forth by Bonaventure and Augustinus, then, theoretical aspects of penance and questions relating to the internal forum—as appear, for instance, in Gratian's *De penitentia*—belong to theology.

Some medieval writers explicitly allocated particular sacramental issues between theologians and canonists. Writing around 1170, Peter of Poitiers assigned the sacrament of orders to canonists but labeled marriage a subject for both theologians and canonists.[36] Simi-

35. Augustinus Triumphus, *Summa de potestate ecclesiastica,* q.108, a.3 (Venice, 1497), quoted in Herbert Kalb, "Rechtskraft und ihre Durchbrechungen im Spannungsfeld von kanonistischem und theologischem Diskurs (Rufin—Stephan von Tournai—Iohannes Faventinus," in *Grundlagen des Rechts,* ed. Helmholz et al., 405–19, at 410–11: "Differunt tamen in modo considerandi quantum ad quinque. Primo quidem quia a theologo determinantur modo subtili et quasi propter quid et modo quo propter quid in theologia assignari potest. In iure vero canonico modo grosso et solum quia. Secundo quia a theologo determinantur principaliter propter veritatis contemplationem; a canonistis vero magis principaliter propter actionem et questionem occurrentium solutionem. Tercio quia a theologo determinantur principaliter de cultu Dei et de his que spectant ad integritatem fidei unius Dei. A canonistis vero magis de ordine ministrorum et ecclesiasticorum negociorum spectantium ad talem cultum. Quartum quia a theologo determinantur canones qualiter piis opitulentur et contra impios defendantur. In iure vero canonico taxatur modus quo opitulentur piis et defendantur contra impios. Quinto quia a theologo determinantur magis universaliter et in foro conscientie in quo agitur causa inter hominem et Deum. A canonistis vero magis particulariter applicando ad particularia negocia in foro exterioris iudicii in quo agitur causa inter hominem et hominem."

36. Peter of Poitiers, *Quinque libri sententiarum* 5.14, in *Patrologiae Cursus Completus, Series Latina,* ed. J.-P. Migne, 217 vols. (Paris: Imprimerie Catholique, 1841–55) [hereafter "PL"], 211, 1257B: "De quinto, id est de ordinibus, nil hic dicendum eo quod decretistis disputatio de his potius quam theologis deservit. Quae circa sextum, id est conjugium a theologis solent inquiri, sub compendio sunt perstringenda; nec enim animus nobis est complectendi omnia quae circa conjugium possunt inquiri, cum pleraque decretistarum potius quam theologorum famulentur inquisitioni." On the date of this sentence collection, see Philip S. Moore and Marthe Dulong, "Introduction," in *Sententiae Petri Pictaviensis,* Publications in Medieval Studies 7 and 11, 2 vols. (Notre Dame, Ind.: University of Notre Dame Press, 1940–50), 1:vi: "written at Paris certainly before 1176 and probably before 1170." Cf. Lauge Olaf Nielsen, *Theology and Philosophy in the Twelfth Century: A Study of Gilbert Porreta's Thinking and the Theological Exposition of the Doctrine of the Incarnation During the Period 1130–1180* (Leiden: Brill, 1982), 281n9, who argues that Peter of Poitiers was probably a pupil of Peter Comestor rather than of Peter Lombard and hence could not have composed his *Sentences* until after 1169.

larly writing in the 1170s, Sicard of Cremona mentions questions on transubstantiation in his *Summa decretorum*, but explicitly declines to answer them, instead leaving their resolution to the theologians.[37] Orders, it would thus appear, is less a theological topic than other sacramental matters, but theoretical questions on the eucharist belong to theology. Moreover, insofar as sacramental and liturgical questions involve the why and not just the how, they too should be considered theological issues according to the criteria mentioned by Bonaventure and Augustinus that were discussed above in connection with penance.

Two relatively recent developments make this book's investigation of Gratian the theologian possible, worthwhile, and opportune. First, the discovery of the first recension offers an opportunity to reassess Gratian as a theologian. Older portraits of Gratian the theologian rely upon the second recension, which, as Winroth has argued and as evidence from chapter 8 of this book likewise suggests, probably had a different author than the first recension.[38] More recent studies based on the first recension, on the other hand, have focused on relatively narrow topics or sections of the *Decretum*.[39] And none of these new assessments has performed a detailed analysis of Gratian on the sacraments (aside from penance and marriage) or liturgy, as part 3 of this book does. Second, this book is the first to take advantage of recently discovered and edited texts that Gratian may have drawn upon in composing *De penitentia*, the most theological section

37. Sicard of Cremona, *Summa decretorum* ad De cons. D.2, ed. V. L. Kennedy, "The Moment of Consecration and the Elevation of the Host," *Mediaeval Studies* 6 (1944): 121–50, at 132: "Item queritur si hoc prolato: *hoc est corpus meum*, facta sit transsubstantiatio panis in carnem antequam proferatur: *hic est sanguis meus*. Diverse sunt opiniones; quidam aiunt utrumque verbum ad utriusque effundatur, vino apposito, repetatur. Alii alterum ad alterius transsubstantiationem sufficere. Item de pronominibus hoc et meum et multis aliis circa hanc formam queritur; hec omnia examini theologico relinquimus."

38. Among the most significant older assessments are: Joseph de Ghellinck, *Le mouvement théologique du XIIe siècle*, 2nd rev. ed. (Bruges: Éditions "De Tempel," 1948); John E. Rybolt, "Biblical Hermeneutics of Magister Gratian: An Investigation of Scripture and Canon Law in the Twelfth Century" (PhD diss., DePaul University, 1978); Marcia L. Colish, *Peter Lombard*, 2 vols. (Leiden: Brill, 1994), esp. in vol. 2.

39. See, e.g., the works cited at pp. 8–9.

of the *Decretum* and the locus for his treatment of penitential theology. As a result, it is able to present new evidence concerning Gratian's background and what he was trying to accomplish in the first recension of the *Decretum* that are absent from other recent studies.[40]

My main conclusion concerning Gratian the theologian is that he was a sophisticated thinker, but interested in relatively few areas of theology. On the one hand, he had a deep knowledge of the Bible and a deep interest in theoretical questions of penitential theology. Indeed, his treatment of penitential theology comprises over ten percent of the first recension. On the other hand, Gratian appears to have cared little for most other (potentially) theological topics, such as the other sacraments and liturgy. The first recension treats the other sacraments aside from penance and marriage exceedingly sparingly and neglects the liturgy almost completely. These different emphases may have been bound up both with Gratian's Italian theological context and his original vision for what his textbook—and perhaps also the fledgling discipline of canon law—should be. Gratian intended his work to be an analytical textbook, a *Concordia discordantium canonum*. It was the redactor of the second recension who was largely responsible for transforming it into a comprehensive compilation of canon law, a *Decretum*.

The Structure of This Book

The rest of this book is divided into three main parts. Part 1, which consists of two chapters, deals with "Gratian the Author and Biblical Exegete." Chapter 1 provides an introduction to "Gratian and His Book(s)," that is, it discusses the evidence for Gratian's biography and his work as an author, devoting particular attention to the *Decretum*'s sources, recensions, and dating. Chapter 2, "The Bible," then looks at Gratian's use of the Bible. The chapter shows how the Bible shaped not only the first recension's language and doctrine, but also its argumentation and structure.

Part 2, which consists of four chapters, turns to "Gratian the Pen-

40. E.g., Larson, *Master of Penance*.

itential Theologian." Chapter 3, "The Practice and Theory of Penance," surveys the development of penance to the early twelfth century and the reception of penitential theology in canonical collections. Its main aim is to provide background information necessary for understanding Gratian's main ideas on penance as presented in *De penitentia*, which I set forth in chapter 4, "Gratian on Penance." Chapter 5, "Critiquing and Correcting the Scholastics," attempts to shed further light on Gratian the penitential theologian by situating the core of *De penitentia* in the context of contemporary theological positions, particularly the ones laid out in three sources stemming from the same Italian theological milieu and which he may have known and used: the tract on charity *Ut autem hoc evidenter* of the sentence collection *Deus itaque summe atque ineffabiliter bonus*, the tract on baptism *Baptizato homine* often found as an appendix to that sentence collection, and the treatise *Augustinus in libro vite*, which is edited in the appendix to this book. Chapter 6, "From Penitential Theology to the Canon Law of Magic," then proposes a new explanation for how and why Gratian integrated *De penitentia* into the *Decretum*. The tract, I suggest, was not a later addition to a pre-existing *causa*, but rather the main reason why Gratian composed *Causa* 33 in the first place, as well as the immediate cause for his decision to incorporate sections on the canon law of magic into the *Decretum*. This chapter is admittedly more speculative than the rest of the book, but not for that reason, I hope, of lesser, little, or no value.

Part 3, which consists of the final two chapters, presents evidence that Gratian was not much of a sacramental or liturgical theologian. Hence the question mark for the title of part 3: "Gratian, a Theologian of the Sacraments and Liturgy?" Chapter 7 examines Gratian's treatment of the sacraments in the first recension. However, the chapter omits penance, since that is the subject of part 2, and marriage, since that would merit a monograph in its own right and furthermore Gratian does not appear to have viewed marriage as a sacrament. Chapter 8 then examines one of the surprising omissions revealed by the investigation in chapter 7, namely the absence of not only liturgical theology but even liturgical law from the first recension.

Part 1

Gratian the Author and Biblical Exegete

1

Gratian and His Book(s)

Prior to turning to our investigation proper of Gratian the theologian, we need to have a basic understanding of Gratian as an author. To that end, this chapter provides an introduction to a number of topics useful for understanding both the contents of this book in general and chapter 2's study of Gratian the biblical exegete in particular. Discussed in turn will be Gratian's biography, the *Decretum*'s sources (both first and second recensions), the two recensions and their dating, the editions used in this study, and the St. Gall manuscript of the *Decretum*.

Gratian's Biography

For many centuries, scholars believed that they knew quite a lot about the author of the *Decretum*. Reference works, surveys, and monographs routinely asserted that he was both a teacher and a monk (more specifically, according to many authors, a member of the Camaldolese Order who resided at the monastery of Saints Felix and Nabor); that he was born at Ficulle near Carraria or at Chiusi; and that he died by 1159 at the latest. These sources sometimes also made other claims about his life, for instance, that he was a bishop and, much more skeptically, that he was related to Peter Lombard, whose *Four Books of Sentences* became the standard textbook of theology used in medieval universities.[1]

In 1979, however, John T. Noonan raised serious doubts about the received biography. Subjecting all the known evidence to critical review, he demonstrated how the earliest witnesses to many of the supposed details of Gratian's life originated many decades, sometimes even centuries, after the compilation of the *Decretum*, and that these witnesses frequently contradicted one another.[2] Only one contemporary document mentions a Gratian who might be identical to the author of the *Decretum* and all it explicitly tells us is that Gratian, together with two other *prudentes*, provided the papal legate Cardinal Goizo with legal advice in Venice in 1143.[3] In Noonan's judgment, only three things could be asserted about Gratian with relative certainty: that he "composed and commented upon a substantial portion of the *Concordia*," was "a teacher with theological knowledge and interests and a lawyer's point of view," and "worked in Bologna in the 1130s and 1140s."[4]

Later scholars have largely accepted Noonan's critique, though many have been more willing to accept evidence that Noonan himself dismissed as "hearsay."[5] Peter Landau, for instance, believes that there is substantial evidence Gratian was a monk, Noonan's criti-

1. Examples of authors who accepted this traditional biography are Alphonse Van Hove, *Commentarium Lovaniense in codicem iuris canonici* 1: *Prolegomena: Editio altera auctior et emendatior* (Rome: H. Dessain, 1945), 339; Alfons M. Stickler, *Historia iuris canonici latini* 1: *Historia fontium* (Turin: Libraria Pontif. Athenaei Salesiani, 1950), 202–3. For comprehensive documentation of what scholars once regarded to be facts about Gratian, see John T. Noonan, "Gratian Slept Here: The Changing Identity of the Father of the Systematic Study of Canon Law," *Traditio* 35 (1979): 145–72. On Peter Lombard's life and work, see Colish, *Peter Lombard*; Philipp W. Rosemann, *Peter Lombard* (Oxford: Oxford University Press, 2004).

2. Noonan, "Gratian Slept Here."

3. Notarial Report of the Judgment of Cardinal Goizo, *Codice diplomatico padovano*, ed. Andrea Gloria, Monumenti storici publicati dalla R. deputazione veneta di storia patria 1st ser., Documenti 4 (Venice, 1879), 313. See also Winroth, *The Making of Gratian's Decretum*, 6; Gundula Grebner, "Lay Patronate in Bologna in the First Half of the 12th Century: Regular Canons, Notaries, and the *Decretum*," in *Europa und seine Regionen: 2000 Jahre Rechtsgeschichte*, ed. Andreas Bauer and Karl H. L. Welker (Cologne: Böhlau, 2007), 107–22.

4. Noonan, "Gratian Slept Here," 172.

5. Ibid.

cisms notwithstanding.[6] A relatively early commentary on the *Decretum*, the *Summa Parisiensis*, reports that Gratian was a monk.[7] In addition, *Causae* 16–20 in both recensions devote considerable attention to monks and their prerogatives.[8]

Winroth, on the other hand, argues that Gratian was more likely a bishop of Chiusi than a monk (or both a bishop and a monk). A relatively early gloss from the third quarter of the twelfth century, which perhaps dates to the time when the first recension was still in use, reports that Gratian was a bishop.[9] Writing around 1180, the abbot and chronicler Robert of Torigni says in particular that Gratian was bishop of Chiusi.[10] Furthermore, an entry in the necrology of the cathedral of Siena, of which Noonan was unaware, confirms that one of the bishops of Chiusi in the mid-twelfth century was named Gratian.[11]

Of course, one major problem with any attempt to rely on outside documents to illuminate the biography of the first recension's author is the uncertainty surrounding that person's name. With one exception, the manuscripts of the first recension and the earliest manuscripts of the second recension do not name the author.[12] It is only later glosses, introductions, and commentaries that refer to the *Decretum*'s author as Gratian, and it is not clear whether they intended to refer to the author of the first or the second recension.

6. Landau, "Gratian and the *Decretum Gratiani*," 24.

7. *Summa Parisiensis* ad C.2 q.7 d.p.c.52 and C.16 q.1 c.61, in *The Summa Parisiensis on the Decretum Gratiani*, ed. Terence Patrick McLaughlin (Toronto: Pontifical Institute of Medieval Studies, 1952), 115 and 181. McLaughlin, *Summa Parisiensis*, xxxii, dates the work to around 1160, but that date is certainly too early. Landau, "Gratian and the *Decretum Gratiani*," 24, places the *Summa Parisiensis* at around 1168; Winroth, *Making*, 6, at "shortly before 1170."

8. Landau, "Gratian and the *Decretum Gratiani*," 24.

9. For an edition of the gloss based on all the known manuscripts, see Rudolf Weigand, "Frühe Kanonisten und ihre Karriere in der Kirche," *ZRG KA* 76 (1990): 135–55, at 153.

10. Richard Howlett, ed., *The Chronicles of the Reigns of Stephen, Henry II, and Richard I* 4: *The Chronicle of Robert of Torigni*, Memorials of Great Britain and Ireland During the Middle Ages ["Rolls Series"] 82 (London: Longman, 1889), 118.

11. Anders Winroth, "Where Gratian Slept: The Life and Death of the Father of Canon Law," *ZRG KA* 130 (2013): 105–28.

12. The manuscript that names Gratian as author of the *Decretum* is Aa = Admont, Stiftsbibliothek, 23 and 43. See Winroth, *Making*, 176.

In his groundbreaking study of the *Decretum,* Winroth argued that Gratian was probably the name of the author of the first recension.[13] He based his conclusion on the testimony of an early introduction to the *Decretum,* known after its incipit as *Hoc opus inscribitur,* and an early gloss. Winroth thought both texts were written for the first recension, since both *Hoc opus inscribitur* and the gloss describe the *Decretum* as being divided into two parts.[14] But as chapter 8 will show, the distinctions and *causae* were expanded into their second-recension form before *De consecratione* was appended. So it is possible that both *Hoc opus inscribitur* and the gloss refer to the second recension before it was augmented with *De consecratione.* Gratian thus might not be the name of the author of the first recension after all, but rather the name of the redactor of the second recension or the name of both authors. The evidence is ambiguous. As I still regard it as more likely than not that Gratian was the name of Winroth's Gratian 1, I will, in the absence of any positive evidence to the contrary, simply refer to the author of the first recension as Gratian.

Gratian's *Decretum*

The Sources of the *Decretum*

For the most part, the canonists responsible for producing the two recensions of the *Decretum* took their authorities not from the "material" sources (the original papal letters, patristic writings, and other sources of the canonical tradition) but rather "formal" sources (intermediate collections compiled by earlier canonists and writers). Almost all the canons in the *Decretum*—both the first and the second recensions—appear to have been taken from just five formal sources:[15]

1. The canonical collection of Anselm of Lucca, originally compiled around 1081–86.[16] The collection exists in four main recen-

13. Ibid., 175–78.

14. Ibid., 178.

15. Landau, "Neue Forschungen"; Landau, "Quellen und Bedeutung."

16. For a problematic edition of book 1 to the beginning of book 11, see Friedrich Thaner, ed., *Anselmi episcopi Lucensis collectio canonum: Una cum collectione minore* (Innsbruck: Wagner, 1906–15; reprinted in Aalen: Scientia Verlag, 1960). For

sions: A, B, Bb, and C.[17] Peter Landau suggests that Gratian's copy of the collection belonged to the early twelfth-century expansion of recension A that he dubs recension A′.[18]

2. The *Tripartita*.[19] Following Paul Fournier, scholars have generally attributed this collection to Ivo of Chartres.[20] The first two books of the *Tripartita*, generally referred to as Collection A of the *Tripartita* or as *Tripartita A*, date to 1093–95 and were the second most important formal source of a canonical collection definitely compiled by Ivo, known as the *Decretum* and dating to the period 1093–95. The third book of the *Tripartita*, often referred to as Collection B of the *Tripartita* or as *Tripartita B*, is an abbreviation of Ivo's *Decretum* and dates to after 1095.[21]

---

a transcription of book 13, see Edith Pasztór, "Lotta per le investiture e 'ius belli': La posizione di Anselmo di Lucca," in *Sant'Anselmo, Mantova e la lotta per le investiture*, Atti del Convegno Internazionale di Studi, ed. Paolo Golinelli (Bologna: Pàtron, 1987), 405–21. On the canonist Anselm of Lucca, not to be confused with his namesake uncle, Pope Alexander II (1061–73), see Kathleen G. Cushing, *Papacy and Law in the Gregorian Revolution: The Canonistic Work of Anselm of Lucca* (Oxford: Clarendon Press, 1998). For a guide to the literature, see Lotte Kéry, *Canonical Collections of the Early Middle Ages (ca. 400–1140): A Bibliographical Guide to the Manuscripts and Literature* (Washington, D.C.: The Catholic University of America Press, 1999), 218–26; Linda Fowler-Magerl, *Clavis canonum: Selected Canon Law Collections before 1140; Access with Data Processing*, MGH Hilfsmittel 21 (Hanover: MGH, 2005), 139–45. For the dating of this text, see Cushing, *Papacy and Law*, 5.

17. For the relationship between the various recensions of Anselm's collection, see Peter Landau, "Die Rezension C der Sammlung des Anselm von Lucca," *BMCL* 16 (1986): 17–54, reprinted in his *Kanones und Dekretalen*, 43*–80*, with retractations at 472*; Landau, "Erweiterte Fassungen der Kanonessammlung des Anselm von Lucca aus dem 12. Jahrhundert," in *Sant'Anselmo*, ed. Golinelli, 323–38, reprinted in Landau, *Kanones und Dekretalen*, 81*–95*, with retractations at 473*.

18. Landau, "Die Rezension C," 28, reprinted in his *Kanones und Dekretalen*, 54*; Landau, "Erweiterte Fassungen," 328, reprinted in his *Kanones und Dekretalen*, 86*.

19. For a working edition of the *Tripartita*, see https://ivo-of-chartres.github.io/tripartita.html. On this collection, see Christof Rolker, *Canon Law and the Letters of Ivo of Chartres* (Cambridge: Cambridge University Press, 2010), 100–107 and 135–37. For a guide to the literature, see Kéry, *Canonical Collections*, 244–50; Fowler-Magerl, *Clavis*, 187–90.

20. Paul Fournier, "Les collections attribuées à Yves de Chartres," *Bibliothèque de l'École de Chartres* 57 (1896): 645–98 and 58 (1897): 26–77, 293–326, 410–44, and 624–76, at 322–25, reprinted in his *Mélanges de droit canonique*, ed. Theo Kölzer, 2 vols. (Aalen: Scientia Verlag, 1983), 1:451–678, at 586–89.

21. See esp. Fournier, "Les collections," *Bibliothèque de l'École de Chartres* 57 (1896): 650.

3. The *Panormia*.[22] The work has long been attributed to Ivo of Chartres, but Christof Rolker argues convincingly that this attribution is incorrect.[23] According to Rolker, the *Panormia* dates to around 1115.[24]

4. The *Polycarpus* compiled by Cardinal Gregory of San Grisogono, which dates to 1104–13.[25]

5. The anonymous *Collection in Three Books* (= 3L), compiled sometime between 1111 and 1123.[26]

As chapter 2 will show, the *Glossa ordinaria* to the Bible was likewise an important formal source for the *Decretum*, though quantitatively less significant.

Other formal sources were employed more restrictively. Isidore of Seville's *Etymologies* or a florilegium based on that work, for instance, served as the primary formal source for the opening four distinctions on natural law found in the first part of the *Decretum*.[27] The main formal source for *Causa* 1 on simony was Alger of Liège's *Liber de misericordia et iustitia*.[28] Much of *De penitentia* derives from sentence

22. For a working edition of the *Panormia*, see https://ivo-of-chartres.github.io/panormia.html. On this collection, see Rolker, *Canon Law*, esp. 123–26 and 248–89. For a guide to the literature, see Kéry, *Canonical Collections*, 253–60; Fowler-Magerl, *Clavis*, 198–202.

23. See Fournier, "Les collections attribuées à Yves de Chartres," 57 (1897): 315–17, reprinted in his *Mélanges*, 1:579–81; Rolker, *Canon Law*, 248–89.

24. Rolker, *Canon Law*, 272–84.

25. For a typescript of Carl Erdmann's unpublished edition, see http://www.mgh.de/datenbanken/kanonessammlung-polycarp/. For an analysis, see Uwe Horst, *Die Kanonessammlung "Polycarpus" des Gregor von S. Grisogono: Quellen und Tendenzen*, MGH Hilfsmittel 5 (Munich: MGH, 1980). For a guide to the literature, see Kéry, *Canonical Collections*, 266–69; Fowler-Magerl, *Clavis*, 229–32. For citations to the *Polycarpus*, I use the numbering in Erdmann's edition, which differs sometimes from the numbering in *Clavis*.

26. Ed. Joseph Motta, *Collectio canonum trium librorum*, 2 vols., MIC.B 8/I-II (Vatican City: BAV, 2005–8). For a guide to the literature, see Kéry, *Canonical Collections*, 269–71; Fowler-Magerl, *Clavis*, 234–35.

27. Isidore of Seville, *Etymologiarum sive Originum libri xx*, ed. W. M. Lindsay, 2 vols. (Oxford: Oxford University Press, 1911).

28. Robert Kretzschmar, *Alger von Luttichs Traktat "De misericordia et iustitia": Ein kanonistischer Konkordanzversuch aus der Zeit des Investiturstreits; Untersuchungen und Edition*, Quellen und Forschungen zum Recht im Mittelalter 2 (Sigmaringen: J. Thorbecke, 1985). For a guide to the literature, see Kéry, *Canonical Collections*, 272–73.

collections associated with the school of Laon.[29] And parts of *De consecratione* derive from the *Sententiae magistri A.* as well as from Peter Abelard's *Sic et non* or a closely related source.[30]

In all likelihood not among the formal sources of the first recension is Justinian's compilation of Roman law, the *Corpus iuris civilis*.[31] Almost all the Roman law excerpts in the first recension derive from earlier canonical collections.[32] Only three may derive directly from the *Corpus iuris civilis* itself rather than from an intermediate source: C.2 q.6 c.28, C.15 q.3 cc.1–3, and C.15 q.3 c.4.[33] The *Corpus iuris civilis* was, however, probably a formal source of the second recension. The second recension contains over forty extracts of Justinianic Roman law not found in any known earlier canonical collection and also displays a greater familiarity with Roman law doctrines and concepts than does the first recension.[34] Since Bologna was already

29. On the relevant texts, see chapter 5 and the literature cited there.

30. On the use of the *Sententiae magistri A.* in *De consecratione*, see Peter Landau, "Gratian und die Sententiae Magistri A," in *Aus Archiven und Bibliotheken: Festschrift für Raymund Kottje zum 65. Geburtstag*, ed. Hubert Mordek (Frankfurt am Main: Peter Lang, 1992), 311–26, at 316–19, reprinted in Landau, *Kanones und Dekretalen*, 161*–76*, with retractations at 474*–75*, at 166*–69*. On the *Sententiae magistri A.*, see Pauline Maas, *The Liber sententiarum magistri A.: Its Place amidst the Sentence Collections of the First Half of the Twelfth Century* (Nijmegen: Centrum voor Middeleeuwse Studies, Katholieke Universiteit Nijmegen, 1997). For a guide to the literature, see Kéry, *Canonical Collections*, 273–74. On the use of the *Sic et non* in *De consecratione*, see Landau, "Appendix II" to "Gratian und die Sententiae Magistri A," 326, reprinted in Landau, *Kanones und Dekretalen*, 176*; John C. Wei, "Appendix" to "The *Collectio sancte Genoveve* and Peter Abaelard's *Sic et non*," *ZRG KA* 94 (2008): 21–37, at 35–37. Cf. Genka, "Zur textlichen Grundlage," 73. The critical edition is Peter Abelard, *Sic et non: A Critical Edition*, ed. Blanche B. Boyer and Richard McKeon (Chicago: University of Chicago Press, 1976).

31. The standard critical edition is Theodore Mommsen et al., eds., *Corpus iuris civilis*, 3 vols. (Leipzig: Weidmann, 1872). On medieval Roman law, see Hermann Lange, *Römisches Recht im Mittelalter*, 2 vols. (Munich: C. H. Beck, 1997). On Roman law in the two recensions of the *Decretum*, see Winroth, *Making*, 146–74; Winroth, "Roman Law in Gratian and the *Panormia*," in *Bishops, Texts and the Use of Canon Law Around 1100: Essays in Honour of Martin Brett*, ed. Bruce C. Brasington and Kathleen G. Cushing (Aldershot: Ashgate, 2008), 183–90. Cf. José Viejo-Ximénez, "Les étapes de l'incorporation des textes romains dans le Décret de Gratien," *Revue de droit canonique* [hereafter "*RDC*"] 51 (2001): 251–60; Viejo-Ximénez, "El derecho romano 'nuevo' en el Decreto de Graciano," *ZRG KA* 88 (2002): 1–19.

32. Winroth, *Making*, 146–53.

33. Ibid.

34. Ibid., 146 and 148–57.

a major center for the study of Roman law in the 1140s, the decade when the second recension was compiled, the redactor of the second recension would have had ready access to the *Corpus iuris civilis*.[35]

The Two Recensions and Their Dating

Four manuscripts and one manuscript folio preserve the first recension of Gratian's *Decretum*, while two manuscripts preserve (different) abbreviations of the first recension.[36] Most other medieval manuscripts and printed editions, including Friedberg's edition, contain the second recension or some reworking thereof. As preserved in the manuscripts, the first recension dates to 1139–50. While none of the first recension's formal sources necessitates such a late dating, a reference in the first recension does. At D.63 d.p.c.34, the first recension mentions a decree of "a general synod of Pope Innocent [II] held at Rome," that is, the Second Lateran Council held in 1139.[37] Since the popes of the era frequently repromulgated legislation from earlier councils, Atria Larson has suggested that this reference could be to an earlier, unknown council held by Innocent at Rome.[38] Her suggestion, however, is implausible. Rome was in the control of the antipope's supporters during most of the Anacletian schism (1130–

35. On the growth of Roman law studies in the twelfth century, see Winroth, *Making*, 157–74; Winroth, "The Teaching of Law in the Twelfth Century," in *Law and Learning in the Middle Ages: Proceedings of the Second Carlsberg Academy Conference on Medieval Legal History 2005*, ed. Helle Vogt and Mia Münster-Swendsen (Copenhagen: DJØF, 2006), 41–55.

36. The manuscripts of the first recension are: Aa = Admont, Stiftsbibliothek, 23 and 43; Bc = Barcelona, Arxiu de la Corona d'Aragó, Santa María de Ripoll 78; Fd = Florence, Biblioteca Nazionale Centrale, Conv. Soppr. A.1.402; P = Paris, Bibliothèque nationale de France [hereafter "BNF"], nouvelles acquisitions latines 1761; Pfr = Paris, BNF, lat. 3884 I-II, fol. 1 (*fragmentum unius paginae*). The abbreviations of the first recension are: Mw = Munich, Bayerische Staatsbibliothek, Clm 22272; Sg = St. Gall, Stiftsbibliothek, 673. On Mw, see Atria A. Larson, "An *Abbreviatio* of the First Recension of Gratian's *Decretum* in Munich?" *BMCL* 29 (2011–12): 51–118. On Sg, see below pp. 27–33.

37. D.63 d.p.c.34 (ed. Winroth, *Making*, 137, on the basis of Aa Bc Fd P and Friedb.): "Nunc autem sicut electio summi pontificis non a cardinalibus tantum immo etiam ab aliis religiosis clericis auctoritate Nicholai pape est facienda, ita et episcoporum electio non a canonicis tantum set etiam ab aliis religiosis clericis, *sicut in generali sinodo Innocentii pape Rome habita constitutum est.*"

38. Atria A. Larson, "Early Stages of Gratian's *Decretum* and the Second Lateran Council," *BMCL* 27 (2007): 21–56. See also Larson, *Master of Penance*, 26–28.

38), so Innocent was almost never there, or even on the Italian peninsula, prior to 1138.[39] The one exception was briefly in 1133, when Lothar III managed to retake part of the city long enough to be crowned emperor.[40] But there is no evidence that Innocent ever promulgated any canons at that time, and it seems unlikely that he did, as he had plenty of other problems on his mind.

More plausible, though similarly unsupported by any outside evidence, is the conjecture that the reference to Lateran II is an interpolation. Winroth thought this idea unlikely back in 2000 because the reference appears in all the extant manuscripts of the first recension.[41] But the suggestion may not be so implausible given the possible descent of three or perhaps even all four of the extant first recension manuscripts from the same defective hyparchetype.[42]

The first recension dates to 1150 at the latest. A Sienese court decision from that year quotes extensively from the second recension, so the first recension also must have been in existence already at that time.[43] Moreover, other texts from around the same date likewise cite the *Decretum*.[44] The first recension could, of course, conceiv-

39. On the schism, see Mary Stroll, *The Jewish Pope: Ideology and Politics in the Papal Schism of 1130* (Leiden: Brill, 1987). One can reconstruct Innocent II's itinerary from Philip Jaffé, *Regesta pontificum romanorum*, 2 vols. (Leipzig: Veit, 1885–88; reprinted in Graz: Akademische Druck- u. Verlagsanstalt, 1956), 1:841–82.

40. Larson, "Early Stages," 40–41. Larson also considers and dismisses the possibility that Innocent held a council immediately after his elevation to the papacy (ibid., 39–40).

41. Winroth, *Making*, 137–38.

42. Anders Winroth, "Critical Notes on the Text of Gratian's *Decretum* 2," https://sites.google.com/a/yale.edu/decretumgratiani/home/critical-notes-2. Cf. Winroth, "Critical Notes on the Text of Gratian's *Decretum* 1," https://sites.google.com/a/yale.edu/decretumgratiani/critical-notes-1.

43. For an edition and analysis of the Sienese judgment, see Paolo Nardi, "Fonti canoniche in una sentenza senese del 1150," in *Life, Law, and Letters: Historical Studies in Honour of Antonio García y García*, ed. Peter Linehan, Studia Gratiana 29 (Rome: Libr. Ateneo Salesiano, 1998), 661–70. See also Anders Winroth, "Recent Work on the Making of Gratian's *Decretum*," *BMCL* 26 (2004–6): 1–29, at 4–5.

44. See Rainer Murauer, "Geistliche Gerichtsbarkeit und Rezeption des neuen Rechts im Erzbistum Salzburg im 12. Jahrhundert," in *Römisches Zentrum und kirchliche Peripherie: Das universale Papsttum als Bezugspunkt der Kirchen von den Reformpäpsten bis zu Innozenz II.*, ed. Jochen Johrendt and Harald Müller (Berlin: De Gruyter, 2008), 259–84, at 268–70; Martina Hartmann, "The Letter Collection of

ably date to much earlier in the 1140s. Peter Landau suggests 1145 as a *terminus ante quem*, which seems possible.[45]

The dating of the second recension is more complicated, because, as will be discussed in chapter 8, it emerged in stages. The first two parts of the *Decretum* (the distinctions and *causae*) were expanded before the addition of *De consecratione*.[46] And even after *De consecratione* was added canonists continued to tinker with the text of the *Decretum* in various ways, for instance, by inserting *paleae* and altering readings in the text.[47] The second-recension form of the distinctions and *causae* appears to date to the period 1139–50 for the same reason that the first recension does. *De consecratione*, on the other hand, may also date to this same period, but may not have been appended to the *Decretum* until 1158, the latest date when Peter Lombard, who borrows extensively from *De consecratione*, could have completed his *Four Books of Sentences*.[48] The chronology of the later additions and alterations to the second recension extends to at least the thirteenth century, if not beyond.[49]

Editions and Manuscripts Employed

To facilitate the analysis of the *Decretum* in the chapters that follow, I will refer to it using the divisions in Friedberg's edition. In citing passages of the *Decretum*, I give the largest division first, followed by the smaller ones. Thus, for instance, I write D.1 c.1 to refer to the first canon in the first distinction of the first part of the *Decretum*; C.1 q.2 c.1 to refer to the first canon in the second question of the first *causa*; De pen. D.2 d.a.c.1 to refer to the beginning (literally the dic-

---

Abbot Wibald of Stablo and Corvey and the *Decretum Gratiani*," *BMCL* 29 (2011–12): 35–49.

45. Landau, "Gratian and the *Decretum Gratiani*," 25.

46. For evidence of this claim, see chapter 8.

47. See John C. Wei, "The Later Development of Gratian's *Decretum*," in *Proceedings of the Fourteenth International Congress of Medieval Canon Law*, MIC.C 15 (Vatican City: BAV, forthcoming).

48. Winroth, *Making*, 142. On the date of the Lombard's *Sentences*, see Ignatius Brady, "Prolegomena" to *Magistri Petri Lombardi Parisiensis episcopi sententiae in IV libris distinctae*, 3rd rev. ed., Spicilegium Bonaventurianum 4, vol. 1 (Grottaferrata, 1971), 128*.

49. Wei, "Later Development."

Table 1-1. Editions Employed

Section of *Decretum*	Edition
D.20	ed. Tatsushi Genka, "Hierarchie der Texte, Hierarchie der Autoritäten: Zur Hierarchie der Rechtsquellen bei Gratian," *ZRG KA* 95 (2009): 100–127, at 126–27.
C.24 q.1	ed. Titus Lenherr, *Die Exkommunikations- und Depositionsgewalt der Häretiker bei Gratian und den Dekretisten bis zur Glossa ordinaria des Johannes Teutonicus* (St. Ottilien: EOS Verlag, 1987), 18–56.
C.27–C.36 (excluding *De penitentia*)	ed. Jean Werckmeister, *Décret de Gratien: Causes 27 à 36; Le mariage* = *RDC* 58–59 (2011).
C.30 qq.1, 3, 4	ed. Enrique de León, *La 'cognatio spiritualis' según Graciano* (Milan: Giuffrè, 1996), 138–68.
remaining sections	ed. Emil Friedberg, *Corpus iuris canonici* 1: *Decretum magistri Gratiani* (Leipzig: Veit, 1879; reprinted in Graz: Akademische Druck- u. Verlagsanstalt, 1959).

tum before the first canon) of the second distinction of *De penitentia*; and De cons. D.3 c.2 to refer to the second canon in the third distinction of *De consecratione*.

In establishing the text of the *Decretum*, I consult the editions shown in table 1-1. I also consult the following first-recension manuscripts:

1. Aa = Admont, Stiftsbibliothek, 22 and 43;[50]
2. Bc = Barcelona, Arxiu de la Corona d'Aragó, Santa Maria de Ripoll 78;[51]
3. Fd = Florence, Biblioteca Nazionale Centrale, Conv. Soppr. A.1.402;[52] and
4. P = Paris, BNF, nouvelles acquisitions latines 1761.[53]

The St. Gall Manuscript (Sg)

This book does not consider the form of the *Decretum* preserved in Sg = St. Gall, Stiftsbibliothek, 673, or otherwise take into account its

50. Aa contains the first recension in its entirety, but with occasional interpolations from the second recension. On the manuscript, see Winroth, *Making*, 23–26.

51. Bc ends after *Causa* 12. On the manuscript, see ibid., 26–28.

52. Fd begins at D.28 d.p.c.13. On the manuscript, see ibid., 28–32.

53. P breaks off in the middle of C.12 q.2 c.39. On the manuscript, see ibid., 32.

text because I reject the view, first advanced by Carlos Larrainzar in 1999, that Sg contains an even earlier stage of the *Decretum* than the first recension.[54] Instead, I have argued, Sg contains an abbreviation or transformation of the first recension with interpolations from the second recension. The main reason why I adopt this view has to do with Sg's contents. While Sg contains an extremely abbreviated form of the *Decretum,* it also contains many texts that do not appear in the first recension but do in the second. Sg, moreover, contains more late texts than the first recension. In addition to containing a reference to the Second Lateran Council, it also includes two late second-recension additions: canons 7 and 8 of the Second Lateran Council (C.27 q.1 c.40) and the decretal *De parentela* (JL 8316, C.35 q.6 c.8) of Pope Innocent II to Bishop Otto of Lucca.[55]

Larrainzar and those who accept his hypothesis have advanced two types of arguments in favor of the chronological priority of the text preserved in Sg.[56] First, they have stressed the alleged logical priority of Sg over the first recension. Sg, they argue, must be chronologically prior to the first recension because its argumentation and structure are simpler, clearer, and less sophisticated than that of the first recension. Second, they have pointed to changes in Sg which could conceivably

54. Carlos Larrainzar, "El borrador de la 'Concordia' de Graciano: Sankt Gallen, Stiftsbibliothek MS 673 (= Sg)," *Ius Ecclesiae* 11 (1999): 593–666. See also Larrainzar, "La formación del Decreto," and "Datos sobre la antigüedad del manuscrito Sg: Su redacción de C.27 q.2," in *"Panta rei,"* ed. Condorelli, 3:205–37.

55. Larson, "Early Stages," 21–56, appears to have been unaware of the presence of C.35 q.6 c.8 in Sg when she argued that the recension represented by Sg dates to around 1133. For further difficulties with the chronology she proposes, see Anders Winroth, "Innocent II, Gratian, and Abbé Migne," *BMCL* 28 (2008): 145–51.

56. Kenneth Pennington, "Gratian, Causa 19, and the Birth of Canonical Jurisprudence," in *"Panta rei,"* ed. Condorelli, 4:339–55; Pennington, "La Causa 19, Graziano, e lo Ius commune"; Enrique de León, "La biografia di Graziano," in *La cultura giuridico-canonica medioevale,* ed. de León and Álvarez de las Asturias, 89–107; Luis Pablo Tarín, "An secularibus litteris oporteat eos esse eruditos? El texto de D.37 en las etapas antiguas del Decreto de Graciano," in ibid., 469–511; José Miguel Viejo-Ximénez, "La ricezione del diritto romano nel diritto canonico," in ibid., 157–209; Atria A. Larson, "The Evolution of Gratian's *Tractatus de penitentia,*" *BMCL* 26 (2004–5): 59–123; Melodie Harris Eichbauer, "St. Gall Stiftsbibliothek 673 and the Early Redactions of Gratian's *Decretum,*" *BMCL* 27 (2007): 105–39; Luis Pablo Tarín, *Graciano de Bolonia y la literatura latina: La distinción treinta y siete del Decreto* (Madrid: Fundación Pastor, 2008), esp. 72–82.

have been the work of an abbreviator, but which they argue that no medieval abbreviator would have made, for instance, reworking the distinctions in the first part of the *Decretum* into a single *causa* or haphazardly omitting rubrics.[57] Because a medieval abbreviator would not have made these changes, they assert, Sg cannot contain an abbreviation and instead must contain an earlier version of the *Decretum.*

Other scholars, however, have drawn attention to not only the methodological flaws and weaknesses of these arguments, but also the substantial body of evidence showing that Sg, far from containing an early version of Gratian's *Decretum,* in fact preserves an abbreviation of the first recension with interpolations from the second recension.[58] First, the redactor of Sg states explicitly in *Causa* 1 that he has abbreviated and altered the order of Gratian's text.[59] In the first and second recensions, C.1 q.6 begins with the words: "What is to be done about those, who unknowingly were ordained by a simoniac (which was asked in the sixth place), is found above, in the *capitulum* of Urban with the incipit *Si qui a symoniacis non symoniace ordinati sunt* (C.1 q.1 c.108)."[60] Sg, however, does not list C.1 q.1 c.108 above (*supra*) in its usual position in C.1 q.1, but instead transposes it to immediately after C.1 q.6 d.a.c.1. The altered version of this dictum

57. It is worth noting in this connection that some abbreviations of Gratian's *Decretum* do radically alter its structure. The thirteenth-century manuscript British Library, Royal 9 A viii, for instance, takes the material in the *causae* and reorganizes it into books and distinctions. I would like to thank Martin Brett for drawing my attention to this manuscript and sharing his notes with me.

58. Titus Lenherr, "Die vier Fassungen von C. 3 q. 1 d.p.c. 6 im Decretum Gratiani: Zugleich ein Einblick in die neueste Diskussion um das Werden von Gratians Dekret," *Archiv für katholisches Kirchenrecht* [hereafter "*AKKR*"] 169 (2000): 353–81; Lenherr, "Ist die Handschrift 673 der St. Galler Stiftsbibliothek (Sg) der Entwurf zu Gratians *Dekret*?: Versuch einer Antwort aus Beobachtungen an D. 31 und D. 32"; Winroth, "Recent Work," 11–22; John C. Wei, "A Reconsideration of St. Gall, Stiftsbibliothek 673 (Sg) in Light of the Sources of Distinctions 5–7 of the *De penitentia,*" *BMCL* 27 (2007): 141–80; Jean Werckmeister, "Le manuscrit 673 de Saint-Gall: Un Décret de Gratien primitif?" *RDC* 60 (2010): 155–70. See also Sommar, "Gratian's Causa VII."

59. This is laid out clearly by Winroth, "Recent Work," 20–21.

60. C.1 q.6 d.a.c.1 (ed. Friedberg, 424): "Quid vero de his fieri debeat, qui ignoranter a symoniacis ordinati sunt (quod sexto loco quesitum est), supra in capitulo videlicet Urbani, quod sic incipit: 'Si qui a symoniacis non symoniace ordinati sunt' requiratur." The translation and Latin text are taken from Winroth, "Recent Work," 20.

(C.1 q.6 d.a.c.1) in Sg explains why. "What is to be done about those, who unknowingly were ordained by a simoniac (which was asked in the sixth place), is said above, in the *capitulum* of Urban, which it was not necessary to put there in its entirety in that context, but which we now bring forth as evidence."[61] The redactor of Sg states that the canon of Urban (C.1 q.1 c.108) was originally found above, that is, in question 1 of *Causa* 1, as it appears in the first and second recensions, but that it was not pertinent enough to quote at that point. For that reason, he only quotes it now, in question 6 of *Causa* 1.

Second, Sg not only references canons not found in its text, something the first recension also does on occasion, but it also refers to absent canons as if they were in fact present in the text.[62] De pen. D.6 d.p.c.2 provides the one example studied to date. This dictum attempts to reconcile the words of Pseudo-Augustine in c.1, who advises penitents to choose a knowledgeable confessor, with canons forbidding priests to hear the confessions of penitents belonging to other parishes.[63] Like all the other excerpts from *De vera et falsa penitentia*, c.1 is not found in Sg. Yet, as table 1-2 shows, d.p.c.2 clearly echoes the language of c.1. What is more, d.p.c.2 even refers to c.1 explicitly as being present in the *Decretum*, stating that "it is one thing to disdain one's own priest out of partiality or hate, which is prohibited by the sacred canons; it is another thing to avoid a blind [priest], which each person is advised to do *by this authority* (*hac auctoritate*), lest, if a blind person leads [another] blind person, both fall into a pit."

The words *hac auctoritate* (*ab hac auctoritate* in Sg), which should be translated as either "the immediately preceding" or "the immediately following" authority, must refer to c.1. Only c.1 advises penitents to avoid ignorant priests. The other two canons in distinction 6 of *De penitentia*, which do not appear in the first recension, treat different

61. C.1 q.6 d.a.c.1 (as it appears in Sg): "Quid autem de his fieri debeat qui ignoranter a symoniacis ordinati sunt (quod quidem sexto loco quesitum est), supra in capitulo Urbani dictum est quod, quia forte ibi quantum ad negotium pertinebat integre poni non fuit necessarium, in presenti ad evidentiam in medium adducamus." The translation and Latin text are taken from Winroth, "Recent Work," 21.

62. Wei, "A Reconsideration of St. Gall," 171–74.

63. The beginning of this authority also appears in De pen. D.1 c.88 §1. Like all the other extracts from *De vera et falsa penitentia*, c.88 is present in the first and second recensions but not in Sg.

Table 1-2. Evidence That Sg Uses and Specifically Refers to De pen. D.6 c.1

De pen. D.6 c.1 (absent from Sg)	**De pen. D.6 d.p.c.2 (version in Sg)**
Qui uult confiteri peccata, ut inueniat gratiam, querat *sacerdotem scientem ligare et soluere,* ne, cum negligens circa se extiterit, negligatur ab illo, qui eum misericorditer	Quod autem dicitur, ut penitens eligat *sacerdotem scientem ligare et soluere,* uidetur esse contrarium ei quod in canonibus inuenitur, ut nemo uidelicet alterius parochianum iudicare presumat. Sed aliud est fauore uel odio proprium sacerdotem contemnere, quod sacris canonibus prohibetur, aliud cecum uitare, quod *hac auctoritate*[a] quisque facere *monetur, ne* si
monet et petit, *ne ambo in foueam cadant,* quam stultus euitare noluit....	cecus ceco ducatum prestet, *ambo in foueam cadant.*
	[b]ab hac auctoritate *Sg*

Note: Left-hand column is from ed. Friedberg, 1242, supported by Aa Fd.

topics. De pen. D.6 c.2 forbids priests to divulge the sins of penitents to others. De pen. D.6 c.3, on the other hand, does not advise penitents to avoid "blind" priests, but rather simply permits penitents to confess their sins to another priest after they have already confessed their sins to their own priest.[64] Yet only these latter two canons, first added in the second recension, are found in Sg.

Third, the canons and authorities in Sg differ more from the formal sources than the corresponding texts in manuscripts of the first recension and sometimes the second recension as well.[65] Sg even acknowledges many of these textual alterations explicitly through the addition of *et cetera* when it abbreviates canons.

Fourth, Sg contains canons that do not appear in the first recension but do in the second recension. Most of these appear in the *causae* on marriage and include some of the chronologically latest material in the second recension, namely canons 7 and 8 of the Second Lateran Council (C.27 q.1 c.40), which date to 1139, and the decretal

64. Defenders of Larrainzar's hypothesis sometimes object that the first recension also contains references to texts not included in the *Decretum.* This is true. But unlike Sg—and this is what is truly noteworthy and in need of emphasis—the first recension never refers to a missing text as *if it were present,* using demonstrative pronouns like *hac,* which here needs to be translated as "the immediately preceding" authority.

65. For examples, see Lenherr, "Ist die Handschrift"; Winroth, "Recent Work," 17–20; Tarín, *Graciano,* 72–73.

De parentela (C.35 q.6 c.8), which dates to 1138–43.[66] That these are not texts that were originally present, then removed, and later put back into the *Decretum* is demonstrated by De pen. D.7 c.2. Source analysis proves that the version of this canon found in Sg must derive from a later redactional stage of the *Decretum* than the form found in the first recension. For as it appears in Sg, the canon is a composite text deriving from two canonical collections.[67] De pen. D.7 c.2 in the first recension contains an abbreviation of 3L 3.19.37. The longer form of De pen. D.7 c.2 found in the second recension consists of the first-recension text plus additions taken from Trip. 3.28.2. The form of De pen. D.7 c.2 found in Sg corresponds to an abbreviation of the second-recension canon, with part of the text deriving from the 3L, part from the *Tripartita*, and *et cetera* tacked on at the end where the scribe has omitted the rest of the second-recension canon.

Fifth, Sg introduces doctrinal distinctions that did not develop until after the publication of the second recension. The most notable instance is in the discussion of the role of consummation in marriage formation. Through the addition of the word *postea* to C.27 q.2 c.34, Sg addresses a question not considered in the first or the second recension: do sexual relations prior to the exchange of consent suffice to turn a *coniugium initiatum* into a *coniugium ratum* or *perfectum*? Sg answers no; only consummation following consent suffices.[68]

66. Werckmeister, "Le manuscrit," 161–68.

67. For the details, see Wei, "A Reconsideration of St. Gall," 148–51, 166–68, and 173–75. Larson, *Master of Penance*, 228–30, agrees with my analysis and hence, it would now seem, with the view that Sg is not an early version of the *Decretum*. Her partial criticism of my argument stems from a misreading of what I wrote. The statement that seems to have caused confusion appears on 170: "The way in which the authorities from the *Tripartita* are layered in distinction 5 and the way in which the authorities from the 3L are layered in distinction 7 suggest that they were added at the same time, apart from—but perhaps inspired by—the use of the first recension as a teaching text." My point was that De pen. D.5 cc.2–5, i.e., the additions in De pen. D.5 deriving from the *Tripartita*, and De pen. D.7 cc.1 and 3–4, i.e., the additions in De pen. D.7 deriving from the 3L, were each added to the *Decretum* in a single sitting as the result of deliberate redactional activity rather than organic growth. I was not claiming that all the second-recension additions in De pen. D.7, that is, the single addition deriving from the *Tripartita* and the three additions deriving from the 3L, were added at the same time. This would be a puzzling assertion to make, for the reasons that Larson sets forth.

68. Werckmeister, "Le manuscrit," 165–66.

In all of the aforementioned instances, the form of Gratian's *Decretum* preserved in Sg postdates the form preserved in the first and sometimes even the second recension. The easiest way to account for this evidence is by acknowledging that Sg does not contain or derive from an early form of the *Decretum*, but rather is an abbreviation or transformation of the first recension with interpolations deriving from a manuscript of the second recension. There are only two ways a proponent of Sg's chronological and redactional priority could explain away such evidence. The first possibility is to argue that Sg does indeed preserve pre-first-recension material, even though portions of it postdate the first and second recensions. The other possibility is to argue that the text preserved in Sg does indeed abbreviate and alter an earlier version of the *Decretum*, but that this earlier version was neither the first recension nor the second recension, but rather a pre-Sg version of the *Decretum* more similar to these two recensions than to the recension preserved in Sg. According to this scenario, there would exist at least four historically reconstructable stages in the development of Gratian's *Decretum*: (1) an Ur-Gratian similar to the first recension; (2) the recension preserved in Sg, which altered Ur-Gratian; (3) the first recension, which largely changed the text preserved in Sg back to the form found in Ur-Gratian; and (4) the second recension. To date, however, proponents of the priority of Sg have been able to adduce no proof for either of these scenarios.

Conclusion

The received biography about Gratian rests on hearsay and legend. We know almost nothing about Gratian's biography save that he existed and taught canon law and that he may later have been elevated to the see of Chiusi. Given this lack of reliable extrinsic evidence, our best source of information about Gratian is his book(s). And, as the following chapters will attempt to show, one of the least exploited aspects of Gratian's book(s) is the theology. The following chapters thus take a closer look at what and how Gratian wrote on theology, beginning with the textual fount and foundation of theology, the Bible.

2

The Bible

Prior to Gratian, the Bible featured in most canonical collections to only a modest extent. While medieval Christians regarded the Bible as the most authoritative source of religious truth, they generally did not treat it as a source of positive law or structure their canonical collections around biblical texts. For the most part, the Bible entered the canonical tradition indirectly, through its quotation in conciliar canons, papal decretals, and patristic texts, rather than through direct incorporation into canonical collections. Only in the seventh and eighth centuries did Irish compilers begin to include biblical excerpts as "canons" in their canonical collections, and most of these never made their way into the broader canonical tradition. More sophisticated importation of biblical principles and motifs into canonical collections occurred occasionally but was not the norm, except when canonists like Pseudo-Isidore and Burchard of Worms "corrected" or forged canonical texts.[1]

This chapter explores how and why Gratian went beyond this earlier tradition. My main claim is that the Bible shapes much of the first recension of the *Decretum*, though sometimes in ways not read-

1. See Jean Gaudemet, "La Bible dans les collections canoniques," in *La moyen âge et la Bible*, ed. Pierre Riché and Guy Lobrichon (Paris: Beauchesne, 1984), 327–69; Greta Austin, *Shaping Church Law Around the Year 1000: The Decretum of Burchard of Worms* (Farnham: Ashgate, 2009), 145–61.

ily apparent from an initial reading of the text. The Bible, of course, occupies the highest place in Gratian's doctrine of the sources of law. And biblical quotations and exempla recur frequently throughout not only the distinctions in the first part of the *Decretum*, but also the *causae* and *De penitentia*. In addition, however, it will be shown, Gratian used biblical texts and commentary to supplement and modify aspects of existing canon law, most notably—and perhaps surprisingly—procedural law. And he used biblical texts and commentary to structure many sections of the *Decretum* as well.

The Bible in Theory

This section looks at Gratian's doctrines of biblical authority and biblical interpretation. Gratian touches upon these issues in numerous places throughout the first recension of the *Decretum*, but most completely and systematically in the so-called *Tractatus de legibus* (DD.1–20) that opens the work.[2] Canonists of the reform period had begun their collections with material on papal primacy, while Ivo of Chartres and canonists dependent on him placed texts on faith and the sacraments at the beginning of their compilations.[3] Gratian broke with both these traditions by prefacing his textbook with an examination of the nature and sources of law.[4] Aside from the *Collectio Caesaraugustana*, which Gratian does not seem to have known or used, no earlier canonical collection begins in this fashion.[5] Gratian's deci-

2. Gratian, *The Treatise on Laws (Decretum DD. 1–20) with the Ordinary Gloss*, trans. Augustine Thompson and James Gordley, with an introduction by Katherine Christensen (Washington, D.C.: The Catholic University of America Press, 1993).

3. Rolker, *Canon Law*, 180–81.

4. Landau, "Gratian and the *Decretum Gratiani*," 38.

5. On the *Collectio Caesaraugustana*'s opening section, see Eloy Tejero, "'Ratio' y jerarquía de fuentes canónicas en la Caesaraugustana," in *Hispania Christiana: Estudios en honor del Prof. Dr. José Orlandis Rovira en su septuagesimo aniversario*, ed. Josep-Ignasi Saranyana and Eloy Tejero (Pamplona: Ediciones Universidad de Navarra, 1988), 303–22. On the *Collectio Caesaraugustana* in general, see Linda Fowler-Magerl, "The Version of the *Collectio Caesaraugustana* in Barcelona, Archivo de la Corona de Aragón, MS San Cugat 63," in *Ritual, Text and Law: Studies in Medieval Canon Law and Liturgy Presented to Roger E. Reynolds*, ed. Kathleen G. Cushing and Richard F. Gyug (Aldershot: Ashgate, 2004), 269–80. For a guide to

sion to begin with the *Tractatus de legibus* and to include a discussion of the Bible therein was thus almost completely unprecedented in the canonical tradition. The move highlights both his jurisprudential orientation and his theological bent.

The Authority of the Bible

Gratian had an exalted view of biblical authority. Like his contemporaries, he regarded the books making up the Bible as more than just the writings of wise human authors. The Bible does not simply record the history of God's dealings with humanity. It also contains and makes known his will. God speaks not only when dictating the Old Law to Moses or when Christ speaks in the gospels, but also when the prophets proclaim his message.[6] God places his words in the mouth of the prophets.[7] When they speak, he speaks through them.[8]

Nevertheless, Gratian was unwilling to recognize the literal interpretation of every biblical passage as law, and in the *Tractatus de legibus* he takes great pains to show how the Bible both is the highest source of law and should not always be followed according to its literal sense. In the *Tractatus de legibus,* Gratian lays the foundation for what

---

the literature on the *Collectio Caesaraugustana,* see Kéry, *Canonical Collections of the Early Middle Ages,* 260–62; Fowler-Magerl, *Clavis,* 239–44. On earlier canonical collections, see Jean Gaudemet, "La doctrine des sources du droit dans le Décret de Gratien," *RDC* 1 (1950): 5–31, at 6–11, reprinted in his *La formation du droit canonique médiéval,* Variorum Collected Studies Series CS111 (London: Variorum, 1980), no. VII.

6. Whence such formulas as *Dominus ait/precepit Moysi/ad Moysen/per Moysen*: C.13 q.1 d.p.c.1 §4 (ed. Friedberg, 718); C.23 q.5 d.p.c.7 (ed. Friedberg, 932); De pen. D.4 d.p.c.7 (ed. Friedberg, 1230); C.35 q.1 d.a.c.1 §2 (ed. Werckmeister, 584); and *Dominus/Christus ait (in euangelio)*: D.21 d.a.c.1 §1 (ed. Friedberg, 67); C.3 q.7 d.p.c.7 (ed. Friedberg, 528); C.23 q.6 d.a.c.1 (ed. Friedberg, 947); De pen. D.1 d.p.c.35 (ed. Friedberg, 1167).

7. D.36 d.p.c.2 §4 (ed. Friedberg, 134, supported by Aa Bc Fd P): "Hinc etiam Dominus prius ponit uerba sua in ore prophete, et postea constituit eum super gentes et regna."

8. Whence the recurrent formula *per prophetam*: C.2 q.7 d.p.c.27 §3 (ed. Friedberg, 490); C.2 q.7 d.p.c.41 §8 (ed. Friedberg, 497); C.23 q.5 d.p.c.49 §1 (ed. Friedberg, 946); C.27 q.1 d.p.c.43 (ed. Werckmeister, 132); De pen. D.1 d.p.c.33 (ed. Friedberg, 1165); De pen. D.1 d.p.c.34 (ed. Friedberg, 1166); De pen. D.1 d.p.c.37 §1 (ed. Friedberg, 1167); De pen. D.4 d.p.c.20 (ed. Friedberg, 1237); C.35 q.1 d.p.c.1 §1 (ed. Werckmeister, 588). See also De pen. D.4 d.p.c.14 (ed. Friedberg, 1236, supported by Aa Fd): "Dominus ait per Ezechielem."

would later become the doctrine of the hierarchy of authorities, that is, a doctrine for what authority to follow when two or more authorities conflict. Gratian divides law into two main categories: natural law and mores.[9] He identifies mores with human law, which he subdivides into two categories: constitution (human law that has been set down in writing) and custom (human law that has not been set down in writing).[10] He equates natural law with "what is contained in the Law and the Gospel" (that is, the Bible), an identification that he supports through a comparison of their content and the testimony of scripture. Natural law prescribes the golden rule in both its positive and negative forms: do unto others what you would wish done to yourself, and do not do to others what you would not wish done to yourself. The Gospel of Matthew, on the other hand, reports that Jesus both prescribed the golden rule in its positive form and identified the golden rule with the Bible. "Whatever you want men to do to you, do so to them. This indeed is the Law and the Prophets."[11]

Gratian's identification of natural law with the Bible was innovative, but also problematic.[12] According to Gratian, natural law takes precedence over mores in not only dignity, but also time. Natural law, he teaches, began with the creation of rational creatures and thereafter has undergone neither change nor variation.[13] It is immutable and

9. On Gratian's conception of natural law, see Rudolf Weigand, *Die Naturrechtslehre der Legisten und Dekretisten von Irnerius bis Accursius und von Gratian bis Johannes Teutonicus*, Münchener theologische Studien 3, Kanonistische Abteilung 26 (Munich: Hueber, 1967), 132–40.

10. D.1 d.p.c.1 (ed. Friedberg, 1, supported by Aa Bc P): "nomine uero legis humane mores iure conscripti et traditi intelligantur"; D.1 d.p.c.5 (ed. Friedberg, 2, supported by Aa Bc P): "Que in scriptis redacta est, constitutio siue ius uocatur; que uero in scriptis redacta non est, generali nomine, consuetudo uidelicet, appellatur."

11. D.1 d.a.c.1 (ed. Friedberg, 1, supported by Aa Bc P): "Humanum genus duobus regitur, naturali uidelicet iure et moribus. Ius nature (naturale *Aa*) est quod in lege et euangelio continetur, quo quisque iubetur alii facere, quod sibi uult fieri, et prohibetur alii inferre, quod sibi nolit fieri. Vnde Christus in euangelio: 'Omnia quecumque uultis ut faciant uobis homines et uos eadem facite illis. Hec est enim lex et prophete.'" Translation of the biblical passage (Mt 7:12) from Gratian, *The Treatise on Laws*, 3.

12. On the natural law theories of earlier Christian writers, see Weigand, *Naturrechtslehre*, 121–32.

13. D.5 d.a.c.1 §1 (ed. Friedberg, 7, supported by Aa Bc P): "Naturale ius inter

unchanging, so human law has no force if it contradicts it.[14] Custom, in contrast, began with the first human cities—before the flood with the city founded by Cain, after the flood with the one established by Nimrod—while (human!) constitutions only began with the decrees that God gave to Moses.[15] But if, as Gratian teaches, the natural law is unchanging and the Bible touches upon both custom and constitution, then can the natural law really be identical to what is contained in the Bible? Gratian answers with a distinction borrowed from the Christian exegetical tradition. The Bible, he states, contains not only moral precepts, but also mystical ones. Moral precepts and the moral meaning of mystical precepts belong to the natural law and are therefore immutable. But the literal meaning of mystical precepts, such as the Jewish ceremonial law, does not belong to the natural law and hence can change (and has changed) over time.[16]

For Gratian, then, the Bible both does and does not occupy the highest place in the doctrine of the sources of law. On the one hand, the Bible is in a certain sense identical to the natural law and thus takes precedence over any human authority.[17] On the other hand, the meaning of the Bible is not always self-evident and thus requires the aid of a human exegete.

---

omnia primatum obtinet et tempore et dignitate. Cepit enim ab exordio rationalis creature, nec uariatur tempore, sed immutabile permanet."

14. D.8 d.p.c.1 (ed. Friedberg, 13, supported by Aa Bc P): "Dignitate uero ius naturale similiter (simpliciter *Friedb.*) preualet consuetudini et constitutioni. Quecumque enim uel moribus recepta sunt, uel scriptis comprehensa, si naturali iuri fuerint aduersa, uana et irrita sunt habenda."

15. D.6 d.p.c.3 (ed. Friedberg, 11); D.7 d.a.c.1 (ed. Friedberg, 12).

16. D.6 d.p.c.3 (ed. Friedberg, 11, supported by Aa Bc P): "In lege et euangelio naturale ius continetur; non tamen quecumque in lege et euangelio inueniuntur, naturali iuri coherere probantur. Sunt enim in lege quedam moralia (precepta *add. Aa*), ut: 'non occides' etc., quedam mistica, utpote sacrificiorum precepta, et alia his similia. Moralia mandata ad naturale ius spectant atque ideo nullam mutabilitatem recepisse monstrantur. Mistica uero, quantum ad superficiem, a naturali iure probantur aliena, quantum ad moralem intelligentiam, inueniuntur sibi annexa; ac per hoc, etsi secundum superficiem uideantur esse mutata, tamen secundum moralem intelligentiam mutabilitatem nescire probantur."

17. Cf. Weigand, *Naturrechtslehre*, 135–36.

Biblical Interpretation

Gratian recognizes the need for human intervention in biblical interpretation most explicitly when he distinguishes between moral and mystical precepts. As the Bible itself generally does not state when it is speaking mystically as opposed to literally and morally, the exegete must decide, first, whether a mystical meaning exists and, second, if he has decided that a mystical meaning exists, what that mystical meaning is. Gratian's doctrine of the Bible provides guidance on the first question, but not the second. A mystical meaning exists, Gratian implies, when the literal meaning of a biblical precept does not correspond to what the exegete knows that the moral law commands today.[18] As Gratian notes repeatedly throughout the first recension, the Old Testament permitted many things that the perfection of grace in the New Testament has abolished.[19] In some cases, Gratian states, biblical exempla should elicit admiration but not imitation. Gratian, for instance, finds admirable Samuel's slaying of Agag, king of the Amalekites, (1 Sm 15:33) and Phineas's slaying of a Jew and a Midianite woman (Nm 25:8). But he argues that Christian ecclesiastics should not imitate their actions and themselves shed blood.[20]

In other instances, Gratian finds formerly permitted biblical practices simply to have been the result of necessity. He argues, for instance, that the Old Testament permitted marriage between siblings and other close relatives not because this practice is or should be normally permitted, but rather from necessity. As all human beings

18. See D.6 d.p.c.3.

19. C.15 q.3 d.a.c.1 (ed. Friedberg, 750, supported by Aa Fd): "(In *add. Friedb.*) ueteri lege multa permittebantur que hodie perfectione gratie abolita sunt." C.26 q.2 d.p.c.1 (ed. Friedberg, 1020, supported by Aa Fd): "Antequam euangelium claresceret, multa permittebantur, que tempore perfectionis (perfectioris *Friedb.*) (et *add. Aa*) discipline penitus sunt eliminata."

20. C.2 q.7 d.p.c.41 §8 (ed. Friedberg, 497, supported by Aa Bc Fd P): "Miracula, (et *add. Aa Fd² Friedb.*) maxime ueteris testamenti, sunt admiranda, non in exemplum nostre actionis trahenda. Multa enim tunc concedebantur, que nunc penitus prohibentur. Tunc enim Samuel Agag pinguissimum regem Amalech in frustra conscidit; nunc nulli ecclesiasticorum iudicium sanguinis agitare licet. Tunc Finees iudeum coeuntem cum Madianita interfecit, et reputatum est ei in iustitiam; hodie sacerdotibus in perniciem sui uerteretur officii."

descend from Adam and Eve, siblings had to marry each other initially if the human race was to survive. However, lack of necessity now makes this practice damnable.[21]

In still other instances, Gratian argues that a formerly permitted practice was the result of human infirmity, which the coming of Christ has eliminated. He gives three examples: David's marrying Bathsheba after committing adultery with her and having her husband killed (2 Sm 11); the permissibility of divorce in the Old Testament (Dt 24:1); and the offering of animal sacrifices (Lv 5).[22] While these practices were permitted in the Old Testament, they are forbidden today.

The exegete's determination of when a mystical meaning exists is complicated, of course, by Gratian's admission elsewhere that the Bible does not contain just precepts, whether moral or mystical, but also sets forth counsels of perfection. This distinction is analogous to one that he introduces for non-biblical authorities, between precept and exhortation. A precept, Gratian writes, imposes necessity on an individual, whereas an exhortation excites his free will.[23] Similarly, Gratian argues, some passages from scripture should be interpreted not as commands, but rather as counsels that we should follow if we wish to be perfect, but which we can, without sin, refrain from doing. Jesus's question to the Jews in John 8:46 ("Which of you shall convince me of sin?") provides one example. Jesus, Gratian argues,

21. C.35 q.1 d.a.c.1 §2 (ed. Werckmeister, 584): "Consanguineorum coniunctiones alias causa necessitatis permisse, alias causa iuste rationis inueniuntur imperate. Cum enim unus ab initio uir, atque una ex latere eius mulier formaretur a Deo, necessario sorores fratribus copulabantur. Quod autem necessitate cogente fit, cessante necessitate pariter cessare oportet. Tanto ergo nunc damnabilius usurpatur consanguineorum coiunctio, quanto minus necessaria probatur."

22. C.31 q.1 d.p.c.7 (ed. Werckmeister, 334): "Sed in ueteri testamento multa permittebantur propter infirmitatem que in euangelii perfectione eliminata sunt: sicut permittebatur quibuslibet dare libellum repudii ne per odium funderetur sanguis innoxius. Quod postea Dominus in euangelio prohibuit dicens uxorem a uiro non esse dimittendam nisi causa fornicationis. Quedam permittebantur causa infirmitatis et sacramenti futurorum: sicut Dominus permisit filiis Israel offerre animalia sibi in sacrificium que in Egipto consueuerant immolare demonibus, malens ea sibi offerri quam idolis et ut essent illis sacramenta futurorum. Sic et Bersabee permissa est duci in uxorem, non magis causa sue infirmitatis quam significatione futurorum."

23. D.4 d.p.c.6 (ed. Friedberg, 7, supported by Aa Bc P): "Decretum uero necessitatem facit, exhortatio autem liberam uoluntatem excitat."

invited the Jews to criticize him not because prelates are obligated to accept criticism from their subordinates, but rather to demonstrate his perfect humility. If Jesus's actions were interpreted as a legal precept, then criminals and infamous individuals would be able to accuse people in court, which the canons do not allow.[24]

In contrast to the fair amount of guidance he provides for determining whether a mystical interpretation exists, Gratian provides no guidance to the exegete when the dispute centers on which of two or more competing mystical interpretations is the correct one. Augustine of Hippo famously made charity or love the litmus test for the correctness of a mystical interpretation. In theory, he accepted any mystical interpretation as correct if it promoted love of God for his own sake and love of oneself and one's neighbors in subordination to God.[25] Perhaps because Gratian often wants to identify a single interpretation as correct rather than acknowledge the possibility of multiple correct mystical meanings, he never refers to this Augustinian teaching in his textbook. Instead of providing and applying any particular theory for resolving conflicts between mystical meanings, Gratian acts opportunistically. When there is a position he prefers, he simply rules out mystical interpretations that go against that position and argues for the mystical interpretations that support it.[26] However, where he is undecided on an issue, he is willing to leave the exegetical question open as well.[27]

24. C.2 q.7 d.p.c.9 §3 (ed. Friedberg, 495, supported by Aa Bc Fd P): "Aliud est quod de rigore cogimur seruare discipline, aliud quod admittitur ex perfectionis consideratione. Christus Iudeos ad se arguendum admisit perfectione humilitatis, non seueritate iuris. Si enim legis rigore essent admissi, hac auctoritate criminosi et infames in accusatione religiosorum essent recipiendi, cum essent sceleratissimi, qui de Christi nece tractantes, innocentem condempnare uolebant. Hoc ergo exemplo prelati non coguntur recipere subditos in accusatione sui, sed permittuntur." On infamy, see the discussion below of procedural law. For another example of the distinction between precept and counsel, see C.35 q.1 d.p.c.1 §2 (ed. Werckmeister, 590).

25. Augustine, *De doctrina christiana* 3.10.14–16 and 15.23, ed. Joseph Martin, CCSL 32 (Turnhout: Brepols, 1962), 86–88 and 91.

26. See, e.g., Gratian's handling of a biblical text and its commentary by Gregory the Great in distinction 3 of *De penitentia*, discussed at p. 133.

27. See, e.g., Gratian's handling of the biblical and other authorities in distinction 1 of *De penitentia*, discussed esp. at pp. 103–19.

The Bible in Practice

Modern scholars have at times judged Gratian's use of the Bible to be largely cosmetic and without consequence for his legal thought.[28] But a broader and more detailed examination of the *Decretum* provides evidence against this view. Many sections of the *Decretum* quote or otherwise refer to the Bible extensively. Biblical passages not only serve as proof texts and authorities, but also lead Gratian to depart from contemporary legal norms. Many of the maxims and exempla in the *Decretum* derive from the Bible, as does the structure underlying various sections of the *Decretum*. In both theory and practice, the Bible occupies a prominent place in the *Decretum*.

Biblical Quotations and Allusions

Different sections of the *Decretum* refer to the Bible to differing degrees (see table 2-1). The *Tractatus de legibus* (DD.1–20) and the so-called *Causae monachorum* (*Causae* 16–20), for instance, rarely quote from the Bible or refer to biblical exempla. The *Tractatus de legibus* elaborates Gratian's doctrine of biblical authority, but buttresses this

28. E.g., Gabriel le Bras, "Les Écritures dans le Décret de Gratien," *ZRG KA* 27 (1938): 47–80, at 76–77: "l'ensemble [of biblical material in the *Decretum*] est moins imposant que le principium du Décret ne le laissait prévoir. Beaucoup d'objections vaines, de jongleries littéraires, sans grande originalité, assez peu de règles et de principes. La raison en est claire: l'Ancien Testament contient des parties légales, de véritables codes, mais adapté au peuple juif, il a été aboli par le Christ, sauf quelques principes éternels; l'Évangile est une prédication morale, où les précisions sont rares; enfin, les communautés que surveillait l'Apôtre Paul étaient trop simples pour que l'on trouvât dans ses Epîtres la constitution qui convenait à la société religieuse du XIIe siècle [The whole of the biblical material in the *Decretum* is less imposing than the principium of the *Decretum* would lead one to predict. Many vain objections, literary sleights of hand, without much originality, rather few rules and principles. The reason is clear: the Old Testament contains legal sections, true codes, but adapted to the Jewish people, they were abolished by Christ, with the exception of some eternal principles; the gospel is a moral teaching, where precisions are rare; finally, the communities that the apostle Paul was supervising were too simple for one to find in his epistles a constitution suitable to the religious society of the twelfth century]." Cf. Gaudemet, "La Bible dans les collections canoniques," 362–64; Christoph H. F. Meyer, *Die Distinktionstechnik in der Kanonistik des 12. Jahrhunderts: Ein Beitrag zur Wissenschaftsgeschichte des Hochmittelalters* (Leuven: Leuven University Press, 2000), 153.

doctrine with only occasional references to scripture. *Causae* 16–20, on the other hand, neither draw on the Bible to any great extent nor discuss how the Bible should be used or studied. Monastic contemplation was rooted in scripture, the canon law of religious life much less so.

Sections of the *Decretum* dealing with the clergy, crime, marriage, and penance, in contrast, are replete with biblical references. In the first recension, *De penitentia* contains 437 biblical references; *Causae* 22–24 on perjury, violence, and heresy, 385 biblical references; DD.21–101 on ordination, 268 biblical references; and *Causae* 27–36 on marriage, 195 references. In the second recension, these same sections continue to exceed other sections of the *Decretum* in the number of their biblical references. *De penitentia* comes in first place with 541 biblical references; *Causae* 22–24 in second place with 494 biblical references; DD.21–101 in third place with 461 references; and *Causae* 27–36 in fourth place with 289 biblical references. *De consecratione*, which deals with the sacraments and liturgy and which one might expect to contain an especially large number of biblical references, in fact comes in fifth place with 277 biblical references. The number is by no means trivial, but nevertheless is less than for the four above mentioned sections (see table 2-1).

To a certain extent, the aforementioned differences in the degree to which the Bible is referenced are due to the fact that different sections are of different length. *De penitentia*, for instance, comprises more than 10 percent of the work in both the first and second recensions, whereas the *Tractatus de legibus* occupies less than 5 percent of the second recension and only slightly more of the first recension. But the canonical tradition that Gratian summed up likewise played an important role. The canons dealing with topics like war and penance draw more heavily on the Bible than those dealing with other issues, like the regulation of monastic life. Sections of the *Decretum* dealing with topics of the former sort thus naturally contain more biblical references than sections dealing with issues of the latter sort.

That said, a somewhat different perspective on the importance of the Bible in the different sections of the *Decretum* emerges if one leaves out the biblical references found in the canons. If one con-

Table 2-1. References to the Bible in the First and Second Recensions

	First Recension			Second Recension		
	Old Test.	New Test.	Total	Old Test.	New Test.	Total
DD.1–20	15 (8)	17 (3)	32 (11)	20 (8)	25 (3)	45 (11)
DD.21–101	102 (36)	166 (63)	268 (99)	191 (38)	270 (67)	461 (105)
C.1	59 (26)	79 (21)	138 (47)	83 (27)	126 (21)	209 (48)
CC.2–6	50 (37)	54 (24)	104 (61)	65 (37)	74 (24)	139 (61)
CC.7–14	45 (12)	57 (20)	102 (32)	103 (19)	145 (40)	248 (59)
C.15	9 (4)	8 (5)	17 (9)	12 (4)	8 (5)	20 (9)
CC.16–20	12 (3)	20 (1)	32 (4)	18 (3)	26 (1)	44 (4)
C.21	0 (0)	7 (0)	7 (0)	0 (0)	8 (0)	8 (0)
CC.22–24	161 (62)	224 (97)	385 (159)	219 (64)	275 (97)	494 (161)
C.25	3 (2)	7 (5)	10 (7)	3 (2)	8 (5)	11 (7)
C.26	23 (7)	21 (5)	44 (12)	31 (7)	31 (5)	62 (12)
CC.27–36	71 (20)	124 (35)	195 (55)	96 (20)	193 (35)	289 (55)
De pen.	188 (86)	249 (63)	437 (149)	248 (87)	293 (64)	541 (151)
De cons.	n/a	n/a	n/a	66 (0)	211 (0)	277 (0)
Total	738 (303)	1030 (341)	1768 (644)	1155 (316)	1693 (367)	2848 (683)

Note: Each column gives, first, the total number of biblical citations and allusions in a given section of the *Decretum*, and second (in parentheses), the number of biblical citations and allusions in just that section's dicta, minus those found in non-biblical texts quoted in the dicta. These numbers are somewhat subjective, since it is to a certain extent arbitrary just what exactly constitutes a single reference. I drew up these numbers with the aid of Franciscus Germovnik, *Index biblicus ad Decretum Gratiani: Secundum editionem Aemilii Friedberg* (Lemont, Ill.: De Andreis Seminary, 1971).

siders only Gratian's dicta, the sections on the clergy, crime, marriage, and penance continue to contain a significant amount of biblical references, but the section dealing with marriage now contains fewer references than *Causae* 2–6 on procedural law. *Causae* 2–6, in fact, have a higher ratio of biblical references in the dicta to the total number of biblical references than does any other section of the *Decretum*. Gratian referred to the Bible in many other sections of the *Decretum* out of necessity, because the canons in these sections did so. He seems to have referred to the Bible in *Causae* 2–6, in contrast, for the opposite reason, because the canons failed to do so.

For the most part, modern scholars of canonical procedure in the

Decretum have focused on its indebtedness to Roman law, with good reason.[29] The procedural norms prescribed by the canon law in the mid-twelfth century derived largely from "vulgar" Roman law, that is, Roman law as simplified and adapted by the Germanic tribes that came to dominate western Europe, rather than the pure(r) Roman law of the *Corpus iuris civilis*, which the emperor Justinian had produced in the sixth century.[30] Many of these vulgar Roman law procedural norms, however, circulated not under their own name but rather in disguise, under the patronage of early popes.[31] In the mid-ninth century, industrious clerics in the province of Reims produced several collections of closely related forgeries, which they combined with authentic material. The chief products were an interpolated version of the *Collectio Hispana*, false capitularies ascribed to an otherwise unknown Benedictus Levita, the so-called *Capitula Angilramni*, and, most notably, the Pseudo-Isidorian or *False Decretals*, so called because they were allegedly compiled by Isidore the Merchant (*Isidorus Mercator*).[32] Because the same forgers were presumably responsible for all these

29. See, e.g., Georg May, "Die Infamie im Decretum Gratiani," *AKKR* 129 (1960): 389–408; Wieslaw Litewski, "Les textes procéduraux du droit de Justinien dans le Décret de Gratien," *Studia Gratiana* 9 (1966): 67–109; Brigitte Basdevant-Gaudemet, "Les sources de droit romain en matière de procédure dans le Décret de Gratien," in her *Église et autorités: Études d'histoire de droit canonique médiéval* (Limoges: Presses Universitaires de Limoges, 2006), 213–51.

30. On the history of the term "vulgar Roman law," see Detlef Liebs, "Roman Vulgar Law in Late Antiquity," in *Aspects of Law in Late Antiquity: Dedicated to A. M. Honoré on the occasion of the Sixtieth Year of His Teaching in Oxford*, ed. A. I. B. Sirks (Oxford: All Souls College, 2008), 35–53.

31. Cf. Basdevant-Gaudemet, "Les sources de droit romain en matière de procédure dans le Décret de Gratien," who demonstrates that much of the Roman law in *Causae* 2–6 derives from the Pseudo-Isidorian forgeries.

32. For an introduction to the Pseudo-Isidorian forgeries, see Eric Knibbs, "The Interpolated Hispana and the Origins of Pseudo-Isidore," *ZRG KA* 99 (2013): 1–71. Also useful, though dated, are Horst Fuhrmann, "The Pseudo-Isidorian Forgeries," in Detlev Jasper and Horst Fuhrmann, *Papal Letters in the Early Middle Ages* (Washington, D.C.: The Catholic University of America Press, 2001), 137–95; Paul Fournier and Gabriel le Bras, *L'histoire des collections canoniques en Occident: Depuis les Fausses Décrétales jusqu'au Décrét de Gratien*, 2 vols. (Paris: Sirey, 1931–32), 1:127–233. On the *Capitula Angilramni*, see Karl-Georg Schon, *Die Capitula Angilramni: Eine prozessrechtliche Fälschung Pseudoisidors*, MGH Studien und Texte 39 (Hanover: MGH, 2006). For a list of editions, manuscripts, and guide to further literature, see Kéry, *Canonical Collections*, 100–124; Fowler-Magerl, *Clavis*, 50–55.

works, the secondary literature generally refers to them collectively as the Pseudo-Isidorian Forgeries and to their compilers as Pseudo-Isidore. Pseudo-Isidore employed a cut-and-paste method when forging capitularies and decretals. He took snippets from earlier works and then rearranged, combined, and altered them to produce new texts that said what he wanted them to say.[33]

The resulting forgeries addressed a wide range of topics, ranging from heresy to the liturgy, papal power, and legal procedure. Of particular concern to the forgers, it is clear, were the rights and prerogatives of bishops.[34] Numerous forgeries expand the power of bishops *vis-à-vis* both laypersons and other clerics. Many false decretals, for instance, condemn the rival office of chorbishop as an abuse and demand its abolition.[35] The false decretals enlarge exceptions to the contemporary prohibition on episcopal translation, that is, the now-regular practice of moving a bishop from one see to another.[36] They insist that laypersons cannot judge clerics, but that only clerics may sit in judgment over other clerics.[37] They repeatedly assert that a metropolitan or archbishop has to act in concert with the other bishops of the ecclesiastical province if he wishes to judge a suffragan bishop. A metropolitan cannot judge a suffragan on his own.[38]

33. See the following texts by Klaus Zechiel-Eckes: "Verecundus oder Pseudoisidor? Zur Genese der Excerptiones de gestis Chalcedonensis concilii," *Deutsches Archiv* 56 (2000): 413–46; "Ein Blick in Pseudoisidors Werkstatt: Studien zum Entstehungsprozeß der falschen Dekretalen mit einem exemplarischen editorischen Anhang," *Francia* 28 (2001): 37–90; "Auf Pseudoisidors Spur, oder: Versuch einen dichten Schleier zu lüften," in *Fortschritt durch Fälschungen? Ursprung, Gestalt und Wirkungen der pseudoisidorischen Fälschungen*, ed. Wilfried Hartmann and Gerhard Schmitz (Hanover: Hahn, 2002), 1–28.

34. See Fuhrmann, "Pseudo-Isidorian Forgeries," 142–43; Agostino Marchetto, *Episcopato e Primato pontificio nelle decretali pseudo isidoriane: Ricerca storico-giuridica* (Rome: Pontificia Università Lateranense, 1971); Fernando Yarz, *El Obispo en la organización eclesiástica de las Decretales pseudoisidorianas* (Pamplona: Universidad de Navarra, 1985).

35. The chorbishop was an office intermediate between bishop and priest that existed for some time in the early Middle Ages. On its history and Pseudo-Isidore's crusade against it, see Marchetto, *Episcopato e Primato*, 41–56; Yarz, *Obispo*, 197–217.

36. Marchetto, *Episcopato e Primato*, 31–40; Yarz, *Obispo*, 188–93.

37. Marchetto, *Episcopato e Primato*, 59–61; Yarz, *Obispo*, 103–30 and 138–88.

38. Marchetto, *Episcopato e Primato*, 62; Yarz, *Obispo*, 217–50.

Numerous false decretals also insist on exspoliation. If a bishop has been "spoliated," ejected from his see, he must be "exspoliated," have his office and property restored to him, before he can stand trial. Only after he has been judicially convicted and sentenced can his office and property be taken away.[39] To give one last example, many forgeries vigorously defend the right of bishops to appeal to Rome at any time during the judicial process.[40] During the Reformation, Protestant scholars generally thought such forgeries proof that Pseudo-Isidore's purpose was to exalt papal power and prerogatives. Modern scholarship, however, has made it clear that Pseudo-Isidore did not promote the papacy as an end in itself, but rather as a means to safeguard and protect bishops against their metropolitans and secular authorities.[41]

Because of their apparent authority and relevance to the concerns of medieval canonists, the Pseudo-Isidorian forgeries proved extremely successful.[42] Both the *False Decretals* and some of the other forgeries associated with Pseudo-Isidore—for example, the *Capitula Angilramni*—achieved a wide diffusion in later canonical collections and feature prominently in the ones that Gratian drew on in producing his textbook. Pseudo-Isidorian forgeries, for instance, comprise approximately 23 percent of Anselm of Lucca's canonical collection and are particularly rich in books 2 and 3 on criminal procedure and appeal.[43] They make up about 30 percent of the canons in book 1 of the *Tripartita*, which is a chronological collection of papal letters.[44] They comprise over 45 percent of the canons in the *Polycarpus*

39. Marchetto, *Episcopato e Primato*, 63–64; Yarz, *Obispo*, 130–38.

40. Marchetto, *Episcopato e Primato*, 69–84; Marchetto, "Diritto di appello a Roma nelle Decretali Pseudo-Isidoriane," in *Scientia veritatis: Festschrift für Hubert Mordek zum 65. Geburtstag*, ed. Oliver Münsch and Thomas Zotz (Ostfildern: Thorbecke, 2004), 191–206.

41. See, e.g., Fuhrmann, "The Pseudo-Isidorian Forgeries," 142–43.

42. On the influence of Pseudo-Isidore, see Horst Fuhrmann, *Einfluß und Verbreitung der pseudoisidorischen Fälschungen*, 3 vols., Schriften der MGH 24 (Stuttgart: Hiersemann, 1973–74).

43. Cushing, *Papacy and Law*, 72 and 203–4; Fuhrmann, *Einfluß*, 2:511.

44. There are 673 canons in book 1 of the *Tripartita*, of which 206 are forgeries deriving from Pseudo-Isidore. Almost all of the canons from Pseudo-Isidore appear in the first third of book 1, which contains forged papal decretals from Clement (88–97) and Anacletus (76–88) to Damasus (366–83).

and 75 percent of book 5 of that collection, which deals with procedure.[45] They make up over 10 percent of the *Panormia* and over half of that collection's fourth book, which deals with papal primacy and the rights of metropolitans and bishops.[46] And they comprise around 19 percent of the 3L if one excludes that collection's appendix, and around 17 percent if one includes the appendix.[47]

Given the prominence of Pseudo-Isidorian forgeries in Gratian's formal sources, it is unsurprising that they likewise appear in great number in the *Decretum*. Around 10 percent of the second recension derives ultimately from Pseudo-Isidore.[48] And in the first recension, canons deriving from Pseudo-Isidore comprise approximately 9 percent of the whole work and 54 percent of *Causae* 2–6.[49]

While the prominence of Pseudo-Isidore in the *Decretum* is not surprising, what Gratian does to Pseudo-Isidore is: he uses the Bible to modify Pseudo-Isidorian prescriptions on procedural law. C.2 q.4 provides one example. This question investigates the number of witnesses needed to condemn a bishop. A Pseudo-Isidorian decretal that Gratian includes as C.2 q.4 c.2 asserts that deposing a bishop requires seventy-two witnesses.[50] But an earlier unforged canon from the Second Council of Braga (572), which Gratian includes as C.2 q.4 c.1,

45. By my count, the *Polycarpus* contains 1,531 canons, of which around 706 are from Pseudo-Isidore, and 109 canons in book 5, of which 82 are from Pseudo-Isidore. In calculating these figures, I used the tables in Horst, *Die Kanonessammlung "Polycarpus,"* 104–98. See also ibid., 69.

46. Fuhrmann, *Einfluß*, 2:555.

47. By my count, the three books of the 3L contain 1,942 canons, of which around 377 are from Pseudo-Isidore. The appendix contains 373 canons, of which 24 are from Pseudo-Isidore. In calculating these figures, I relied on Joseph Motta, ed., *Collectio canonum trium librorum*, 2 vols., MIC.B 8/I-II (Vatican City: BAV, 2005–8).

48. Fuhrmann, *Einfluß*, 2:566–67.

49. By my count, the first recension contains 2,072 canons, of which 194 derive from Pseudo-Isidore, and *Causae* 2–6 contain 221 canons in the first recension, of which 120 derive from Pseudo-Isidore. In drawing up these figures, I rely upon the tables in Friedberg's edition and the appendix to Winroth, *The Making of Gratian's Decretum*, 196–227.

50. C.2 q.4 c.2 (ed. Friedberg, 466, supported by Aa Bc Fd P): "Presul non dampnetur (dampnatur *Aa*) nisi cum LXXII testibus." The material source is Pseudo-Silvester, *Ex synodalibus gestis*, c.2, ed. Paul Hinschius, *Decretales Pseudo-Isidorianae et Capitula Angilramni* (Leipzig: B. Tauchnitz, 1863), 449.

states that just two or three witnesses are required for deposing clerics.[51] To decide between these competing procedural norms, the first recension looks to the Bible. The council fathers at Braga had justified their requirement of just two or three witnesses by appealing to the apostle Paul. Gratian goes even further. In support of the requirement of just two or three witnesses, he point to not only Paul, but also Jesus, whom he quotes directly, and Moses, whose legislation on the matter is referred to in the other biblical passages he quotes.[52] Gratian explains the conflicting norm set forth by Pseudo-Isidore in two ways. The requirement of seventy-two witnesses to condemn a bishop, sixty-four to condemn a priest, twenty-seven to condemn a deacon, and seven to condemn those in minor orders found in Pseudo-Isidore, he suggests, may be a special privilege unique to the clerics of the Roman church. Alternatively, this rule may have been set forth on account of the shamelessness of those who, because their own lives and knowledge were unexamined, accused clergy over hastily. But, Gratian maintains, just two or three witnesses suffice when the witnesses are such as live praiseworthily, concerning whose assertions no doubt can arise.[53]

51. C.2 q.4 c.1 (ed. Friedberg, 465, supported by Aa Bc Fd P): "Placuit, ut si quis aliquem clericorum maculatione fornicationis impetit, secundum preceptum Pauli apostoli duo uel tria testimonia requirantur ab illo." The material source is Second Council of Braga, c.8, ed. José Vives, *Concilios Visigóticos e Hispano-Romanos* (Barcelona: Consejo Superiod de Investigaciones Científicas, Instituto Enrique Flórez, 1963), 8.

52. C.2 q.4 d.a.c.1 (ed. Friedberg, 465, supported by Aa Bc Fd P): "Quod uero quarto loco querebatur: An duorum testimonio episcopus sit condempnandus, multorum auctoritate probatur. Sicut enim in euangelio Iohannis [Jn 8:17] legitur, ait Christus ad Iudeos: 'In lege uestra scriptum est, quoniam duorum hominum testimonium uerum est.' Hinc consequenter argumentatur contra eos, dicens: 'Si duorum hominum testimonium uerum est, quare testimonium meum et Patris (mei *add. Fd*[1]) non accipitis?' Item Paulus in epistola ad Corinthios [2 Cor 13:1]: 'In ore duorum uel trium testium stabit omne uerbum.' Item in epistola ad Hebreos [Heb 10:28]: 'Quis preuaricans legem Moysi, duobus uel tribus testibus conuictus, sine miseratione lapidabatur.'" The relevant passage in the Pentateuch mentioned by the Epistle to the Hebrews is Dt 17:6.

53. C.2 q.4 d.p.c.3 (ed. Friedberg, 465, supported by Aa Bc Fd P): "Sed hoc uel speciali priuilegio de clericis Romane ecclesie intelligitur, uel propter inprobitatem quorumdam, qui, cum non sint spectate uite et scientie, in accusatione (accusationem *Aa*) ministrorum Dei repente prosiliunt. Quorum uero uita adeo laudabilis est, ut omnibus imitanda appareat, de quorum assertione nulla dubitatio nasci poterit,

C.3 q.7 provides another example of how Gratian appealed to the Bible to modify procedural law derived from Pseudo-Isidore. This question investigates whether the sentence of a judge who is guilty of the same or a greater crime than the one being sentenced should be obeyed. Gratian quotes or alludes to two Pseudo-Isidorian forgeries (c.1, d.p.c.2) and three patristic texts (cc.3, 4, 5) that, he claims, appear to indicate the answer is no, although none of the authorities is in fact strictly on point. The Pseudo-Isidorian forgeries, taken from the *Capitula Angilramni* and the decretals of Pseudo-Felix, respectively, simply forbid those suffering from infamy from serving as procurators, attorneys, or accusers in criminal cases.[54] Infamy was a legal condition under Roman law that affected people who had been convicted of certain crimes, like engaging in sodomy, or who belonged to certain professions, for instance, prostitutes. Infamous persons were prohibited from representing others in court, testifying, making wills, or performing numerous other legal acts and services.[55] First through the Germanic law codes and Pseudo-Isidore, then later directly through Justinian's *Corpus iuris civilis,* the concept of infamy entered the canonical tradition, eventually giving rise to a canonical doctrine of infamy distinct and in many ways different from the original Roman law doctrine.[56]

Like the Pseudo-Isidorian forgeries that he quotes, the three patristic texts that Gratian adduces in C.3 q.7 similarly provide no direct support for the view that the sentence of a judge who is guilty of the same or a greater crime than the one being sentenced should not be obeyed. All three texts deal only with the moral qualifications for being a judge. An excerpt from Gregory's *Moralia in Iob* admonishes judges to correct their own vices before they attempt to cor-

---

eorum testimonio duorum uel trium testium (*om. Aa Fd*[1]) quilibet iure conuinci et dampnari poterit."

54. C.3 q.7 c.1 (ed. Friedberg, 524) = *Capitula Angilramni* c.3(s), ed. Schon, 108.3–4; C.3 q.7 d.p.c.2 (ed. Friedberg, 526) alludes to C.3 q.5 c.11 (ed. Friedberg, 517) = JK †230 = Pseudo-Felix II, *Epistolae* 1.15, ed. Hinschius, 487.

55. For a general introduction, see Vincent Tatarczuk, *Infamy of Law: A Historical Synopsis and Commentary* (Washington, D.C.: The Catholic University of America Press, 1954).

56. On this development, see Peter Landau, *Die Entstehung des kanonischen Infamiebegriffs von Gratian bis zur Glossa ordinaria* (Cologne: Böhlau, 1966).

rect the vices of others.[57] A passage from Ambrose stresses the same point, while also emphasizing the need for judges to follow the law rather than their own wills and desires.[58] Finally, a pastiche of texts by Gregory and from the Bible denies the efficacy of having a sinful person intercede with God on one's behalf. For the pleas of an intercessor to bear fruit, the intercessor must be free from sin.[59]

Gratian responds to these authorities not by pointing out the mismatch between what they say and what they purportedly prove, but rather with a consideration of biblical exempla that he feels demonstrate the contrary view. The sentence of a judge, Gratian writes, should be obeyed so long as the church tolerates him. For after Saul had already been condemned by the Lord, he continued to judge the Israelites and the people continued to seek his judgment (1 Sm 15). David, similarly, despite being guilty of adultery and murder, when asked by the prophet Nathan, nevertheless passed sentence on the rich man who had stolen the poor man's sheep (2 Sm 12). Solomon and Ahab both judged the tribes of Israel while worshipping other gods (1 Kgs 11 and 16). And Jesus in the gospels recognized the authority of the Scribes and Pharisees when he affirmed that they occupied the "seat of Moses" (Mt 23:2).[60]

57. C.3 q.7 c.3 = Gregory the Great, *Moralia in Iob* 14.29.34, ed. Marcus Adriaen, CCSL 143A (Turnhout: Brepols, 1979), 718.32–719.46.

58. C.3 q.7 c.4 = Ambrose, *Expositio de psalmo CXVIII* 20.31, 36, and 39, ed. Michael Petschenig, CSEL 62 (Vienna: F. Tempsky, 1913), 460.6–10, 462.8–15, 463.19–20, and 464.1–2.

59. C.3 q.7 c.5 = Gregory the Great, *Moralia in Iob*, praefatio 3.8, ed. Marcus Adriaen, CCSL 143 (Turnhout: Brepols, 1979), 14.51–53; Gregory the Great, *Regula pastoralis* 1.10, ed. Floribert Rommel, Sources Chrétiennes 381 (Paris: Éditions du Cerf, 1992), 164.35–37; JE 1757; Eccl 34:23; Prov 15:8.

60. C.3 q.7 d.p.c.7 (ed. Friedberg, 528, supported by Aa Bc Fd P): "Sed obicitur: Saul cum a Domino esset reprobatus, populum Dei iudicabat, et eius iudicium uniuersus populus expetebat. Item, Dauid, cum esset adulter et homicida interrogatus a propheta, sententiam in diuitem dedit, qui ouem pauperis rapuit, dicens: 'Iudicium mortis est uiro huic.' Item, Salomon, cum amore mulierculorum deos gentium coleret, tamen uniuersa plebs Israelitica ad eius iudicium confluebat. Sic et Achab, quamuis coleret Baal, tamen x. tribus iudicabat. Multi etiam alii tam in ueteri testamento (*post* nouo *tr. Bc P*) quam in nouo inueniuntur, quorum uita cum esset blasphemabilis, tamen eorum sententia, quia ex officio suo seruata iudiciarii ordinis integritate processit, inuenitur seruata. Vnde et Dominus ait in euangelio. 'Super cathedram Moysi sederunt scribe et Pharisei' etc.

Finally, the Bible also plays an important role in C.5 q.5. This question investigates whether someone who reveals another person's crime should be judged malevolent.[61] Two Augustinian texts which Gratian quotes (cc.1, 2) suggest that the answer is no, as Christians have a duty to point out the faults of others. But a decretal from Pseudo-Isidore (c.4) suggests that the answer is yes, since it forbids those who have confessed the crimes of others to testify against bishops.[62] And Proverbs 11:13 and 25:8 likewise condemn those who reveal others' secrets. Gratian resolves this contradiction by introducing a distinction that he supports with four quotations from Proverbs and that may have stemmed from his reading of this biblical book.[63] There is a difference, he writes, between revealing others' crimes out of charity, so that those whom we are unable to correct through secret admonition may be corrected by a judicial sentence, and insidiously making false objections or by mocking to reprove truthful things. The first is a work of charity, the second a work of impiety.[64]

Maxims and Exempla

Three characteristics of Gratian's biblical references and exegesis are worthy of note. First, only occasionally does he exploit the Bible as a source of maxims or general principles, and when he does it is often to qualify their applicability. Gratian invokes Psalm 75:12

Hinc liquido constat, quod mali pastores, dum sententia iusti examinis aliorum crimina feriunt, sibi ipsis nocent, dum sine exemplo sue emendationis aliorum uitia corrigere curant; subditis uero prosunt, si, eorum increpatione correcti uel sententia coherciti uitam suam in melius commutare didicerint. Ac per hoc, dum ab ecclesia tollerati fuerint, eorum iudicium subterfugere non licet."

61. C.5 q.5 d.a.c.1 (ed. Friedberg, 549, supported by Aa Bc Fd P): "Nunc autem queritur, an sit aliquis iudicandus maliuolus (inimicus *Aa*), quia crimen indicat alterius."

62. JK †163 = Pseudo-Eusebius, *Epistolae* 1.3, ed. Hinschius, 231 = C.5 q.5 c.4 (ed. Friedberg, 550, supported by Aa Bc Fd P): "Illi, qui aut in fide catholica, aut inimicitia suspecti sunt, ad pulsationem episcoporum non admittantur. Nec illi, qui aliorum sponte crimina confitentur."

63. Prov 12:17, 12:19, 13:3, and 13:5.

64. C.5 q.5 d.p.c.5 (ed. Friedberg, 550, supported by Aa Bc Fd P): "Sed aliud est ex caritate aliorum crimina deferre, ut quos secreta admonitione corrigere non possumus conuictos iudicis sententia corripiat, atque aliud insidiando falsa obicere, uel insultando uera facile exprobrare. Illud autem caritatis, hoc uero impietatis est officium."

("Vow ye, and pay to the Lord your God"), for instance, as an argument that all vows must be fulfilled,[65] but then goes on to distinguish between simply deciding to do something and formally making a vow.[66] He quotes Matthew 5:37 ("let your speech be yes yes, no no") and James 5:12 ("swear not, neither by heaven, nor by the earth, nor by any other oath") as authorities against the taking of oaths. Yet instead of concluding that oaths should therefore be forbidden, he distinguishes between taking oaths voluntarily and taking oaths to affirm one's innocence, confirm a peace agreement, or persuade listeners that one is speaking the truth.[67] Furthermore, Gratian relativizes Jesus's admonition to turn the other cheek and other New Testament passages forbidding violence by arguing that they apply to one's inward disposition rather than to outward actions.[68] The def-

65. C.17 q.1 d.a.c.1 (ed. Friedberg, 812, supported by Aa Fd): "Quod a uoto discedere non liceat, multis auctoritatibus probatur. Ait enim Propheta: 'Vouete et reddite Domino Deo uestro' [Ps 75:12]."

66. C.17 q.1 d.p.c.4 (ed. Friedberg, 813, supported by Aa Fd): "His ita respondetur: Aliud est propositum corde concipere, et etiam ore enuntiare; aliud est subsequenti obligatione se reum uoti facere. Quia ergo iste propositum sui cordis ore simpliciter enuntiauit, non autem monasterio aut abbati se tradidit, nec promissionem scripsit, nequaquam reus uoti habetur."

67. C.22 q.1 d.a.c.1 (ed. Friedberg, 861, supported by Fd): "Quod iuramentum prestandum non sit, auctoritate probatur canonice scripture. Ait enim Christus in euangelio apostolis: 'Sit sermo uester: Est est, non non; quod autem amplius est a malo est' [Mt 5:37]. Item Iacobus in epistola: 'Ante omnia, fratres mei, nolite iurare omnino' [Jam 5:12]. Vtraque auctoritate iuramentum prohibemur prestare. Sed aliud est ad iurandum sponte accedere, aliud uel ad asserendam innocentiam suam, uel ad federa pacis confirmanda (firmanda *Fd*), uel ad persuadendum auditoribus, quando pigri sunt credere quod eis utile est, iuramentum offerre. Primum prohibetur, secundum conceditur. Non enim iurare omnino peccatum est."

68. C.23 q.1 d.a.c.1 (ed. Friedberg, 890, supported by Aa Fd): "Quod militare alienum uideatur ab euangelica disciplina, hinc uidetur posse probari, quia omnis militia uel ob iniuriam propulsandam, uel propter uindictam inferendam est instituta, iniuria autem uel a propria persona, uel a socio repellitur, quod utrumque euangelica lege prohibetur. Cum enim dicitur: 'Si quis te percusserit in unam maxillam, prebe ei et alteram' et item (iterum *Friedb.*): 'Qui angariauerit te (ire *add. Fd*) mille passus, uade cum eo duo milia (alia duo *Fd*)' [Mt 5:41]; item cum Apostolus dicat ad Romanos: 'Non uos defendentes, carissimi, sed date locum ire' [Rom 12:19], quid aliud prohibemur, quam proprie persone iniuriam repellere?" C.23 q.1 d.p.c.1 (ed. Friedberg, 890, supported by Aa Fd): "His ita respondetur: Precepta patientie non tam ostentatione corporis quam preparatione cordis sunt retinenda."

erence that Gratian gives to biblical maxims and principles in *Causae* 2–6 on procedural law is thus not representative.

The second noteworthy feature of Gratian's biblical exegesis is his focus on exempla. Gratian exploits the Bible less as a source of precepts and more as a source of apparently authoritative examples concerning permissible and prohibited actions. The Levites, for instance, provide Gratian with an argument about contemporary tithing practices. Just as the Levites accepted tithes only from those for whom they offered prayers and sacrifices (Lv 16:11), so should parishioners pay tithes to those priests who actually minister to their needs.[69] On the other hand, Christ's observation of the precepts of the Old Law (for example, Lk 2) despite his occasional dispensation from them (for example, Mt 12) provides, according to Gratian, a model for papal behavior. Like Jesus, popes should, as a general rule, observe the laws they lay down, even though they are free to dispense from them when they need to.[70] The apostle Paul's failure to fulfill his promise to the Corinthians that he would visit them again (1 Cor 16:5) serves as a counterexample to the claim that swearing something false is the same as perjury. For swearing something false is one thing, swearing with the intention to deceive something else.[71]

69. C.13 q.1 d.p.c.1 §1 (ed. Friedberg, 718, supported by Aa Fd): "Non accipiebant filii Leui decimas, nisi ab eis, pro quibus offerebant preces et sacrificia. Quia ergo nos seruimus Domino in tabernaculo offerendo pro istis preces et sacrificia, et ipsi debent nobis persoluere decimas et primitias."

70. C.25 q.1 d.p.c.16 §1 (ed. Friedberg, 1011, supported by Aa Fd): "Ita ergo canonibus auctoritatem prestat, ut se ipsam non subiciat eis. Sed sicut Christus, qui legem dedit, ipsam legem carnaliter impleuit, octaua die circumcisus, quadragesimo die in templo cum hostiis est (*om. Friedb.*) presentatus, ut in se ipso eam sanctificaret, postea uero, ut se dominum legis ostenderet, contra litteram legis leprosum tangendo mundauit.... Sic et summe sedis pontifices canonibus a se siue ab aliis sua auctoritate conditis reuerentiam exhibent, et eis se humiliando ipsos custodiunt, ut aliis obseruando exhibeant. Nonnumquam uero seu iubendo, seu diffiniendo, seu decernendo, seu aliter agendo, se decretorum dominos et conditores esse ostendunt."

71. C.22 q.2 d.p.c.2 §2 (ed. Friedberg, 867, supported by Aa Fd): "Sed aliud est falsum iurare, aliud iurare in dolo. Non enim omnis qui aliter (qualiter omnis *Fd*[1]) facturus est quam promittit in dolo iurat. Licet enim Apostolus aliter facturus esset (erat *Aa*) quam Corinthiis promitteret in prima epistola (epistola sua prima *Aa*), cum ait: 'Veniam ad uos' [1 Cor 16:5], non tamen in dolo iurauit, aut mendaciter promisit."

And the destruction of the Sodomites (Gn 19), Amalekites (1 Sm 15), and followers of Dathan and Abiram (Nm 16) provide apparent biblical support for the view that an entire family can be excommunicated for the sin of just one of its members.[72]

Third and finally, despite Gratian's focus on the mystical sense in the *Tractatus de legibus*, throughout most of the first recension he in fact focuses on the literal sense. Gratian often references biblical passages and exempla because he finds their literal meaning pertinent to the argument at hand. The biblical passage may directly address an issue, like the biblical maxims and principles described above. Or they may provide an apparently authoritative example in support of a particular practice or proposition, as with the exempla just discussed. In either case, what Gratian generally focuses on is the literal sense, and what he tries to explain is why the literal sense does not conflict with other biblical and non-biblical authorities rather than trying to prove that these texts do not have a literal meaning.

For this reason, Gratian frequently does not make use of the interpretive techniques discussed in the first part of this chapter, but instead handles biblical texts in the same way that he handles non-biblical texts: by applying to them the scholastic method for reconciling contradictory authorities. Gratian harmonizes biblical passages with each other and with non-biblical texts by introducing distinctions—most often between multiple senses of the same word.[73] Thus C.27 q.2 d.p.c.39, for instance, explains that just as Joseph is called Jesus's father because he cared and provided for Jesus like a father, not because Joseph actually was Jesus's father biologically (since Jesus was conceived of Mary by the power of the Holy Spirit), so too is Joseph called Mary's husband because he cared and provided for her

72. C.24 q.3 d.a.c.1 (ed. Friedberg, 988, supported by Aa Fd): "Quod autem pro peccato alicuius tota familia excommunicanda sit, multorum exemplis probatur. Pro peccato namque Sodomitarum paruuli eorum, qui beneficio etatis paterna flagitia nesciebant, celesti igne (igni *Friedb.*) sunt consumpti. Item, pro peccato Amalechitarum, non solum paruuli eorum, sed etiam bruta animalia usque ad mingentem ad (in *Fd*) parietem iussa sunt a Domino deleri. Item, Dathan et Abiron auctores scismatis fuerunt contra Moysen et Aaron, nec tamen (tantum *Friedb.*) ipsi soli, sed omnis substantia eorum cum ipsis descendit ad inferos."

73. Meyer, *Distinktionstechnik*, 169–74.

like a husband, not because he actually knew her carnally.[74] Similarly, C.29 q.1 d.a.c.1 uses the distinction between precedent and subsequent consent to explain why Jacob's marriage to Leah (Gn 29:16–26) does not prove that consent is unnecessary to marriage. Precedent consent, Gratian argues, was lacking when Jacob married Leah, but subsequent consent was not.[75]

Gratian's preferred harmonization technique, distinguishing between multiple senses of the same word, was known to earlier canonists like Bernold of Constance, but only with Gratian did canonists begin to make extensive use of it. Gratian's immediate predecessors, Ivo of Chartres and Alger of Liege, favored a different method for reconciling contradictions: the distinction between justice and mercy, which they assimilated to strict application of the law and dispensation from its application.[76] While Gratian knew and used this technique, he did so to a far lesser extent than they did.[77] More importantly for the purposes of this chapter, Gratian never explicitly applied this distinction to the Bible. Gratian recognized that the literal sense of the Bible should not always be followed, but he avoided using dispensation as an explanation for why. Certain Old Testament practices like marriage between close relatives and divorce were the result of necessity or infirmity and thus, in a sense, dispensations from the natural law.[78] However, Gratian never suggested that present-day popes or judges could dispense from still-valid biblical commands and practices. God, he seems to have thought, may be able to dispense from biblical law, but the church and her ministers cannot.

The Church Fathers and the *Glossa Ordinaria*

In many instances, what Gratian finds pertinent about a biblical exemplum is the practice or episode itself. But what frequently gives

74. C.27 q.2 d.p.c.39 §2 (ed. Werckmeister, 184): "sicut Ioseph pater Domini dictus est non effectu geniture sed officio et cura prouidendi: sic et coniux matris eius appellatus est non coniugii effectu sed subministratione necessariorum et indiuidue mentis affectu."

75. C.29 q.1 d.a.c.1 §3 (ed. Werckmeister, 256): "Iacob ergo et Liam non fecit coniuges precedens consensus, sed subsequens."

76. Meyer, *Distinktionstechnik*, 129–43.

77. Ibid., 162–65.

78. See pp. 39–40.

the exemplum force or makes it pertinent is the Christian exegetical tradition, particularly the tradition of Christological and allegorical exegesis. These two approaches to the Bible, which had developed already in the New Testament period, encouraged Christians to look for and impart new meanings to biblical passages. The earliest Christians interpreted persons, places, and events described in the Old Testament as signifying and foretelling various aspects of the New Testament. Later Christians went even further by endowing almost every single biblical passage, from not only the Old Testament but also the New Testament, with a moral or doctrinal significance. Individual verses came to form the basis for elaborate doctrines that might bear only a tenuous connection to the biblical text. Christian exegetes did not ignore the literal interpretation of the Bible, but prior to the twelfth century literal interpretation often took a backseat to allegorical exegesis.[79]

The primary repositories of the Christian exegetical tradition were the same as the sources of canon law: conciliar canons, papal decretals, and above all the writings of the Church Fathers. Councils and popes appealed to the Bible to justify their legal decisions or to add rhetorical flourish to their legislative texts.[80] But it was the Church Fathers and later theologians who most thoroughly developed the exegetical framework and imagery that shaped Gratian's reading of the Bible and whose views he expressly acknowledges should be preferred concerning questions of exegesis.[81]

In D.20, at the very end of the *Tractatus de legibus*, Gratian consid-

79. For an introduction, see Beryl Smalley, *The Study of the Bible in the Middle Ages*, 3rd rev. ed. (Oxford: Blackwell, 1983); Henri de Lubac, *Medieval Exegesis*, trans. Mark Sebanc, 3 vols. (Grand Rapids, Mich.: Eerdmans, 1998–2009).

80. Jean Gaudemet, "La Bible dans les conciles (IVe–VIIe s.)," in *Le monde latin antique et la Bible*, ed. Jacques Fontaine and Charles Pietri (Paris: Beauchesne, 1985), 289–310; Gaudemet, "La Bible dans les collections canoniques," 334–35. The two articles are republished as chapters 3 and 4 of Jean Gaudemet, *La formation du droit canonique et gouvernement de l'église de l'antiquité à l'âge classique: Recueil d'articles* (Strasbourg: Presses Universitaires de Strasbourg, 2008).

81. On the Church Fathers in canon law, see Charles Munier, *Les sources patristiques du droit de l'église du VIIIe au XIIIe siècle* (Mulhouse: Salvator, 1957); Jean Werckmeister, "The Reception of the Church Fathers in Canon Law," in *The Reception of the Church Fathers in the West* 1: *From the Carolingians to the Maurists*, ed. Irena Backus (Leiden: Brill, 1997), 51–81.

ers the problem of the relative authority of popes and theologians. Canonical collections had long complained about the numerous contradictions in the canonical tradition and proposed various solutions to the problem, for instance, that in case of a conflict the "older and stronger authority" take precedence. Gratian, however, was the first to broach explicitly the problem of the relative authority of two special types of legal authorities, namely, popes and theologians.[82] Many expositors of sacred scripture such as Augustine and Jerome, Gratian writes, appear to possess greater authority than popes. Popes occupy a higher position in the ecclesiastical hierarchy, but the expositors of sacred scripture often possess a greater share of the grace of the Holy Spirit and thus excel popes in both knowledge and their adherence to reason. To resolve this question, Gratian introduces a distinction between deciding cases and diligently interpreting the scriptures. In order to decide cases, one needs not only knowledge, but also power. Christ conferred on Peter, the first pope, two keys: not only one of knowledge, to discern between different types of "leprosy," but also a key of power, to bind and to loose. For this reason, Gratian writes, popes possess greater authority than Church Fathers in judicial cases. In matters of biblical interpretation, however, the Church Fathers enjoy precedence.[83]

82. Munier, *Les sources patristiques*, 95–119; Werckmeister, "Reception," 73.

83. D.20 d.a.c.1 (ed. Genka, 126): "Decretales itaque epistole canonibus conciliorum pari iure exequantur. Nunc autem queritur de expositoribus sacre scripture, an exequentur, an subiciantur eis. Quo enim quisque magis ratione nititur, eo maioris auctoritatis eius uerba esse uidentur. Plerique autem tractatorum, sicut pleniori gratia Spiritus sancti, ita ampliori scientia aliis precellentes rationi magis adhesisse probantur. Unde nonnullorum Pontificum constitutis Augustini, Ieronimi atque aliorum tractatorum dicta eis uidentur esse preferenda. Sed aliud est causis terminum imponere, aliud scripturas sacras diligenter exponere. Negotiis diffiniendis non solum est necessaria scientia, sed etiam potestas. Unde Christus dicturus Petro: Quodcumque ligaueris super terram et cetera. Prius dedit sibi claues regni celorum, in altera dans ei scientiam discernendi inter lepram et lepram, in altera dans sibi potestatem eiciendi aliquos ab ecclesia uel recipiendi. Cum ergo quelibet negotia finem accipiant uel in absolutione innocentium uel in condempnatione delinquentium, absolutio uero uel dampnatio non scientiam tantum, sed etiam potestatem presidentium comitantur, apparet, quod diuinarum scripturarum tractatores, etsi scientia Pontificibus premineant, tamen, quia dignitatis eorum apicem non sunt adepti, in sacrarum scripturarum expositionibus eis preponuntur, in causis uero diffiniendis secundum post eos locum merentur."

It is not entirely clear why Gratian wished to stress the authority of popes over theologians. Charles Munier argued that Gratian was not trying to deny or cut back on the authority of the Church Fathers, whose legal authority he in fact explicitly affirms, but instead wished simply to affirm the jurisdictional primacy of Rome.[84] Tatsushi Genka, on the other hand, suggests that Gratian had a more specific purpose. He wished to combat the view, championed by some contemporary canonists and theologians, that authority and personal merit must go hand in hand. As Genka notes, Gratian never explicitly affirms the superior authority of councils over theologians, although this hierarchy of authorities follows from what he says in the *Tractatus de legibus*. D.19 argues that papal letters have the same legal authority as conciliar canons, while D.20 emphasizes that papal decretals take precedence over the writings of theologians in deciding judicial cases. Gratian's failure to discuss or even note explicitly the superiority of councils to theologians, Genka suggests, reflects the fact that his concern was not to construct a comprehensive hierarchy of authorities, but rather to refute contemporary attempts to tie together authority and personal merit. Such attempts endangered papal authority, since popes did not always possess grace or knowledge. But they did not undermine conciliar authority, since councils were collective bodies.[85]

For the most part, Gratian appears to have encountered patristic interpretations of the Bible not through their original writings but rather through excerpts incorporated into intermediate works. Research since the 1970s has made it increasingly clear that the majority of canons in the two recensions of the *Decretum*, including the patristic texts, derive from just a handful of relatively recent canonical collections, plus the *Glossa ordinaria* to the Bible.[86] Already in the early Middle Ages, it was common for manuscripts containing bibli-

84. Munier, *Les sources patristiques*, 183–88.

85. Tatsushi Genka, "Hierarchie der Texte, Hierarchie der Autoritäten: Zur Hierarchie der Rechtsquellen bei Gratian," *ZRG KA* 95 (2009): 100–127, at 122–25.

86. For an overview of Gratian's sources, see pp. 20–24. On the sources of the patristic texts in the *Decretum*, see Munier, *Les sources patristiques*, 125–82; Peter Landau, "Patristische Texte in den beiden Rezensionen des *Decretum Gratiani*," *BMCL* 23 (1999): 77–84.

cal books to include marginal and interlinear commentary. Over the course of the twelfth century, a particular set of these glosses became standardized, becoming thereby the *Glossa ordinaria* rather than just a *glossa* to the Bible.[87] These glosses were taken from the writings of ecclesiastical authors, particularly the Church Fathers, but also included the opinions or *sententiae* of "modern"—that is, contemporary—masters like Anselm of Laon, his brother Ralph, and Gilbert the Universal. These three masters are generally credited with having begun the ambitious project of glossing the entire Bible rather than just individual biblical books. For many biblical books, the earliest form of the *Glossa ordinaria* is attributed to one or the other of them. But there remains much uncertainty on the authorship of the *Glossa ordinaria* to individual biblical books.[88]

While it is unclear exactly which glossed books Gratian had access to, he certainly knew and used glossed copies of at least the Psalms and Pauline epistles, which derive in their earliest form from Anselm of Laon. The first recension contains numerous references to the *Glossa ordinaria* to both biblical works. Gratian, for instance, structures much of the first part of the *Decretum* (DD.25–48), which deals with the qualifications for becoming a bishop, around the *Glossa or-*

87. For an introduction to the *Glossa ordinaria*, see Smalley, *Study of the Bible*, 46–66; Titus Lenherr, "Die 'Glossa ordinaria' zur Bibel als Quelle von Gratians Dekret: Ein (neuer) Anfang," *BMCL* 24 (2000): 97–129; Alexander Andrée, *Gilbertus Universalis: Glossa ordinaria in Lamentationes Ieremie prophete; Prothemata et Liber I; A Critical Edition with an Introduction and a Translation* (Stockholm: Almqvist and Wiksell International, 2005); Lesley Smith, *The "Glossa ordinaria": The Making of a Medieval Biblical Commentary* (Leiden: Brill, 2009). For an uncritical edition of the *Glossa ordinaria*, see Margaret T. Gibson and Karlfried Froehlich, eds., *Biblia latina cum glossa ordinaria: Facsimile Reprint of the Editio princeps: Adolph Rusch of Strassburg 1480/81*, 4 vols. (Turnhout: Brepols, 1992). For critical editions to some biblical books, see Andrée, *Gilbertus Universalis*; Mary Dove, *In canticum canticorum*, CCCM 170 (Turnhout: Brepols, 1997). The defective and highly misleading edition of the *Glossa ordinaria* printed in PL 113 and 114 should not be used.

88. Smith, *Glossa ordinaria*, 17–38, provides a comprehensive summary on what is known about the authorship of the *Glossa ordinaria* to the various biblical books. On Anselm's relationship to the *Glossa ordinaria* and other biblical works, see Cédric Giraud, *Per verba magistri: Anselme de Laon et son école au XIIe siècle* (Turnhout: Brepols, 2010), 84–99; Alexander Andrée, "Anselm of Laon Unveiled: The *Glosae super Iohannem* and the Origins of the *Glossa ordinaria* on the Bible," *Mediaeval Studies* 73 (2011): 217–60.

dinaria to Paul's letters to Timothy and Titus. According to 1 Timothy 3:2–4, a bishop must "be blameless, the husband of one wife, sober, prudent, of good behavior, chaste, given to hospitality, a teacher, not given to wine, no striker, but modest, not quarrelsome, not covetous, but one that rules well his own house, having his children in subjection with all chastity." Titus 1:7–9 teaches much the same, declaring that "a bishop must be without crime, as the steward of God: not proud, not subject to anger, not given to wine, no striker, not greedy of filthy lucre, but given to hospitality, gentle, sober, just, holy, continent, embracing that faithful word which is according to doctrine, that he may be able to exhort in sound doctrine, and to convince the gainsayers." Gratian refers to both lists of qualities but interprets them in light of the gloss apparatus by Anselm that became the basis for the *Glossa ordinaria*.[89] Paul, for instance, merely states that a bishop should be "of one wife." Following the *Glossa ordinaria,* Gratian interprets this requirement as referring more explicitly to marriage after baptism. A man is unfit to be bishop if he has been married more than once after baptism, but no similar unsuitability arises from multiple marriages contracted prior to baptism.[90]

Similarly, Paul states that a bishop should be prudent, but does not explain why or how. The marginal gloss notes that this requirement is directed against those who try to excuse the stupidity of priests by calling them simple, while the interlinear gloss states that a bishop should be prudent "in doing all things."[91] Gratian incorporates the

89. D.25 d.p.c.3 §1 (ed. Friedberg, 92, supported by Aa Bc P): "qualem oporteat eum (*om. P*) esse, qui in episcopum est ordinandus, diligenter inuestigemus, Apostoli regulam secuti, quam in huiusmodi re Timotheo et Tito scribit"; *Glossa ordinaria* ad 1 Tim 3:2–4 (ed. Lenherr, "Die 'Glossa ordinaria' zur Bibel," 123–25; ed. Rusch, 4:408) and Ti 1:7–9 (ed. Rusch, 4:419; Cologne, Dombibliothek, fol. 96v).

90. *Glossa ordinaria* ad 1 Tim 3:2 v. *unius uxoris uirum* (ed. Lenherr, 123): "idest monogamum post baptismum. Si enim et ante coniugem habuit que obierit, non ei imputatur, cui prorsus nouo nec stupra nec alia que ante fuerunt iam obsunt." D.26 d.a.c.1 (ed. Friedberg, 95, supported by Aa Bc P): "Sequitur in utraque epistola: 'unius uxoris uirum' post baptisma uidelicet, non ante baptisma (baptismum *Friedb.*)."

91. *Glossa ordinaria* ad 1 Tim 3:2 v. *prudentem* (ed. Lenherr, 123): "Contra eos qui sub nomine simplicitatis excusant stulticiam sacerdotum"; ibid. (ed. Lenherr, 124): "in omnibus agendis."

marginal gloss almost verbatim and interprets the interlinear gloss as requiring bishops to be not only learned, but also wise in the management of secular affairs.[92] Moreover, Paul states that a bishop should be *ornatus* ("of good behavior" according to the Douay-Reims translation), but does not specify in what way. The *Glossa ordinaria* connects this quality to the possession of virtues, graceful behavior, and decent dress.[93] Gratian adopts the same interpretation.[94] To give one final example from DD.25–48, Paul states that a bishop should not be given to wine. The interlinear gloss qualifies this prohibition by stating that a bishop should not be inebriated *frequently*.[95] And Gratian repeats this laxer interpretation.[96]

While Gratian draws upon the *Glossa ordinaria* most extensively in DD.25–48, he also exploits this source elsewhere in the *Decretum*, most notably in C.17 q.1. *Causa* 17 considers a priest who, on account of infirmity, says that he wishes to become a monk and thus renounces his church and benefice. After recovering, however, he refuses to enter the religious life and attempts to recover the things he renounced. The first question that Gratian investigates is whether the aforementioned priest committed perjury.[97] Two considerations

92. D.36 d.a.c.1 (ed. Friedberg, 133, supported by Aa Bc Fd P): "Oportet etiam esse ordinandum prudentem. Quod contra eos notandum est, qui sub nomine simplicitatis excusant stultitiam sacerdotum. Prudentem autem oportet episcopum intelligi non solum litterarum peritia, uerum etiam secularium negotiorum dispensatione."

93. *Glossa ordinaria* ad 1 Tim 3:2 v. *ornatum* (ed. Lenherr, 123): "Vel uirtutibus uel motu et incessu, habitu et sermone communi."

94. D.40 d.a.c.1 (ed. Friedberg, 145, supported by Aa Bc Fd P): "Oportet quoque episcopum esse ornatum et hospitalem. Ornamenta episcopalia uirtutes debent intelligi." D.41 d.a.c.1 (ed. Friedberg, 148, supported by Aa Bc Fd P): "Scilicet preterea oportet illum (sacerdotem *Aa*) esse ornatum in exterioribus, habitu uidelicet et incessu: habitu, ut nec fulgidis, nec sordidis se uestibus ornet. Vt enim ait Ieronimus, nec affectate sordes, nec exquisite delicie laudem pariunt (pariant *Aa*), quod tam de uestibus quam de cibis intelligendum est."

95. *Glossa ordinaria* ad 1 Tim 3:3 v. *non uinolentum* (ed. Lenherr, 124): "qui hoc agat frequenter."

96. D.35 d.a.c.1 §2 (ed. Friedberg, 131, supported by Aa Bc Fd P): "Quod autem uinolentus esse prohibetur, non semel, sed frequenter uino repletus debet intelligi."

97. C.17 pr. (ed. Friedberg, 812, supported by Aa Fd): "Quidam presbiter infirmitate grauatus se fieri uelle monachum dixit; ecclesie et beneficio in manu aduocati renuntiauit. Postquam conualuit, mox se futurum monachum negauit,

lead Gratian to argue initially that the answer is yes. First, many authorities prove that one may not break a vow. Psalm 75:12 declares: "Vow and pay to the Lord your God."[98] The gloss to this passage, taken from Cassiodorus and incorporated by Gratian into the first recension as C.17 q.1 c.1, explains that there are some things which we ought not do even if we promise to do them, like murder, but that there are other things which we are not compelled to do unless we so promise, like remaining a virgin.[99] And an authority that Gratian falsely attributes to Jerome, taken from the *Glossa ordinaria* to Paul's epistle to Timothy, declares that not only marrying, but even wishing to be married is damnable to those who have made a vow.[100]

The second consideration that leads Gratian to argue initially that the priest in the case statement committed perjury are two glosses apparently taken from the *Glossa ordinaria* to Psalm 31:5 that he quotes in a combined form in C.17 q.1 d.p.c.4 §1 and that he also reproduces at De pen. D.1 c.5.[101] The glosses refer to David's verbal

---

ecclesiam et beneficium reposcit. Hic primum queritur utrum reus uoto (*add. sup. lin. Aa*, uoti *Friedb.*) teneatur, an liceat ei a proposito sui cordis discedere?"

98. C.17 q.1 d.a.c.1.

99. *Glossa ordinaria* ad Ps 75:12 (ed. Rusch, 2:550; Cologne, Dombibliothek, 7, fol. 83r): "Quedam sunt que nec promittentes debemus soluere, ut non occides et huiusmodi. Alia sunt que nisi uouemus, non cogimur implere, ut uirginitatem seruare. Ad hec ergo uouenda inuitat." = C.17 q.1 c.1 (ed. Friedberg, 812, supported by Aa Fd): "Sunt quedam, que etiam non uouentes debemus; quedam etiam, que nisi uouerimus, non debemus, sed postquam ea Deo promittimus, necessario (reddere *add. Friedb.*) constringimur." The material source is Cassiodorus, *Expositio psalmorum* 75:12, ed. Marcus Adriaen, CCSL 98 (Turnhout: Brepols, 1958), 696.213–19.

100. *Glossa ordinaria* ad Tim 5:12 (ed. Rusch, 4:410; Cologne, Dombibliothek, 25, fol. 92r): "Voventibus uirginitatem uel uiduitatem non solum nubere sed et uelle damnabile est. Omnis huiuscemodi similis est uxori Loth que retro aspexit." C.17 q.1 c.2 (ed. Friedberg, 812, supported by Aa Fd): "Vouentibus non solum nubere, sed etiam (ipsum *add. Aa*) uelle damnabile est." On the authorship of this passage, see the note of the Correctores Romani to D.27 c.4 (ed. Friedberg, 99).

101. *Glossa ordinaria* ad Ps 31:5 (ed. Rusch, 2:490–91; Munich, Bayerische Staatsbibliothek, Clm 5257a, fol. 40r; Clm 6231, fol. 30v). The first gloss reads: "Dixi enim prius, id est deliberaui apud me. Magna pietas, ut ad solam promissionem dimiserit. Votum enim pro operatione iudicatur." The second gloss reads: "Nondum pronuntiat, promittit pronuntiaturum, et Deus iam dimittit, quia hoc ipsum dicere quoddam pronuntiare est corde. Nondum est uox in ore, ut homo audiat confessionem et Deus audit." The material source for these two glosses is Cassiodorus, *Expositio psalmorum* ad Ps 31:5, ed. Marcus Adriaen, CCSL 97 (Turnhout:

declaration as a vow (*uotum*). The priest's verbal declaration, Gratian argues, should thus similarly qualify as a vow.[102]

Only Gratian's solution to this problem does not derive from the *Glossa ordinaria* but is instead a distinction that he perhaps came up with on his own. One must distinguish, Gratian argues, between simply conceiving a proposal in one's heart and even declaring this proposal orally, on the one hand, and, on the other hand, making a morally and legally binding vow. The priest in the case statement made a simple verbal declaration, but not a vow because he never gave himself to a monastery or set down his promise in writing.[103]

Elsewhere, Gratian uses the *Glossa ordinaria* simply to draw out the legal implications of biblical texts or to endow biblical passages with legal meanings, as in C.9 q.3. This question considers whether an archbishop can condemn or absolve one of his suffragan's clerics without consulting the suffragan.[104] Gratian first quotes authorities that appear to suggest the answer is yes (c.1) and then authorities that appear to suggest the answer is no (d.p.c.3–c.9), before giving his own answer to the question in the final dictum: it depends on whether the archbishop acts out of temerity or necessity.[105] Originally, C.9 q.3 probably

Brepols, 1958), 278.151–58. The combined form is found at C.17 q.1 d.p.c.4 §1 (ed. Friedberg, 813, supported by Aa Fd): "Quod autem inter uouentes iste computandus sit, patet ex uerbis Augustini dicentis: '"Dixi, confitebor"' etc. Magna pietas (Dei est *add. Friedb.*), ut ad solam promissionem peccata dimittat. Nondum enim pronuntiat ore, et tamen Deus iam audit in corde; uotum enim pro opere reputatur." The same form is reproduced at De pen. D.1 c.5 (ed. Friedberg, 1159).

102. C.17 q.1 d.p.c.4 (ed. Friedberg, 813, supported by Aa Fd): "Si ergo post uotum quisque necessario cogitur soluere quod uouit; si uouentibus non solum nubere, sed etiam uelle damnabile est: patet, quod sacerdos iste ad executionem (excusationem *Fd*[1]) sui uoti cogendus est, et non solum non fieri, sed etiam uelle (nolle *Aa Fd*) monachum non (*om. Aa*) fieri sibi damnabile est.... Sicut ergo Propheta inter uouentes reputatur, quia dixit: 'Ego confitebor,' sic et iste inter eosdem computandus est, quia dixit: 'Fiam monachus.'"

103. Ibid.: "His ita respondetur. Aliud est propositum corde concipere (incipere *Aa*), et etiam ore enuntiare; aliud est subsequenti obligatione se reum uoti facere. Quia ergo iste propositum sui cordis ore simpliciter enuntiauit (enuntiauerit *Fd*), non autem monasterio aut abbati se tradidit, nec promissionem scripsit, nequaquam reus uoti habetur."

104. C.9 q.3 d.a.c.1 (ed. Friedberg, 606, supported by Aa Fd): "Quod archiepiscopus clericos sui suffraganei illo inconsulto dampnare ualeat uel absoluere, sic uidetur posse probari."

105. C.9 q.3 d.p.c.21 (ed. Friedberg, 612, supported by Aa Fd): "Sed aliud

consisted of just the three authorities discussed in the question's dicta: c.1, a text from the capitulary of Martin of Braga but misattributed to Pope Martin; the example of the fornicator described in 1 Corinthians 5:5; and an excerpt from the *Glossa ordinaria* to the Apocalypse.[106] Apocalpyse 2:1 simply commands its author to "write to the angel of the Church of Ephesus." Only in the *Glossa ordinaria* does this passage acquire an ecclesiastical slant: "He writes to the bishop, from whose hand he seeks out sins and without whose counsel he ought not to judge [his] subordinates."[107] The *Glossa ordinaria* thus sometimes transforms a biblical passage into a legal argument.

Conclusion

Gratian was a biblical exegete. He knew the Bible well, which he studied in the context of the *Glossa ordinaria*, and his knowledge of the Bible exercised a deep influence on his thought and work. The Bible occupies the highest place in his doctrine of the hierarchy of authorities, though it remains subject in theory and particularly in practice to the judgment and skill of the interpreter. While the Bible only occasionally serves as a direct source of law, when it does, Gratian uses it to great effect, as in *Causae* 2–6 on procedural law. Moreover, the Bible provides the underlying structure for various parts of his textbook, most notably DD.25–48 on the qualifications for bishop and C.17 q.1 on perjury.

---

est quod ex temeritate assumitur presumptionis, aliud quod ex necessitate geritur caritatis. Cum suffraganei archiepiscoporum subditis suis ad malum fauere ceperunt, atque circa eorum correctionem negligentes extiterint, tunc licet metropolitanis preter illorum uoluntatem et ligandos dampnare et reconciliandos absoluere. Cum uero episcopi zelo diuine caritatis accensi bonos uerbo et exemplo edificant, maiorum uitia aspera increpatione redarguunt, absque talium consilio non licet metropolitanis in eorum parrochia aliquid agere uel disponere."

106. Martin of Braga, *Capitula*, c.4, ed. C. W. Barlow, *Martini episcopi Bracarensis opera omnia*, Papers and Monographs of the American Academy in Rome 12 (New Haven, Conn.: Yale University Press, 1950), 125; *Glossa ordinaria* ad Apoc 2:1 (ed. Rusch, 4:551): "Episcopo scribit: De manu cuius peccata subditorum requirit et sine cuius consensu subditos iudicare non presumit ipse Iohannes."

107. C.9 q.3 c.9 (ed. Friedberg, 609, supported by Aa Fd): "Item Beda super apocalipsim 'Et angelo ecclesie Ephesi scribe.' Episcopo scribit (scribe *Fd*[1]) de cuius manu peccata requirit, nec sine cuius consilio subditos iudicare debebat (debeat *Friedb.*)."

Part 2

Gratian the Penitential Theologian

3

The Practice and Theory of Penance

Partly because he was a biblical exegete, Gratian was also a penitential theologian. Many questions of penitential theology originated as problems of biblical exegesis and would have attracted the interest of biblical exegetes like Gratian for that very reason. But two other factors, this chapter argues, were just as if not more important for the growth in attention to penitential theology in the twelfth century. First, twelfth-century thinkers possessed a poor understanding of the seismic shifts that had transformed the practice and theory of penance over the centuries. Biblical, patristic, and medieval texts employed mostly the same words (*penitentia, confessio, satisfactio*) in talking about the remission of sin. They used these words, however, to refer to very different practices and rites. As a result, the authorities dealing with penance contained numerous real and apparent contradictions that contemporaries had to address. Second, by Gratian's day, penance not only had become widespread, but was also being reworked and re-theorized into a more effective tool for religious reform. These attempts to transform penance were at times highly controversial and raised numerous theoretical and practical puzzles that demanded resolution. Theologians led the way in this reconceptualization of penance, but canonists—particularly in Italy—were also aware of these developments and paid attention to them.

The present chapter sketches the history of penitential practice and theory from its beginnings in the New Testament through the early twelfth century. Gratian and his contemporaries were aware that penance had changed dramatically between Jesus's day and their own, but did not always understand exactly how or to what extent this shift had occurred. To understand why Gratian was interested in penance, then, and why he argues what he does concerning this rite, we must first understand what his biblical, patristic, and medieval sources really say, as well as the perspective from which Gratian approached them.

This chapter has five sections. The first section sketches the history of penance from New Testament times to Gratian's day, with a focus on the rise of a private, repeatable form of penance. The second section then examines the impact that this private form of penance had on religious practice, arguing against revisionist views that attempt to minimize its significance. The third section turns to changes in penitential theology that began to emerge in the eleventh and twelfth centuries, which elevated contrition over works of satisfaction and which provides the main theoretical backdrop to Gratian's examination of penance. The fourth section studies two further issues, the permanence of charity and the return of sins, that theologians began to explore at around this same time and which Gratian treats in *De penitentia*. The fifth and final section looks at evidence that twelfth-century canonists, particularly in Italy, were aware of and cared about these contemporary developments in penitential theology, even though none of them composed their own tract on penitential theology like Gratian later would.

The Rise of Private Penance

The gospels report that Jesus announced God's coming kingdom and the need to prepare for it through repentance.[1] He performed many acts of physical and spiritual healing and conferred this power

1. Despite much excellent recent work on penance, any attempt at providing its history must still begin with the standard narratives found in Bernhard Poschmann, *Handbuch der Dogmengeschichte* 4.3: *Buße und letzte Ölung* (Freiburg: Herder, 1951); the revision of this work by Herbert Vorgrimmler, *Handbuch der*

on his disciples. Matthew 16:19 states that Jesus granted the apostle Peter the power "to bind and to loose," and Matthew 18:18 says that he did the same for the other disciples. Matthew does not explain just what exactly this "power of the keys," as it later came to be called, entailed, but medieval commentators generally associated it with the power of excommunication and reconciliation as well as penance and absolution. As Jesus declares in John 20:23, "Whose sins you forgive are forgiven them; whose sins you retain are retained."[2]

In time, the power of the keys became one of the main biblical foundations for the sacrament of penance, a rite not explicitly mentioned in the New Testament. Although the New Testament frequently mentions μετάνοια (repentance/penance), it speaks of μετάνοια as a fundamental conversion and reorientation away from sin toward the God preached by Jesus and attested by his life, death, and resurrection, not as a repeatable rite for righting one's relationship with God each time one falls into serious sin. Similarly, although the New Testament frequently mentions ἐξομολόγησις (confession), it generally does so as an admission of guilt to and before God rather than as verbal communication of one's sins to another human being, such as a priest. The main exception is James 5:16, "Confess your sins to one another," which became one of the main biblical loci and authorities for confession.[3]

Only in the post-apostolic period did an ecclesiastical rite for remitting post-baptismal sin develop. Generally referred to in the secondary literature as canonical penance but since the fourth century also known as public penance, this unrepeatable liturgical rite was an ex-

Dogmengeschichte 4.3: *Buße und Krankensalbung* (Freiburg: Herder, 1978); Cyrille Vogel, *Le pécheur et la pénitence au Moyen Âge* (Paris: Éditions du Cerf, 1969), 15–36.

2. On modern exegesis of these passages, see Vorgrimmler, *Buße und Krankensalbung*, 12–19; Karl-Josef Klär, *Das kirchliche Bußinstitut von den Anfängen bis zum Konzil von Trient* (Frankfurt am Main: Peter Lang, 1990), 61–67. On patristic and early scholastic exegesis of these passages, see Ludwig Hödl, *Die Geschichte der scholastischen Literatur und der Theologie der Schlüsselgewalt*, Beiträge zur Geschichte der Philosophie und Theologie des Mittelalters [hereafter "BGPTM"] 38.4 (Münster: Aschendorff, 1960).

3. Amédée Teetaert, *La confession aux laïques dans l'église latine depuis le VIIIe jusqu'au XIVe siècle: Étude de théologie positive* (Paris: J. Gabalda, 1926); Paul Anciaux, *La théologie du sacrement de pénitence au XIIe siècle* (Louvain: E. Nauwelaerts, 1949).

traordinary means for obtaining God's forgiveness and reconciliation with the church. It was reserved for those who had committed the most serious of crimes—apostasy, adultery, and murder are the triad generally mentioned in the sources—yet repented of their actions and wished to remain a part of the Christian community.[4] Canonical penance was not intended for those who had committed only slight sins or even for those who had committed what later ages would categorize as less heinous "mortal" sins. For these other sins, there existed other, informal means of reparation, such as sorrow for sin, almsgiving, fasting, recitation of the Lord's Prayer, and private prayer.[5]

Canonical penance involved five components: the penitent's private confession of sins to the bishop, humiliation before the local congregation, the enrollment into a formal order of penitents, performance of penance/works of satisfaction, and the reconciliation of the penitent with the church—not always in that order. Sometimes the enrollment into the order of penitents and performance of satisfaction preceded the confession of sin and humiliation before the local congregation; at other times they occurred only afterwards. The period of penance was always long, in some cases perpetual. Before their readmission into the community, penitents had to engage in strenuous prayer and fasting, and were excluded from the celebration of the eucharist. Moreover, both during and after the period of penance, penitents had to abstain from conjugal relations and were prohibited from bearing arms, serving in public office, or becoming clerics.[6]

Modern historians have traditionally described the history of ca-

4. Bernhard Poschmann, *Paenitentia secunda: Die kirchliche Buße im ältesten Christentum bis Cyprian und Origenes; Eine dogmengeschichtliche Untersuchung* (Bonn: P. Hanstein, 1940); Poschmann, *Die abendländische Kirchenbuße im Ausgang des christlichen Altertums* (Munich: J. Kösel and F. Pustet, 1928).

5. On some of these alternative means of penance, see Klär, *Das kirchliche Bußinstitut,* 71–131; Richard Price, "Informal Penance in Early Medieval Christendom," in *Retribution, Repentance, and Reconciliation,* ed. Kate Cooper and Jeremy Gregory, *Studies in Church History* 40 (2004): 29–38; Kevin Uhalde, "Juridical Administration in the Church and Pastoral Care in Late Antiquity," in *A New History of Penance,* ed. Abigail Firey (Leiden: Brill, 2008), 97–120; Claudia Rapp, "Spiritual Guarantors at Penance, Baptism, and Ordination in the Late Antique East," in ibid., 121–48.

6. See Cyrille Vogel, *La discipline pénitentielle en Gaule: Des origines à la fin du VIIe siècle* (Paris: Letouzey et Ané, 1952), 30–47; Enrico Mazza, *La liturgia della penitenza nella storia: Le grandi tappe* (Bologna: EDB, 2013), 67–69.

nonical penance after the fifth century as one of decline.[7] According to this view, the roots of which stretch back to patristic critiques of the post-Constantinian Christian masses, the unrepeatability and stringency of canonical penance proved a grave problem in the early medieval period. In the early church, adult baptism was the norm and almost every believer was a committed Christian. The rise of infant baptism, however, and the mass conversion, first of the Romans and then of the various barbarian tribes, led to a sharp decline in church discipline. Under these new social conditions, various churchmen complained, the number of Christians who committed multiple grave sins after baptism increased dramatically, as did the number of violations of the severe prohibitions debilitating penitents both during and after the performance of canonical penance, for instance, marriage, remarriage, and bearing arms. Wishing both to maintain the canons in all their stringency and to minimize the chance that penitents would sin after performing canonical penance, various sources suggest, the clergy chose to deny canonical penance to all but the old and dying. As a result, canonical penance became less and less common, except as a deathbed ritual, and ordinary Christians became deprived of the only certain means for obtaining remission for their sins during the period of their lives that they needed it most.[8]

More recent research, however, suggests less that canonical penance ceased being practiced as that it ceased being practiced according to the fourth- and fifth-century canons. As Mayke de Jong has pointed out, numerous sources from the sixth to eighth centuries describe rituals and practices that look very much like canonical penance, though sometimes imposed on clerics and not always imposed by bishops in an episcopal church.[9] "Canonical" penance, penance according to the canons of the late Roman era, may have become a deathbed ritual in the early Middle Ages, but "public" penance, the practice of making

7. See, e.g., Poschmann, *Buße und letzte Ölung*, 54–57; Vogel, *La discipline pénitentielle en Gaule*; Vogel, *Le pécheur et la pénitence dans l'église ancienne* (Paris: Éditions du Cerf, 1966).

8. Vogel, *Le pécheur et la pénitence au Moyen-Âge*, 18.

9. Mayke de Jong, "Transformations of Penance," in *Rituals of Power: From Late Antiquity to the Early Middle Ages*, ed. Frans Theuws and Janet L. Nelson (Leiden: Brill, 2000), 184–224, esp. 202–20.

reparation to God publicly, by no means died out. Instead, it survived not only through its increasing assimilation to monastic conversion, but also as a political weapon, most notably in the deposition of bishops and the sentencing of political enemies to monastic exile.[10]

The transformation of canonical penance into a preparatory rite for death, on the one hand, and its assimilation to monastic conversion, on the other hand, may have opened up space for the emergence of alternative penitential practices that would eventually lead to the rise of private penance, as has traditionally been argued. But the prevalence of informal, non-clerical means of penance and the restricted role that, by its very nature as a remedy for extraordinary sins, canonical penance occupied in the early church make such an explanation seem unlikely.[11] Somewhat more probable is an argument advanced by Peter Brown linking the emergence of alternative forms of penance with the decline of Roman imperial power. According to Brown, late Roman Christians generally conceived of God as a late Roman emperor, who expressed his absolute power through mercy, indulgence, and amnesty. With the decline of the Roman state, such imagery lost its meaning, and in its place other ways of conceiving of God were able to come to the fore. The result was what Brown calls the "peccatization" of the world, that is, "the definitive reduction of all experience, of history, politics, and the social order quite as much as the destiny of individual souls, to two universal explanatory principles, sin and repentance," and a western Europe receptive to new, more scrupulous forms of penance.[12]

10. Mayke de Jong, "Power and Humility in Carolingian Society: The Public Penance of Louis the Pious," *Early Medieval Europe* 1 (1992): 29–52, at 43–52; de Jong, "What was *Public* about Public Penance? *Paenitentia Publica* and Justice in the Carolingian World," in *La Giustizia nell'alto Medioevo (Secoli IX–XI)*, Settimane di Studio del Centro Italiano di Studi sull'Alto Medioevo 44.2 (Spoleto: Centro Italiano di Studi sull'Alto Medioevo, 1997), 863–902, at 867–87.

11. Price, "Informal Penance," 31: "Conventional histories of penance have laid stress on the influence of the Celtic and Anglo-Saxon penitentials.... But it would be a mistake to see the penitentials as filling a gap left by the virtual demise of public penance, since the latter had never been applied to more than a small range of sins, and the notion that the prime remedy for sin was works of penance was already well established."

12. Peter Brown, "The Decline of the Empire of God: Amnesty, Penance, and the Afterlife from Late Antiquity to the Middle Ages," in *Last Things: Death and*

The most important of these new penitential practices was one that emerged around the beginning of the sixth century in Ireland.[13] Generally referred to as tariff penance, this new form of penance may have been related to or derived from the lay confession commonly practiced in monastic communities. It did not require a bishop or involve formal admission into an order of penitents with debilitating canonical penalties. Instead, penitents simply confessed their sins to a priest, who then prescribed penances based on tariffs, that is, private disciplinary rules, contained in books known as penitentials.[14] These penances consisted mainly of more or less rigorous forms of fasting, but sometimes entailed other penalties, such as abstinence from conjugal relations or, for particularly heinous crimes like incest, exile. For those who wished to complete these penances more quickly or who had little time left in this life, a system of commutations and redemptions existed, whereby long, easier penances could be exchanged for shorter, harder ones or, in some cases, defined money sums in almsgiving. Some penitentials furthermore permitted the prescribed penances to be fulfilled not by the penitent, but by one or more substitutes.[15] It is unclear whether this form of penance originally included a ceremony of reconciliation and, if it did, when it took place. In the ninth and tenth centuries, reconciliation seems to have taken place at varying points in the penitential process: sometimes only at the end of the period of penance, as in canonical penance, but sometimes earlier, when the penitent had only completed a part of the assigned penance.[16]

---

the Apocalypse in the Middle Ages, ed. Caroline Walker Bynum and Paul Freedman (Philadelphia: University of Pennsylvania Press, 2000), 41–59, quotation at 58.

13. On the Irish origins of the new penance, see Allen J. Frantzen, *The Literature of Penance in Anglo-Saxon England* (New Brunswick, N.J.: Rutgers University Press, 1983), 19–60; Raymund Kottje, "Busspraxis und Bussritus," in *Segni e riti nella chiesa altomedievale occidentale*, Settimane di Studio del Centro Italiano di Studi sull'Alto Medioevo 33.1 (Spoleto: Centro Italiano di Studi sull'Alto Medioevo, 1987), 369–95, at 372–74.

14. For an introduction to the penitentials, see Cyrille Vogel, *Les "Libri paenitentiales,"* Typologie des Sources du Moyen Âge Occidental 27 (Turnhout: Brepols, 1978), with a supplemental volume by Allen J. Frantzen (Turnhout: Brepols, 1985). For editions of many of the penitentials, see CCCM 156, 156A, and 156B.

15. Bernhard Poschmann, *Die abendländische Kirchenbuße im frühen Mittelalter* (Breslau: Müller and Seiffert, 1930), 1–57; Vogel, *Libri paenitentiales*, 34–39.

16. Poschmann, *Die abendländische Kirchenbuße im frühen Mittelalter*, 102–15.

Thanks to the efforts of first Irish and then later Anglo-Saxon missionaries, tariff penance quickly spread to other parts of Europe.[17] It had a mixed reception. Some continental bishops welcomed tariff penance, whereas others condemned it and affirmed the sole legitimacy of canonical penance. Canon 11 of the Third Council of Toledo (589) appears to have been the earliest reaction against this new form of penance. It declared an "execrable presumption" that "in certain Spanish churches people perform penance not according to the canons, but wickedly, so that however many times they sin, just as often do they demand reconciliation from a priest."[18] Canon 8 of the Council of Châlons (ca. 647–53), on the other hand, approved of the new form of penance. "Concerning the remission of sins, however, which is the marrow of the soul, we judge it to be useful to everyone; and the university of priests is known to consent that, confession having been made, penance is enjoined on penitents by priests."[19]

Both canonical penance and tariff penance became the subject of intense scrutiny and reform efforts under Charlemagne and his successors.[20] In a series of reform synods convened in 813, the Carolingian episcopate demanded both the renewal of canonical penance, which, they claimed, had fallen into disuse, and the reform of tariff penance, which, they similarly complained, often failed to accord with the canons. The Carolingian Council of Châlons articulated this reform program in particular detail. Canon 25 of the council declared

17. Ibid., 58–72.

18. Third Council of Toledo, c. 11, ed. Vives, *Concilios Visigóticos e Hispano-Romanos*, 128: "Quoniam conperimus per quasdam Spaniarum ecclesias non secundum canones sed foedissime pro suis peccatis homines agere poenitentiam, ut quotiens que peccare voluerit totiens a presbytero se reconciliari expostulent; et ideo pro coercenda tam execrabili praesumtione id a sancto concilio iubetur, et secundum formam canonicam antiquorum detur poenitentiam."

19. Council of Châlons, c. 8, ed. Charles de Clercq, *Concilia Galliae a. 511–a. 695*, CCSL 148A (Turnhout: Brepols, 1963), 304.40–43: "De poenitentia uero peccatorum, quae est medilla animae, utilem omnibus hominibus esse censemus; et ut poenitentibus a sacerdotibus data confessione indicatur poenitentia, uniuersitas sacerdotum nuscetur consentire." French translation in Vogel, *Le pécheur et la pénitence au Moyen-Âge*, 192.

20. Poschmann, *Die abendländische Kirchenbuße im frühen Mittelalter*, 73–101. On Carolingian church reform in general, see Rosamond McKitterick, *The Frankish Church and the Carolingian Reforms, 789–985* (London: Royal Historical Society, 1977).

that "the performance of penance according to the ancient constitution of the canons has gone out of use in many places, and the order of the old custom of excommunication and reconciliation is not kept." To resolve this problem, it commanded that henceforth "if anyone sins publicly, let him perform public penance and let him be excommunicated and reconciled according to the order of the canons in accord with his merits."[21] For secret or hidden sins, however, the council endorsed the continued use of tariff penance, which now generally came to be referred to as secret or hidden penance, only more rarely in this period as private penance, though the council did not express similar approval of the penitentials in use up until that time.[22] Canon 38 declared that "the manner of penance should be imposed on those confessing their sins either according to the institution of the ancient canons, the authority of sacred scripture, or ecclesiastical custom, just as it was said above, those little books which they call penitentials having been repudiated, whose errors are certain but authors uncertain."[23] Indeed, disapproval of the old peniten-

21. Council of Châlons, c. 25, ed. Albert Werminghoff, *Concilia aevi Karolini*, MGH Conc. 2.1 (Hanover: MGH, 1906), 278.20–24: "Paenitentiam agere iuxta antiquam canonum constitutionem in plerisque locis ab usu recessit, et neque excommunicandi neque reconciliandi antiqui moris ordo servatur. Ut a domno imperatore impetretur adiutorium, qualiter, si qui publice peccat, publica multetur paenitentia et secundum ordinem canonum pro merito suo et excommunicetur et reconcilietur."

22. It has been pointed out that the term "private" penance is an anachronism when applied to early medieval tariff penance. Penitentials, councils, and capitularies speak instead of "secret" (*secreta*) or "hidden" (*occulta*) penance. But as later sources do often use the term "private penance," it seems least confusing to retain the use of the term "private penance" rather than speak of "secret penance" as a number of recent studies have done. Since private penance seems to have occurred in public spaces, usually churches, it was hardly secret. But it does seem to have been private in the sense that confession occurred out of earshot of others.

23. Council of Châlons, c. 38, ed. Werminghoff, MGH Conc. 2.1, 281.9–17: "Modus autem paenitentiae peccata sua confitentibus aut per antiquorum canonum institutionem aut per sanctarum scripturarum auctoritatem aut per ecclesiasticam consuetudinem, sicut superius dictum est, imponi debet, repudiatis ac penitus eliminatis libellis, quos paenitentiales vocant, quorum sunt certi errores, incerti auctores, de quibus rite dici potest: *Mortificabant animas, quae non moriebantur, et vivificabant animas, quae non vivebant*; qui, dum pro peccatis gravibus leves quosdam et inusitatos imponunt paenitentiae modos, *consuunt pulvillos* secundum propheticum sermonem *sub omni cubito manus et faciunt cervicalia sub capite universae aetatis ad capiendas animas*."

tials was so great that the Council of Paris (829) went so far as to demand "that those little books that they call penitentials, because they oppose canonical authority, be completely abolished" and "that each bishop should diligently search out those erroneous little books in his parish and consign them to be burned."[24]

In response to these and other decrees, Carolingian churchmen produced a number of new canonical collections and penitentials that drew upon known and recognized authorities. The most influential of these works were the canonical collection and penitential that Halitgar of Cambrai compiled at the request of Archbishop Ebbo of Reims, the two penitentials of Hrabanus Maurus, and the *Quadripartitus*.[25] These works included not only conciliar canons and papal decretals, but also many excerpts from the writings of the Church Fathers, which had not previously been used as authorities to regulate penance. The wide diffusion of these new ninth-century canonical collections and penitentials supports the view that the Carolingian reforms had a real impact on the practice of penance, even though they failed to eliminate completely older penitentials and the tariffs deriving from them. Not only did the Carolingian reform penitentials themselves continue to include older tariffs, but older, non-authoritative penitentials also continued to be copied and reworked.[26] Through the canonical collections of Regino of Prüm and

24. Council of Paris, c. 32, ed. Albert Werminghoff, *Concilia aevi Karolini*, MGH Conc. 2.2 (Hanover: MGH, 1908), 633.12–17 and 19–21: "Ut codicelli, quos penitentiales vocant, quia canonicae auctoritati refragantur, poenitus aboleantur. Quoniam multi sacerdotum partim incuria, partim ignorantia modum paenitentiae reatum suum confitentibus secus, quam iura canonica decernant, imponunt, utentes scilicet quibusdam codicellis contra canonicam auctoritatem scriptis, quos paenitentiales vocant, et ob id non vulnera peccatorum curant, sed potius foventes palpant ... omnibus nobis salubriter in commune visum est, ut unusquisque episcoporum in sua parroechia eosdem erroneos codicellos diligenter perquirat et inventos igni tradat, ne per eos ulterius sacerdotes imperiti homines decipiant."

25. Raymund Kottje, *Die Bussbücher Halitgars von Cambrai und des Hrabanus Maurus: Ihre Überlieferung und ihre Quellen* (Berlin: De Gruyter, 1980); Franz Kerff, *Der Quadripartitus: Ein Handbuch der karolingischen Kirchenreform* (Sigmaringen: J. Thorbecke, 1982). For a guide to the literature on the *Quadripartitus*, see Kéry, *Canonical Collections of the Early Middle Ages*, 167–69; Fowler-Magerl, *Clavis*, 59–60.

26. Allen Frantzen, "The Significance of the Frankish Penitentials," *Journal of Ecclesiastical History* 30 (1979): 409–21; Kottje, *Bussbücher*, 173, 185–90, 204–12, and 251–53.

Burchard of Worms, moreover, many of the older penitential tariffs entered later canonical collections, including the foundational textbook of the new academic discipline of canon law that emerged in the mid-twelfth century, Gratian's *Decretum*.[27]

The normative nature of the sources makes it difficult to determine how extensively the Carolingian reforms actually affected penitential practice. But it seems clear that the Carolingians did not succeed in their stated goal of renewing the ancient practice of canonical penance. Instead, what they actually did was to create a new and rather different dual penitential system.[28] Canonical penance had been intended for serious sins, whereas tariff penance had been intended for all sins whatsoever, regardless of their gravity. The new Carolingian dichotomy, however, reserved public penance solely for public sins and private penance for secret or hidden sins.[29] As actually practiced, moreover, both public and private penance combined elements from canonical and tariff penance. Public penance borrowed many tariffs from tariff penance and private penance employed as tariffs canons originally intended for canonical penance. Indeed, the same penitentials were often used to determine punishments in both episcopal courts and private confession.[30] Liturgically as well, *ordines* for public

27. Kottje, *Bussbücher*, 128–29; Ludger Körntgen, "Fortschreibung frühmittelalterlicher Bußpraxis: Burchards 'Liber corrector' und seine Quellen," in *Bischof Burchard von Worms 1000–1025*, ed. Wilfried Hartmann (Mainz: Selbstverlag der Gesellschaft für Mittelrheinische Kirchengeschichte, 2000), 199–226. See also the alphabetical index of sources in Hartmut Hoffmann and Rudolf Pokorny, *Das Dekret des Bischofs Burchard von Worms: Textstufen—Frühe Verbreitung—Vorlagen*, MGH Hilfsmittel 12 (Munich: MGH, 1991), 269–72.

28. Poschmann, *Die abendländische Kirchenbuße im frühen Mittelalter*, 164.

29. This is stated explicitly in a significant amount of legislation from the period, e.g., Council of Reims, c. 31, ed. Werminghoff, MGH Conc. 2.1, 256.21–22: "Ut discretio servanda sit inter paenitentes, qui publice et qui absconse paenitere debent"; Capitulary of Theodulf of Orleans, ed. Peter Brommer, *Capitula episcoporum* 1, MGH Capit. episc. 1 (Hanover: MGH, 1984), 166.36–167.3: "Quod autem supra diximus, de his agatur, qui publice ad confessionem venerint et publice penitentiam egerint. Quod si occulte actum est et occulte ad sacerdotem venerint et puram confessionem fecerint, occulte poenitere debent."

30. Franz Kerff, "Mittelalterliche Quellen und mittelalterliche Wirklichkeit: Zu den Konsequenzen einer jüngst erschienenen Edition für unser Bild kirchlicher Reformbemühungen," *Rheinische Vierteljahrsblätter* 51 (1987): 275–86; Kerff, "*Libri paenitentiales* und kirchliche Strafgerichtsbarkeit bis zum *Decretum Gratiani*: Ein Diskussionsvorschlag," *ZRG KA* 75 (1989): 23–57, at 40–46.

penance adapted elements from *ordines* for private penance and vice versa.[31]

The Impact of Private Penance

The development of multiple forms of penance, all employing more or less the same vocabulary, is one reason why Gratian and his contemporaries could devote so much attention to penance. A second reason is the sheer importance of private penance by the early twelfth century. By the beginning of the twelfth century, private penance had become extremely widespread and common. It was a practice that was both familiar to the laity and of increasing concern to a clergy ever more interested in the spiritual health of the ordinary Christian.

Largely to be rejected are revisionist attempts to question the impact of private penance on medieval religious life prior to the twelfth century, indeed prior to 1215, when the Fourth Lateran Council issued the famous canon *Omnis utriusque sexus*, commanding all Christians who had reached the age of discretion to confess their sins annually to their own parish priest.[32] Franz Kerff has argued that the penitentials, the main source for private penance prior to the twelfth century, were used primarily as aids to episcopal representatives in the administration of public justice. Ordinary rural clergy, as is well known, were poorly trained, and most, Kerff argues, would not have possessed the requisite skills for using penitentials. In addition, the contents and manuscript transmission of penitentials he has studied, which are often found together with legal texts, suggest that they were used for judicial rather than pastoral purposes.[33]

Building on Kerff's ideas, Alexander Murray has argued that the dual nature of clergy in the central Middle Ages as pastors and policemen makes it unlikely that private penance, which entailed the detailed confession of sins, could have been a widespread practice. Only

31. Sarah Hamilton, *The Practice of Penance, 900–1050* (Woodbridge: Royal Historical Society, 2001), 104–72.

32. For the text of *Omnis utriusque sexus*, see *Decrees of the Ecumenical Councils*, ed. Norman P. Tanner, 2 vols. (London: Sheed and Ward, 1990), 1:245.

33. Kerff, "Mittelalterliche Quellen," 278–86; Kerff, "*Libri paenitentiales.*"

"the separation of secular and ecclesiastical jurisdictions, with the genesis of 'feudal monarchy' after the millennium ... left churchmen free to specialise, whether on outward lay observance in the *forum externum*, or on the consciences of the *forum internum*." In support of this view, Murray points to the absence of regular confession by laypeople in miracle literature before the early twelfth century and argues that when it does appear in the sources, it does so in connection with learned members of religious orders, who were particularly interested in promoting the practice beyond the confines of the monastery.[34]

The results of recent studies, however, argue against the conclusions of Kerff and Murray. First, a more comprehensive examination of surviving penitentials undermines one of the main pieces of evidence they adduce in support of their position: the claim that penitentials were used mainly as penal codes for episcopal courts rather than as handbooks for priests hearing confessions or textbooks for priests learning how to administer penance. Through an analysis of their prologues and prescriptions, Raymund Kottje shows that the tariffs found in penitentials were overwhelmingly intended as penances (disciplinary measures intended to improve and reconcile the penitent) rather than as punishments (sanctions to prevent future misbehavior or as retribution for misdeeds).[35] Similarly, from an analysis of manuscripts containing tripartite penitentials, most of which date to the ninth century, Rob Meens concludes that they were probably intended for use by "simple priests in the daily work of pastoral care." Not only do these penitentials frequently appear together with other pastoral works, but in appearance they are often "simple, small, unadorned and originally often unbound, but sometimes still bear marks that show heavy use."[36] For penitentials from the tenth

34. Alexander Murray, "Confession Before 1215," *Transactions of the Royal Historical Society*, sixth series 3 (1993): 51–81, quotation at 61–62.

35. Raymund Kottje, "Buße oder Strafe? Zur 'Iustitia' in den 'Libri Paenitentiales,'" in *La giustizia nell'alto medioevo (Secoli V–VIII)*, Settimane di Studio del Centro Italiano di Studi sull'Alto Medioevo 42.1 (Spoleto: Centro Italiano di Studi sull'Alto Medioevo, 1995), 443–68.

36. Rob Meens, "The Frequency and Nature of Early Medieval Penance," in *Handling Sin: Confession in the Middle Ages*, ed. Peter Biller and A. J. Minnis (Woodbridge: York Medieval Press, 1998), 35–61, at 39–47, quotations at 41 and 47.

and eleventh centuries, on the other hand, various studies by Adriaan Gaastra and Ludger Körntgen, as well as by Meens, suggest that they were used less frequently as handbooks for direct pastoral care and more frequently for educational purposes, to instruct priests on how they should hear confession and administer penances.[37]

Recent studies have also found positive indications that private penance was widespread and common in many areas even prior to the twelfth century. David Bachrach points to evidence drawn from a variety of literary genres to show that Carolingian soldiers confessed their sins individually to priests not only before, but also after battle. Every Carolingian military unit was required to have a priest capable of hearing confessions and assigning penances. Sermons directed at Carolingian soldiers take for granted that regular confession was a part of military life, and narrative sources confirm that Carolingian soldiers did indeed confess their sins on at least a few occasions.[38] As Catherine Cubitt demonstrates, moreover, a substantial body of textual and manuscript evidence exists for the practice of penance in certain parts of Europe, such as late Saxon England. The Old English vernacular possessed specialized terms for confession and penance. Old English homilies take for granted that the administration of penance was part of a priest's ordinary duties. And there is evidence for the production of vernacular penitential texts, including three Old English penitentials that may have been used as handbooks for confessors.[39]

While revisionist scholarship appears to have been incorrect in claiming that confession and private penance only became widespread in the twelfth century or even later, it does seem to have been justified in questioning the frequency and quality of early medieval

37. Rob Meens, "Penitentials and the Practice of Penance in the Tenth and Eleventh Centuries," *Early Medieval Europe* 14 (2006): 7–21; Adriaan H. Gaastra, "Penance and the Law: The Penitential Canons of the *Collection in Nine Books*," ibid., 85–102; Ludger Körntgen, "Canon Law and the Practice of Penance: Burchard of Worms' Penitential," ibid., 103–17.

38. David Bachrach, "Confession in the Regnum Francorum (742–900)," *Journal of Ecclesiastical History* 54 (2003): 3–22.

39. Catherine Cubitt, "Bishops, Priests and Penance in Late Saxon England," *Early Medieval Europe* 14 (2006): 41–63, at 44–55.

confession. Just because private penance was common and widespread, it does not follow that there was a general obligation or custom of confessing to a priest one or more times a year. As Meens points out, "It was not the frequency of lay confession that worried the Frankish episcopacy, but the way it was done. Councils worried whether priests heard confession and administered penances according to the rules laid down in a penitential. They also worried about the type of penitential priests used. Their main concern was the uniformity of penitential practice, not its frequency."[40]

The sparse evidence makes it impossible to determine how frequently laypersons confessed. Since confession seems to have been closely linked to receiving communion and since legislation from the Carolingian era onward generally demanded laypersons to communicate between one and three times a year, annual or even more frequent confession may have been common in some areas.[41] But even if confession took place regularly, the quality of spiritual guidance which ordinary Christians in the early and central (or even the high and late) Middle Ages received may not have been particularly good, and the average Christian was, one legitimately suspects, not particularly devout. It is thus entirely possible, as many scholars since Jean Delumeau have argued, that the average baptized person was Christian in only the most superficial sense of the word.[42] But if the European Middle Ages really were to a large extent still non-Christian, then they were so in spite of the availability of religious rites like private penance rather than because such practices were lacking.

40. Meens, "Frequency," 37.

41. Ibid., 37–38. Cf. Martin Ohst, *Pflichtbeichte: Untersuchungen zum Bußwesen im Hohen und Späten Mittelalter* (Tübingen: J. C. B. Mohr, 1995), 14–49, who argues, not always convincingly, that the Fourth Lateran Council invented the obligation of annual confession. Prior to 1215, he claims, there were attempts to promote regular confession, but no attempts to impose an *obligation* of confessing sins on a regular basis. To explain away legislation or statements that suggest either an obligation or a custom of annual confession, he argues that the laypersons mentioned in these texts refer not to laypersons in general but to *conversi* or people attached to cathedrals or religious houses or that they refer only to laypersons who believe they have committed a mortal sin.

42. Jean Delumeau, *Catholicism between Luther and Voltaire: A New View of the Counter-Reformation*, trans. Jeremy Moiser (London: Burns and Oates, 1977).

Pseudo-Augustine and the Scholastic Turn

As tariff penance became more and more widespread, theologians and reformers from the late eleventh century onward began to rethink its theoretical underpinnings and how it might better promote spiritual renewal. Their solution was to downplay external works of satisfaction and focus instead on interior contrition for sin. Penitentials, liturgical texts, and other sources from before this period, of course, also stress the importance of contrition and repentance.[43] But none of them suggests, as later theologians do, that contrition alone effects the remission of sins or that confession is a form of satisfaction, indeed the most important form.

The earliest writer to promote this reconceived form of penance appears to have been the author of the Pseudo-Augustinian *De vera et falsa penitentia*. This treatise is usually dated to the eleventh or early twelfth century, but could conceivably have been written as late as the 1140s, since its only firm *terminus ante quem* is 1150, the date by which the first recension of Gratian's *Decretum*, the first work to draw on *De vera et falsa penitentia*, is known to have been published.[44] *De vera et falsa penitentia* takes the form of a letter to a "prudent heroine," at whose request Pseudo-Augustine, following a common literary topos, claims to have written the work. The author states that he will write "everything he believes about penance" and that he will address not only present-day errors, but also more ancient ones.[45]

43. Pierre J. Payer, "The Humanism of the Penitentials and the Continuity of the Penitential Tradition," *Mediaeval Studies* 46 (1984): 340–65; Sarah Hamilton, "Penance in the Age of Gregorian Reform," in *Retribution, Repentance, and Reconciliation*, ed. Cooper and Gregory, 47–73, at 47–67.

44. Karen Teresa Wagner, "*De vera et falsa penitentia*: An Edition and Study" (PhD diss., University of Toronto, 1995), 187–89, summarizes the evidence for the date of *De vera et falsa penitentia*, concluding only that the treatise was composed in the period 1000–1140. On the date of the first recension of the *Decretum*, see pp. 24–26.

45. Pseudo-Augustine, *De vera et falsa penitentia* 1.2, PL 40, 1113: "Haec omnia, provida virago, sensisti, quae hoc tantum bonum tenere dilexisti.... Itaque voluntatem tuam, quam super hoc bono cognovi, libenter adjuvo: et suavem laborem super hac re, ut rogasti, desideranter suscipio.... Tuae itaque trado dilectioni, quidquid de poenitentia sentio, auctoritate patrum et illustratione sancti Spiritus. Nec modo hujus temporis tantum impugnamus errores, sed etiam de impugnatis per copiam rationum conamur tibi tradere dulcedinem suavitatis: ut

Polemic is particularly frequent throughout the first third of the treatise, which focuses on refuting the claim that those who have been baptized cannot perform penance and that penance cannot be repeated.[46] No sin, Pseudo-Augustine argues, is too heinous to be forgiven.[47] On the contrary, because God hates sin and iniquity, he is always ready to destroy them through penance.[48] Those who claim otherwise try to take away from the church the power that Jesus gave it to forgive sins and, what is even worse, impose a limit on the infinite God.[49] God does not deny the grace of forgiveness to any sinner who repents and seeks pardon, even, Pseudo-Augustine emphasizes, undoubtedly with an eye to patristic and early medieval regulations on public penance, if that sinner should happen to be a priest.[50] Canonical penance was originally administered to both clerics and laypersons, but from the fourth century onward church councils began to forbid its administration to clerics, who were instead simply deposed.[51] Pseudo-Augustine was undoubtedly familiar with these regulations and with the fact that clerics were not forbidden from performing private penance. Indeed, towards the end of the treatise, he explicitly mentions the contradictory nature of the canons on this point.[52]

---

integritas tuae mentis, quae Deo dante omnes repulit falsitates, super fugatis ratiocinando laetetur."

46. Ibid., 2.3–7.18, PL 40, 1114–19.

47. Ibid., 3.5–5.11, PL 40, 1114–17.

48. Ibid., 5.11, PL 40, 1117: "Imo constat ei peccata multum displicere, qui semper praesto est ea destruere. Si enim ea amaret, non ita semper destrueret, sed conservaret, atque ut sua munera foveret."

49. Ibid., 5.13, PL 40, 1117: "Scimus autem primos patres, et in omni tempore Ecclesiam Dei semper usque septuagies septies, quod est semper, peccata dimittere. Quam potestatem illi ab Ecclesia Dei conantur auferre." Ibid., 5.15, PL 40, 1118: "Adhuc qui diffidit, et suam nequitiam Dei benignitati comparat, finem imponit Dei virtuti, dans finem infinito, et perfectionem divinitatis auferens Deo; cui nihil deest, quod etiam excogitari non potest."

50. Ibid., 5.13, PL 40, 1117: "Et quod omnibus promisit indulgentiam, aliis promissionibus declarat: *Qui me confessus fuerit coram hominibus*, id est, omnis quantumcumque et quotiescumque peccator, cujuscumque ordinis, etiamsi fuerit sacerdos; *confitebor et ego eum coram Patre meo*." Ibid., 5.16, PL 40, 1118: "Non itaque etiamsi sacerdos peccaverit, desperare debet."

51. Poschmann, *Buße und letzte Ölung*, 57–61.

52. Pseudo-Augustine, *De vera et falsa penitentia* 20.36, PL 40, 1130: "Caveat

While polemic fills the treatise's opening sections, pastoral advice and admonition dominate the last two-thirds of *De vera et falsa penitentia,* which sets forth the author's views on what penance is and how it should be performed.[53] Pseudo-Augustine stresses first and foremost the penitent's inner disposition, although he also repeatedly affirms the importance of the priestly power to bind and loose, as well as the great intercessory power of the church. By itself, he argues, baptism cleanses only original sin. To purge actual sins, suffering (*dolor*)—by which Pseudo-Augustine seems to mean psychological anguish, as felt, for instance, in contrition and shame—is also required.[54] True penance cannot be the result of regret or fear of punishment. Instead, it must proceed from faith and charity and must take place within the unity of the church.[55] Furthermore, true penance cannot be halfhearted. It must involve regret for all one's sins, not just some of them.[56]

Pseudo-Augustine locates the power of confession in the shame that it causes. Shame is a sort of satisfaction, which makes venial what was criminal.[57] Indeed, the shame which confession causes is

---

[sacerdos] ne corruat, ne juste perdat potestatem judiciariam. Licet enim poenitentia ei possit acquirere gratiam, non tamen mox restituit in potestatem primam. Licet enim Petrus post lapsum restitutus fuerit, et saepe lapsis sacerdotibus reddita sit dignitatis potestas; non est tamen necesse, ut hoc omnibus concedatur quasi ex auctoritate. Invenitur enim auctoritas quae concedit, et quasi imperat. Invenitur et alia quae minime concedit, sed vetat."

53. Ibid., 8.19–20.37, PL 40, 1119–30.

54. Ibid., 8.19, PL 40, 1119: "Poenitentia enim baptizandis non est necessaria; sed baptizatis de majoribus et minoribus peccatis dolendum sive poenitendum est. Per fidem enim Ecclesiae sola remittuntur peccata, quae contraxit homo in origine: ut sicut a patre peccante damnationem accepit, ita per matris Ecclesiae fidem consequatur remissionem. Sed qui per se peccavit, per dolorem proprium et per fidem Ecclesiae indulgentiam acquisivit. Haec per Baptismum ita reddunt hominem mundum et novum, ut nihil remaneat quod Deo displiceat. Sine poenitentia nulli profuit Baptismus, qui peccavit spontaneus."

55. Ibid., 9.23, PL 40, 1121: "Sunt enim quos peccasse poenitet propter praesentia supplicia. Displicent enim latroni peccata, quando operantur poenam. Deficit vindicta; revertitur ad crimina. Ista poenitentia non ex fide procedens, nec charitate vel unitate, sterilis manet et sine misericordia."

56. Ibid., 9.24, PL 40, 1121: "Sunt plures quos poenitet peccasse, sed non omnino, reservantes sibi quaedam in quibus delectentur: non animadvertentes Dominum simul surdum et mutum a daemonio liberasse: per hoc docens nos nunquam nisi de omnibus sanari."

57. Ibid., 10.25, PL 40, 1122: "In hoc enim quod per se ipsum dicit sacerdoti,

so powerful that it suffices to confess to a layperson if a priest is lacking. Desire for a priest, Pseudo-Augustine teaches, makes up for the fact that laypersons do not possess the power of the keys.[58]

Pseudo-Augustine lavishly praises the benefits of private penance. At the same time, however, he continues to acknowledge the usefulness, indeed the necessity of public penance, which, in contrast to the scholastics, he attempts to justify theologically. To this end, Pseudo-Augustine allegorically interprets an episode from the gospels (Mk 5:21–43; Mt 9:18–25; Lk 8:40–56). Confession to a priest, Pseudo-Augustine says, suffices to remit hidden sins. For in the resurrection of Jairus's daughter, few people were present. She was not yet buried, not yet carried outside the gate of the city, not yet carried outside the house where others could see. Jesus revived her indoors, where he found her. The only others present were the apostles Peter, James, and John, as well as the father and mother of the girl, in whom are allegorically prefigured priests of the church. However, those whom Jesus found outside, that is, in public, says Pseudo-Augustine, he healed before other people. A crowd wept for the widow's son; Martha and Mary wept for their brother; and the crowd that Mary followed wept. In all of these examples, Pseudo-Augustine argues, we are taught that the merits of public sinners do not suffice to wipe away their sins, but that such people require the merits of the church if they are to obtain forgiveness from God. Thus, he says, apparently describing the liturgy of public penance, one who is dead (in sin) should lie prostrate and show himself to be dead, publicly announcing his death and publicly showing the fruits of his penance so that a crowd may weep for him who is lost and dead. Christ will be moved by these tears and return to the mother her only son. If he does not show himself to be dead through fruits of penance, so much the more necessary is it to

---

et erubescientiam vincit timore Dei offensi, fit venia criminis: fit enim per confessionem veniale, quod criminale erat in operatione.... Et quoniam verecundia magna est poena, qui erubescit pro Christo, fit dignus misericordia."

58. Ibid.: "Tanta itaque vis confessionis est, ut si deest sacerdos, confiteatur proximo. Saepe enim contingit quod poenitens non potest verecundari coram sacerdote, quem desideranti nec locus nec tempus offert. Et si ille cui confitebitur potestatem solvendi non habet, fit tamen dignus venia, ex desiderio sacerdotis, qui socio confitetur turpitudinem criminis."

seek the aid not only of Martha but also of Mary. He should do this, Pseudo-Augustine says, by afflicting himself and showing himself as one suffering and dead, so that those hearing and watching may pray for mercy for him. For he who offends many in sinning must placate many in satisfying. In this way, the church, which was previously offended by guilt, may, in conversion, turn to mercy, praying for him who was dead and by praying obtain pardon from the Lord.[59] Penance, Pseudo-Augustine concludes, must therefore take place within the unity of the church. The church's alms, prayers, and works of justice and mercy assist the penitent in transforming his or her life and achieving salvation. Judas was damned not because he did not perform penance, but because he went to the Pharisees rather than to the apostles.[60]

De vera et falsa penitentia had an enormous influence on scholastic

59. Ibid., 11.26, PL 40, 1123: "Si peccatum occultum est, sufficiat referre in notitiam sacerdotis, ut grata sit oblatio muneris. Nam in resurrectione filiae principis pauci interfuerunt qui viderent. Nondum enim erat sepulta, nondum extra portam civitatis delata, nondum extra domum in notitiam deportata. Intus resuscitavit, quam intus invenit, relictis solis Petro et Joanne et Jacobo et patre et matre puellae, in quibus figuraliter continentur sacerdotes Ecclesiae. Quos autem extra invenit, animadvertendum est quomodo suscitavit. Flebat autem turba post filium viduae; flevit Martha et Maria supplicantes pro fratre, flebat et turba quae Mariam fuerat secuta, lacrymis Mariae admonita: in quo docemur publice peccantibus non proprium, sed Ecclesiae sufficere meritum. Sic itaque mortuus jaceat, sicque se mortuum ostendat, publice mortem suam praedicando, publice fructus poenitentiae ostendendo, ut turba ploret amissum, et defleat quem dolet mortuum. Istis lacrymis movebitur Dominus, qui reddet matri unicum filium suum. Si minus perseveraverit, si se mortuum per fructus poenitentiae non declaraverit; tanto plus oportet addere, unde lacrymas excitet, non solum Marthae, sed etiam Mariae. Tantum se affligat, tantum se dolere et se mortuum sentire ostendat, ut audientes et contemplantes plorando orent veniam, quorum fletum imitetur Ecclesia. Qui enim multos offendit peccando, placare multos oportet satisfaciendo: ut Ecclesia prius offensa per culpam, in conversione flectatur in misericordiam, orans pro ipso quem defunctum dolebat, unde Deus flectetur ad veniam, qui prius adhibuit misericordiam."

60. Ibid., 12.27, PL 40, 1123: "Nisi unitas Ecclesiae succurrat, nisi quod deest peccatori, sua opitulatione compleat, de manibus inimici non eripietur anima mortui. Credendum est enim, et pietas fidei expostulat credere, quod omnes eleemosynae totius Ecclesiae et orationes et opera justitiae et misericordiae succurrant recognoscenti mortem suam ad conversionem suam. Ideoque nemo digne poenitere potest, quem non sustineat unitas Ecclesiae. Ideoque non petat sacerdotes per aliquam culpam ab unitate Ecclesiae divisos. Judas enim poenitens ivit ad Pharisaeos, reliquit Apostolos."

theology after its inclusion in the first recension of Gratian's *Decretum* and then Peter Lombard's *Four Books of Sentences*, but it does not seem to have had any impact or readership before that time. Interest in penance in the early twelfth-century French schools of theology developed independently from Pseudo-Augustine. The early scholastics treat some of the same questions as Pseudo-Augustine, but also many new ones, such as the problem of the return of sins, that is, the doctrine that forgiven sins in some sense return when one later commits another sin. In addressing these issues, however, the early scholastics, like Pseudo-Augustine, emphasize the overwhelming importance of contrition, present confession as a form of satisfaction, and downplay the performance of traditional works of satisfaction. At the same time, they also introduce terminological changes and begin to categorize penance differently. Rather than referring to secret penance, the early scholastics tend to speak of private penance, while they refer to public penance as either public penance or solemn penance. A uniform terminology, however, appears only in the thirteenth century, if even then.

The earliest identifiable theologian to examine penance in the new scholastic manner was Anselm of Laon, the leading teacher of theology in the late eleventh and early twelfth century.[61] Following the rather harsh judgment of Peter Abelard, modern scholars have often downplayed Anselm's theological acumen as well as his significance. However, as Cédric Giraud has shown, Anselm was in fact a skilled and highly influential theologian. He began the glossing activity that resulted in the *Glossa ordinaria* to the Bible and may have been involved with inventing or at least popularizing the sentence collection as a genre of theological literature.[62] His emphasis on applying patristic texts to contemporary theological questions may account in part for their overwhelming use in early scholastic treat-

61. On Anselm, see Giraud, *Per verba magistri*.

62. On the *Glossa ordinaria*, see the discussion in chapter 2, pp. 59–65. Regarding Anselm and sentence collections, see Giraud, *Per verba magistri*, 179–436; Giraud, "Le recueil de sentences de l'école de Laon *Principium et causa*: Un cas de pluri-attribution," in *Parva pro magnis munera: Études de littérature tardo-antique et médiévale offertes à François Dolbeau par ses élèves*, ed. Monique Goullet (Turnhout: Brepols, 2009), 245–69; Wei, *"Deus non habet initium uel terminum,"* 1–118.

ments of penance as well as the corresponding neglect of Carolingian conciliar decrees and penitential tariffs.

Anselm's views on penance must be reconstructed mainly from the various, often brief *sententiae* attributed to him in contemporary florilegia and sentence collections. Two of these deal directly with penance, more specifically the necessity of confession, and both take as their starting point patristic texts. Bede in his commentary on Luke, says Anselm, appears to state that fraternal discord, Judaizing, heresy, and gentile superstition are the only sins that need to be confessed; all other sins can be forgiven in one's conscience (*in sola conscientia*).[63] However, Anselm argues, Bede needs to be understood as talking about public and private confession. Fraternal discord, Judaizing, heresy, and gentile superstition must be confessed publicly. All other sins are to be confessed in private.[64]

Anselm's other sentence on penance deals with the relationship between contrition and confession. Ambrose in his commentary on Luke states that he "read of Peter's tears, but not of his [performing] penance; tears wash away sins, which it is shameful to confess out loud."[65] He thus appears to teach that tears suffice to wipe away sin if one is too ashamed to confess them. However, Anselm argues, this interpretation of Ambrose is contrary to the faith. A person who, out of shame, does not confess, possesses pride, and no one who possesses pride is saved. Instead, Anselm argues, penance necessarily involves both God and a priest. God remits sin whenever a sinner calls out to him in shame (*pudor*), what later theologians generally refer to as contrition (*contritio*). But just as Jesus commanded his disciples

63. Bede, *In Lucae evangelium expositio* 5.17.14, ed. David Hurst, CCSL 120 (Turnhout: Brepols, 1960), 312.682–313.685.

64. Anselm, *Sententiae*, no. 65, ed. Odon Lottin, *Psychologie et morale aux XIIe et XIIIe siècles* 5: *L'école d'Anselme de Laon et de Guillaume de Champeaux* (Gembloux: Duculot, 1959), 57: "Beda dicit de quibusdam debere confiteri, ut de fraterno scismate, iudaica perfidia, heretica prauitate, gentili superstitione, cetera uero in sola conscientia relaxari. Sed intelligendum est illum loqui de publica et priuata confessione. Nam illa in sola conscientia dixit relaxari, que priuatim confitemur."

65. Ambrose, *Expositio evangelii secundum Lucam* 10.88, ed. Marcus Adriaen, CCSL 14 (Turnhout: Brepols, 1957), 371.845–49: "Petrus doluit et fleuit, quia errauit ut homo. Non inuenio quid dixerit, inuenio quod fleuerit. Lacrimas eius lego, satisfactionem non lego; sed quod defendi non potest ablui potest. Lauent lacrimae delictum, quod uoce pudor est confiteri."

to free Lazarus after he had been raised from the dead, so too are sinners already forgiven by God required to confess their sins to a priest. Priests, in Anselm's words, unbind (*soluere*) the sinner.[66]

Later theologians devoted considerable attention to the problems raised by Anselm's simultaneous insistence on the necessity of confession and the expiatory power of contrition. If God indeed remits sins in contrition, then how can priests be said to forgive sins in confession? And even if it is prideful to neglect confessing to a priest, why should God or the church have established such a precept in the first place?[67]

Peter Abelard provided one of the most popular solutions to these interrelated questions. According to Abelard, sin is an imputable fault that occurs whenever one consents to a sinful intention. It is a willful turning away from God, contempt for God.[68] Contrition is displeasure with sin that stems from love of God rather than fear of punishment.[69] God instituted confession, Abelard says, to instill humility in people. Because man placed under his own control abandoned God, it was fitting that he should return to God by being placed under someone else's power.[70] Those who fail to confess their sins out of contempt or negligence will thus be punished eternally, but those

66. Anselm, *Sententiae*, no. 65, ed. Lottin, 56–57: "Inueniuntur quedam in scripturis que ueritati obuiare uidentur, ut uerbi gratia in Ambrosio super lucam: Lacrimas Petri lego, penitentiam non lego; lacrime delent peccata, que pudor est uoce confiteri. Ecce plane uidetur uelle, quod si aliquem pudeat confiteri, fletus tamen impetrat. Quod contra fidem est. Si enim pro pudore dimittit confiteri superbia est, in qua nemo potest saluari. Iterum resuscitato Lazaro dicitur discipulis: *Soluite eum.* In quo monstratur aperte, quia peccator ingemiscens a Deo uiuificatur, sed nunquam nisi per ministros ecclesie soluitur. Agit igitur superior scriptura de eo quod Dominus per se facit ad hominem, id est, dimittit peccata, sic tamen ut ille soluatur a sacerdote. Sic enim dimittitur peccatum, ut pena soluatur cuius initium est pudor qui in confessione habetur. Cum autem dicitur: lacrime delent peccatum quod uoce pudor est confiteri, illud tamen Deus dimittit, postquam peccatorem uere penituerit, ita tamen ut ille penitens a sacerdote soluatur."

67. Anciaux, *Théologie de pénitence*, 164–353, remains the most detailed study of this problem for the twelfth century.

68. Robert Blomme, *La doctrine du péché dans les écoles théologiques de la première moitié du XIIe siècle* (Louvain: Publications Universitaires de Louvain, 1958), 115–28.

69. *Peter Abelard's Ethics*, ed. and trans. D. E. Luscombe (Oxford: Clarendon Press, 1971), 76.22–25; *Sententie Magistri Petri Abaelardi* 279, ed. D. E. Luscombe, CCCM 14 (Turnhout: Brepols, 2006), 145.3323–28.

70. *Abelard's Ethics*, ed. Luscombe, 98.10–15 and 19–24; *Sententie Magistri Petri Abaelardi* 281, ed. Luscombe, 146.3345–53.

who because of sudden death are unable to confess will not be punished on that account.[71] In addition, Abelard creates an exception to the general rule requiring confession for cases that might cause scandal.[72] If the confession of fault may bring about scandal, then, Abelard says, it can be omitted without sin, provided that one does so out of concern for the good of the church rather than from a sense of personal shame or embarrassment.[73]

Despite the general necessity of confession to a priest, however, Abelard, like Anselm, teaches that priests do not actually possess the power to forgive sins. As far as sins are concerned, Christian priests are like the priests of the Old Testament, who merely declare clean or unclean what God has healed or left unhealed through his own power. They (should) possess the discretion to discern who should be bound or unbound, but are unable themselves to cleanse from sin.[74] The power of the keys Abelard interprets in two different, though not necessarily mutually exclusive, ways. The keys, he says, can be understood to refer to the power of imposing and remitting penance, that is, works of satisfaction. Taken in this sense, the keys have not been granted to all bishops, but rather only to the apostles and those who imitate their morally upright behavior.[75] The other way to understand the keys is as the power to excommunicate and reconcile sinners in the this-worldly church. In this sense, says Abelard, the keys have been granted to all bishops and priests. Anyone excommunicated by one bishop or priest is held to be excommunicated in all the other churches, regardless of whether the sentence is just or unjust. Such a sentence of excommunication has force only in this world; it is unable to exclude from grace someone who has not merited eternal punishment through his own sin.[76] Since the keys un-

71. *Sententie Magistri Petri Abaelardi* 282, ed. Luscombe, 146.3354–62.

72. *Abelard's Ethics*, ed. Luscombe, 100.14–17; *Sententie Magistri Petri Abaelardi* 282, ed. Luscombe, 147.3368–70.

73. *Abelard's Ethics*, ed. Luscombe, 100.24–30; *Sententie Magistri Petri Abaelardi* 284, ed. Luscombe, 148.3388–98.

74. *Abelard's Ethics*, ed. Luscombe, 114.17–25; *Sententie Magistri Petri Abaelardi* 288, ed. Luscombe, 150.3456–151.3458 and 151.3470–86.

75. *Abelard's Ethics*, ed. Luscombe, 112.2–9, 114.25–29, and 116.31–118.7.

76. *Abelard's Ethics*, ed. Luscombe, 122.19–124.4; *Sententie Magistri Petri Abaelardi* 289, ed. Luscombe, 151.3486–152.3500.

derstood in this latter sense can be exercised without discretion, Abelard rejects the traditional idea that there are two keys, discretion and power. Instead, he proposes, there is only one key, the power to excommunicate and reconcile in the this-worldly church, which is said to be plural on account of its dual effects.[77] Abelard's position was commonsensical. If bishops and priests did in fact receive two keys in ordination and one of those keys was discretion, then there would be no such thing as a foolish bishop or priest. Yet the contrary is true: in ordination bishops and priests do not gain any special insight that they previously lacked, but rather remain as wise or foolish as before.

Many of Abelard's teachings were accepted without much debate and became common currency in the schools, but his ideas about the power of the keys were not among them. Far from gaining a following, they drew much criticism. Indeed, they were one of the "heresies" that spurred William of St. Thierry and Bernard of Clairvaux to press for his condemnation at the Council of Sens (1140/1141).[78] Abelard's idea that there was only one key was innocuous enough and was particularly well received among canonists.[79] But his assertion that not all priests possessed the power to bind and loose met with complete rejection. Later scholastic theologians firmly dismissed this idea, teaching instead that all priests receive the power of the keys.[80]

Abelard's ideas about how a priest can be said to forgive sin, which he shared to a large degree with Anselm of Laon, fared much

77. *Abelard's Ethics*, ed. Luscombe, 124.18–22: "Claues itaque regni celorum apostolis uel Petro traditas potestatem accipimus aperiendi uel claudendi regnum celorum, hoc est, presentem ecclesiam subiectis, ut diximus, suis tanquam una clauis sit reserandi, altera obseruandi." *Sententie Magistri Petri Abaelardi* 290, ed. Luscombe, 152.3500–3505.

78. On the disputed date of the council, see Constant J. Mews, "The Council of Sens (1141): Abelard, Bernard, and the Fear of Social Upheaval," *Speculum* 77 (2002): 342–82. On the heresy accusations, see *Capitula haeresum Petri Abaelardi*, ed. E. M. Buytaert, CCCM 12 (Turnhout: Brepols, 1969), 455–80; Constant J. Mews, "The List of Heresies Imputed to Peter Abelard," *Revue Bénédictine* 95 (1985): 73–110, reprinted in his *Abelard and His Legacy* (Aldershot: Ashgate, 2001), no. IV.

79. See Brian Tierney, *Origins of Papal Infallibility 1150–1350: A Study on the Concepts of Infallibility, Sovereignty and Tradition in the Middle Ages* (Leiden: Brill, 1972), 43–44. Cf. D. E. Luscombe, *The School of Peter Abelard: The Influence of Abelard's Thought in the Early Scholastic Period* (Cambridge: Cambridge University Press, 1969), 177, 248, and 297.

80. Luscombe, *School*, 152–53, 169, 249, 257, and 279.

better in the twelfth century, proving to be more popular than the main alternative position sketched out by his contemporary Hugh of St. Victor and adopted by their common pupil, the author of the *Summa sententiarum,* who may have been Bishop Otto of Lucca.[81] While Anselm and Abelard maintained that those who neglect confession to a priest commit sins of pride or contempt, Hugh treated such reasoning as insufficient and attempted to show how and why confession is essential to remitting sin.[82] God himself, Hugh says, made priests "sharers in His power, that they might fulfill His office by receiving the confession of penitents and might exercise His power by forgiving the sins of those who repent and confess."[83] God's purpose in doing this was to heal the wounds of sin more effectively.

Since then every sin is committed through pride, it is necessary for all repentance to be tempered through humility, in order that obedience may crush disobedience and the devotion of humility suppress the swelling of elation. Therefore, it is very fitting that we who have been insolent to God by sinning be suppliants also to the servants of God by repenting to men, and that man who did not need a mediator to preserve the grace of God be unable now to recover it except through man as a mediator.[84]

To explain how both God and man forgive sins, Hugh argues that sin gives rise to two bonds: obduracy or darkness of the mind, and the debt of future damnation. God removes obstinacy of the mind when sinners repent, while priests remove the debt of future damnation when they confess.[85] For this reason, neither contrition alone nor confession alone suffices for wiping away a penitent's sins. In order to be saved, both are required. In his mercy, says Hugh, God dispenses from the requirement of confession and looses the debt of eternal

81. On the attribution and dating of the *Summa sententiarum,* see Ferruccio Gastaldelli, "La 'Summa sententiarum' di Ottone da Lucca: Conclusione di un dibatto secolare," *Salesianum* 42 (1980): 537–46, reprinted in Gastaldelli, ed., *Scritti di letteratura, filologia e teologia medievali* (Spoleto: Centro italiano di studi sull'alto Medioevo, 2000), 165–74.

82. Hugh of St. Victor, *De sacramentis* 2.14.8, PL 175, 564C–565A.

83. Hugh, *De sacramentis* 2.14.1, PL 175, 551D. English translation taken from Roy J. Deferrari, trans., *Hugh of St. Victor on the Sacraments of the Christian Faith: De sacramentis* (Cambridge, Mass.: Medieval Academy of America, 1951), 403.

84. Hugh, *De sacramentis* 2.14.8, PL 175, 569A–B. English translation taken from Deferrari, *Hugh of St. Victor on the Sacraments,* 421.

85. Hugh, *De sacramentis* 2.14.8, PL 175, 565B–D.

damnation himself when the penitent lacks the opportunity to confess, though, according to Hugh, this possibility is the exception rather than the rule.[86]

Further Questions Relating to Penitential Theology

The relationship between contrition and confession, the role of the priest in the remission of sins, and the power of the keys were some of the main problems concerning penance that the early scholastics debated, but not the only ones. Two other problems also stimulated much controversy: whether those who possess charity, that is, the love of God, can lose it; and whether forgiven sins return when one later commits another mortal sin. The scholastics treated only the second question in connection with penitential theology, but I will treat both questions here on account of their inclusion by Gratian in *De penitentia*.

The Permanence of Charity

As with so many problems debated by the scholastics, the first question had its roots in contradictory biblical and patristic passages. Abelard's *Sic et non* collects eighty-two authorities pro and contra the permanence of charity, an impressive but far from complete list of all the texts drawn on by his contemporaries.[87] Some theologians, including the author of the treatise *Ut autem hoc evidenter*, one of Gratian's probable theological sources, taught that charity can never be lost.[88] But most early scholastic theologians held the contrary view, and they harmonized the many contradictory texts on the subject by distinguishing between multiple forms of charity. Texts which affirm that charity cannot be lost, they argued, speak of perfect charity, which one encounters rarely or not at all in this life, while texts affirming the contrary refer to some form of imperfect charity.[89]

86. Ibid., 567B–C.

87. Abelard, *Sic et non*, ed. Boyer and McKeon, 470–84.

88. See Wei, "A Twelfth-Century Treatise," 1–50, as well as the discussion of *Ut autem hoc evidenter* in chapter 5, esp. pp. 155–60.

89. Artur Michael Landgraf, *Dogmengeschichte der Frühscholastik*, 4 vols. in 8 parts (Regensburg: Friedrich Pustet, 1952–56), 1.2:136–61.

Since most theologians generally accepted the incompatibility of charity and serious sin, they accepted as corollaries that, in sinning, those who possess imperfect charity lose it and that those who possess perfect charity cannot sin criminally. A considerable number of theologians, however, of whom Abelard is one of the few we know by name, held a different position.[90] Because they defined charity as a virtue, that is, a constant habit of the mind, they argued that a person could both possess charity and commit certain serious sins resulting from weakness. Abelard mentions as examples King David's adultery with Bathsheba and his murder of her husband Uriah (2 Sm 11).[91] When David sinned, he spurned God in this respect, but, Abelard argues rather anachronistically, without losing Christ as his foundation. For if David had been given the choice between letting himself be killed or denying Christ, he would have chosen death.[92]

The Return of Sins

Like the permanence of charity, the return of sins also originated as a problem of biblical exegesis. The key text was the parable of the unforgiving servant (Mt 18:23–35). In that parable, a king had mercy on a servant who owed him a large sum of money, forgiving the debt completely. That servant, however, refused to behave in a similar fashion toward a fellow servant who owed him a far lesser sum. The unforgiving servant had his fellow servant thrown into prison until he could repay the debt in full. When the king heard how the unforgiving servant had treated his fellow servant, the king delivered the unforgiving servant "to the torturers, until he paid all the debt" (Mt 18:34).

Early medieval exegetes like Bede often interpreted this parable allegorically of the Jews: God delivered the Jewish people to the Romans for their transgressions. But occasionally early medieval exe-

90. Ibid., 146–51.

91. David, of course, did not kill Uriah personally, but rather engineered his death in battle. He ordered his commander Joab to place Uriah in the front lines of the Israelite army, which was besieging the Ammonite city of Rabbah. Joab placed Uriah where the fighting was thickest, but then had the other soldiers draw back. Uriah died in the fighting.

92. *Sententie Magistri Petri Abaelardi*, ed. Luscombe, 131.2963.

getes also took this story as an indication that forgiven sins, like the debts of the unforgiving servant, return after a person falls back into sin. They did not, however, explore this view or its theological implications in any great detail.[93]

In the early twelfth century, with the rise of scholasticism, the return of sins became a subject of intense debate in the schools.[94] Abelard judged it important enough that he devoted a whole question to the problem in his *Sic et non*.[95] Yet he himself rejected the idea that sins could in any way return. In both *Scito te ipsum* and his *Sentences*, Abelard advances a different understanding of the parable of the unforgiving servant. The story does not, he argues, show that forgiven sins return. Rather, it shows that we who have received God's mercy must likewise show mercy by forgiving others and that if we do not, we become guilty and worthy of being punished even more harshly than before. God's forgiveness, according to Abelard, is not conditional or temporary. The sins he forgives remain forgiven for all eternity, but God is justified in punishing and in fact does punish new sins, such as contempt for divine mercy, and he does so more harshly after one has already received his forgiveness.[96]

Abelard's explanation was popular and found many followers throughout the twelfth century.[97] But many other theologians were not as willing to dismiss or interpret away the numerous testimonies affirming that forgiven sins return. Of Abelard's contemporaries, it was once again Hugh of St. Victor who provided the most spirited defense of the doctrine. There is nothing unjust, Hugh argues, about God punishing previously forgiven sins when a person falls back into the same sin. For God has promised forgiveness to the repentant and punishment to the unrepentant. God does not punish any sins for which a person has performed worthy satisfaction, but no worthy

93. Landgraf, *Dogmengeschichte der Frühscholastik*, 4.1:194–95.

94. For an overview, see Francesco Carpino, *Il 'reditus peccatorum': Nelle collezioni canoniche e nei teologi fino ad Ugo da S. Vittore* (Rome: Istituto grafico tiberino, 1937); Artur Michael Landgraf, "Die frühscholastische Streitfrage vom Wiederaufleben der Sünden," *Zeitschrift für katholische Theologie* 61 (1937): 509–94.

95. Abelard, *Sic et non* 148, ed. Boyer and McKeon, 508–9.

96. *Abelard's Ethics*, ed. Luscombe, 90.31–34; *Sententiae Magistri Petri Abaelardi* 286–87, ed. Luscombe, 149.3427–151.3455.

97. Landgraf, *Dogmengeschichte der Frühscholastik*, 4.1:195–210.

satisfaction remains for one who falls back into sin.[98] Hugh's remarks suggest that he envisioned the return of sins as applying only to the specific case where a person performs penance for and then falls back into the same or a similar sin. His pupil Peter Lombard certainly understood the doctrine in this more restricted fashion.[99]

It is unclear exactly why Hugh felt so strongly about the return of sins. It is possible that he recognized the doctrine's pastoral implications, although neither he nor almost any scholastic before Peter the Chanter bothers to spell them out explicitly. If sins do indeed return, then every time one sins, one should not only confess and perform works of satisfaction for sins committed since one's last confession, but also for all one's previous sins.[100] Peter the Chanter himself was unsure what advice to give for this presumably common situation. (Peter affirmed clearly and explicitly that forgiven sins return.)[101] But at least some later writers, like Pseudo-Praepositinus, were more definite. Sinners should always confess all their sins anew.[102]

Scholastic Penitential Theology in Canon Law

Prior to Gratian, theologians were the ones primarily responsible for investigating questions of penitential theology in the new scholastic fashion. But contemporary canonists also took an interest in these matters, particularly, it would seem, in Italy. The anonymous 3L, an Italian canonical collection compiled between 1111 and 1123 and one of Gratian's main formal sources, provides an early witness.[103] Its third book and its appendix each contain a title devoted to

98. Hugh, *De sacramentis* 2.14.9, PL 176, 576D–578A.

99. Peter Lombard, *Sententiae in IV libris distinctae* 4.26.1.1, ed. Ignatius Brady, 3rd ed. (Grottaferrata: Editiones Collegii S. Bonaventurae ad Claras Aquas, 1971–81), 2:386: "Cumque multis auctoritatibus supra sit assertum in vera cordis contritione peccata dimitti, ante confessionem vel satisfactionem, ei etiam qui aliquando in crimen relapsurus est, quaeritur, si post cordis contritionem confiteri contempserit vel in peccatum idem vel simile reciderit, an peccata dimissa redeant."

100. Peter the Chanter, *Summa de sacramentis et animae consiliis*, ed. Jean-Albert Dugauquier (Louvain: Nauwelaerts, 1954–67), 2:21.126–35.

101. Ibid., 2:24.198–206.

102. Hödl, *Schlüsselgewalt*, 277 and 296.

103. See Joseph Motta, ed., *Collectio canonum trium librorum*, 2 vols., MIC.B 8/I-II (Vatican City: BAV, 2005–8) and the discussion of this collection above p. 22.

penance.[104] In addition to the penitential canons and tariffs common in earlier canonical collections, they contain many patristic texts not found in the earlier canonical tradition.[105] The majority of these simply aim at explaining why sinners need to confess their sins or perform penance.[106] But a number also take up hotly debated questions of scholastic penitential theology, such as the role of intention in the genesis of sin, the sufficiency of contrition without confession, and even the return of sins.[107]

Some minor canonical collections similarly contain patristic texts used by the scholastics, most notably the canonical collection found in Mantua, Biblioteca Comunale, 266 (C.I.4) and the *Collection in Five Books* of Vat. lat. 1348.[108] Both collections are of Italian origin and date to the twelfth century. The Mantua manuscript used to belong to the monastery of San Benedetto in Polirone. The *Collection in Five Books*, on the other hand, which consists primarily of an abbreviation of the *Liber canonum diversorum sanctorum patrum* or *Collectio sancte Marie Novelle*, was compiled in Tuscany, perhaps at Florence.[109] The texts they contain deal, among other matters, with the relationship between contrition and confession, the repeatability of penance, and the return of sins. These patristic authorities are similar to—but not always identical with—the ones debated in the French schools.

The space devoted to penitential theology in these Italian canoni-

104. 3L 3.19, ed. Motta, 2:209–52; 3L App. 40, ed. Motta, 2:341–57.

105. This is evident from a perusal of the apparatus fontium. As the collection was only recently edited, it was not studied in Munier, *Les sources patristiques*.

106. E.g., 3L 3.19.55, 58, 81, 100, 103, and 110, ed. Motta, 2:229, 238, 245–46, and 249–50.

107. 3L 3.19.63 and 3.19.78–80, ed. Motta, 2:231 and 237–38; 3L App. 40.23, ed. Motta, 2:349; 3L 3.19.64, ed. Motta, 2:231.

108. For the penitential material, see fols. 33v–34v of the Mantua manuscript and canons 2.25.1–12 of the *Collection in Five Books*, ed. Joseph Motta, *Liber canonum diuersorum sanctorum patrum siue Collectio in CLXXXIII titulos digesta*, MIC.B 7 (Vatican City: BAV, 1988), 314–15.

109. On these collections, see Giuseppe Motta, "I codici canonistici di Polirone," in *Sant'Anselmo, Mantova e la lotta per le investiture*, ed. Paolo Golinelli (Bologna: Pàtron, 1987), 349–74; Motta, ed., *Liber canonum diversorum sanctorum patrum*, 303–24; Motta, "I rapporti tra la Collezione canonica di S. Maria Novella e quella in Cinque Libri: Firenze, Bibl. Naz. Conventi Soppressi MS A.4.269 e Bibl. Vaticana, Vat. lat. 1348," *BMCL* 7 (1977): 89–94; Kéry, *Canonical Collections*, 216–18; Fowler-Magerl, *Clavis*, 101–4 and 132–33.

cal collections provides a partial explanation for Gratian's own decision to incorporate an extensive treatise on penitential theology, *De penitentia*, into his textbook of canon law, the first recension of the *Decretum*: he believed the subject would be of interest to contemporary canonists. Particularly in a period when the curricula in theology and canon law had yet to emerge, such a crossing of disciplinary boundaries would have seemed unremarkable. As chapter 5 will argue, however, Gratian had additional reasons to incorporate *De penitentia* into the *Decretum*, reasons related to his Italian theological context.

Conclusion

A wide variety of factors led to the emergence of two different forms of penance by the twelfth century: a (theoretically) unrepeatable form administered publicly by a bishop, which emphasized public humiliation and the performance of works of satisfaction, and a repeatable form performed in a more private setting, which emphasized interior contrition. The early scholastics focused their attention almost exclusively on this latter form, which they tried to understand in light of biblical and patristic texts rather than the Irish penitential tariffs and Carolingian legislation that had given rise to it. Their efforts led them to explore a whole constellation of theoretical questions with important implications for penitential practice, such as the relationship between contrition and confession, the necessity of confession, the nature and number of the keys granted to the apostles and their successors, the repeatability of penance, the permanence of charity, and the return of sins. While theologians were the primary ones to busy themselves with the new penitential theology, canonists, particularly in Italy, also took an interest in the subject. This historical context provides a partial explanation for why Gratian included a treatise on penitential theology—as opposed to just penitential law—in his canon law textbook. However, more specific reasons exist for why Gratian did what he did as well. The following chapters take a closer look at these.

4

Gratian on Penance

Gratian was not the first canonist to include material on scholastic penitential theology in a canonistic work.[1] But he was the first canonist to engage with the questions and problems of scholastic penitential theology by composing a treatise on the subject, namely the tract *De penitentia*. *De penitentia* corresponds to the third question of the thirty-third *causa* in the second part of Gratian's *Decretum*. It was originally a continuous theological treatise, but was later divided by the schools into seven distinctions, each of which treats a more or less well-defined theological problem.[2] Distinctions 5–7 are the least original and interesting; in the first recension, distinctions 5 and 6 simply present, without debate or discussion, excerpts from the Pseudo-Augustinian *De vera et false penitentia* on what confessors should consider when ministering to penitents in the confessional and what penitents should look for in good confessors, respectively, while distinction 7 briefly examines whether those who are near death can repent or per-

1. See the discussion of scholastic penitential theology in canon law at the end of chapter 3.

2. That the division into distinctions arose only later is evident from a cross-reference introduced by the redactor of the second recension referring to the first *quaestio* rather than the first distinction of *De penitentia*. See C.11 q.3 d.p.c.24 §1 (ed. Friedberg, 651): "require infra causa Maleficiis impeditus quest. i. de penitentia." On the absence of any distinction markers in the early manuscripts, see Larson, *Master of Penance*, 100, 136, and 168.

form penance. Longer, more intricate, and more revealing about Gratian the penitential theologian are the first four distinctions. Distinction 1 examines two interrelated and not always clearly distinguished questions. First, is it contrition, a feeling of repentance, which brings about the remission of post-baptismal sin, or is it confession and/or the performance of works of satisfaction? Second, regardless of what causes the remission of sins, is it really true that the penitent needs to confess sins? Distinction 2 examines whether the theological virtue of charity can be lost. In other words, can those who love God ever stop loving him? Gratian's contemporaries treated this question separately from penitential theology. Gratian's innovation was to relate it to contemporary debates about penance. Distinction 3 examines the repeatability of penance. It focuses not so much on the practical question of whether someone who has already performed penance once can be permitted or ordered to perform penance again, as on the theoretical question of whether the previously performed penance of a person who later sins again ever actually qualified as a valid penance. In other words, did such a relapsed sinner ever perform true penance and obtain forgiveness from God? Finally, distinction 4 examines the return of sins, that is, the doctrine that forgiven sins in some way return when one later commits another mortal sin.

As will be discussed below, modern interpretations of Gratian's answers to these questions have not been uniform. While scholars agree that Gratian denies the permanence of charity in distinction 2 and affirms the repeatability of penance in distinction 3, they disagree on whether he intended to question the necessity of confession in distinction 1 and whether he affirms or denies the return of sins in distinction 4. The present chapter attempts to resolve these debates by performing a careful reading of distinctions 1–4 of *De penitentia* as found in the first recension of the *Decretum*. In the process, it will also highlight some of the ways in which Gratian's arguments and positions differ from those of his sources and well-known contemporary theologians. Chapter 5 will then take a closer look at one of the main reasons for the differences between Gratian and his more well-known contemporaries, a reason already alluded to in chapter 3: Gratian's indebtedness to an Italian theological milieu.

Distinction 1

Considerable controversy surrounds what Gratian was trying to accomplish in distinction 1 of *De penitentia*. Some scholars have interpreted the distinction as investigating whether penitents need to confess their sins to a priest.[3] Other commentators, in contrast, have argued that Gratian presupposed the necessity of confession and that the distinction instead attempts to clarify only the point in time at which a penitent receives forgiveness for his or her sins—at the moment of contrition or when a penitent actually confesses to a priest.[4] Both interpretations would make sense in the historical context. As shown in chapter 3, contemporary practice and theory had elevated contrition over the performance of works of satisfaction. This development both undermined the traditional *raison d'être* of confession and was difficult to reconcile with many older authorities, which stressed confession and satisfaction over contrition.[5]

Neither interpretation, however, accords entirely with the text of distinction 1. As will be shown below, distinction 1 investigates both the necessity of confession to a priest and whether it is contrition rather than confession (or satisfaction) that remits sin. Although these two questions can be logically distinguished and were logically distinguished by many contemporary and later theologians, Gratian did not do so. The reason, I will argue, apart from Gratian's unfamiliarity with much contemporary French theology and the distinctions it invented, is that Gratian viewed the two questions as equivalent, not, as various scholars have argued, because he intended to investigate only when in the penitential process sins are forgiven.[6]

3. See, e.g., Charles Henry Lea, *A History of Auricular Confession and Indulgences in the Latin Church*, 3 vols. (Philadelphia: Lea Brothers, 1896), 1:135; Jean Gaudemet, "Le débat sur la confession dans la Distinction I du 'de penitentia' (Décret de Gratien, C.33, q.3)," *ZRG KA* 71 (1985): 52–75.

4. For the most detailed defense of this position, see A. Debil, "La première distinction du *De paenitentia* de Gratien," *Revue d'histoire ecclésiastique* 15 (1914): 251–73 and 442–55. For the most recent such defense, see Larson, *Master of Penance*, 35–40.

5. See chapter 3, pp. 84–95.

6. Cf. Larson, *Master of Penance*, 35–40.

The Two Questions

There are two textual sources of confusion regarding the purpose of distinction 1. First, Gratian provides two different formulations for the question under investigation. In the case statement to *Causa* 33, Gratian frames the question as "whether a crime can be erased by confession of the heart alone," which could be interpreted as being about either the necessity of confession or the point in the penitential process when a penitent receives the remission of sins.[7] However, at the beginning of *De penitentia*, Gratian restates the question as "whether anyone can satisfy God by contrition of the heart alone and secret satisfaction without confession of the mouth," which is most naturally interpreted as being about the necessity of confession.[8]

Second, in expounding the contritionist position, the view of "those who say that anyone can merit forgiveness for a crime without confession to the church and priestly judgment," and in refuting the confessionist position, the view of "those who say that no one can be cleansed from sin without confession of the mouth and works of satisfaction, if he has time to perform satisfaction," Gratian adopts two different lines of attack.[9] He argues that penitents can receive forgiveness from God *even if* they do not confess their sins to a priest. However, Gratian also argues that penitents receive forgiveness from God *before* they confess to a priest. Scholars who assert that Gratian never questioned the necessity of confession are forced to conflate

7. C.33 pr. (ed. Werckmeister, 488): "Tertio, si sola confessione cordis crimen possit deleri?"

8. De pen. D.1 d.a.c.1 (ed. Friedberg, 1159, supported by Aa Fd): "utrum sola cordis contritione et secreta satisfactione absque oris confessione quisque possit Deo satisfacere." Cf. Larson, *Master of Penance*, 39, who argues that "sine/absque confessione" and "ante confessionem" are equivalent in meaning because other, later writers, many of whom were trying to harmonize Gratian's text with their own conceptions of orthodoxy, apparently did so. For an alternative and, I would argue, better explanation, see below pp. 108–10.

9. De pen. D.1 d.a.c.1 (ed. Friedberg, 1159, supported by Aa Fd): "Sunt enim qui dicunt quemlibet criminis ueniam sine confessione ecclesie et sacerdotali iudicio posse mereri (promereri *Friedb.*)," De pen. D.1 d.p.c.37 §1 (ed. Friedberg, 1167, supported by Aa Fd): "Alii econtra testantur dicentes sine confessione oris et satisfactione operis neminem a peccato posse emundari, si tempus satisfaciendi habuerit."

these two types of arguments. Nevertheless, they are distinct, and, as will be shown below, some of the contritionist and many of the confessionist arguments that Gratian advances make sense only under the assumption that the contritionists are arguing that penitents need not always confess their sins to a priest.

The following sections will provide a more comprehensive discussion of the evidence that the contritionist position as presented by Gratian does in fact question the necessity of confession. Here, I would simply like to flag two of them. First, both the advocates of the contritionist position and the advocates of the confessionist position admit that the apostle Peter did not confess his sins to a priest. The contritionists quote two texts to this effect (cc.1, 2) when first presenting their position. And in d.p.c.87 the confessionists explicitly concede this point, but try to limit its force by arguing that Peter was an exception to the general rule.

Second, the contritionists try to explain various texts referenced by the confessionists by arguing that they exhort but do not command confession and to neutralize the remaining texts that do command confession by distinguishing between internal confession to God and external confession to a priest. However, these distinctions would be meaningless if distinction 1 always presumed that penitents must confess their sins to a priest.[10] If Gratian—and the contritionists whose position he is presenting—never question the necessity of confession, then the subtleties that he introduces in distinction 1 serve

10. Larson, *Master of Penance*, 78, concedes as much when she writes: "much of what follows could be construed as the proponents of the first position denying the necessity of confession altogether, not just for the remission of sins." But she then tries to explain away this conclusion by stating that "Gratian certainly did not mean to encourage the abandonment of confession" (which is probably true but beside the point; as Martin Luther shows, one can believe that confession is not necessary but still not want to abolish it) and noting that "the advocates of the first position distinguished confession to a priest and satisfaction according to his judgment from confession to God and self-imposed satisfaction" (which is likewise true, but also beside the point because the contritionists introduce this distinction to explain those authorities where confession is a command rather than an exhortation). On the survival of private penance in the Lutheran tradition, see Ronald K. Rittgers, *The Reformation of the Keys: Confession, Conscience, and Authority in Sixteenth-Century Germany* (Cambridge, Mass.: Harvard University Press, 2004).

no purpose. The contritionists can simply agree that the authorities adduced by the confessionists do assert the necessity of confession, but then point out that that is not the issue in dispute. Distinction 1—according to this (erroneous) interpretation—would be about whether contrition rather than confession effects the remission of sins, not whether confession is necessary. But Gratian does not make this very basic point, which suggests that he did indeed understand the contritionist position as questioning the necessity of confession.

The Contritionist Position

Gratian begins his exposition of the contritionist position by quoting five biblical and patristic authorities (cc.1–5). Two of these authorities (cc.1, 2) imply both that contrition remits sin and that penitents do not need to confess their sins to a priest. Speaking of the apostle Peter's denial of Christ, Pseudo-Leo affirms in c.1 that he "read that Peter cried, but not that he performed satisfaction," and Pseudo-Chrysostom asserts in c.2 that "tears wash away what it is shameful to confess."[11] The other three authorities (cc.3–5), in contrast, merely emphasize the existence of a direct relationship between penitents and God. They imply that third parties, such as confessors, are not necessary for obtaining forgiveness from God, but do not explicitly state that confession to a priest is unnecessary. They thus can be interpreted in three ways: (1) in support of the view that distinction 1 is about the necessity of confession; (2) in support of the view that it is about when in the penitential process sin is remitted; or (3) in support of the view that it is about both.

11. The denial of Christ is found in Mt 26:33–35; Mk 14:29–31; Lk 22:33–34; and Jn 13:36–38. De pen. D.1 c.1 (ed. Friedberg, 1159, supported by Aa Fd). The text of the canon in the first recension differs somewhat from the text of the canon in the second recension. The first-recension canon is attributed to Pope Leo the Great instead of Ambrose and reads: "Lacrimas Petri lego, satisfactionem non lego." The material source is Ambrose, *Expositio evangelii secundum Lucam* 10.88, quoted in chapter 3, p. 90n65. De pen. D.1 c.2 (ed. Friedberg, 1159, supported by Aa Fd). The text of the canon in the first recension differs somewhat from the text in the second recension. The first-recension canon reads: "Lacrime lauant quod pudor est confiteri." Both the first and second recensions misattribute the canon to John Chrysostom. The material source is in fact Ambrose, *Expositio evangelii secundum Lucam* 10.88.

In c.30 §1 and d.p.c.30, which follow immediately upon c.5 in the first recension, Gratian concludes that the remission of sins is effected by contrition of the heart rather than confession of the mouth. He does not expressly state here that auricular confession is unnecessary for obtaining forgiveness from God, but c.32 does refer explicitly to the absence of human knowledge about one's sins, which, the context suggests, should be interpreted as referring to auricular confession.

They will placate God more easily who, not convicted by human judgment, acknowledge their crime voluntarily, because they either make it public by their own confessions or they lay a sentence of excommunication upon themselves, *with others unaware of how their [true characters] have been concealed* ... certain that, reconciled by the fruits of efficacious penance they will not only receive what they have lost from God but even be transformed into citizens of the supernal city and arrive at sempiternal joys.[12]

Later on in d.p.c.87 §2, Gratian, speaking in the persona of a supporter of the confessionist position, attempts to interpret this text as really being about secret as opposed to public confession. "Similarly, the text of Prosper is understood [thus]: ... others unaware, that is, confessing their sin by secret confession, not making [it] known publicly."[13] However, Gratian, speaking in the persona of a supporter of the contritionist position, points out how implausible this reading of c.32 is. The interpretation of the confessionists, Gratian says, distorts the meaning of this text. For the authority does not say that "everyone," that is, the public, is unaware of the penitent's sin, but rather that "others [are] unaware."[14] The text thus indicates that the

12. De pen. D.1 c.32 (ed. Friedberg, 1165, supported by Aa Fd): "Facilius Deum sibi placabunt illi, qui non humano convicti iudicio, sed ultro crimen agnoscunt, quia aut propriis illud confessionibus produnt, aut *nescientibus aliis quales occulti sint* ipsi in se excommunicationis sententiam ferunt ... certi quod reconciliati sibi efficacis penitentie fructibus a Deo non solum amissa recipiant, sed etiam ciues superne ciuitatis effecti ad gaudia sempiterna perueniant."

13. De pen. D.1 d.p.c.87 §2 (ed. Friedberg, 1185, supported by Aa Fd): "Similiter et illud Prosperi [c.32] intelligitur: 'Qui crimen suum ultro agnoscunt et aut propriis illud confessionibus produnt aut nescientibus aliis quales occulti sint' etc. Aliis nescientibus, id est occulta confessione istis peccatum suum confitentibus, non publice illud manifestantibus."

14. De pen. D.1 d.p.c.87 §4 (ed. Friedberg, 1185, supported by Aa Fd): "Econtra, auctoritas illa Iohannis Crisostomi [an authority introduced at De pen. D.1 d.p.c.87 §1] et Prosperi [c.32] contra mentem auctoris extorta uidetur.... Prosper

penitent has not made his sin known to any other human being, including a priest, not just that he has not performed public penance for his sin, as the confessionists would have it.

Up to this point in distinction 1, Gratian's canons and dicta tend to assume that penitents receive forgiveness from God even though they do not confess their sins to a priest. From d.p.c.32 onward, however, the assumption changes: the canons and dicta presuppose the practice of auricular confession. Thus, the allegorical exegesis of the lepers healed by Jesus (Lk 17:12–19) and the resurrection of Lazarus (Jn 11) found in d.p.c.34 presuppose the practice of auricular confession.[15] And d.p.c.37 appears to take for granted that confession will occur as an exterior sign of the forgiveness that one has already received through contrition.[16]

This shift in presuppositions is one reason why the most recent and careful student of *De penitentia,* Atria Larson, feels that distinction 1 must concern only when in the penitential process sins are forgiven and that Gratian could not have questioned the necessity of confession. Reading Gratian otherwise, Larson argues, would destroy the unity and consistency of Gratian's presentation of the contritionist position.[17] But there is a perfectly reasonable explanation—one

---

enim non ait 'omnibus' sed simpliciter 'aliis nescientibus.' Vnde euidentissime datur intelligi quod sine confessione oris peccata possunt deleri."

15. De pen. D.1 d.p.c.34 (ed. Friedberg, 1166, supported by Aa Fd): "Hinc etiam leprosi illi quibus Dominus precepit, ut ostenderent se sacerdotibus in itinere, antequam ad sacerdotes uenirent, mundati sunt.... Hinc etiam Lazarus de monumento uiuus prodiit." On allegorical exegesis, see chapter 2, pp. 56–57.

16. De pen. D.1 d.p.c.37 (ed. Friedberg, 1167, supported by Aa Fd): "Fit itaque confessio ad ostensionem penitentie, non ad impetrationem venie. Sicut circumcisio data est Abrahe in signum iusticie, non in causam iustificationis, sic sacerdoti offertur in signum uenie accepte, non in causa remissionis accipiende."

17. Larson, *Master of Penance,* 44n28: "[In his dissertation, John] Wei acknowledged that much of the following section assumes the normal practice of confession following contrition, and yet he argued that this first position is about the nonnecessity of confession, not which element of penance remits sins. He argued that Gratian here modified his presentation of this position; in the first several canons, he was arguing that confession is not necessary at all, but now he attempted only to make the weaker argument that confession is not necessary for the remission of sins. The problem with Wei's reading is that Gratian gave no indication that he was moderating the first position; he presented the position as a consistent whole focused on the issue of remission."

that does not destroy the unity and consistency of Gratian's presentation—for why the first part of Gratian's discussion of the contritionist position should argue that penitents receive forgiveness from God *even though* they do not confess their sins to a priest, while the second part of Gratian's presentation argues that contrition remits sin *even if* penitents later confess to a priest. The answer is not, as the contrary position defended by Larson and others implies, that Gratian was sloppy and really meant to investigate only when in the penitential process sin is remitted even though his words imply otherwise. Rather, I would argue, the answer is that Gratian believed confession could be necessary only if confession rather than contrition remits sin and that his exposition of the contritionist position thus sets forth two separate and independently valid arguments for why confession is not necessary. The first argument is that penitents can and do receive forgiveness from God even if they do not confess to a priest. The second argument is that, even if penitents do confess to a priest, remission of sins in fact occurs earlier in the penitential process, when a penitent becomes contrite for his sins.

This twofold line of attack explains how and why Gratian can conclude in d.p.c.36 that "sin is remitted by just contrition of the heart *without* confession of the mouth" immediately after he establishes that "we are resuscitated by grace and made sons of light *before* confession."[18] Larson argues that this statement shows Gratian thought "without confession" and "before confession" equivalent in meaning.[19] But there is no need to rewrite Gratian's Latin. Gratian's syllogism is indeed false and makes no sense if one believes, as many contemporary and later theologians did, that confession can be required of Christians even if it does not contribute to the remission of sins.[20] However, Gratian's syllogism follows perfectly if, like Gratian and the contritionists whose position he is recounting, one holds that confession can be necessary if and only if confession—

18. De pen. D.1 d.p.c.36 (ed. Friedberg, 1167, supported by Aa Fd): "Cum ergo ante confessionem, ut probatum est, simus (sumus *Friedb.*) resuscitati per gratiam et filii lucis facti, euidentissime apparet quod sola contritione cordis sine confessione oris peccatum remittitur."

19. Larson, *Master of Penance*, 39.

20. On the views of contemporary scholastics, see chapter 3, pp. 90–95.

rather than or in addition to contrition—remits sin. If the necessity of confession entails that confession remits sin and vice versa, then the fact that contrition remits sin before confession will necessarily imply that contrition remits sin without confession.

Most of the arguments that Gratian adduces in support of the sufficiency of contrition are arguments from authority or arguments based on allegorical exegesis. Only one argument—to which, however, Gratian devotes considerable attention—actually attempts to explain *why* contrition rather than confession should remit sins: only those in a state of grace are able to confess their sins. Basing his argument on three biblical quotations (Ps 87:11, Eccl 17:26, and Ps 6:2, 5, 6), Gratian argues that those who are dead to God are unable to confess their sins. Consequently, infers Gratian, only those who are alive to God can confess their sins. Positively, living to God entails God's indwelling in the soul. Negatively, it entails freedom from sin and eternal punishment. One who confesses, argues Gratian, must therefore have already obtained forgiveness from God prior to his or her confession.[21] And if remission occurs prior to confession, then confession cannot be necessary.[22]

21. De pen. D.1 d.p.c.34 (ed. Friedberg, 1166, supported by Aa Fd): "Hinc etiam medici negantur resuscitare aliquem, ut resuscitatus confiteatur [biblical quotations omitted].... Si ergo nullus confitetur nisi suscitatus, nemo autem uiuit eterne geenne filius et perpetua dampnatione dignus, patet quod antequam quisque confiteatur peccatum, a reatu sue preuaricationis quo eterna sibi debebantur supplicia, per gratiam interne compunctionis absoluitur. Si antequam quisque confiteatur, a Domino resuscitatur, uel resuscitatus uiuit, dum confitetur, uel post resuscitationem iterum mortuus est et confitetur. Sed sicut antequam resuscitaretur mortuus confiteri non poterat, sic post resuscitationem mortuus confiteri non ualet. Restat ergo ut resuscitatus uiuat, dum peccatum confitetur. Habet itaque resuscitatorem suum sibi presentem seque inhabitantem." De pen. D.1 d.p.c.35 (ed. Friedberg, 1166–67, supported by Aa Fd): "Cum enim Deus sit uita anime, anima uero uita corporis, sicut corpus uiuere non potest anima absente, ita non nisi Deo presente anima uiuere ualet. Habet itaque anima sibi Deum presentem per gratiam, que uiuens peccatum suum confitetur eamque uita que Deus est inhabitat, quam inhabitando uiuere facit. Si autem illam inhabitat, ergo templum Spiritus sancti facta est, ergo illuminata est, ergo a tenebris peccatorum expiata est, ergo templum diaboli esse desiit, que ad lucem uenit, cuius respectus tenebras fugat. Nulla enim, ut ait Apostolus, conuentio Christi et Belial, nulla participatio lucis ad tenebras, nulla communicatio iustitie et iniquitatis, nullus consensus templo Dei cum idolis."

22. See above pp. 108–9 and De pen. D.1 d.p.c.36.

The Confessionist Position

After setting forth the contritionist position, Gratian presents the contrary position, that "no one can be cleansed from sin without confession of the mouth and works of satisfaction, if he has time to perform satisfaction."[23] He quotes thirteen authorities in support of this position, all of which are excerpts or allegedly excerpts from the writings of Church Fathers. Only the first two of these authorities (cc.38, 39) assert clearly and unambiguously the necessity of confession for the remission of sins, although c.40, an excerpt falsely attributed to John Chrysostom, which describes the nature of fruitful penance, can be interpreted as implying the necessity of auricular confession as well. Canons 42 and 43, both extracts from Augustine, assert the necessity of penance (*penitentia*), but make no mention of confession itself or of satisfaction. Canons 44, 49, and 51 stress the power of the church to bind and loose sins. The remaining authorities (cc.50, 52, 54–56), all taken from the same section of Ambrose's *De penitentia*, simply describe various aspects of confession and satisfaction. Only with difficulty can they be interpreted as affirming the necessity of confession and satisfaction to the remission of sins. Nevertheless, they stress aspects of confession and satisfaction that Gratian, speaking in the persona of a supporter of the confessionist position, goes on to argue in d.p.c.87 support the necessity of confession.

Based on the preceding thirteen authorities, d.p.c.60—which follows immediately after c.56 in the first recension—concludes that sins cannot be remitted without auricular confession and satisfaction: "From these [authorities] it is clear that sin is not remitted without confession of the mouth and works of satisfaction."[24] The dictum then discusses examples from the entirety of biblical history to prove the intimate connection between confession and the remission of sins: Adam and Eve (Gn 3), the serpent (Gn 3), Cain (Gn 4:9), the

23. De pen. D.1 d.p.c.37 §1 (ed. Friedberg, 1167, supported by Aa Fd): "Alii econtra testantur dicentes sine confessione oris et satisfactione operis neminem a peccato posse mundari (emundari *Friedb.*), si tempus satisfaciendi habuerit."

24. De pen. D.1 d.p.c.60 (ed. Friedberg, 1174, supported by Aa Fd): "Ex his itaque apparet quod sine confessione oris et satisfactione operis peccatum non remittitur."

kings who sinned against Abraham (Gn 12 and 26), the Mosaic regulations concerning lepers (Lv 13–14), Saul (1 Sm 16:23), David (2 Sm 12:13), Ahab (1 Kgs 21:27–29), Nineveh (Jon 3), Nebuchadnezzar (Dn 4 and 9), John the Baptist (Mt 3), and even events from the life of Christ (for example, Jn 8, Lk 17, Mt 9, Mk 2).

Thirteen patristic authorities (cc.61–68, 78–81, §2 and 87) follow d.p.c.60 in the first recension. They can be aptly characterized as a digression, since only one of these authorities (c.61) mentions confession explicitly and only one (c.63) mentions satisfaction.

The Dialogue of d.p.c.87

After setting forth the reasons for and against the necessity of confession, Gratian next discusses counterarguments and objections to the proposed arguments. This critique takes the form of a dialogue between advocates of the views that Gratian has just set out. Both sides employ the same terminology—which is to some degree forced upon them by their authorities—but give these shared terms different meanings. For instance, whereas advocates of the sufficiency of contrition equate secret satisfaction with self-imposed satisfaction, advocates of the necessity of confession equate it with satisfaction imposed by a priest yet performed in secret. As a result of these divergent interpretations of the same terms, the dialectical back and forth in d.p.c.87 leads to clarifications and concessions, but not to any final resolution concerning the questions at issue: whether confession to a priest is necessary and whether contrition rather than confession remits sin.

D.p.c.87 begins with Gratian, speaking in the persona of a confessionist, attempting to explain the authorities quoted by the contritionists in support of their position.[25] The apostle Peter, the confessionist concedes, did not confess his sins to a priest and never performed satisfaction for his sins. But, he argues, Peter had no need to do these things as his threefold confession of love for the Lord and satisfaction of tears had already completely wiped away the sin of his threefold de-

25. De pen. D.1 d.p.c.87 (ed. Friedberg, 1184, supported by Aa Fd): "Vnde premisse auctoritates quibus uidebatur probari sola contritione cordis ueniam prestari, aliter interpretande sunt quam ab eis exponantur."

nial. For the confessionists, the text by Pseudo-Leo in c.1 does indeed prove that Peter did not perform satisfaction for his sins. In their view, however, this exception does not argue against the general necessity of satisfaction. Instead, they argue, Pseudo-Leo merely shows that satisfaction is unnecessary for individuals who, like Peter, "renounce the world and completely root out from their bodies the fomes of sin."[26]

To explain other authorities adduced by the contritionists, the confessionists introduce the Carolingian dichotomy.[27] Pseudo-Chrysostom in c.2 and another authority actually by John Chrysostom that Gratian introduces here for the first time, they argue, "should not be understood [as claiming] that sins are said to be forgiven without confession of the mouth, but rather without public satisfaction. For secret sins are purged by secret confession and hidden satisfaction. Nor is it necessary that we confess anew what we have already confessed to a priest, but we ought constantly to confess them before the true judge with the tongue of the heart, not the flesh."[28] Similarly, the confessionists explain the text of Prosper in c.32 by glossing "others unaware" (*aliis nescientibus*) to mean "confessing their sin by secret confession rather than making it publicly known."[29]

The confessionists explain most of the remaining authorities adduced by the contritionists by clarifying that confession by itself does not effect the remission of sins; contrition also plays a role. Speaking in the persona of a confessionist, Gratian interprets the authorities in cc.4 and 5 as affirming that contrition renders a sin remissible, but

26. Ibid.: "Negationem namque Petri secuta est satisfactio lacrimarum et trina confessio dominice dilectionis, qua penitus deleuit peccatum trine negationis. Non ergo illa auctoritate Leonis pape [c.1] satisfactio penitentie negatur esse necessaria cuilibet delinquenti, sed ei tantum qui beatum Petrum imitatus, huic seculo penitus abrenuntiat, et cunctorum uitiorum fomitem in se funditus mortificat."

27. See chapter 3, esp. pp. 79–80.

28. This other authority is John Chrysostom, *Homiliae in epistolam ad Hebreos* 31, in *Patrologiae Cursus Completus, Series Graeca*, ed. J.-P. Migne, 161 vols. (Paris: Imprimerie Catholique, 1857–66) [hereafter "PG"], 63, 436. De pen. D.1 d.p.c.87 §1 (ed. Friedberg, 1184, supported by Aa Fd): "[These authorities] non ita intelligendum est, ut sine confessione oris peccata dicantur dimitti, sed sine publica satisfactione. Secreta namque peccata secreta confessione et occulta satisfactione purgantur, nec est necesse ut, que semel sacerdoti confessi fuerimus, denuo confiteamur, sed lingua cordis non carnis apud uerum iudicem ea iugiter confiteri debemus."

29. De pen. D.1 d.p.c.87 §2 (ed. Friedberg, 1185), quoted above p. 107n13.

does not actually remit the sin itself; the authority in c.30 as affirming that contrition makes a "work" (*opus*)—presumably confession or satisfaction or both—worthy of remuneration; and the authorities in cc.33 and 34 as demonstrating that exterior satisfaction without interior satisfaction, that is, contrition, cannot placate God.[30] Gratian also proposes an alternative interpretation of Lazarus's resurrection and Luke's miracle story concerning lepers. John 11:43–44 reports how Jesus first raised Lazarus, then commanded his disciples to unwind the funeral sheets, while Luke 17:14 reports how Jesus told lepers to present themselves to the Jewish priests, but healed them along the way before they had arrived. According to contritionists, these episodes demonstrate allegorically that the remission of sins occurs in contrition, before the performance of auricular confession and satisfaction. The alternative exegesis advanced by confessionists applies these same events to contrition of the heart rather than to the remission of sins. Obstinacy of the soul and contempt of confession, confessionists argue, can be interpreted as forms of death or leprosy, from which one is resuscitated or healed when, by the grace of God, one repents and resolves to confess one's sins. In other words, contrition is only the first step to obtaining forgiveness from God. Confession to a priest is also necessary.[31] The confessionists draw an analogy to original sin. "For just as sin is remitted in baptism, though its punishment is not, thus through contrition of the heart is a person said to be revived to God, even though still bound by the guilt of sin."[32]

30. De pen. D.1 d.p.c.87 §2 (ed. Friedberg, 1185, supported by Aa Fd): "Item illud prophete: 'Dixi confitebor et tu remisisti' [c.4], id est remissibile iudicasti, 'impietatem peccati mei.' Ita et illud Augustini [c.5] intelligitur: 'Magna pietas Dei ut ad solam promissionem peccata dimiserit,' id est remissibilia iudicauerit." Ibid.: "Item: 'Voluntas remuneratur non opus' [c.30] ita intelligitur: Voluntas facit opus remunerabile, non opus uoluntatem." Ibid.: "Ita et illud intelligitur: 'Conuertimini ad me' [c.34] etc. Item: 'Scindite corda uestra et non uestimenta uestra' [c.33]. Eis dicitur qui nulla interiori satisfactione, precedente sola exteriori, se Deum posse placare confidunt."

31. Ibid.: "Item cuncta que de leprosis mundatis uel de Lazaro resuscitato inducuntur ad contritionem cordis non ad ueniam remissionis referenda sunt. Obstinatio enim animi et confessionis contemptus quedam mors est impietatis et lepra superbie, a qua quisque reuiuiscit, dum sibi per gratiam dolor delicti et uotum confessionis inspiratur."

32. De pen. D.1 d.p.c.87 §3 (ed. Friedberg, 1185, supported by Aa Fd): "Sicut

These arguments, however, do not convince proponents of the contritionist position. As Gratian points out, the text actually by Chrysostom and the authority of Prosper in c.32 can only with difficulty be interpreted as referring to public confession rather than to auricular confession in general.[33] For advocates of the sufficiency of contrition, then, these two authorities provide clear proof that sins can be remitted even without confession.

The authorities adduced in support of the necessity of confession do not, in the view of advocates of the sufficiency of contrition, pose any real difficulty. Some of these authorities, they point out, only exhort confession; they do not command it. And almost all the authorities that do command confession or penance or both, they argue, refer to confession of the heart rather than to confession of the mouth, while almost all the authorities that mention satisfaction refer to secret satisfaction rather than to satisfaction meted out by a priest. In support of the view that satisfaction refers to secret satisfaction, Gratian quotes numerous extracts from Augustine that connect the remission of sins with self-imposed satisfaction.[34] He then gives voice to the view of the Carolingian reformers, who attempted to resolve the conflict between canonical penance and tariff penance by creating a dual penitential system.[35] Only in the case of public and manifest crimes, he asserts, are public auricular confession and public satisfaction necessary. Venial and secret sins require only secret satisfaction.[36]

The confessionists agree partially with this more nuanced state-

---

enim in baptismate peccatum remittitur et tamen eius pena reseruatur, sic per contritionem cordis quisque a Deo resuscitari dicitur, licet adhuc peccati reatu teneatur."

33. De pen. D.1 d.p.c.87 §4, quoted above p. 107n14.

34. De pen. D.1 d.p.c.87 §6 (ed. Friedberg, 1186, supported by Aa Fd): "aliud est peccatum sacerdoti confiteri et eius arbitrio de peccato satisfacere atque aliud Deo corde confiteri et secreta satisfactione peccatum in se ipso punire."

35. See chapter 3, esp. pp. 79–80.

36. De pen. D.1 d.p.c.87 §7 (ed. Friedberg, 1186, supported by Aa Fd): "Hec ergo secreta satisfactio leuium siue occultorum criminum Deo offerenda est, nec sine pena relaxari probantur, que sic expiari creduntur. Ea uero que de publica satisfactione uel oris confessione dicuntur, in publicis et manifestis criminibus intelligenda sunt."

ment of the contritionist position. No one, they agree, can obtain remission for sins without contrition of the heart. Secret sins require secret satisfaction—which they interpret as satisfaction imposed by a priest but performed in secret rather than as self-imposed satisfaction—and manifest sins require manifest satisfaction. The confessionists disagree, however, with their opponents' claim that mortal sin can be forgiven without auricular confession, if the opportunity for confession should be available. If, aside from the case when no priests are available, forgiveness for grave sins could be obtained without confession, then, contrary to the words of Pope Leo the Great in c.49, priestly intercession would not be necessary to obtain the forgiveness of sins; contrary to the words of Augustine in c.44, the power of the keys would be pointless; and contrary to the words of Ambrose in c.51, the power of the keys would not be the sole preserve of priests, but would in fact belong even to laypersons.[37] Gratian finishes this long exposition by adducing two more reasons for the necessity of confession. First, priests are responsible for setting the duration of one's satisfaction, a task they are unable to perform unless they first learn of a penitent's sins through auricular confession. Second, refusal to confess one's sins is a form of pride, which is incompatible with humility, and without humility it is impossible to obtain the remission of sins.[38]

37. De pen. D.1 d.p.c.87 §§9–12 (ed. Friedberg, 1186–87, supported by Aa Fd): "Econtra ea que in assertione huius sententie dicta sunt, partim ueritate nituntur, partim pondere carent. Sine contritione etenim cordis nullum peccatum posse dimitti. Occulta uero peccata secreta satisfactione, publica quoque manifesta penitentia expiari debere firmissima constat ratione subnixum. Porro sine confessione oris, si facultas confitendi non defuerit, aliquod graue delictum expiari auctoritati penitus probatur aduersum. Quomodo enim secundum auctoritatem Leonis pape [c.49] sine supplicationibus sacerdotum indulgentia nequit optineri, si sine confessione oris a peccato possumus emundari? Quis enim supplicabit pro peccato quod nescit? Item: Quomodo secundum Augustinum [c.44] frustrat claues ecclesie, qui sine arbitrio sacerdotis penitentiam agit, si sine oris confessione criminis indulgentia impetratur? Item: Quomodo secundum Ambrosium [c.51] ius ligandi et soluendi solis sacerdotibus a Domino creditur permissum, si quisque suo arbitrio se ipsum peccando ligat uel secreta penitentia secundum Prosperum in se ipso sententiam profert excommunicationis atque post satisfactionem absque sacerdotali iudicio se ipsum Deo uel altario eius reconciliat? Non sunt hec premissis auctoritatibus consentanea, sed multorum exemplis probantur aduersa."

38. De pen. D.1 d.p.c.87 §§14–15 (ed. Friedberg, 1187, supported by Aa Fd):

Gratian's Indecision

Gratian presents more authorities in favor of the confessionist position than he does in favor of the contritionist position and also devotes more space to elaborating the counterarguments to the sufficiency of contrition in d.p.c.87 than he does to explicating the objections to the necessity of confession. Contrary to what this imbalance might lead one to expect, however, Gratian does not end distinction 1 by coming down in favor of the general necessity of confession. Instead, he leaves the choice up to his readers: "We have briefly set forth the authorities and reasons upon which the two positions [regarding] confession and satisfaction rest. [The choice of] which of these should rather be adhered to is reserved to the judgment of the reader, however, since both have wise and religious supporters."[39] To clarify his refusal to take sides, Gratian then appends the following canon, which he misattributes to Archbishop Theodore's penitential.

Some say that we should confess sins to God alone, like the Greeks. Others, however, think that sins must be confessed to priests, like *almost* the entire holy church. Because both [practices] occur not without great benefit within the holy church, we shall confess our sins to God, who is the redeemer of sins, and this concerns the perfect, and we shall say with Da-

---

"Cum ergo, ut ex premissis colligitur, tempora penitentie sacerdotis arbitrio diffiniantur, euidentissime apparet sine confessione proprie uocis peccata non dimitti. Quis enim tempora penitentie alicui prefiget, nisi primum peccata sua sibi manifestare curauerit. Item: Taciturnitas peccati ex superbia nascitur cordis. Ideo enim peccatum suum quisque celare desiderat, ne iniquitas sua aliis manifesta fiat, ne talis reputetur apud homines foris, quales se iamdudum exhibuit diuino conspectui. Quod ex fonte superbie nasci nulli dubium est. Species etenim superbie est se uelle iustum uideri qui peccator est atque ypocrita conuincitur qui ad imitationem primorum parentum uel tergiuersatione uerborum peccata sua leuigare contendit uel sicut Cayn peccatum suum reticendo penitus supprimere querit. Vbi autem superbia regnat uel ypocrisis, humilitas locum habere non ualet. Sine humilitate uero alicui ueniam sperare non licet, nec ergo ubi est taciturnitas confessionis uenia speranda est criminis."

39. De pen. D.1 d.p.c.89 (ed. Friedberg, 1189, supported by Aa Fd): "Quibus auctoritatibus uel quibus rationum firmamentis utraque sententia confessionis et satisfactionis nitatur, in medium breuiter proposuimus. Cui autem harum potius adherendum sit, lectoris iudicio reseruatur. Vtraque enim fautores habet sapientes et religiosos."

vid: "I have made my crime known to you and I have not hidden my injustice. I said, I will confess my injustice against myself to the Lord and you have forgiven the impiety of my sin" (Ps 31:5). But nevertheless we ought to follow the institution of the apostle [James], so that we confess our sins to each other and pray for each other that we may be saved (cf. Jam 5:16). Therefore confession that occurs to God alone, which concerns the just, purges sins. Confession that is made to a priest, however, teaches how sins are purged. For God, the source and giver of health and sanctity, often grants this *medicine* of his own penance by invisible means [and] often by the working of medical doctors.[40]

The material source of c.90 is c.33 of the Council of Châlons (813).[41] Gratian probably took the text from the *Tripartita*, the only one of Gratian's known formal sources to contain the canon. Gratian's text contains two interpolations *vis-à-vis* the formal source: "almost" (*fere*) and "medicine" (*medicinam*). The insertion of "almost" (*fere*) is immensely significant.[42] As Gratian makes clear in d.p.c.89, the purpose of c.90 is to provide authority for his claim that orthodox Catholics may decide for themselves whether sinners have to confess their sins to a priest. The version of c.90 found in the *Tripartita* lauds both confession to God alone and confession to a priest as good and useful practices. For confession to God purges sins, while confession to a

40. De pen. D.1 c.90 (ed. Friedberg, 1189, supported by Aa Fd): "Quidam Deo solummodo confiteri debere dicunt peccata, ut Greci. Quidam uero sacerdotibus confitenda esse percensent, ut *fere* tota sancta ecclesia. Quod utrumque non sine magno fructu intra sanctam fit ecclesiam, ita dumtaxat ut Deo, qui remissor est peccatorum peccata nostra confiteamur, et hoc perfectorum est, et cum Dauid dicamus: 'Delictum meum cognitum tibi feci, et iniustitiam meam non abscondi. Dixi, confitebor aduersum me iniustitiam meam Domino et tu remisisti impietatem peccati mei.' Sed tamen Apostoli institutio nobis sequenda est, ut confiteamur alterutrum peccata nostra, et oremus pro inuicem, ut saluemur. Confessio itaque que soli Deo fit, quod iustorum est, peccata purgat. Ea uero que sacerdoti fit, docet qualiter ipsa purgentur peccata. Deus namque salutis et sanctitatis auctor et largitor, plerumque prebet hanc sue penitentie *medicinam* inuisibili administratione, plerumque medicorum operatione" (emphasis added).

41. Council of Châlons, c.33, ed. Albert Werminghoff, *Concilia aevi Karolini*, MGH Conc. 2.1 (Hanover: MGH, 1906), 280.1–10. On this Carolingian reform council, see chapter 3, pp. 76–77.

42. The word "fere" does not appear in Burchard's *Decretum*. Nor is it found in any manuscript of the Ivonian *Decretum* or the *Tripartita* collated thus far for Martin Brett's provisional editions of these two works. In contrast, every manuscript of Gratian's *Decretum* that I have consulted contains this word.

priest teaches how sins ought to be purged. Clear bias toward the necessity of confession to a priest, however, emerges through the *Tripartita*'s association of confession to God alone with the Greeks (*ut Greci*), who were usually viewed as schismatics or heretics, but confession to priests with the entire "holy church" (*ut tota sancta ecclesia*), as well as through the qualification of confession to God alone as concerning "the perfect" and "the just." Confession to God alone, the canon suggests, is an exceptional practice suitable only for heretics and extraordinary saints, not ordinary Catholics.

The insertion of "almost" (*fere*) changes the character of the canon. Whereas the version of c.90 found in the *Tripartita*, which opposes the (schismatic/heretical) Greeks to the entire church, can be read as an endorsement of the necessity of confession, Gratian's modified version of the canon cannot. Instead, it appears to be an objective observation: *Almost* the entire church, that is, all of Gratian's Catholic contemporaries and numerous patristic authorities, support the practice of auricular confession. However, the Greeks—whom Gratian never explicitly identifies as schismatics or heretics in the first recension—plus many of the patristic authorities quoted at the beginning of the distinction, advocate confession to God alone. So far as is known, the word "almost" is absent from the pre-Gratian manuscript tradition of this canon. So Gratian himself may have been the one to make this insertion. If this hypothesis is correct, then Gratian may well have found the contritionist position more compelling than the relatively short amount of space devoted to that position might lead one initially to conclude. Gratian rarely altered or modified the text of his canons except to abbreviate them. But he appears to have felt strongly enough about the merits of the contritionist position to make a rare exception here.[43] Far from not questioning the necessity of confession, Gratian in fact found the arguments against its necessity compelling, if not clearly to be preferred over the arguments in favor of the opposing position.

43. For another apparent exception, see Titus Lenherr, "*Reos sanguinis* [*non*] *defendat ecclesia*: Gratian mit einem kurzem Blick erhascht," in *Medieval Church Law*, ed. Müller and Sommar, 71–94.

Distinction 2

With distinction 2 begins what Gratian acknowledges is a digression from the original topic of C.33 q.3. Because he has begun discussing penance, he has found it sensible to probe the subject more deeply.[44] The main problem he wishes to address is whether penance can be performed only once or whether it can be repeated. However, he ends up focusing in distinction 2 on what appears at first glance to be a digression within a digression, the permanence of charity. The reason for this second digression, Gratian explains, is that theologians who deny the repeatability of penance—a topic he does not formally address until distinction 3—support their position with two arguments based on the characteristics of charity. First, they claim, no adult can obtain the remission of sins without charity. Second, they assert, one who will commit a mortal sin in the future does not possess true charity in the here and now.[45] The first of these claims, that charity is necessary for the remission of sins, was a consensus position in the twelfth century, and Gratian seems to have thought it self-evident since he makes no attempt to prove it. It was the second claim, that one who will later commit a mortal sin does not possess true charity in the here and now, that Gratian and his contemporaries found controversial and which prompts the extended analysis of charity in distinction 2.[46]

Unlike with distinction 1, there exists little controversy over the question that Gratian was trying to answer in distinction 2 or what his position was. Commentators universally agree that distinction 2 concerns whether charity can be lost and that Gratian answered this question affirmatively. For that reason, this chapter's presentation of distinction 2 will be brief.

44. De pen. D.2 d.a.c.1 (ed. Friedberg, 1190, supported by Aa Fd): "Quia uero de penitentia semel cepit sermo haberi, aliquantulum altius repetendum uidetur, diuersorum sententias ceteris auctoritatibus munitas in medium proponentes."

45. Ibid.: "Alii dicunt penitentiam semel tantum esse utilem, unica enim est, nec reiterari potest. Si uero reiteratur, precedens penitentia non fuit, et si de sententia iudicis eius merito peccata uidentur esse remissa, apud tamen eius prescientiam (presentiam *Friedb.*), cui omnia futura presentia sunt, numquam habentur remissa.... Item, sine caritate nulli adulto peccatum remittitur. Non autem habet caritatem qui aliquando peccaturus est criminaliter."

46. On contemporary debates about the permanence of charity, see pp. 95–96.

Charity Cannot Be Lost

Gratian begins distinction 2 by quoting eleven biblical and patristic authorities in support of the view that charity, once possessed, cannot subsequently be lost (cc.2–12), followed by an excerpt from Augustine in support of the view that one who possesses charity can never sin (c.13). Taken together, Gratian notes, these two claims imply that one who sins mortally has never possessed charity and, as a further corollary, that the reprobate never possess charity.[47] For if the reprobate do ever come into the possession of charity, then according to this position they will never be able to lose it. And if they possess charity at the moment of death, they will be saved rather than damned. However, by definition the reprobate are not saved. Consequently, they can never possess charity.

Charity Can Be Lost

After setting forth the view that charity cannot be lost, Gratian turns to the contrary view, that charity can be lost. He adopts a twofold strategy to demonstrate the correctness of this latter position. First, he provides alternative interpretations for the authorities adduced in support of the permanence of charity. Second, he adduces arguments and authorities to demonstrate expressly that charity can be lost. Probably because acting otherwise would have undermined his preferred position, Gratian leaves unchallenged the text of Augustine in c.13 purporting to show that charity and sin are incompatible, that one cannot both possess charity and commit a mortal sin. As noted in the chapter 3, the majority of Gratian's contemporaries accepted the incompatibility of charity and sin, but there were exceptions, such as Peter Abelard.[48] Gratian avoids engaging with

47. De pen. D.2 d.p.c.13 (ed. Friedberg, 1194, supported by Aa Fd): "Cum ergo qui criminaliter peccat caritatem numquam habuisse probatur, euidenter colligitur, penitentiam non agere, qui quandoque criminaliter peccauit." De pen. D.2 d.p.c.14 (ed. Friedberg, 1194, supported by Aa Fd): "Reprobus ergo cum eternis mancipatus incendiis in eternum sitiat, quomodo bibet (bibat *Aa*, bibit *Fd*) aquam uiuam aut quomodo potabit aquam salientem in uitam eternam, qui quasi plumbeus demersus in ima, penas luit dampnationis eterne?"

48. See the discussion in chapter 3, pp. 95–96.

these contrary arguments and authorities, instead resting his own view on the authority of Augustine in c.13.

To neutralize the authorities adduced in support of the permanence of charity, Gratian appeals to the scholastic distinction between perfect and imperfect charity.[49] Just as there are gradations between different virtues, Gratian argues, so too are there gradations in the same virtue. Reaching the summit of a virtue such as charity does not occur instantly, but rather takes place over time.[50] In support of this idea, Gratian quotes an extract from Gregory's Homily 15 on Ezekiel (c.15), followed by five patristic authorities (cc.16–20). These authorities do not always classify the different grades of charity in the same way, but they all distinguish between an imperfect and a more perfect form of charity.

According to Gratian, authorities that appear to show that charity cannot be lost refer to perfect charity, while those that appear to demonstrate the contrary refer to imperfect charity.[51] To prove that imperfect charity can be lost, Gratian adduces two kinds of evidence. First, he quotes authorities from Augustine and the Bible in support of the general proposition that those who possess charity can sin mortally (d.p.c.24–d.p.c.29). Second, he provides concrete examples from the Bible of this same phenomenon, including Adam, Moses, Aaron, and David (c.30–d.p.c.39).

Gratian concludes this section of his argument by pointing out an additional problem with the view that charity cannot be lost: it implies that those who sin mortally have never received the remission of sins in baptism. No adult can receive the remission of sins without

49. On this distinction, see chapter 3, pp. 95–96.

50. De pen. D.2 d.p.c.14 §1 (ed. Friedberg, 1194, supported by Aa Fd): "Exordia uero caritatis enutriuntur, ut crescant, et conculcantur, ut deficiant. Nemo enim repente fit summus, sed in bona conuersatione, que sine caritate nulla est, a minimis quisque inchoat, ut ad magna perueniat. Sunt itaque gradus non solum inter uirtutem et uirtutem, sed etiam in eadem uirtute."

51. De pen. D.2 d.p.c.14 §1 (ed. Friedberg, 1194, supported by Aa Fd): "Hec que de caritate dicuntur, de perfecta intelligi possunt, que semel habita numquam amittitur." De pen. D.2 d.p.c.24 §1 (ed. Friedberg, 1198, supported by Aa Fd): "Hec itaque caritas que in Petro ante negationem herba fuit et in singulis nascitur antequam roboretur, ante sui perfectionem, amittitur et reparatur."

possessing the love of God.[52] But the view that those who sin mortally were never truly baptized is a heretical belief, as Gratian demonstrates by quoting a long passage from Jerome's *Epistola adversus Iovinianum* (c.40). Jerome composed this polemical tract in 392/393 to refute the teachings of Jovinian, a Christian writer from the fourth century. According to Jerome, Jovinian argued that those who have been baptized by water alone can sin, but that those who have been baptized by both water and the Spirit cannot. In the process of refuting these views, *Adversus Iovinianum* demonstrates that those who later sin still receive the forgiveness of sins in baptism.[53] That is why Gratian introduces Jerome's text here.

Gratian does not point it out explicitly, but a corollary of the view that baptism remits the sins of only those who will not sin criminally afterwards is that baptism does not wash away the sins of the reprobate. Bernard of Clairvaux accused Bishop Gilbert of Poitiers of teaching this opinion at the Council of Reims in 1148.[54] According to John of Salisbury, Gilbert denied the allegation, suggesting instead that this heretical idea stemmed from some of his erstwhile students, one of who was then in France, the other who was in England.[55] It is conceivable that Gilbert's misguided pupils influenced or were

52. De pen. D.2 d.p.c.39 §4 (ed. Friedberg, 1202, supported by Aa Fd): "Item, secundum hanc sententiam qui criminaliter delinquit ueram peccatorum remissionem in baptismo consecutus non est, si adultus ad baptisma accessit, quia Dei amorem non habuit, sine quo nemo umquam gratiam inuenit, atque ita secundum heresim Iouiniani, si uere ex aqua et Spiritu quis renatus est, ulterius criminaliter peccare non potest, uel, si criminaliter peccat, aqua tantum, non Spiritu probatur esse renatus." There is an interesting difference between the two recensions. In the first recension, Gratian writes that his opponents hold that adults who later sin have not received the forgiveness of sins in baptism. The redactor of the second recension changes "si adultus ad baptisma accessit" to "siue in annis infantie siue adultus ad baptisma accessit." The scribe of Aa gives both readings one after the other.

53. Jerome, *Adversus Iovinianum*, PL 23, 211–338.

54. John of Salisbury, *Historia Pontificalis—Memoirs of the Papal Court*, ed. and trans. Marjorie Chibnall (London: Clarendon Press, 1956), 22; Otto of Freising, *Gesta Friderici Imperatoris*, lib. 1, c. 50, ed. Georg Heinrich Pertz, MGH SS 20 (Hanover: MGH, 1868), 379; H. C. van Elswijk, *Gilbert Porreta: Sa vie, son oeuvre, sa pensée* (Leiden: Spicilegium Sacrum Lovaniense, 1966), 114–17.

55. John of Salisbury, *Historia Pontificalis*, 22.

known to Gratian or that Gratian's attack on this doctrine contributed to Bernard's heresy hunting at Reims. But no explicit evidence for any such connection exists, and the doctrine is probably not distinctive enough that scholars should rush to posit one.[56]

Charity and the Reprobate

The generally accepted view that the predestined can lose charity so long as they eventually repent and die in a state of grace leads Gratian to address one final problem in distinction 2: whether the reprobate can possess charity. In addressing this issue, Gratian considers extracts from the Bible, Augustine, and Gregory the Great (cc.41–45). His conclusion is that the reprobate can possess charity. The reprobate, says Gratian, truly possess charity and not just the works of charity for the time that they are among the faithful. Unlike the predestined, however, the reprobate are not rooted in charity. Invoking eucharistic imagery, Gratian remarks that the reprobate only "eat" and "drink" Christ; they do not "taste" him.[57] Similarly, argues Gratian, God created the devil in the truth, but the devil did not remain in the truth. Through pride the devil fell from grace. Before the Fall, he possessed charity, for without charity the devil would not have been created in the truth, nor would it be possible to say that he had been created equal to or more excellent than all other creatures.[58] The difference between good and evil angels stems from their exercise of free will, not from the way that they were created by God.[59]

56. Cf. Chodorow, *Christian Political Theory,* who argues that Bernard and Gratian belonged to the same political "party."

57. De pen. D.2 d.p.c.44 (ed. Friedberg, 1208, supported by Aa Fd): "Quod uero reprobi negantur comedere panem, qui de celo descendit, uel bibere aquam uiuam, non sic accipiendum est, ut a caritate penitus credantur alieni, sed ut in caritate radicem figere non intelligantur. Aliud est enim manducare uel bibere, atque aliud degustare."

58. De pen. D.2 d.p.c.44 §1 (ed. Friedberg, 1208, supported by Aa Fd): "Hinc etiam diabolus in ueritate stetisse, non in ea creatus esse negatur. Fuit enim in ueritate conditus; sed, dum de se superbiendo presumpsit, ab ea alienus factus est."

59. De pen. D.2 d.p.c.44 §1 (ed. Friedberg, 1209, supported by Aa Fd): "Vnde autem hec differentia inter bonos et malos angelos processit? Si ex creante, iniustus uidetur Deus, qui ante peccatum infert penam, uel qui hoc punit, quod creando infudit. Si autem non ex creante, cum non ex traduce, restat, ut ex proprie libertatis arbitrio uicium superbiae in angelicam naturam processerit."

The Concluding Dictum

The concluding dictum provides a reconsideration of c.12 ("charity that can be abandoned in adversity is fictive") in light of the immeasurable distance between God and creatures.[60] In comparison to God, who is immutable, every creature can be called flawed due to being mutable. Similarly, in comparison with the divine charity, which can never fail, charity that can fail is denied to be true, even though it is true in its own, lesser way.[61]

Gratian's ultimate conclusion in distinction 2, then, is that charity is not permanent. While in this life, those who possess charity can still sin and by sinning lose charity. The contrary view, Gratian maintains, leads to numerous errors, including the heretical view that baptism does not wash away the sins of the reprobate and that the reprobate can never possess charity.

Distinction 3

Although some of the proponents of the view that penance cannot be repeated defend their claim by arguing that charity can never be lost and that those who possess charity cannot commit mortal sins, others employ different arguments. For this reason, Gratian does not simply conclude at the end of distinction 2 that penance

60. De pen. D.2 c.12 (ed. Friedberg, 1193, supported by Aa Fd): "Ficta caritas est, que deserit in aduersitate."

61. De pen. D.2 d.p.c.45 (ed. Friedberg, 1210–11, supported by Aa Fd): "Caritas autem, que in aduersitate deseritur, ficta, id est fictilis et fragilis, esse perhibetur, sicut fides, ex qua caritas procedit, ficta, id est fragilis, apud Apostolum esse negatur. Similiter caritas, que in aduersitate deseri potest, dicitur numquam uera fuisse.... Sicut ergo eius comparatione, qui mutabilitatem nescit, omnis creatura uitiosa dicitur (est *Aa*), quia mutabilitatis est capax ... sic comparatione eius creature, que mutationem non recipit, omnis creatura que permutatur, non uera sed uana (falsa *Aa*) esse probatur.... Sic ergo comparatione diuine caritatis nulla uirtus uera probatur, aut comparatione eius, que non deseritur, illa, que amittitur, uera esse negatur. Sicut autem omnis creatura suo modo bona et uere (uera *Friedb.*) esse dicitur, sic et caritas, que deseritur, suo modo uera esse monstratur: alioquin, a nullo desereretur, si nullo modo in eo esset (si ... esset *ante* a nullo *tr. Friedb.*). Quod enim nullo modo uere est nullo modo deseri potest. Quod si aliquo modo uere deseritur, et aliquo modo id uere esse oportet."

can be repeated, but instead goes on to discuss the repeatability of penance in its own right in distinction 3.

In approaching this question, Gratian does not, as one might expect, focus on the practical question of whether a person can perform the rite(s) of penance multiple times. Instead, he deals with the theoretical issue of whether a penance performed by a person who later commits another mortal sin actually qualified as penance. In other words, distinction 3 concerns not so much what a penitent needs to do going forward, after he has committed another sin—although it by no means ignores this topic—as opposed to the metaphysical status of the penances that penitents perform before falling back into mortal sin.

As with distinction 2, there exists little controversy over the question that Gratian was trying to answer in distinction 3 or what his position was. Commentators universally agree that distinction 3 concerns the repeatability of penance and that Gratian answered this question in the affirmative. The following treatment of distinction 3 must nevertheless be longer than the preceding discussion of distinction 2, since other aspects of distinction 3, most notably its structure, are poorly understood. One puzzle is the shift in topic that occurs partway through the distinction. The first half of distinction 3 presents the authorities that appear to support the unrepeatability of penance (cc.1–17), before moving on to refute these authorities (d.p.c.17–d.p.c.22), and present the authorities that support the contrary position (d.p.c.22 §2–d.p.c.33). The remainder of distinction 3, however, turns to what appear at first glance to be two only somewhat related issues: the nature of true penance (d.p.c.33–d.p.c.39) and whether a person can perform penance for just one of many sins (d.p.c.39–c.49). Chapter 5 will propose an explanation for this structure. As a prelude to the analysis set forth there, this section will examine Gratian's arguments in each part of the distinction.

Penance Cannot Be Repeated

Gratian begins distinction 3 by setting forth the position that he will go on to refute. Some people, says Gratian, argue that, just as true charity can never be lost, so too can true penance be performed only once, after which one can never again commit mortal sin. If a penitent should commit a sin later on, then his penance was not true penance.[62] Gratian quotes sixteen authorities (cc.1–6, 8–17) that appear to support this position. (Canon 7 was added only in the second recension.) These authorities are taken almost entirely from the writings of the Church Fathers—Ambrose, Augustine, Gregory, Isidore, and John Chrysostom—but also include an excerpt from the writings of Smaragdus, a Carolingian monk who died in 843. At this point in the distinction, Gratian does not bother to analyze these authorities or to provide any arguments from reason in support of the unrepeatability of penance.

Refuting Authorities for the Unrepeatability of Penance

Immediately after quoting cc.1–6 and 8–17, Gratian proceeds to show how they do not, in fact, support the unrepeatability of penance. His main technique for explaining these authorities is a grammatico-linguistic argument, which he explains through an analysis of c.6. The canon, an excerpt from a homily of Gregory the Great, reads:

> We cannot worthily perform (*agere*) penance, unless we know the mode of this same penance. Indeed, performing penance is to weep for perpetrated evils and no longer to perpetrate what we must weep over. For he who weeps over some [sins] in such a way that he nevertheless commits (*committat*) other [sins], either is still ignorant of how to perform penance or feigns [penance]. For what does it profit someone to weep over the sins of luxury and nevertheless still to pant after the passions of avarice?[63]

62. De pen. D.3 d.a.c.1 (ed. Friedberg, 1211, supported by Aa Fd): "Hec de caritate breuiter scripsimus propter eos qui penitentiam negant reiterari posse, asserentes quod sicut caritas semel uere habita numquam amittitur, ita penitentia semel uere celebrata nulla sequenti culpa maculatur. Si uero criminalis culpa illam aliquando sequitur, uera penitentia non fuit nec ueniam a Domino impetrauit. Quod si ex diffinitione ipsius penitentie et multorum auctoritatibus probare contendit."

63. De pen. D.3 c.6 (ed. Friedberg, 1212, supported by Aa Fd): "Penitentiam agere digne non possumus, nisi modum quoque eiusdem penitentie cognoscamus. Penitentiam quippe agere est et perpetrata mala plangere et plangenda non perpetrare. Nam qui sic alia deplorat ut tamen (tantum *Fd*) alia committat, adhuc penitentiam agere aut ignorat aut dissimulat. Quid enim prodest si peccata quis luxurie defleat et tamen adhuc auaritie estibus anhelat?" The material source is Gregory the Great, *Homiliae in euangelia* 34.15–16, ed. Raymond Étaix, CCSL 141 (Turnhout: Brepols, 1999), 314.417–23.

The verbs (*agere, committat*) of the definition of penance in c.6, says Gratian in d.p.c.17, do not refer to different times, such as the present and the future, but rather to the same time, the moment when one performs penance. The authority thus does not claim that those who perform true penance will never sin again, but rather only that they resolve never to sin again at the moment they perform penance.[64]

This grammatico-linguistic argument clearly applies to c.1 as well as c.6, since c.1 consists of nothing more than a single sentence from a Pseudo-Ambrosian sermon, which Gregory and Gratian reproduce in c.6.[65] And Gratian states explicitly that the grammatico-linguistic argument applies to the authorities in cc.3, 5, and 9–16.[66] To reinterpret the remaining authorities adduced in support of the unrepeatability of penance, however, Gratian employs different techniques. He refers the authorities in cc.2 and 22 to "solemn penance," which, according to some people, he says, can only be celebrated once.[67] Such an explanation was historically accurate, as the penance to which these two authorities—one by Ambrose (c.2), the other by Augustine (c.22)—were referring was the unrepeatable canonical penance of the patristic era.[68] It is doubtful, however, whether Gra-

64. De pen. D.3 d.p.c.17, quoted in chapter 5, p. 171n59.

65. Compare De pen. D.3 c.1 (ed. Friedberg, 1211, supported by Aa Fd): "Penitentia est et mala preterita plangere et plangenda iterum non committere" and De pen. D.3 c.6 (ed. Friedberg, 1212, supported by Aa Fd): "Penitentiam quippe agere est et perpetrata mala plangere et plangenda non perpetrare." It should be noted that De pen. D.3 c.1 is an abbreviation of the longer citation found in De pen. D.1 c.39 (ed. Friedberg, 1167–68). The material source is Pseudo-Ambrose, *Sermones Sancto Ambrosio hactenus ascripti* 25.1, PL 17, 655A.

66. De pen. D.3 d.p.c.21 (ed. Friedberg, 1215, supported by Aa Fd): "Ex persona huiuscemodi penitentis etiam illud Smaragdi [c.9] intelligitur ... et illud Augustini [c.10] ... et illud Ysidori [c.11] ... et illud Ysaie [cited in c.14, part of the single authority by Gregory comprising cc.13–16] ... Idem illud soliloquiorum [c.12].... Similiter illud Gregorii [c.13]." De pen. D.3 d.p.c.22 (ed. Friedberg, 1215, supported by Aa Fd): "'Satisfactio quoque penitentie' [c.3] et 'Vade et amplius noli peccare' [c.5], eundem cum diffinitione intellectum habent."

67. De pen. D.3 d.p.c.21 (ed. Friedberg, 1215, supported by Aa Fd): "Illud autem Ambrosii [c.2]: 'Reperiuntur' etc. non secundum generalem sed secundum specialem consuetudinem ecclesie de sollempni penitentia dictum intelligitur, que apud quosdam semel celebrata non reiteratur." De pen. D.3 d.p.c.22 (ed. Friedberg, 1215, supported by Aa Fd): "Hac auctoritate [c.22] et illud Ambrosii [c.2] determinatur, et iterum peccaturo per primam penitentiam uenia dari monstratur; alioquin nequaquam iterum parceret Deus, qui necdum pepercisset."

68. See chapter 3.

tian fully understood how much penance had changed since late antiquity.

Gratian employs yet another distinction to explain the authorities in cc.4 and 8. Just as there exist three levels of charity—beginner, intermediate, and perfect—so too, says Gratian, do there exist three corresponding levels of penance: penance performed by beginners, penance performed by the intermediate, and penance performed by the perfect. Comparison with baptism, Gratian argues, shows that even the penance of beginners forgives sins. Just as the sins of one possessing only imperfect charity are remitted in baptism, even if he or she should later commit a mortal sin, so too is forgiveness not denied to a beginner in penance. The penance of such a beginner can be termed both perfect and imperfect: perfect on account of contrition, imperfect on account of its impermanence. Gratian interprets the authority in c.8 as referring to the first mode of perfect penance, that is, penance which is not permanent, while he interprets the authority in c.4 as referring to the second mode of perfect penance, penance that will persevere to the end.[69]

A slight aside occurs at the end of d.p.c.22, where Gratian examines in greater detail the interpretation of a single sentence from c.5: "If penance ends, nothing of mercy remains." He offers two interpretations. If one accepts the return of sins, says Gratian, then the sentence can be taken to mean that forgiven sins return. Just as someone in just servitude who has been manumitted and then later re-enslaved on account of ingratitude is truly free for the brief period of time between his manumission and his re-enslavement, so too are sins which later return truly forgiven for the period of time before they return. If

69. De pen. D.3 d.p.c.22 (ed. Friedberg, 1215, supported by Aa Fd): "Illud autem quod in libro de penitentia [c.4] dicitur, de perfecto intelligendum est. Sicut enim caritas alia est incipiens, alia proficiens, alia perfecta, sic et penitentia alia est incipientium, alia proficientium, alia perfectorum. Sicut autem caritati, licet nondum perfecte, in baptismo datur uenia peccatorum, ut quamuis postea grauiter aliquis sit peccaturus, tamen tunc intelligatur esse renatus non aqua tantum sicut Iouinianus tradidit, sed et aqua et spiritu, sicut Ieronimus contra eum scribit: sic et incipientium penitentie uenia non negatur, que quadam ratione perfecta dici potest, quia toto corde gemit et dolet, licet alia ratione dicatur imperfecta, quia non usque in finem duratura. Secundum primum modum perfectionis intelligitur illud Iohannis os aurei [c.8].... Iuxta secundum modum perfectionis illud Augustini [c.4] intelligitur."

one rejects the return of sins, one can interpret the sentence to mean that nothing remains of the purity of life and hope for eternal beatitude that one obtained along with the forgiveness of sins.[70]

Proving the Repeatability of Penance

After demonstrating that the authorities adduced in support of the unrepeatability of penance do not really support that position, Gratian presents authorities in support of the contrary position, the repeatability of penance. As in his proof that imperfect charity can be lost, Gratian's strategy here is twofold. He proves the correctness of the general rule that penance can be repeated (cc.23, 32, 33), and he provides concrete examples of persons who performed true penance but nevertheless later sinned again. These concrete examples are all taken from the Bible: David (2 Kgs 11:1–12:15), Ahab (3 Kgs 21), and the people of Nineveh (Jon 3).

The Nature of True Penance and Performing Penance for Just One of Many Sins

The remainder of distinction 3 deals with what seem to be two only somewhat related issues: the nature of true penance and whether a penitent can repent and perform penance for just one of many sins. Well-known contemporary masters active in the schools of northern France did not treat these topics together. However, as chapter 5 will show, works from the Italian theological milieu that Gratian was addressing did.

Beginning with d.p.c.33, Gratian examines the nature of true pen-

70. De pen. D.3 d.p.c.22 §1 (ed. Friedberg, 1215, supported by Aa Fd): "Illud autem 'Si penitentia finitur, nichil de uenia relinquitur' [c.5], dupliciter intelligi potest (intelligitur *Aa*). Si enim iuxta quorundam sententiam peccata dimissa redeunt, facile est intelligere nichil de uenia relinquitur, quoniam peccata que prius erant dimissa iterum replicantur. Sicut enim ille qui ex iusta seruitute in libertatem manumittitur, interim uere liber est, quamuis ob ingratitudinem in seruitutem postea reuocetur, sic et penitenti peccata uere remittuntur, quamuis ob ingratitudinem uenie eisdem postea sit implicandus. Si autem peccata dimissa non redeunt, dicitur nichil relinqui de uenia, quia nichil sibi relinquitur de uite munditia et spe eterne beatitudinis, quam cum uenia assecutus est. Sicut enim argento perfecte purgato nichil sui decoris relinquitur, si sequenti erugine fedatur, non prima tamen sed subsequenti sordidatur, sic expiato per penitentiam nichil de uenia dicitur relinqui, cum tamen non iam deletis sed adhuc expiandis coinquinetur."

ance. The two authorities that he quotes in this regard, cc.34 and 35, are extracts from the commentaries of Origen and Pseudo-Hesychius on Leviticus 10:16.[71] This passage from the Old Testament tells how Moses grew angry upon finding an already-burned sin offering of a goat, which was supposed to be eaten by Aaron's sons in the holy of holies. Both Origen and Pseudo-Hesychius interpret the verse allegorically of penance. Both authorities understand the sacrifice of the goat as refering to penance, which should have been eaten in the holy of holies.[72] Origen focuses on the destruction of the goat by an alien fire, which he interprets as "libido, avarice, and every depraved cupidity."[73] Pseudo-Hesyschius, on the other hand, focuses on the failure of Aaron's sons to eat the sacrifice in the holy of holies, that is, the church.[74] Both authorities, however, come to more or less the same conclusion about what the penitent should do: he should perform true penance. Pseudo-Hesyschius notes that "just as true penance merits forgiveness, so too does false penance anger God."[75] Origen, for his part, exhorts him who would be purified to "remove every alien fire" and offer himself to the fire that destroys guilt rather than man.[76] Priests, he

71. Hesyschius of Jerusalem (also spelled Esitius) was a presbyter and exegete, probably from the early fifth century. He did not write the commentary on Leviticus printed in PG 93, 787–1180, which is extant only in Latin and which Gratian quotes in De pen. D.3 c.35 through the intermediary of the *Glossa ordinaria* ad Lv 10:16 (ed. Rusch, 1:235; Munich, Bayerische Staatsbibliothek, Clm 4574, fols. 34v–35r).

72. De pen. D.3 c.34 (ed. Friedberg, 1222, supported by Aa Fd): "combusta est enim furore et fumo iniquitatis. Inde irascitur, et dicit deuorandam fuisse penitentiam in sanctis sanctorum; sacerdotes quasi segnes increpat." De pen. D.3 c.35 (ed. Friedberg, 1222, supported by Aa Fd): "Quia non commederunt filii Aaron quod (qui *Aa Fd*) pro peccato erat in loco sancto, id est penitentiam commissi peccati in ecclesia peragi non fecerunt."

73. De pen. D.3 c.34 §1 (ed. Friedberg, 1222, supported by Aa Fd): "Quomodo autem poterat, ubi ignis alienus erat, peccatum exuri et in conspectu Domini, cui cuncta aperta, quasi non complacet Deo, qui iniustitiam corde inclusam tenet et se penitentiam agere perhibet. Ignis alienus libido, auaricia, et omnis cupiditas praua.... Qui ergo uult mundari, ignem alienum remoueat."

74. De pen. D.3 c.35 (ed. Friedberg, 1222, supported by Aa Fd): "Debet autem commedi hoc sacrificium in loco sancto, scilicet in ecclesia, in propitiationem peccatorum."

75. De pen. D.3 c.35 (ed. Friedberg, 1222, supported by Aa Fd): "sicut uera penitentia ueniam promeretur, ita simulata Deum irritat."

76. De pen. D.3 c.34 §2 (ed. Friedberg, 1222, supported by Aa Fd): "Qui ergo

says, cannot remove the guilt of one who offers himself deceptively. Only a true and sincere sacrifice is acceptable to God.[77]

Based on these two authorities, Gratian concludes that one cannot obtain forgiveness for one crime without simultaneously repenting of and performing penance for one's other crimes.[78] Proponents of the contrary view, says Gratian, rely for the most part on Nahum 1:9: "God will not judge the same [crime] twice." These opponents argue that whomever a priest judges, God judges, and that whoever is punished by a priest, cannot be punished again by God.[79] Gratian, however, explicitly rejects this line of reasoning. According to Gratian, Nahum 1:9 applies only to those who perform penance for their sins and reform their lives after having been punished by God.[80] These people alone will God refrain from punishing in the next life. Of sinners who become more hardhearted on account of their punishment, such as Pharaoh, Antiochus, and Herod, their present punishments simply represent the beginning of their eternal damnation. Gratian adds, however, that temporal punishments are not entirely without profit for those who fail to repent; for temporal punish-

---

uult mundari, ignem alienum remoueat. Illi (et *praem. Aa*$^{sup. lin.}$ *Friedb.*) igni se offerat, qui culpam exurit, non hominem."

77. Ibid.: "Culpam ergo eius non auferunt sacerdotes qui dolose offert (se *add. Friedb.*).... Non est acceptum Deo sacrificium, nisi uerum et sincerum."

78. De pen. D.3 cc.36–39 are all second-recension additions. De pen. D.3 d.p.c.39 (ed. Friedberg, 1224, supported by Aa Fd): "His auctoritatibus, que sit uera, que falsa penitentia ostenditur, et false nulla indulgentia dari probatur. In quo illorum sententia destruitur, qua cum qui pluribus irretitus fuerit, asseritur unius penitentia eiusdem ueniam a Domino consequi sine alterius criminis penitentia."

79. De pen. D.3 d.p.c.39 (ed. Friedberg, 1224, supported by Aa Fd): "Quod etiam multorum auctoritatibus probare conantur. Quarum prima est illa Naum prophete: 'Non iudicabit Deus bis in idipsum.' Sed quem sacerdos iudicat, Deus iudicat, cuius personam in ecclesia gerit. Qui ergo a sacerdote semel pro peccato punitur, non iterum pro eodem peccato a Deo iudicabitur."

80. De pen. D.3 d.p.c.42 (ed. Friedberg, 1225–26, supported by Aa Fd): "Auctoritas illa Naum prophete: 'Non iudicabit Deus' etc., non ostendit omnia que temporaliter puniuntur non ulterius a Deo punienda.... Intelligitur ergo illud Ieronimi de his tantum qui inter flagella penitentiam egerunt, quam et si breuem et momentaneam tamen non respuit Deus, sicut et illud prophete: 'Non iudicabit Deus bis in idipsum' de his tantum intelligi oportet, quos presentia supplicia commutant, super quos non consurget duplex tribulatio."

ments purge and punish venial sins, even if eternal punishment is reserved for mortal sins.[81]

The other two authorities that, according to Gratian, are often adduced in support of the view that one can receive forgiveness for repenting of just one of many sins are the texts he quotes in cc.40 and 41. He spends a significant amount of time explaining both texts. The extract from Gregory quoted in c.40, says Gratian, should be understood as referring to the detestation of a crime rather than to forgiveness for a crime. "'God rains over one city and does not rain over another city; and over the same city he rains in part and leaves dry in part' (Amos 4:7). When he who hates his neighbor removes himself from other vices, one and the same city receives rain in part and remains dry in part, because there exist those who, when they check certain vices, persist seriously in others."[82] A city is said to receive rain, says Gratian, because a penitent begins to detest his sin, not because he receives forgiveness for it. The detestation of sin is likened to rain because it is instilled into our hearts from the fount of divine grace, so that by it one can reach true penance or at least be punished less by God, since the longer one perseveres in sin, the greater the punishment one accumulates for oneself.[83]

81. De pen. D.3 d.p.c.42 (ed. Friedberg, 1226, supported by Aa Fd): "Qui autem inter flagella duriores et deteriores fiunt, sicut Pharao, qui flagellatus a Domino durior, factus est, presentibus futura connectunt, ut temporale supplicium sit eis eterne dampnationis initium." De pen. D.3 d.p.c.43 (ed. Friedberg, 1226, supported by Aa Fd): "Hoc contra illos notandum est, qui dicunt non iudicabit Deus bis in idipsum ad omnia pertinere flagella, quia quidam hic flagellis emendantur, alii hic et in eternum puniuntur, sicut Antiochus et Herodes. Quod autem super eundem locum de adulterio infideli Ieronimus sentire uidetur, ex uerbis eiusdem falsum esse probatur. Exemplo enim illius qui Israelite maledixerat et qui ligna in Sabbato collegerat, ostendit parua peccata breuibus et temporalibus suppliciis purgari, magna uero diuturnis et eternis suppliciis reseruari."

82. De pen. D.3 c.40 (ed. Friedberg, 1224, supported by Aa Fd): "'Pluit Dominus super unam ciuitatem et super alteram non pluit, et eandem ciuitatem ex parte compluit, et ex parte aridam relinquit.' Cum ille qui proximum odit ab aliis uitiis se corrigit, una eademque ciuitas ex parte compluitur et ex parte arida manet, quia sunt qui cum uitia quedam resecant, in aliis grauiter perdurant."

83. De pen. D.3 d.p.c.44 (ed. Friedberg, 1226–27, supported by Aa Fd): "Illud autem Gregorii: 'Pluit Dominus super unam ciuitatem' etc. [c.40], non ad criminis ueniam sed ad eius detestationem referendum est, ut ideo pars ciuitatis dicatur esse compluta, quia crimen quod dilexerat detestari incipit (incepit *Fd*),

Gratian's reinterpretation of c.41 focuses on the last sentence: "Even if faith is absent, punishment satisfies." Gratian interprets "faith" (*fides*) as referring to consciousness of one's own sins rather than to the theological virtue of faith. The sentence thus does not mean that punishments will satisfy God's judgment even if one lacks faith, but rather that punishments will satisfy God's judgment even if we do not know what we have done to merit such punishment. Only when we repent of *all* our sins, says Gratian, will we actually obtain the fruit (*fructus*) of penance.[84]

Gratian supports his interpretation by quoting cc.45 and 46, which affirm that God always rewards sinners for their good works. He also admits, however, that one can interpret these texts differently. The reward spoken of in c.46 need not be eternal life. It can also refer to a temporal reward (c.47) or simply a diminishment of the punishment that one will receive in hell (c.49).[85]

---

non quod eius ueniam consequatur. Criminis autem detestatio pluuia uocatur, quia ex fonte diuine gratie cordi nostro instillatur, ut uel sic quisque ad ueram penitentiam perueniat, aut eo minus a Deo puniatur, quo diuturniori delectatione peccati maius sibi supplicium accumulasset. Si uero ad indulgentiam criminis pluuia referatur, euangelice sententie contraire uidebitur. Si enim per odium fraternum et que dimissa sunt replicantur ad penam, multo magis que nondum sunt dimissa ad uindictam reseruari probantur."

84. De pen. D.3 d.p.c.44 §2 (ed. Friedberg, 1227, supported by Aa Fd): "Item, illud Ambrosii: 'et si fides desit, pena satisfacit' [c.41] non de ea fide intelligitur, de qua dicitur 'fides sine operibus mortua est,' sed de ea de qua Apostolus ait: 'Omne quod non est ex fide,' id est omne quod contra conscientiam fit, 'peccatum est.' Deest ergo fides, cum (cui *Aa*) non subest conscientia peccati. Sed quia delicta omnia nullus intelligit, est aliquando in homine peccatum cuius non habet conscientiam.... Cuius ergo peccati deest conscientia, illius pena, si patienter feratur, satisfacit et releuat grauatum. Quod autem in fine obicitur, 'si satisfactio illa fuit, ueniam impetrauit; si autem ueniam non impetrauit, satisfactio non fuit; si autem satisfactio non fuit, adhuc sibi pena imponenda est,' non procedit argumentatio. Satisfactio namque est dum illius peccati pena exciditur, et eius suggestionibus aditum non indulgetur. Sed eius fructus non percipitur, impeditus peccato quod nondum deseritur. Percipitur autem, cum eius penitentia fuerit subsecuta, sicut ad lauacrum ficte accedens regenerationis sacramentum accipit. Non tamen in Christo renascitur. Renascetur autem uirtute sacramenti quod perceperat, cum fictio illa de corde eius recesserit, ueraci penitentia."

85. De pen. D.3 d.p.c.48 (ed. Friedberg, 1228, supported by Aa Fd): "Potest etiam referri memoria bonorum ad mitiorem penam habendam, ut bona que inter multa mala fiunt non proficiant ad presentis uel future uite premium obtinendum, sed ad tolerabilius extremi iudicii supplicium subeundum."

Concluding Dictum

Gratian concludes distinction 3 by summing up the preceding discussion. Penance, says Gratian, does not help those who persevere in sin. Nevertheless, penance must never be denied to anyone because penitents will always receive the fruit of their penance the moment that they repent of their remaining sins.[86] Concerning solemn penance, Gratian repeats his earlier judgment that its unworthy celebration brings no profit whatsoever and removes the opportunity for a second solemn penance according to the custom of certain churches. To this form of penance alone does the statement apply: "A second opportunity for penance does not exist."[87]

Distinction 4

Because of its connection with the previously considered issues, the return of sins attracts Gratian's attention in distinction 4. Do forgiven sins in some way return when one later commits another mortal sin? Modern scholars have at times suggested that Gratian answers this question in the negative.[88] But, as other scholars have recognized, the contrary is in fact true: Gratian affirms the return of sins.[89]

86. De pen. D.3 d.p.c.49 (ed. Friedberg, 1228, supported by Aa Fd): "Penitentia ergo, ut ex premissis apparet, nulli in peccato perseueranti utilis est, non tamen alicui deneganda est, quia sentiet fructum eius, cum alterius criminis penitentiam egerit."

87. De pen. D.3 d.p.c.49 (ed. Friedberg, 1228, supported by Aa Fd): "Illud autem Ambrosii: 'Penitentia semel usurpata nec uere celebrata, fructum prioris aufert et usum sequentis ammittit' de solempni intelligitur, que cum non uere celebrata fuerit, et fructum prioris, id est sui ipsius secuturam precedentis, amittit, quia ueniam, quam impetrare potuit, contempsit, et usum sequentis aufert secundum consuetudinem quarundam ecclesiarum, apud quas penitentie sollempnitas non reiteratur. De hac eadem penitentia etiam illud inteligitur: 'Non est secundus locus penitentie.'" The first authority by Ambrose does not appear in the first recension of the *Decretum*, though it is added to the second recension as De pen. D.3 c.37. The second authority is also cited at D.50 d.p.c.61 (already in the first recension).

88. Joseph de Ghellinck, "La reviviscence des péchés pardonnés à l'époque de Pierre Lombard et de Gandulphe de Bologne," *Nouvelle revue théologique* 41 (1909): 400–408, at 400–401 and 405; Albert Michel, *Dictionnaire de théologie catholique*, 15 vols. (Paris: Letouzey et Ané, 1908–50), 13.2:2644–53, at 2647, s.v. "Reviviscence des péchés."

89. Landgraf, "Die frühscholastische Streitfrage," 534; Francis Courtney, *Car-*

The Two Versions of the Return of Sins

Gratian begins his investigation of the view that forgiven sins return when one later commits a grave sin by quoting authorities that appear to support it. As discussed in chapter 3, this issue had originated as a problem of biblical exegesis surrounding the parable of the unforgiving servant, but soon came to encompass other texts and authorities. The two biblical passages that Gratian quotes in support of the return of sins are Psalm 108:14 ("May the iniquity of his fathers return in the sight of the Lord"), a text more typically cited in connection with the inheritance of parental sin, and Matthew 18:32 ("Wicked servant, I forgave you all the debt"), a passage from the parable of the unforgiving servant.[90] The patristic and pseudo-patristic authorities that he quotes are attributed to Augustine, Bede, Gregory, and Hrabanus Maurus, but are not all authentic (cc.1–7). All of these authorities can be interpreted to mean that forgiven sins return when a person later commits any kind of mortal sin. Some theologians, such as Hugh of St. Victor and Peter Lombard, understood a sin as returning only when a person later commits the same or a similar sin.[91] Gratian's phrasing—both in his opening dictum and later on in distinction 4—makes clear that he understood the doctrine more broadly, as affirming that forgiven sins return whenever a person commits any other mortal sin. On his understanding, then, a forgiven sin of adultery would return if a penitent later committed perjury and a forgiven sin of gluttony would return if a penitent later committed murder.

After presenting the authorities supporting the return of sins, Gratian distinguishes between two versions of the doctrine. According-

---

dinal Robert Pullen: An English Theologian of the Twelfth Century (Rome: Apud Aedes Universitatis Gregorianae, 1954), 246; Larson, *Master of Penance*, 194 and 194n55.

90. De pen. D.4 d.a.c.1 (ed. Friedberg, 1228, supported by Aa Fd): "Quia uero multorum auctoritatibus supra monstratum est penitentiam uere celebrari et peccata uere dimitti ei qui aliquando in crimen recasurus est, queritur an peccata dimissa redeant. Huius questionis diuersorum uaria est sententia, aliis asserentibus, aliis econtra negantibus peccata semel dimissa ulterius dimissa replicari ad penam. Quod autem peccata dimissa redeant, multorum probatur auctoritatibus, quarum prima est illa prophete (Ps 108:14): 'In memoria redeat iniquitas patrum eius' etc. Secunda illa euangelii (Mt 18:32): 'Serve nequam, omne debitum dimisi tibi' etc."

91. See the discussion in chapter 3, pp. 97–98.

ing to Gratian in d.p.c.7, certain proponents of the return of sins hold that forgiven sins which later return are only forgiven according to justice (*secundum iustitiam*) but not according to prescience (*secundum prescientiam*). In other words, forgiven sins that return are in a certain respect never fully forgiven. On the other hand, other proponents of the return of sins, says Gratian, argue that sinners always receive full and unconditional remission for their sins, even when these sins later return.[92]

An analogous distinction between being written in the book of life according to justice and according to prescience, to which Gratian makes reference, can be found in Ambrosiaster's *Commentary on Romans*, which was written in the late fourth century and widely known in the twelfth century.[93] The justice/prescience distinction as applied to the forgiveness of sins, however, was not similarly widespread and does not appear in the writings of any of Gratian's French compeers, such as Abelard or Hugh.[94] For this reason, modern commentators have sometimes suggested that no one actually defended the view that forgiven sins which later return are forgiven only according to justice but not according to prescience and that Gratian introduces it purely for pedagogical reasons.[95] Chapter 5 will argue that these suggestions are probably incorrect. Gratian himself may well have been the one to invent this distinction, but he did so for more than pedagogical reasons. He wanted to disprove the complaint, voiced in *Baptizato homine* and likely shared by other theologians, that those who defend the return of sins could not give a

92. De pen. D.4 d.p.c.7 (ed. Friedberg, 1230, supported by Aa Fd): "Horum uero qui hanc sententiam secuntur, alii dicunt quod peccata reditura dimittuntur secundum iusticiam sed non secundum prescientiam (presentiam *Fd*[ac]), sicut nomina discipulorum qui retro abierunt erant scripta in libro uite propter iusticiam, cui deserviebant, non secundum prescientiam que in numero saluandorum eos non habebat."

93. Larson, *Master of Penance*, 172–79, provides a detailed discussion of the history of the *secundum iustitiam/secundum prescientiam* distinction.

94. See chapter 3, pp. 96–98.

95. E.g., Larson, *Master of Penance*, 182–83: "Gratian set up this debate probably more as a pedagogical exercise for harmonization or reconciliation than as a reflection of actual, current debate (no evidence yet exists to suggest this was a real point of conflict among Gratian's contemporaries)." See also ibid., 193.

reasoned defense of their position, but simply appealed to God's inscrutable justice.

According to Gratian, the long excerpt from Augustine's *De correptione et gratia* found in c.8 offers support for both versions of the return of sins.[96] For the end of c.8 appears to support the view that such sins are only forgiven according to justice but not according to prescience.[97] The beginning of the authority, however, seems to support the view that sins which later return are fully forgiven at the moment when they are forgiven, since if one of the non-predestined were to die while in a state of grace, he would, according to the beginning of c.8, be saved.[98]

In order to resolve this apparent contradiction, Gratian investigates the doctrine of predestination. More specifically, he investigates what it means to be written in or deleted from the book of life. Being written in the book of life according to prescience, says Gratian, is being predestined to life, which is done from eternity.[99] Being deleted from the book of life according to prescience is being foreknown to death not to life, which is likewise done from eternity.[100] Being written in the book of life according to justice is being granted

96. De pen. D.4 c.8 (ed. Friedberg, 1230, supported by Aa Fd): "Si ex bono in malum deficientes bona uoluntate moriuntur, respondeant, si possunt, cur illos Deus cum fideliter et pie uiuerent, non tunc de uite huius periculis rapuerit, ne malicia mutaret intellectum eorum et ne fictio deciperet animas eorum."

97. De pen. D.4 d.p.c.8 (ed. Friedberg, 1232, supported by Aa Fd): "Finis huius auctoritatis eorum sententie concordat qui peccata dicunt remitti secundum iustitiam, non secundum prescientiam."

98. De pen. D.4 d.p.c.8 (ed. Friedberg, 1232, supported by Aa Fd): "Alii uero, quamuis fateantur peccata redire, tamen seu per baptisma seu per penitentiam asserunt omnino peccata remitti, et plena fide accedentem ad lauacrum renasci non aqua tantum sed etiam spiritu sancto, et si postea peccaturus sit, deinde penitentem et si aliquando recasurus sit, tamen tempore sue penitentie ita perfecte expiatum affirmant ut, si tunc moreretur, salutem inveniret eternam. Quorum sententie eiusdem auctoritatis principium consentit."

99. De pen. D.4 d.p.c.8 (ed. Friedberg, 1232, supported by Aa Fd): "Vt ergo finis principio conueniat, ne sibi ipsi contraire uideatur, diffiniendum est quid sit scribi in libro uite uel de eodem deleri secundum iustitiam, quid secundum prescientiam. Secundum prescientiam scribi est ad uitam preordinari, quod ab eterno factum est."

100. De pen. D.4 d.p.c.9 (ed. Friedberg, 1232, supported by Aa Fd): "Similiter secundum prescientiam deleri est ad mortem non ad uitam presciri, quod et ipsum ab eterno factum est."

the grace of doing things by which one merits being worthy of eternal salvation.[101] And being deleted from the book of life according to justice is to have God's grace subtracted from oneself so that one is permitted to do things by which one merits eternal damnation.[102] If we apply these distinctions to the forgiveness of sins, says Gratian, then it becomes apparent that the sins of the predestined are forgiven both according to justice and according to prescience, but that the sins of the non-predestined are only ever forgiven according to justice. Sins are forgiven according to prescience when God prepares grace from all eternity to justify sinners so that they may be glorified. Sins are forgiven according to justice when someone receives baptism in full faith or performs penance with all his or her heart.[103]

To clarify this idea yet further, Gratian discusses the doctrine that there exist two predestinations: predestination to present justice and predestination to eternal life. All those who are predestined to eternal life are necessarily predestined to present justice, since only by dying in a state of grace can someone obtain eternal life. In other words, God makes all those predestined to eternal life worthy of eternal life by transforming them into morally good people, that is, predestining them to present justice. Not all those who are predestined to present justice, however, are able to persevere until the end, since not all of these people are predestined to eternal life. In other words, God sometimes allows those whom he has not predestined to eternal life to lead morally good lives—something they can do only because God grants them the grace to live well, that is, has predestined them to present justice—even though God does not permit these people to persist in his grace to the very end. If one of the non-predestined

101. De pen. D.4 d.p.c.10 (ed. Friedberg, 1233, supported by Aa Fd): "Porro secundum iusticiam scribi est Deo auctore ea operari, quorum merito sit dignus eterna salute."

102. De pen. D.4 d.p.c.11 (ed. Friedberg, 1233, supported by Aa Fd): "Secundum iustitiam deletur, qui gratia subtracta ea operari permittitur, quibus eternam dampnationem meretur."

103. Ibid.: "Sic itaque peccata secundum prescientiam remittuntur, cum ab eterno gratia preparatur, qua uocatus iustificetur, iustificatus tandem eternaliter glorificetur. Secundum iustitiam uero peccata remittuntur, cum uel baptisma plena fide accipitur uel penitentia toto corde celebratur. Que remissio et ipsa secundum prescientiam non inconuenienter fieri dicitur."

were to die while reconciled to God, he would indeed be saved. Because he is not predestined to eternal life, however, he will necessarily die estranged from God and thus merit eternal punishment.[104]

Gratian denies the claim that those who are predestined to present justice but not to eternal life only appear to be good but are in fact always evil. Instead, he argues that, in the same way that those who are predestined to eternal life are really sinners before they are reconciled to God through baptism or penance, so too are the future damned really children of God for the time that they live pious and holy lives.[105]

Based on these considerations, Gratian argues that those who support the return of sins must hold that forgiven sins which later return are forgiven according to justice but not according to prescience.

> Therefore, they who assert that forgiven sins return must confess that sins are forgiven according to justice but not according to prescience, just as sins are imputed to the eternal damnation of those who will be saved according to justice [but] not according to prescience, because each [sin] will be returned to the punishment of those who turn from good to evil [but] no [sin] will be imputed to the punishment of those persevering in good to the very end.[106]

The return of sins, this dictum makes clear, is a doctrine restricted to the non-predestined. Because it concerns the future punishment

104. De pen. D.4 d.p.c.11 §1 (ed. Friedberg, 1233, supported by Aa Fd): "Vt enim ex premissa auctoritate Apostoli datur intelligi, due sunt preordinationes: una qua quisque preordinatur hic ad iustitiam et remissionem peccatorum percipiendam; altera qua aliquis predestinatur ad uitam eternam in futuro obtinendam. Harum effectus sunt presens iustificatio et futura glorificatio, que omnia in premissa auctoritate conuenienter distinguntur."

105. De pen. D.4 c.12 (really a *dictum Gratiani*, not a canon) (ed. Friedberg, 1234–35, supported by Aa Fd): "Sicut ergo isti, quamuis sint futuri filii Dei, tamen prius sunt filii diaboli; sic hi de quibus sermo habetur, quamuis recedendo a iustitia sint futuri filii perditionis eterne, tamen cum pie et fideliter uiuunt, uere sunt filii Dei et iusti et eterna beatitudine digni."

106. De pen. D.4 c.12 §2 (really a *dictum Gratiani*, not a canon) (ed. Friedberg, 1235, supported by Aa Fd): "Qui ergo peccata dimissa redire fatentur, secundum iustitiam non secundum prescientiam ea dimitti necesse est ut confiteantur, sicut saluandis peccata secundum iustitiam ad eternam dampnationem imputantur non secundum prescientiam, quia et illis a bono in malum deficientibus singula replicabuntur ad supplicium et his usque in finem in bono perseuerantibus nulla imputabuntur ad penam."

that God will mete out to sinners, the doctrine has no application to the predestined. While Gratian could develop further distinctions and subtleties to explain what would happen to one of the predestined who performed penance, then committed a grave sin, and then died before performing penance again, any such effort would be otiose because it deals with an impossible counterfactual. By definition the predestined will be saved. Hence they will not be punished eternally for their sins. As Gratian states at the end of the above-quoted dictum, "no [sin] will be imputed to the punishment of those persevering in good to the very end."

The Non-Return of Sins

After setting forth the position of those who support the return of sins, Gratian next quotes Gregory and Prosper in favor of the opposing view, that forgiven sins do not return (cc.13, 14). Immediately, however, he comes across a difficulty. Even though the beginning of c.14 seems to deny the return of sins (non-italicized portion), the end of c.14 appears to affirm it (italicized portion).[107] "He who recedes from Christ and finishes this life estranged from [Christ's] grace, where, if not into perdition, does he depart? Yet he does not fall back into that which was already forgiven, nor will he be damned on account of original sin; and *nevertheless he is afflicted by that death which was owed on account of what was forgiven him.*"[108] As Gratian notes, the return of sins is nothing other than having to suffer punishment owed for sins that were previously forgiven.[109] Canon 14 thus seems to con-

107. De pen. D.4 d.p.c.14 (ed. Friedberg, 1236, supported by Aa Fd): "Finis huius auctoritatis principio contraire uidetur."

108. De pen. D.4 c.14 (ed. Friedberg, 1235–36, supported by Aa Fd): "Qui recedit a Christo et alienus a gratia finit hanc uitam, quid nisi in perditionem uadit? Sed non in id quod remissum est recidit, nec originali peccato dampnabitur, *qui tamen ea morte afficitur que ei propter dimissa debebatur*" (emphasis added). The material source is Prosper of Aquitaine, *Pro Augustino Responsiones ad Capitula obiectionum gallorum calumniantium*, c. 2, PL 51, 153B.

109. De pen. D.4 d.p.c.14 (ed. Friedberg, 1236, supported by Aa Fd): "Neque enim aliud est peccata dimissa redire uel in originali peccato dampnari, quam penam peccato debitam post eiusdem remissionem excipere." Medieval commentators often misinterpret Gratian on this point, attributing to him the view that the guilt (*culpa*) and essence (*essentia*) of previously forgiven sins return, when someone later commits another mortal sin. Gratian's medieval commentators do not

tradict itself, since it simultaneously affirms that a Christian who dies in mortal sin is not damned on account of original sin and previously forgiven sins, and that such a Christian is punished for previously forgiven sins.

To resolve this difficulty, says Gratian, opponents of the return of sins interpret the last phrase in a different way, analogous to the interpretation adopted by Abelard.[110] According to this alternative interpretation, a penitent who later sins again displays ingratitude toward the mercy that God has shown in pardoning the penitent's previous sins, and the punishment due for this ingratitude is as great as the punishment due for the penitent's previously forgiven sins. The punishment that this sinner will suffer in hell is thus as great as what he would have had to suffer had he never confessed his sins in the first place. For this reason, one can say that forgiven sins return, when a penitent later commits another mortal sin, even though neither the guilt of, nor the punishment due for these previously forgiven sins actually returns.[111]

Gratian's Preferred Position

Gratian does not find the aforementioned explanation of c.14—or, in fact, any of the arguments against the return of sins—to be very convincing. He writes: "But the former position [*illa sententia*] appears more favorable because it is supported by more authorities and confirmed by more evident reason."[112] Consequently, Gratian

---

make clear what the difference is between the guilt and essence of a sin. See Landgraf, *Dogmengeschichte der Frühscholastik*, 4.1:223: "Wir haben gesehen, daß Gratian nach der Überzeugung seiner Erklärer einer Wiederkehr der sünden nach ihrer Wesenheit das Wort geredet haben soll [We have seen that, according to his commentators, Gratian is supposed to have advocated a return of sins according to their essence]."

110. See p. 97.

111. De pen. D.4 d.p.c.14 (ed. Friedberg, 1236, supported by Aa Fd): "Auctoritates uero sibi contrarias, assertores huius sententie ita determinant: peccata dimissa redire dicuntur, quia quisquis post acceptam remissionem ad uomitum redierit tanto grauius punietur, quanto magis benignitate Dei abusus singulorum remissioni accepte ingratus extitit."

112. De pen. D.4 d.p.c.14 (ed. Friedberg, 1236, supported by Aa Fd): "Verum illa sententia fauorabilior uidetur, quia pluribus roboratur auctoritatibus et euidentiori ratione firmatur." *Illa* here refers to the opinion that Gratian first di-

does not dwell any further on the view that forgiven sins do not return, but moves instead to reasons and authorities concerning the death and reviviscence of good works and the reviviscence of parental sin.

Reviviscence of Good Works and the Reviviscence and Return of Parental Sins

Modern scholars have sometimes used the phrase "reviviscence of sins" to describe the scholastic doctrine that forgiven sins return.[113] But Gratian throughout most of *De penitentia* speaks simply of the return of sins. Only toward the end of distinction 4 of *De penitentia* does he begin using the word "revive" (*reuiuiscunt*), which he applies almost exclusively to good works and parental sins. The concluding dictum is the sole place where Gratian appears to speak of the reviviscence—as opposed to just the return—of an individual's own forgiven sins.[114]

The last dictum of distinction 4 suggests that Gratian investigates the reviviscence of good works because it offers an argument *a contrario* for the return of sins. Just as good works "die" through sin, that is, they become worthless in God's sight, so too do they "revive" through penance, that is, they once again become sources of merit for an eternal reward.[115] Gratian quotes five biblical and patristic authorities (cc.15–19) which affirm that sinning makes one's previously committed good deeds invalid, before going on to provide authorities for the reviviscence of good works. Gratian refers to two authorities previously quoted in distinction 3 of *De penitentia* that to his mind show that just as one's previous good deeds become dead by sinning, so too do they revive through penance.[116] He ar-

---

scussed, i.e., the view that sins do return, as noted by Larson, *Master of Penance*, 194n55.

113. E.g., de Ghellinck, "La reviviscence des péchés pardonnés"; Michel, *Dictionnaire de théologie catholique*, s.v. "Reviviscence des péchés"; Landgraf, "Die frühscholastische Streitfrage."

114. De pen. D.4 d.p.c.24 (ed. Friedberg, 1238, supported by Aa Fd): "Sicut si ergo bona, que peccato moriuntur, per penitentiam reuiuiscunt ad premium: sic et mala que per penitentiam delentur reuiuiscunt ad supplicium."

115. Ibid.

116. De pen. D.4 d.p.c.19 (ed. Friedberg, 1236–37, supported by Aa Fd): "Dicens opera mortua priora bona significat, que per sequens peccatum erant mor-

gues that a text from the epistle to the Hebrews, included in distinction 4 of *De penitentia* as c.19, demonstrates the same.[117] And, finally, he quotes Ezekiel 18:21–22: "But if the wicked do penance for all his sins which he has committed, and keep all my commandments, and do judgment, and justice, living he shall live, and shall not die. I will not remember all his iniquities that he has done: in his justice which he has wrought, he shall live."[118]

After quoting this last biblical authority, Gratian turns his attention to the doctrine that God punishes sinners for the sins of their parents. Contemporary masters active in the schools of northern France treated this issue separately from the return of sins, as does Gratian himself in other sections of the *Decretum*.[119] At the end of distinction 4, however, Gratian also addresses the reviviscence of parental sin as part of his exposition of the return of sins, apparently because the reviviscence of parental sins functions analogously to the reviviscence of good works. Hosea 7:13–15 (c.20), Gratian points out, indicates that parental sins

---

tua, quia hii peccando priora bona irrita fecerunt. Hec, sicut peccando fiunt irrita, ita per penitentiam reuiuiscunt, et ad meritum eterne beatitudinis singula prodesse incipiunt, etiam illa que peccatis inueniuntur admixta. Vnde Augustinus: 'Pium est credere' etc. [De pen. D.3 c.45]. Et Ieronimus: 'Non est iniustus Deus' etc. [De pen. D.3 c.46]."

117. De pen. D.4 d.p.c.19 (ed. Friedberg, 1237, supported by Aa Fd): "Apostolus etiam scribens ad Hebreos, cum fidem et dilectionem et bona opera eorum breuiter commemorasset, horum omnium mercedem quam peccando amiserant post penitentiam a Domino eos recepturos ostendit."

118. Ibid.: "Porro, qui per prophetam dixit: 'Si auerterit se iustus a iustitia sua' etc. [Ezek 18:24], ipse per eundem prophetam premisit (promisit *Friedb.*) dicens: 'Si impius egerit penitentiam ab omnibus peccatis suis que operatus est, et custodierit uniuersa precepta mea, et fecerit iudicium et iustitiam, uita uiuet et non morietur. Omnium iniquitatum eius quas operatus est non recordabor. In iustitia sua, quam operatus est, uiuet' [Ezek 18:21–22]."

119. Cf. Larson, *Master of Penance*, 197: "At the beginning and end of D.4, when Gratian connected what I have here called the individual and intergenerational return of sins, he was in fact doing something original. The latter issue most often appeared separately and under some question like, 'Are sons punished for the sins of their fathers?' The question undoubtedly led to a discussion of original sin and then of actual sins of parents." As the following chapter will demonstrate, Larson's statement is not entirely accurate. Gratian was doing something different from the masters in the schools of northern France, but not from masters active in northern Italy. See pp. 164–65, 179, and 181. Gratian treats the punishment of parental sin in C.1 q.4 d.p.c.9 (ed. Friedberg, 420); C.1 q.4 d.p.c.11 (ed. Friedberg, 420–22); C.24 q.3. d.a.c.1 (ed. Friedberg, 987–88).

can revive.[120] But other authorities, namely Hosea 7:2 (c.21) and texts by Jerome found in the *Glossa ordinaria* to that passage of the Bible (cc.22, 23), seem to indicate that parental sins do not revive.[121] Gratian interprets those authorities (cc.21–23) which suggest that God does not punish sinners for the sins of their parents as applying only to those cleansed from original sin who imitate the sins of their parents. Such sons are not punished because their fathers sinned, but rather because they imitated their fathers' sins.[122] The reviviscence of parental sins is thus like the reviviscence of good works. Good works that die through sin will not benefit one just because the good works were performed, but rather because they revive through penance.[123]

Gratian goes on to indicate that this general principle applies to the authority of Augustine in c.1 and the authority of Gregory the Great in c.13.[124] Augustine in c.1 affirms that the iniquity of Judas's parents would not have applied to him had he remained true to his calling, but since he chose the iniquity of his old race, the iniquity of his parents returned to him.[125] Gregory in c.13 states that sins return because,

120. Commenting on Hos 7:13–15 = De pen. D.4 c.20, Gratian in De pen. D.4 d.p.c.20 (ed. Friedberg, 1237, supported by Aa Fd) writes: "Antiqua peccata parentum filiis improperat sermo diuinus, et propterea principes eorum in gladio casuros predicit."

121. *Glossa ordinaria* ad Hos 7:2 (ed. Rusch, 3:362); De pen. D.4 d.p.c.20 (ed. Friedberg, 1237, supported by Aa Fd): "Sed per eundem prophetam contra se Dominus facere ostendit dicens."

122. De pen. D.4 d.p.c.24 (ed. Friedberg, 1237, supported by Aa Fd): "Sed his auctoritatibus [cc.21–23] docentur filii ab originali peccato expiati non ideo puniendi quia patres peccauerunt, sed ideo peccata patrum in eos redire quia eorum culpam secuntur." On the history of this "imitation theory," see Artur Michael Landgraf, "Die Vererbung der Sünden der Eltern auf die Kinder nach der Lehre des 12. Jahrhunderts," *Gregorianum* 21 (1940): 203–47.

123. De pen. D.4 d.p.c.24 (ed. Friedberg, 1237, supported by Aa Fd): "Sic et bona que peccato moriuntur non proficient ad premium, quia facta sunt, sed quia per penitentiam reuiuiscunt."

124. Ibid.: "Tale est et illud Augustini in libro psalmorum intelligitur: 'Si Iudas teneret adoptionem etc. [c.1]. Sic etiam illud Gregorii in Moralibus [c.13] intelligitur: 'Quid est quod dicitur: reddis iniquitatem patrum' etc."

125. De pen. D.4 c.1 (ed. Friedberg, 1229, supported by Aa Fd): "Si Iudas teneret illud ad quod uocatus est, nullomodo ad eum uel sua preterita uel parentum iniquitas pertineret. Quia ergo non tenuit adoptionem in familia Dei, sed iniquitatem uetusti generis potius elegit, rediit iniquitas patrum eius in conspectu Domini, ut in eo etiam ipsa puniretur."

unless freed through the grace of baptism, a person carries both original sin and the sins of his parents, and that sins do not return because, when freed from original sin through baptism, he henceforth has only the guilt deriving from the sins that he himself has committed.[126]

Interpreting Gregory's remarks, Gratian goes on to state in d.p.c.24: "For the iniquity of [one's] fathers return to those who are therefore punished because they derived the bitterness of sin in [their] root. [But the iniquity of one's fathers] is said not to return to those in whom, by the merits of one's own iniquity, the sins of [one's] father revive."[127] The first sentence indicates that, following Gregory, Gratian viewed punishment for original sin as a sort of return of parental sins. The second sentence is more problematic as it appears to affirm that sins do not return to those in whom, as a result of one's own iniquity, the sins of one's father revive, whereas the beginning of d.p.c.24 states that parental sins return to those who imitate the sins of their fathers. The solution would seem to lie in Gratian's exact phrasing: the iniquity of one's fathers "is said not to return" by Gregory in c.13 when "by the merits of one's own iniquity, the sins of [one's] father revive." But, as the parental sins revive, Gratian probably thinks that these sins also really do return, which is what he states at the beginning of d.p.c.24 as well.

Gratian concludes distinction 4 by relating the reviviscence of good works back to the return of sins, which he now refers to as the reviviscence of sins. "Just as good works die through sin and revive with regards to reward through penance," he states, "so too do evil works that are erased through penance revive with regards to punishment."[128]

126. De pen. D.4 c.13 (ed. Friedberg, 1235, supported by Aa Fd): "Quid est quod dicitur: 'qui reddis iniquitatem filiis ac nepotibus'? Peccatum scilicet originale a parentibus trahimus et nisi per gratiam baptismi soluamur, etiam parentum culpam portamus, quia unum cum illis sumus. Reddet iniquitatem patrum in filiis, dum pro culpa parentis ex originali peccato anima polluitur prolis. Et rursus non reddet iniquitatem patrum in filiis, quia cum ab originali culpa per baptismum liberamur, non iam parentum culpas, sed quas ipsi committimus habemus."

127. De pen. D.4 d.p.c.24 (ed. Friedberg, 1237–38, supported by Aa Fd): "Illis namque parentum iniquitas redditur, qui propterea puniuntur, quia in radice traxerunt amaritudinem peccati. Illis autem non reddi dicitur in quibus merito sue iniquitatis (non *add. Friedb.*) reuiuiscunt peccata parentis."

128. De pen. D.4 d.p.c.24 (ed. Friedberg, 1238, supported by Aa Fd): "Sicut

Conclusion

Gratian approaches penitential theology in the same way as he approaches canon law: through a study of the authorities *pro* and *contra*. In contrast to such contemporary theologians as Abelard and Hugh, who generally proceed from philosophical and theological first principles, Gratian relies more on textual analysis to develop and elaborate his views. *De penitentia* adduces numerous texts for and against the various theses considered, only coming to a conclusion after careful and at times painstakingly detailed textual analyses. For this reason, modern scholars have not always fully understood what he argues or appreciated the nuances of his doctrine.

Contrary to the claims of several modern scholars, Gratian wanted to know whether sinners had to confess their sins to a priest to obtain the remission of sins, not just whether contrition will remit sin prior to confession. But Gratian was unsure what the correct answer was and left the ultimate choice to his reader. Nevertheless, he seems to have felt strongly enough about the merits of the minority view, that confession is not necessary, to do something common for earlier canonists, but atypical for himself—to make a substantive alteration to the text of an authority.

In contrast to his indecisiveness on the necessity of confession, Gratian was sure that charity could be lost, that penance could be repeated, and that forgiven sins return. Gratian's doctrinal positions here were similar to those of contemporary masters active in the schools of northern France, but the way in which Gratian arrived at two of these positions differed from theirs in several respects. Unlike contemporary French masters, Gratian explicitly links the repeatability of penance to the nature of true penance and the question whether a person can perform penance for just one of many sins. In addition, he treats the reviviscence of parental sin in connection with the return of sins. Chapter 5 explores the significance of these differences, together with other links between Gratian and anonymous theological works of apparently Italian origin, in greater detail.

---

ergo bona, que peccato moriuntur, per penitentiam reuiuiscunt ad premium: sic et mala que per penitentiam delentur reuiuiscunt ad supplicium."

5

Critiquing and Correcting the Scholastics

Gratian's decision to treat penitential theology has long puzzled modern scholars. Why would a jurist, even an ecclesiastical jurist, decide to include a treatise on this subject (*De penitentia*) in a textbook on canon law (the *Decretum*)? Most modern scholars writing before 1996, when the discovery of the first-recension *Decretum* was announced, erroneously believed *De penitentia*—or at the very least its more theological core, distinctions 2–4—to be a later addition possibly compiled by a different author. As a result, they generally argued that Gratian did not have any particular interest in penitential theology.[1] Since the discovery that *De penitentia* does indeed belong to the original form of Gratian's textbook, the first recension of the *Decretum*, the few scholars who have addressed this issue have tended to suggest that Gratian's interest in penitential theology was pedagogical. Atria Larson, for instance, writes that Gratian "recognized areas of inquiry which needed further integration. Just as he appears to have decided that his students needed a greater introduction to the idea of 'law' and so wrote the *Tractatus de legibus*, so he appears to have realized the lack of a solid and definitive treatment of penance

1. See, e.g., Munier, *Les sources patristiques*, 135–36; Wojtyła, "Le traité 'De penitencia,'" 357–90; Hödl, *Die Geschichte*, 163–65; Rambaud, "Le legs," 82–90; Landau, "Gratian und die Sententiae Magistri A.," 311–26, reprinted in Landau, *Kanones und Dekretalen*, 161*–76*, with retractations at 474*–75*.

and so wrote the *Tractatus de penitentia*."[2] Similarly, Joseph Goering has proposed that, in writing on penitential theology, Gratian and his contemporaries "were attempting to introduce a long and rich tradition to students who wanted to master it. Instead of taking sides in a dispute and proposing their own unique solutions, the masters in the schools regularly used disputes to illustrate a common, if complicated, view of penance and give students the tools they needed if they were to engage the entire tradition of which they were the inheritors."[3]

This chapter extends and challenges such explanations for the composition of *De penitentia*. In writing on penitential theology, this chapter proposes, Gratian did indeed have pedagogical aims. His main goal, however, was not to provide "a solid and definitive treatment of penance," as Larson suggests, nor, with the possible exception of distinction 1, to "introduce a long and rich tradition to students who wanted to master it," as Goering argues. Rather, Gratian's aim in writing *De penitentia* was to critique and correct several scholastic ideas about penance that were prevalent or becoming prevalent in his day.

As noted in chapters 3 and 4, *De penitentia* does not provide a comprehensive treatment of penance, but instead focuses on controversial issues. In including topics, Gratian was selective and idiosyncratic, choosing to deal with questions that earlier theologians did not treat in connection with penance, such as whether charity can be lost, and excluding others that they did frequently examine when treating penance, such as the nature and number of the priestly keys. The reason, this chapter will attempt to show, can be found in Gratian's sources and theological milieu. The questions comprising the core of *De penitentia*, distinctions 2–4, were the subject of much debate in the twelfth century, and in examining these problems a significant number of theologians attacked and rejected what Gratian

2. Larson, "Evolution," 118. Larson's article should be used with caution, since much of her interpretation rests and falls with the erroneous hypothesis of Carlos Larrainzar that Sg contains the earliest preserved version of the *Decretum*. On Sg, see chapter 1, pp. 27–33.

3. Joseph Goering, "The Scholastic Turn (1100–1500): Penitential Theology and Law in the Schools," in *A New History of Penance*, ed. Abigail Firey (Leiden: Brill, 2008), 219–37, at 220.

in *De penitentia* would later come to argue was true and Catholic doctrine. Gratian's theological opponents were not fictitious *quidam* and *alii*, but rather anonymous masters belonging at least in part to the school of Laon and whose views have been preserved in numerous manuscripts and sentence collections. It is unclear whether Gratian knew any of these theologians personally. But there is evidence that he may have known and used their writings, and he certainly knew the authorities and arguments that they adduced in support of their views. What these were and how Gratian went about critiquing and correcting them will be the focus of the pages that follow.

The Tract *De penitentia* and Gratian's Theological Sources

For the most part, Gratian's formal sources for *De penitentia* differ from the ones he used in the rest of the *Decretum*. Gratian took almost all of the *Decretum*'s canons from just five formal sources: the canonical collection of Anselm of Lucca, the *Tripartita*, the *Panormia*, the *Polycarpus*, and the 3L. But he also made relatively frequent use throughout of the *Glossa ordinaria* to the Bible. Even when Gratian does not quote this work, or rather collection of works, directly, his exegesis of biblical passages often reflects knowledge of its contents. In addition to or sometimes instead of these six normal formal sources, Gratian occasionally drew on other works, particularly for sections of the *Decretum* devoted to more specialized topics like penance.[4]

For *De penitentia*, the first recension draws predominantly on theological works used rarely or not at all in the rest of the *Decretum*. As already mentioned, the Pseudo-Augustinian *De vera et falsa penitentia* was an important source, particularly in distinctions 5–7.[5] For distinctions 2–4, on the other hand, Gratian drew heavily on a florilegium of patristic texts on penance that circulated together with a number of theological and canonistic compilations.[6] The most complete of these

4. See the discussion of Gratian's sources in chapter 1, pp. 20–24, and of the *Glossa ordinaria* to the Bible in chapter 2, pp. 59–65.

5. See pp. 101–2; Wei, "A Reconsideration of St. Gall," 148.

6. Portions of this florilegium are preserved in Florence, Biblioteca Medi-

is found together with the *Sententiae magistri A.* in F (= Florence, Bibl. Medicea Laurenziana, Plut. V. sin 7), which I will refer to on occasion in the pages that follow. In addition, Gratian also appears to have made extensive use of two anonymous theological treatises: *Ut autem hoc evidenter*, which circulated together with the anonymous sentence collection *Deus itaque summe* as its tract on charity; and *Baptizato homine*, which likewise circulated together with *Deus itaque summe* as its tract on penance.[7] Both treatises are remarkably similar to *De penitentia*, and it is clear that these texts are related literarily. However, philological, doctrinal, and structural features rule out the possibility that *Ut autem hoc evidenter* and *Baptizato homine* depend on *De penitentia*. Instead, *De penitentia* must draw on these texts directly or these works must depend on one or more shared, treatise-like sources. I make this qualification ("treatise-like") because these works do draw on at least one common florilegium, the one preserved in the F manuscript. As with all anonymous texts, it is impossible to rule out completely the possibility that the similarities between *Ut autem hoc evidenter* and *Baptizato homine*, on the one hand, and *De penitentia*, on the other, stem solely from unknown common sources. However, no textual or doctrinal features require postulating such sources, and both treatises appear to have been popular enough in Gratian's Italy for him to have known these texts themselves. Both treatises survive in a sizeable number of manuscripts from the general region: seven extant manuscripts preserve *Ut autem hoc evidenter* and ten preserve *Baptizato homine*.[8] Approximately half of these manuscripts are of Italian origin

---

cea Laurenziana, Plut. V. sin 7, fols. 70ra–72va and 78rb–82rb; Zurich, Zentralbibliothek, C 111 (390), fols. 98va–101rb and 103vb–104ra; Mantua, Biblioteca Comunale 266 (C.I.4), fols. 33v–34v; *Sententiae Sidonis* 9.2.34–56 (Vat. lat. 1345); and *Collection in Five Books* 2.25.1–13 (Vat. lat. 1348).

7. For a description, analysis, and edition, see Wei, "A Twelfth-Century Treatise," 1–50. For an analysis of the relationship between *Ut autem hoc evidenter* and Gratian, see Wei, "Gratian and the School of Laon," 279–322, and Wei, "*Deus non habet initium uel terminum*," 1–118. On *Baptizato homine*, see Wei, "Penitential Theology in Gratian's *Decretum*," 78–100; Wei, "*Deus non habet.*"

8. For the manuscripts containing *Ut autem hoc evidenter*, see Wei, "A Twelfth-Century Treatise," 2–3; for the manuscripts containing *Baptizato homine*, see Wei, "Penitential Theology," 89, and Rome, Biblioteca Vallicelliana, Ms. C.64, fols. 13v–21r. A description of the Vallicelliana manuscript can be found in George Polycarpus Götz, ed., *Liber Quare*, CCCM 60 (Turnhout: Brepols, 1983), C.

or provenance, while most of the remaining manuscripts are of south German or Austrian origin or provenance.

Ut autem hoc evidenter and *Baptizato homine* have generally been attributed to or associated with the school of Anselm of Laon.[9] Both treatises contain parallels with other works of this school, and neither betrays much, or perhaps even any, knowledge of the doctrines of somewhat later scholastic theologians active in northern France, such as Peter Abelard and Hugh of St. Victor. The same can be said of Gratian's *Decretum*. It has often been claimed that Gratian knew the works of Abelard and/or Hugh, and even that he learned the scholastic method for reconciling contradictory authorities from the former.[10] But in fact there is little to no evidence connecting Gratian with either theologian. The only probable use of Abelard's *Sic et non* occurs in the tract *De consecratione*, which was added only in the second recension and almost certainly by a person other than the author of the first recension.[11] In contrast, the *Decretum* exhibits no clear signs of having borrowed material from any of Hugh's works.[12]

9. On the relationship between *Ut autem hoc evidenter*, which is simply the tract on charity of *Deus itaque summe*, and the school of Laon, see Giraud, *Per verba magistri*, 358–63; Wei, "A Twelfth-Century Treatise," 25–30. The traditional association of *Baptizato homine* with the school of Laon stems from its presence as the tract on charity of *Deus itaque summe*. For the first such association, see Artur Michael Landgraf, "Werke aus dem Bereich der Summa Sententiarum und Anselms von Laon," *Divus Thomas* 14 (1936): 209–16, at 213–14, who examined the treatise as found in the perhaps chronologically latest manuscript, the Fulda manuscript. See also Anciaux, *La théologie*, 293–95, who examines the portion of the treatise that was incorporated into the *Sententiae Sidonis*.

10. On Gratian's supposed familiarity with Abelard, see Heinrich Denifle, "Die Sentenzen Abaelards und die Bearbeitungen seiner Theologia vor Mitte des 12. Jhs.," *Archiv für Literatur- und Kirchengeschichte des Mittelalters* 1 (1885): 402–624, at 619–20; Friedrich Thaner, *Abälard und das canonische Recht: Die Persönlichkeit in der Eheschliessung; Zwei Festreden* (Graz: Leuschner and Lubensky, 1900), 5–29; Kuttner, "Zur Frage," 243–68; Ghellinck, *Le mouvement théologique du XIIe siècle*, esp. 207 and 494–95; Luscombe, *The School of Peter Abelard*, 214–23; Meyer, *Die Distinktionstechnik*, 174–77. On his alleged familiarity with Hugh, see Kuttner, "Zur Frage," 268; Weigand, *Die Naturrechtslehre*, 133; Giuseppe Mazzanti, "Graziano e Rolando Bandinelli," *Studi di storia del diritto* 2 (1999): 79–103; Anders Winroth, "Neither Slave nor Free: Theology and Law in Gratian's Thoughts on the Definition of Marriage and Unfree Persons," in *Medieval Church Law*, ed. Müller and Sommar, 97–109, at 103–5.

11. On the use of the *Sic et non* in *De consecratione*, see chapter 1, p. 23.

12. The one parallel identified by Winroth, "Neither Slave nor Free," 103–5, could just as well have been due to a common source.

Chapter 4 noted a possible point of contact between *Ut autem hoc evidenter*, Gratian, and a doctrine perhaps erroneously attributed to Gilbert of Poitiers by Bernard of Clairvaux. Yet, on the whole, Gratian appears to have been familiar only with works associated with the school of Laon.[13]

Master Anselm of Laon was the most well-known and respected teacher of theology in the late eleventh and early twelfth centuries.[14] He taught many students throughout his long career and continued to claim admirers even after his death. These intellectual heirs comprised a school in the sense that they regarded Anselm as an authority and attempted to do theology in the tradition that he established, but not in the sense that they all subscribed to the same doctrinal positions or even to the same doctrinal positions that Anselm did. The school of Laon was not monolithic. Despite the close literary relationship between the school's extant works, there was much diversity and even at times debate and controversy.[15]

The following sections will explore some of these doctrinal conflicts as they relate to penance and how they appear to have influenced Gratian's thought. As will be seen, a number of theologians belonging to the school of Laon defend doctrinal positions that Gratian rejects in distinctions 2–4 of *De penitentia*.

Members of the school of Laon and those who can be affiliated only more loosely with the school argue that those who possess charity can sin without losing it, that only the predestined can possess charity, that charity cannot be lost, that people can perform penance for just one of many sins, and that forgiven sins do not return when one later commits another sin, and they do so using many of the same texts and arguments as Gratian. Particularly interesting is the relationship between *Ut autem hoc evidenter* and *Baptizato homine*, on the one hand, and Gratian, on the other. Despite Gratian's probable dependence on the former two works, both they and Gratian defend significantly different, sometimes diametrically opposed doctri-

13. Wei, "Gratian and the School of Laon," esp. 316–21; Atria A. Larson, "The Influence of the School of Laon on Gratian: The Usage of the *Glossa ordinaria* and the Anselmian *Sententiae* in *De penitentia* (*Decretum* C.33 Q.3)," *Mediaeval Studies* 72 (2010): 197–244; Larson, *Master of Penance*.

14. See chapter 2, p. 60.

15. See Giraud, *Per verba magistri*, 339–436.

nal positions. Earlier scholars have often attempted to assign Gratian to one or another theological school based on his alleged knowledge of their texts and ideas. Yet in *De penitentia*, the one place where actual evidence for his theological formal sources aside from the *Glossa ordinaria* to the Bible exists, textual dependence and doctrinal independence go hand in hand. With the exception of the *Glossa ordinaria*, which was mainly a reference work, it is unclear if Gratian knew Anselm's doctrinal opinions and writings, much less whether he held Anselm in esteem or considered himself to be one of Anselm's intellectual heirs.[16] But it is clear that Gratian disagreed with aspects of the Anselmian theological tradition, and it seems likely that he composed the core of *De penitentia* to address these differences. However much Gratian may have owed to the Laon tradition in general, he did not accept that tradition wholesale and uncritically. Modern scholars have rarely rated Gratian's theological acumen very highly, and indeed his theology often lacks the philosophical sophistication and theological vision of his French compeers. But Gratian was nevertheless a creative theologian, one with strong convictions and enough self-confidence and independence to challenge what he regarded as mistakes in the teachings of his contemporaries.

The Possession of Charity

The interrelated theses that charity cannot be lost, the reprobate cannot possess charity, and those who possess charity can sin criminally were fairly popular among members of the school of Laon. Anselm himself may have rejected this constellation of ideas.[17] But

16. Larson, "The Influence of the School of Laon on Gratian," and *Master of Penance*, 271–97, argues that Gratian had direct knowledge of Anselm's *sententiae* and teachings. But what the evidence she adduces demonstrates is simply that Gratian was familiar with the *Glossa ordinaria*, which was just a reference work, and with works belonging to or associated with the school of Laon.

17. Only one known *sententia* attributed to Anselm deals with this subject, and in this case there are reasons to doubt the attribution, which is found in only one of the three manuscripts of the *Liber Pancrisis*. See Robert Wielockx, "La sentence *de caritate* et la discussion scolastique sur l'amour," *Ephemerides Theologicae Lovanienses* 58 (1982): 50–86, 334–56 and 59 (1983): 26–45. The text of the *sen-*

many of his followers found these theses compelling and sought to show how they accorded with scripture, the Fathers, and reason.[18] One of the most influential and widely diffused works belonging to the school of Laon, *Principium et causa*, which was sometimes attributed to Anselm, seems to have been most responsible for popularizing these theses.[19] This sentence collection argues that just as there is an unforgivable sin, the incurring of which rules out the possibility of salvation, so too is there a supreme virtue, charity, which ensures that one will not fall irreparably and be damned. Only the predestined can possess charity. The reprobate cannot, for if they could, it would be impossible for them to fall irreparably and be damned. The most that the reprobate can possess is a purely natural form of affection, which, though good, does not help one towards salvation.[20]

A number of sentence collections dependent on *Principium et causa*, such as *De conditione angelica et humana*, the *Sententiae Atrebatenses*, and *Prima rerum origo*, demonstrate that other masters found these arguments convincing.[21] So too do works textually independent of

tentia is edited by Wielockx at 82.19–21: "Secundus vero status caritatis perfectior est, in quo etiam perseveranti salus acquiritur; sed a quibusdam ad tempus habetur, et postea discedit ab eis et damnantur." It is also printed as Anselm, *Sententiae* no. 73, ed. Lottin, *Psychologie et morale*, 64.20–22.

18. See Landgraf, *Dogmengeschichte der Frühscholastik*, 1.2:139–45.

19. On this work, see Giraud, "Le recueil de sentences de l'école de Laon *Principium et causa*"; Giraud, *Per verba magistri*, 367–78.

20. *Principium et causa*, ed. Franz Bliemetzrieder, *Anselms von Laon Systematische Sentenzen*, Beiträge zur Geschichte der Philosophie des Mittelalters [hereafter "BGPM"] 18.2–3 (Münster i. W.: Aschendorff, 1919), 82–83.

21. *De conditione angelica et humana*, ed. Yves Lefèvre, "Le *De conditione angelica et humana* et les *Sententie Anselmi*," *AHDLMA* 34 (1959): 249–75, at 274–75; on its connection to the school of Laon, see Giraud, *Per verba magistri*, 354–58. *Sententiae Atrebatenses*, ed. Lottin, *Psychologie et morale*, 420.137–60; on its connection to the school of Laon, see Giraud, *Per verba magistri*, 341–48. *Prima rerum origo*, Munich, Bayerische Staatsbibliothek, Clm 2598, fols. 54r–v (author's transcription): "Queritur si postquam aliquis semel suscipit caritatem, amittat eam uel dampnetur. Quod quibusdam uidetur, quia ad (*male pro* a) dampnandis interdum fueri<n>t opera caritatis. Alii autem hoc negantes has adducunt auctoritates. Si quis edificauerit domum suam supra firmam petram ueniant flumina et uenti et non possunt eam dimouere. Et iterum et Dauid. Cum ceciderit non collidetur q<uia> D<ominus> s<upponit> m<anum> s<uam>. Et Augustinus tractans de tunica Domini dicit per caritatem fieri unitatem ecclesie in qua qui maneat sit securus, cum nemo eum possit superare. Idem Augustinus testatur caritatem esse unic-

Principium et causa, such as *Ut autem hoc evidenter*. This latter treatise or a common source appears to have provided Gratian with over half of distinction 2 (and part of distinction 3) of *De penitentia*.[22] Both *De penitentia* and *Ut autem hoc evidenter* quote many of the same authorities, often in the same order and in the same abbreviated form, and they also share many dicta. Yet despite this extensive overlap, distinction 2 of *De penitentia* and *Ut autem hoc evidenter* defend completely different theological positions.

Like *Principium et causa* and the various works dependent on it, *Ut autem hoc evidenter* endorses the view that charity can never be lost, only the predestined can possess charity, and those who possess charity can sin without losing it. The treatise considers three positions concerning charity: (1) charity cannot be lost, and those who possess it are unable to commit mortal sins; (2) charity cannot be lost, but those who possess it are able to commit mortal sins; and (3) charity can be lost. The treatise never explicitly states which position the author favored, but the differential treatment of the objections to each position reveals that it was the second position. The treatise makes no attempt to refute the numerous objections to the first position that it

um fontem de quo non communicet alienus cum omnibus aliis sacramentis ecclesie cunctisque sancti Spiritus donis boni et mali pariter participare possint.... Hic queritur si illi qui habent caritatem crimen possint committere. Quod posse fieri patet in Petro dicente ex dilectione: Si o<portuerit> m<e> m<ori> t<ecum> etc. Qui postea negando Christum peccauit. Patet etiam in Dauid qui post unctionem Goliam uincens adulterium et homicidium commisit. Videntur ergo contraria in his duobus simul fuisse, sed attende quod uirtus per habitum mentis bene constitute difficile mobilem fundata uicium per habitum secum non patitur. Vnde dici potest quod in Petro et Dauid non caritatis contrarium sed quedam iniquitatis exercitio quasi per transitum eos ad malum illexit sopita caritate cum econuerso opus caritatis sepius fiat a malis, nec tamen ideo sunt boni sicut pallens, si quandoque rubet, pallex tamen dicitur. Sed opponitur de his uerbis Augustinus: Vbi est caritas mala opera esse non possunt, que separant a regno Dei. Ergo karitas non fuit in Dauid qui fecit homicidium. Sed hic nulla contrarietas inuenitur, si uerba auctoritatis diligenter inspiciuntur. Nam homicidium tam cita penitentia deletum non separauit Dauid a regno Dei." On *Prima rerum orgio,* see Heinrich Weisweiler, *Das Schrifttum der Schule Anselms von Laon und Wilhelms von Champeaux in deutschen Bibliotheken,* BGPTM 33.1–2 (Münster i. W.: Aschendorff, 1936); specific page references are listed in the index on 406.

22. Wei, "Gratian and the School of Laon"; Wei, "A Twelfth-Century Treatise," 20–23.

raises. And while it makes one attempt to refute the objections to the third position, it characterizes the solution as the *solutio* of the *auctores huius sententie*. Only the objections to the second position receive detailed consideration, and *Ut autem hoc evidenter* provides an unqualified *solutio* to every single one.[23]

In contrast to the aforementioned works from the school of Laon, distinction 2 of *De penitentia* defends the third position from *Ut autem hoc evidenter*, that charity can be lost and that even the reprobate can possess charity. Like his formal source, Gratian begins his exposition by setting forth the authorities and arguments in favor of *Ut autem hoc evidenter*'s first position. But unlike his formal source, Gratian largely sidesteps the second position discussed in that treatise. He is able to adopt this approach because he refutes the distinguishing feature of the second position, its claim that those who possess charity can sin without losing it, at the very outset. Because Pseudo-Augustine in c.13 expressly affirms the incompatibility of charity and sin,[24] it is, Gratian notes, impossible for a person to possess charity and sin without losing possession of it.[25]

Almost all Gratian's arguments and texts against the permanence of charity appear in *Ut autem hoc evidenter*.[26] Many of the borrowings serve the same purpose in both contexts. In presenting its first position, for instance, *Ut autem hoc evidenter* raises numerous objections to the related propositions that those who possess charity cannot sin and that charity cannot be lost. Gratian quotes these same authorities and uses them to the same end.[27] But on other occasions Gratian

23. I base this summary on the more detailed analysis in Wei, "A Twelfth-Century Treatise," 13–16.

24. De pen. D.2 c.13 (ed. Friedberg, 1194, supported by Aa Fd): "Quia radix omnium malorum est cupiditas, et radix omnium bonorum est caritas, et simul ambe esse non possunt, nisi una radicitus euulsa fuerit, alia plantari non potest. Sine causa aliquis conatur ramos incidere, si radicem non contendit euellere." The material source is Pseudo-Augustine, *Sermones supposititios* 270.1, PL 39, 2248.

25. De pen. D.2 d.p.c.13, quoted in chapter 4, p. 121n47.

26. For a list of all the parallels, see Wei, "A Twelfth-Century Treatise," 20. There is one mistake in the table. For De pen. D.2 d.p.c.24–d.p.c.29, the corresponding lines should read 108–30.

27. De pen. D.2 d.p.c.24–d.p.c.29 = *Ut autem hoc evidenter*, ed. Wei, 36.108–

uses material found in *Ut autem hoc evidenter* to very different purposes. In defending the second position, for instance, *Ut autem hoc evidenter* quotes a long series of texts showing that there are different levels of charity. Authorities that affirm the incompatibility of charity and sin, the treatise argues, refer to perfect charity. Those who possess imperfect charity can sin without losing it.[28] Gratian quotes these same texts but uses them to show that authorities affirming the permanence of charity refer to perfect charity and that those who possess imperfect charity can lose it.[29] In Gratian's hands, then, this material becomes an argument against the permanence of charity rather than serving as further support for that position.

Likewise in defending the second position, *Ut autem hoc evidenter* considers two authorities that appear to support the view that the reprobate can possess charity: "Moreover, Augustine. 'It must be wondered why God gives faith operating through love to certain sons of perdition' etc. Furthermore: 'Their faith which operates through love either does not fail or, if it fails, is restored' etc."[30] And: "Augustine. 'If they had remained in that which they had accepted, they would be saved.'"[31] Like *Principium et causa, Ut autem hoc evidenter* explains away both authorities by asserting the existence of different types of love of God. The first authority, the treatise claims, fails to show that the reprobate can possess charity since not all love of God qualifies as charity.[32] The second authority similarly fails in this regard, since it refers

---

38.130; De pen. D.2 cc.31–32 = *Ut autem hoc evidenter*, ed. Wei, 33.45–34.57; De pen. D.2 c.33–d.p.c.39 = *Ut autem hoc evidenter*, ed. Wei, 34.61–36.98; De pen. D.2 c.41–d.p.c.41 = *Ut autem hoc evidenter*, ed. Wei, 38.138–39.154.

28. *Ut autem hoc evidenter*, ed. Wei, 45.278–46.300.

29. De pen. D.2 d.p.c.14 §1, quoted in chapter 4, p. 122n51.

30. *Ut autem hoc evidenter*, ed. Wei, 46.311–47.313: "*Amplius Augustinus*. 'Mirandum est quare deus det fidem operantem per dilectionem quibusdam filiis perditionis' etc. *Iterum*. 'Eorum fides que per dilectionem operatur, aut non deficit, aut si deficit reparatur' etc." The material source appears to be Augustine, *De correptione et gratia* 8.18, ed. Georges Folliet, CSEL 92 (Vienna: Verlag der österreichischen Akademie der Wissenschaften, 2000), 239.1–3.

31. *Ut autem hoc evidenter*, ed. Wei, 47.313–14: "Sed de eisdem adhuc opponitur *secundum Augustinum* 'Si in eo permansissent quod acceperant, salui essent.'" The material source is Augustine, *De correptione et gratia* 7.16, ed. Folliet, CSEL 92, 236.4–6.

32. *Ut autem hoc evidenter*, ed. Wei, 47.314–15: "*Solutio*. Non omnis dilectio dei

not to charity, but rather to a lesser form of love often misleadingly called inchoate charity. According to the treatise, inchoate charity is a type of affect that precedes charity, whether imperfect or perfect, and is found even in the reprobate. In contrast to true charity, which is an unchanging habit of the mind (*habitus animi*) and a movement of the mind (*motus animi*) towards loving oneself, one's neighbor, and God because of God, inchoate charity varies frequently.[33]

Gratian rejects this sort of reasoning in d.p.c.43, which instead presumes the identity of love of God and charity. Quoting the first of the aforementioned authorities plus two related authorities found at the end of *Ut autem hoc evidenter*, Gratian argues that at least some of the reprobate do indeed possess charity at some point in their lives but lose it before they die.[34] Gratian admits, of course, that some authorities really do affirm the fictitiousness of the love possessed by some reprobates. But he argues that these texts refer to hypocrites in particular, not to any and all of the reprobate in general.[35] As a result, there are no good reasons for affirming that none of the reprobate can possess charity. Gratian affirms that they can, but that not all of them in fact do at some point in their lives.

---

caritas est, quia *iuxta Augustinum* diligitur deus et ab infidelibus secundum illud: 'Confitebitur tibi cum benefeceris ei.'"

33. Ibid., 47.323–48.334: "*Solutio*. Si in illa dilectione permansissent, innata esset caritas qua saluarentur. Est enim quidam affectus qui inchoata caritas solet appellari, qui precedit caritatem, qui etiam in reprobis est et frequenter uariatur, cum quo etiam mali plerumque multa bona faciunt. Caritas autem est habitus animi immobilis, et est caritas quidam motus animi ad se et proximum et deum diligendum propter ipsum deum. Dicitur etiam sic. Caritas est dilectio dei et proximi. Dilectio autem dei sine dilectione proximi non ualet, et econuerso. Frequenter tamen in scripturis ponitur alterum pro utroque. Diligere autem deum et proximum est actus quidam sine quo caritas est multotiens, qui sic solet ostendi. Homo semper est rationalis, non autem semper rationatur. Immo quandoque contingit contrarius actus, ut insanire. Et ideo non conceditur quod omnis qui habet caritatem diligat uel econuerso."

34. The two related authorities are: *Ut autem hoc evidenter*, ed. Wei, 49.357 = De pen. D.2 d.p.c.42 (ed. Friedberg, 1207); *Ut autem hoc evidenter*, ed. Wei, 49.358 = De pen. D.2 c.43 (ed. Friedberg, 1207).

35. De pen. D.2 d.p.c.43 §1 (ed. Friedberg, 1207, supported by Aa Fd): "Illud autem Gregorii, 'qui seduci quandoque non reuersuri possunt' etc. non de omnibus generaliter reprobis, sed de ypocritis specialiter intelligendum est. Quod ex uerbis eiusdem euidenter datur intelligi."

Gratian provides one other reason for rejecting the proposition that the reprobate cannot possess charity: doing so would make God the cause of sin. The devil, Gratian points out, was created in the truth.

But how could he be said to be created in the truth if it is shown that he was created without love of his creator? Or how is he asserted to be created good by God, if he accepted nothing of divine love in his creation? How did he exist without vice before the movement of pride, if he by no means loved his own creator? Or how is he said to have been created equal to or more excellent than all other creatures if he was made devoid of love for Him when others were created in love of God? Whence did this difference between good and bad angels proceed? If from the creator, then God, who metes out punishment before sin is committed or who punishes what he infused in creating, appears unjust. But if not from the creator and not from parents, there remains that the vice of pride proceeded into the angelic nature from free will. Therefore [the angelic nature] was created good, which by its own vice was changed from good to evil. But how could [the angelic nature] be good, if it completely lacked love? For the angel was not made similar to us, whom infirmity oppresses up until a certain age, before which time neither virtue nor vice occupies any place in us. Therefore [the devil] received love in his creation.[36]

For Gratian, then, the thesis that charity can never be lost is to be rejected not only because it contradicts everyday experience, but also because it makes God the cause of sin. If charity can never be lost, then God is responsible for the evil of the devil and fallen angels, as well as of the reprobate. God would never impart to the reprobate the forgiveness of sins in baptism, nor ever give them a chance to be good and freely choose evil.

36. De pen. D.2 d.p.c.44 §1 (ed. Friedberg, 1208–9, supported by Aa Fd): "Aut quomodo bonus a Deo conditus asseritur, si nichil diuine dilectionis in sui creatione accepit? Quomodo ante superbie motum sine uicio extitit, si conditorem suum nullatenus dilexit? Aut quomodo par, siue excellentior ceteris creatus dicitur, si, nonnullis eorum in Dei amore conditis, hic ab eius dilectione uacuus factus est? Vnde autem hec distantia (differentia *Friedb.*) inter bonos et malos angelos processit? Si ex creante, iniustus uidetur Deus, qui ante peccatum infert penam, uel qui hoc punit, quod creando infudit. Si autem non ex creante, cum non ex traduce, restat, ut ex proprie libertatis arbitrio uitium superbie in angelicam naturam processerit. Bona ergo condita est, que suo uitio a bono in malum commutata est. Sed quomodo bona esse potuit, si dilectione penitus caruit? Neque enim angelus nobis similis factus est, quos usque ad certum tempus etatis infirmitas grauat, ut neque uirtus, neque uitium ullum locum in nobis optineat. Accepit ergo dilectionem in sui creatione."

The Repeatability of Penance and Performing Penance for Just One of Many Sins

Like the permanence of charity, the repeatability of penance also stimulated much debate in the early twelfth century. While the earliest quasi-systematic sentence collections belonging to the school of Laon do not, for the most part, deal with penance, a variety of shorter treatises, some of which appear to have been composed by theologians connected with Laon, do. Two of these works, which I shall refer to as *Augustinus in libro vite* and *Baptizato homine* after their incipits, are of particular interest for understanding Gratian's concerns in *De penitentia*. Both emerged in the same theological milieu as Gratian and evince many similarities to his work.[37]

Like Gratian in distinctions 3 and 4, *Augustinus in libro vite* and *Baptizato homine* explicitly connect the repeatability of penance, the nature of true penance, performing penance for just one of many sins, and the return of sins and, in addition, engage with many of the same authorities and arguments. Unlike Gratian, however, both works affirm that people can perform penance for just one of many sins and that forgiven sins do not return. *Augustinus in libro vite* is particularly critical of those who, like Gratian, defend the contrary views, while *Baptizato homine*, which Gratian may have known and been responding to, seems to have thought simply that the contrary positions were weaker than the ones it preferred.

Augustinus in libro vite is an anonymous treatise that circulated in Italy in the mid-twelfth century and which may be of Italian origin.[38] The work may well predate Gratian, since it circulated together with pre-Gratian canonical and theological sentence collections, and there are no traces of the influence of *De penitentia* or other sections of Gratian's work. A few texts quoted or referred to in *Augustinus in libro vite* are also found in *Ut autem hoc evidenter* and *De penitentia*, but do not appear to derive from either work. For the purposes of this chap-

37. I make this statement based on the overlap in the positions they discuss and the authorities they cite, many of which appear only in the works of French masters after Gratian.

38. The full text can be found in the appendix. I provide line numbers to the edition in the summary and discussion that follows.

ter, *Augustinus in libro vite* is of interest as a witness to the debates on penance in Gratian's theological milieu, particularly for demonstrating the existence of masters who vigorously defended positions criticized by Gratian in distinctions 3 and 4 of *De penitentia*.

Augustinus in libro vite begins by describing the different types of penance and their respective purposes. Baptism can be said to be a form of penance because it transforms one into a new person and wipes away all previous sin (lines 2–4). Sorrow over the ephemerality of this world is also a type of penance. It preserves one from pride and stimulates humility (lines 5–15). A third type of penance embraces those actions one performs with a contrite heart for the remission of post-baptismal sin (lines 16–23). Prayer and almsgiving suffice to remit venial sins perfectly, that is, sins committed out of invincible necessity, such as in immoderate drinking, eating, speaking, and laughing. And prayer and almsgiving can be performed as often as required, although enough venial sins, the treatise states, "kill us and separate us from the embrace of the beautiful spouse," that is, Jesus (lines 25–32). Perfect penance for sins against the Decalogue, however, such as murder and adultery, cannot be performed unless one abandons all of one's crimes. One who persists in adultery cannot perform perfect penance for fornication. One cannot perform perfect penance for theft while persisting in sacrilege, nor can one perform perfect penance for murder while persisting in perjury (lines 33–54).

One can, however, perform imperfect penance for one sin while remaining in other sins, and *Augustinus in libro vite* explicitly criticizes those who teach otherwise, though it does so, interestingly enough, within the larger context of a discussion of the return of sins (lines 56–61).

On account of the words "there is only one perfect penance" I hear certain [supposedly] wise men (*quosdam sapientes*) argue more subtly than usefully that if someone commits a crime and repents of it and performs satisfaction according to the command of a priest but later commits another crime and dies without performing penance for it, he will suffer punishment eternally and without any remission for both the sin for which he performed satisfaction and the sin for which he did not.

According to *Augustinus in libro vite*, these anonymous *quidam* defend this version of the return of sins with five main authorities and arguments. First, penance performed for the earlier crime must have been either true or false. It cannot have been true penance because if it had been, the person would not have committed another crime. Therefore it must have been false penance. But remission of pain does not accompany false penance (lines 62–64). Second, there is only one penance for many crimes. The *quidam* criticized by *Augustinus in libro vite* interpret this common statement as meaning not that sinners have only one opportunity to perform public or solemn penance, but rather that the satisfaction which a person performs does not count as penance until one has performed satisfaction for all of one's criminal sins. Someone who dies without having performed satisfaction for a crime, whether performed at the same time as or later than one's other crimes, thus cannot be said to have ever performed penance and thus never obtained remission for any sin (lines 65–68). Third, these *quidam* invoke the parable of the unforgiving servant, who, after having been forgiven his debt by the king, was forced to repay it in its entirety when he himself refused to forgive his fellow servant. The parable, they assert, shows that we will be punished for both original and actual sins after death if we do not forgive our brother (lines 69–75). Fourth, Augustine teaches that children will be punished for not only their own sins, but also the sins of their parents that they imitate and love (lines 76–78). Fifth, Ezekiel 18:24 declares that "if the just man sins, I will forget all his justices" (lines 79–80).

None of these arguments convinces the author of *Augustinus in libro vite*, who condemns them for disseminating an impious and irreligious image of God. "We, believing in a pious, merciful, and just God, preach holily and religiously that if a person performs satisfaction in this life according to the measure of the sin and the command of a priest, he will not be punished for it any further" (lines 84–88). True penance, the treatise agrees, entails not committing further criminal sins in the future. But it rejects the idea that true penance alone results in the remission of punishment. False penance, the treatise argues, does as well. Removing one part of a description does not entail removing all the other parts. Just because someone does not refrain from committing further sins does not mean that he does not have sorrow over past sins and, the treatise implies, the benefits resulting from such sorrow. A person suffering from many injuries is cured but then wounded anew and dies. Do these subsequent events really mean, the treatise asks, that the person in question was never healed? (lines 91–98). The other arguments adduced in favor of the return of sins come in for similar criticism. If it is conceded, the treatise argues, that a person can be a murderer and not an adulterer or an adulterer and not a perjurer, then one must believe that a murderer could perform penance for adultery and not perjury. Such a penance would not contribute to eternal salvation, but it would bring remission of punishment (lines 100–105).

The parable of the unforgiving servant, on the other hand, *Augustinus in libro vite* explains in a different fashion. Because God does not punish what he has already forgiven, the king in the parable must be understood as punishing the unforgiving servant not for his old sins but rather for a new one, the hardness of heart he displayed towards his fellow servant (lines 111–15). The treatise's solution is similar to the one advanced by Abelard, among others, though not entirely the same. Abelard argues that the unforgiving servant's new sin is contempt of God's mercy as evinced by his conduct toward his fellow servant.[39] *Augustinus in libro vite*, on the other hand, makes no mention of contempt, instead identifying the sin with hardness of heart towards his fellow servant.

Finally, *Augustinus in libro vite* points out, neither Augustine's statement on the punishment meted out for the sins of one's parents, nor Ezekiel 18:24 demonstrate the truth of the return of sins. Augustine states simply that children will suffer the punishment due for those parental sins that they love and imitate. He does not teach that children suffer the punishment due for all the sins of their parents. So one cannot make an *a fortiori* argument that if the damned suffer the punishment due even for the sins of their parents, they must also suffer the punishment due for their own sins for which they have performed satisfaction (lines 117–26). Ezekiel 18:24, on the other

39. See chapter 3, p. 97.

hand, *Augustinus in libro vite* simply interprets, probably correctly, as meaning that previous good works will not prevent someone who commits a mortal sin from suffering damnation (lines 128–30).

For *Augustinus in libro vite*, God is eminently just and merciful. Just as he leaves no sin unpunished, so too does he leave no good unrewarded, no matter how small. Those who try to show otherwise, for instance, by arguing that nothing is good except that which leads to eternal salvation, are refuted by the example of the Hebrew midwives in Exodus 1:15–21. These pious women refused to obey Pharaoh's order to kill male newborns. Yet, not being completely morally upright, they lied when questioned about their actions, saying that Israelite women were stronger than Egyptian women and thus always gave birth before the midwives arrived on the scene to kill the infants if they were male, as Pharaoh had commanded. In commenting on this passage, Gregory the Great declares that the midwives were punished for their lying, but rewarded for their piety. Yet the good that they did, *Augustinus in libro vite* stresses, was not such a one that led to eternal salvation (lines 132–53).

We do not know how popular the theses defended by *Augustinus in libro vite* were in the Italy of Gratian's day, but another anonymous treatise, *Baptizato homine*, advances basically the same position.[40] This treatise contains even more points of overlap with Gratian and, indeed, may have been among his formal sources.[41] Gratian drew most of the canons in distinctions 3 and 4 of *De penitentia*, which treat the same issues as *Augustinus in libro vite* and *Baptizato homine*, from a flo-

40. Landgraf, *Dogmengeschichte der Frühscholastik*, 4.2:203–4 comes to basically the same conclusion about the theological preferences of *Baptizato homine*, which he examined in the manuscripts Vat. lat. 1345 and Fulda, Landesbibliothek, Aa 36 4°: "Es scheint nun, als ob damals eine Strömung bestanden hätte, die auf der einen Seite sich zur Nichtrückkehr der Sünden bekannt, auf der anderen Seite aber noch angenommen hätte, daß sogar Sünde und Genugtuung nebeneinander bestehen könnten. Ihr steht der Verfasser unserer Sentenzen [i.e., *Baptizato homine*] wohlwollend gegenüber, wie er denn auch im allgemeinen—er führt wenigstens gegen sie nicht, wie er den anderen gegenüber tut, Gegengründe auf, die er nicht erledigen wollte—der Ansicht derjenigen zu sein scheint, die behaupten, daß einer nach getaner Buße rückfällig werden kann und daß ihm für diesen Fall die geleistete Buße nützt, selbst wenn er in Sünden stirbt, und daß auch die Sünden nicht zurückkehren."

41. Wei, "Penitential Theology."

rilegium of patristic texts on penance found in F (= Florence, Bibl. Medicea Laurenziana, Plut. V. sin 7). But he seems to have organized both distinctions around and in response to the exposition on penance found in *Baptizato homine.* Both distinctions reflect a knowledge of *Baptizato homine*'s arguments. Furthermore, on several occasions they also employ the same words and phrases.

Like the *Decretum, Baptizato homine* proceeds in a dialectical fashion. For each topic, it sets forth a thesis, the arguments and authorities normally adduced in support of the thesis, and then objections to these arguments and authorities. The very beginning of *Baptizato homine* discusses the parts of penance, the assignment of penance, the remission of sins, and the role that priests play in obtaining forgiveness from God. Penance, the treatise affirms, consists of three parts: confession of the mouth, contrition of the heart, and the correction of depravity. Confession is not just any outward expression of sin, but rather self-accusation and the cursing of one's past misdeeds; contrition is interior suffering over one's sin; while satisfaction refers to fasting, prayer, almsgiving, and other forms of emendation.[42] In hearing confessions, *Baptizato homine* insists, clerics must exercise discretion. The confessor must consider the quality, quantity, and manner of sin, as well as the age, condition, sex, status, and economic means of the penitent.[43] The effect of penance is defined by the treatise as the remission of sins, which is defined as God not meting out eternal punishment to a sin in consideration of baptism, penance, or some temporal punishment.[44] Both God and priests, it

42. *Baptizato homine* §3, ed. Wei, 90.9–10: "In penitentia autem ista sunt consideranda: oris confessio, cordis contritio, prauitatis correctio. Confessionem autem appellamus non quamlibet propalationem peccati, quia et leccatores siue ridendo siue iactando seu etiam improperando profitentur, sed proprii actus cum sui accusatione execrationem; contritionem uero de peccato corde compungi et angi; satisfactionem per ieiunium, orationes, elemosinas, et ceterorum erroris emendationem."

43. Ibid. §4, ed. Wei, 90.17–21: "Sunt quoque ista in penitentia consideranda: qualitas, quantitas, et modus, que a sacerdote competenter iudicanda secundum etates, conditiones, sexus, officia uirium seu diuitiarum facultates, ut pro modo personarum sit discretio penarum."

44. Ibid. §5, ed. Wei, 90.22–91.26: "Sed quia per penitentiam peccata dimitti credimus, uidendum est quid sit hoc dicere: 'peccatum dimittitur.' Et sic exponi-

teaches, remit sin, God by actually forgiving sin, priests by showing that sins are forgiven.[45] Priests are able to show that sins are forgiven because they have received two keys from God: discretion and office, what other contemporaries generally refer to as power. Indiscriminately binding or loosing means that a priest lacks one or the other key.[46]

In the view of its author, *Baptizato homine*'s treatment of these topics is uncontroversial, merely reproducing what is "commonly said about penance."[47] If this sentence was written in earnest, and there is no reason to think that it was not, then the author of *Baptizato homine* was unfamiliar with the teachings of Abelard and Hugh, perhaps because he was geographically removed from them (the manuscript diffusion suggests that *Baptizato homine* may have been composed in Italy), or perhaps because he composed the treatise before they developed their more distinctive ideas on penance in the 1130s.[48] As discussed in chapter 3, Hugh objected vehemently to the view that a priest in confession does no more than show that sins are forgiven and developed his doctrine of two bonds—one of obduracy, the other of future damnation—to counteract this idea. Abelard, on the other hand, expressly denied that priests receive two keys in ordination because ordination fails to make the wise wiser or the foolish less foolish. Instead, he advanced the idea that priests possess only one

tur: baptismate uel penitentia uel aliqua temporali pena efficiente ad eternam penam non reseruatur. Bonis etiam operibus peccata delentur."

45. Ibid. §8, ed. Wei, 91.44–46: "sacerdos dimittit peccatum, quod interius a deo gestum est, exterius ostendit. Et est 'quorum remiseritis peccata, remittuntur eis,' id est quorum ostendetis dimissa esse."

46. Ibid. §9, ed. Wei, 91.48–92.52: "Unde colligitur quod non est aliud soluere quam solutum ostendere, ligare, ligatum ostendere. Ad hoc due claues dantur sacerdotibus: discretio scilicet et officium. Et qui indiscrete ligat uel soluit, altera caret."

47. Ibid. §10, ed. Wei, 92.58: "Sed cum illa predicta communiter dicantur de penitentia."

48. There are nine manuscripts of *Baptizato homine*. Four manuscripts are of Italian provenance and perhaps of Italian origin as well. On these manuscripts, see Wei, "The Sentence Collection *Deus non habet*," 9 (Fp), 12 (Co), 12–13 (Fa), and 18 (Ox). Three manuscripts are of South German or Austrian provenance. See ibid., 11–12 (Vi) and 13–14 (Fu and Pr). One manuscript is from Sidon in the Holy Land. See ibid., 21–22. One manuscript is today located in Zurich. See Maas, *Liber sententiarum*, 49–51.

key, the power to bind and loose, which is said to be plural in number on account of its two effects.[49] *Baptizato homine* reveals no knowledge of these ideas. Like Gratian, the treatise seems to have belonged to a different theological milieu, one familiar with only some of the debates of the French schools.

The remainder of *Baptizato homine* focuses on what its author expressly recognizes to be disputed theses.[50] It considers three positions in turn. The first position affirms that a person cannot sin again after performing penance and if he does sin again, then his original penance was not valid, in fact was not actually penance, and furthermore that forgiven sins return.[51] The second and third positions both affirm that after a person performs penance, he can still fall into sin and his preceding penance will still be valid and profitable even if he should die in mortal sin. But proponents of the second position hold that forgiven sins do not return, whereas proponents of the third position hold that forgiven sins do return.[52]

Baptizato homine does not expressly state which position its author favored, but the differential treatment of the objections to each position reveals that it was the second position. *Baptizato homine* leaves all the objections to the first position unrefuted and says of the third position that its proponunts ascribe the return of sins to God's justice, yet confess themselves to be ignorant of the sort of justice by which sins return.[53] In contrast, *Baptizato homine* shows how each and every objection to the second position can be refuted, generally introducing

49. On Hugh and Abelard, see chapter 3, pp. 91–95.

50. *Baptizato homine* §10, ed. Wei, 92.59: "hec deinceps est attendenda diuersitas."

51. Ibid., ed. Wei, 92.59–62: "Dicunt quidam quod, postquam aliquis semel penituerit, numquam amplius in crimen recidet, et si reciderit, non ualuit penitentia, immo non fuit penitentia." Ibid. §17, ed. Wei, 93.84: "Est iterum in hac sententia quod dimissa redeunt."

52. Ibid. §30, ed. Wei, 96.167–70: "Quidam aliter sentiunt. Dicunt enim quod, postquam aliquis egerit penitentiam, [quod] recidit in crimen et quod precedens penitentia prodest etiam si in crimine moriatur. Preterea, dimissa non redeunt." Ibid. §41, ed. Wei, 99.245–47: "Sunt autem alii qui concedunt similiter quod post peractam penitentiam aliquis peccat, sed si peccat, id quod dimissum erat per penitentiam statim redit."

53. Ibid., ed. Wei, 100.252–53: "Si autem queritur quomodo hoc fiat, iustitie dei hoc ascribunt; qua autem iustitia fiat, hoc se ignorare dicunt."

its solutions with *solutio, sic respondeatur, istis oppositionibus sit una responsio,* and *iste oppositiones soluuntur secundum predictam auctoritatem.*[54]

As demonstrated in chapter 4, Gratian defends the same basic position as *Baptizato homine* with regards to the repeatability of penance in distinction 3 of *De penitentia.* Where he and *Baptizato homine* differ, and what I argue Gratian is critical of and tries to correct in distinction 3, is the way in which *Baptizato homine* defends their shared belief in the repeatability of penance. Because *Baptizato homine* accepts the permissibility of performing penance for just one of many sins, it cannot effectively neutralize all the authorities adduced in support of the unrepeatability of penance. Gratian, I argue, structures distinction 3 to correct this defect in *Baptizato homine.*

Baptizato homine encounters the problem just identified in considering a text by Gregory examined in chapter 4, "We cannot worthily perform (*agere*) penance...."[55] *Baptizato homine* attempts to show that this text does not support the unrepeatability of penance by subjecting the verbs to careful analysis. The verbs "to perform" (*agere*) and "to commit" (*committere*), it claims, must refer to either the present or the future. If both verbs refer to the present, then the sense of the passage seems to be that "he who performs penance does not sin."[56] *Baptizato homine* finds this interpretation problematic, however, because another extract from Gregory seems to affirm that people can perform penance for one sin while continuing to indulge in other sins.[57]

54. In two instances, *Baptizato homine* does not preface its explanation of how objections to the second position can be neutralized with any special word or phrase. See ibid. §§32, 40, ed. Wei, 97.178–81, 99.240–44. On *solutio,* see ibid. §§31, 36, 37, ed. Wei, 97.172, 98.213, 98.219. On *sic respondeatur,* see ibid. §§33, 34, ed. Wei, 97.186–87, 98.196. On *istis oppositionibus,* see ibid. §35, ed. Wei, 98.203–4. On *iste oppositiones,* see ibid. §38, ed. Wei, 99.224–25.

55. De pen. D.3 c.6 = *Baptizato homine* §13, ed. Wei, 92.69–75. See 127n63.

56. Ibid. §18, ed. Wei, 93.88–92: "Primum opponitur illi parti: 'Penitentiam agere est etc.' 'Agere' et 'committere' uel sunt presentis temporis, uel sunt futuri, uel unum presentis et alterum futuri. Si presentis temporis sunt, talis uidetur esse sensus, quod qui penitet non peccat."

57. Ibid., ed. Wei, 93.92–97: "Sed huic expositioni opponitur de eodem Gregorio super Ezechiel: '"Pluit dominus super unam de ciuitatibus" etc. (Am 4:7). Cum ille qui proximum odit ab aliis uitiis se corrigit, una eademque ciuitas ex parte compluitur et ex parte arida manet, quia sunt qui cum quedam uitia resecant, in aliis grauiter perdurant.'"

A little further on, *Baptizato homine* considers the possibility that both verbs refer to the future: "he who will perform penance will not sin." But it dismisses the idea immediately because no one, it claims, holds this position. The only remaining possibility, it concludes, is that one verb refers to the present and the other to the future. The sense of the passage would thus have to be either that "he who sins will not perform penance" or "he who performs penance will not sin." *Baptizato homine* calls the first of these two interpretations manifestly false. If true, it would mean that no sinner could ever perform penance. Yet *Baptizato homine* also finds the second of these interpretations problematic because it is conceivable that a person could commit another grave sin only many years after first performing penance.[58] A person of this sort seems to offer clear proof that a sinner can perform true penance but then later fall back into sin. Given the long gap between his penance and his later sinning, there are few grounds for impugning the sincerity of such a penitent's conversion. The long years of morally upright behavior would seem to argue against the conversion having been false.

At this point, *Baptizato homine* simply abandons its attempt to reinterpret Gregory. Its efforts to show that his words do not support the unrepeatability of penance end in failure. *Baptizato homine* proposes, but then rejects as unacceptable four supposedly exhaustive interpretations of what Gregory is really saying.

Gratian too, I would suggest, noticed this conundrum, since he addresses it explicitly in distinction 3 and, indeed, structures the distinction in such a way as to meet this problem head on. As discussed in chapter 4, distinction 3 begins by quoting sixteen authorities in favor of the view that penance cannot be repeated (cc.1–6, 8–17). Most of these authorities assert that true penance entails not sinning again. They thus appear to imply that people who will commit a grave sin in the future cannot perform true penance in the here and

58. Ibid. §19, ed. Wei, 93.98–94.103: "Quod autem utrumque sit futuri temporis nemo dicit. Si uero unum presentis et alterum futuri, talis est sensus: qui peccat non penitebit. Hoc autem falsum est. Uel sic: qui penitet non peccabit. Sed huic expositioni opponitur quare ille qui post decem annos peccaturus est non peniteat. Sed dicant quod qui postea peccaturus est non uere dolet, non habet contritionem, idcirco non penitet."

now. In other words, only those who will never sin again can perform true penance.

To refute this interpretation, Gratian in the immediately following dictum, d.p.c.17, has recourse to a variant of *Baptizato homine*'s linguistic approach.

The words of the definition do not refer to diverse times but to the same time, i.e., so that at the time one weeps over the evils which one committed, one does not commit that which would force one to weep even more. This is understood from the following words of the same authority, where it is said: "For he who weeps over some [sins] in such a way that he nevertheless commits other [sins], either is still ignorant of how to perform penance or feigns [penance]."[59]

According to Gratian, the verbs in the definition of penance all refer to the same time. The definition does not affirm that people perform true penance at time A if and only if they do not sin again at any later time B. Rather, it really states that people perform true penance at time A if and only if they also refrain from sinning at this same time A.

The way in which Gratian phrases this argument suggests that he was familiar with *Baptizato homine*. Although it appears after c.17, internal evidence makes it clear that Gratian originally formulated d.p.c.17 in connection with c.6, the text from Gregory to which *Baptizato homine* applied its linguistic analysis. We know that Gratian also had this authority in mind because he states that "the following words of the same authority" prove the correctness of his interpretation, whereupon he then quotes from c.6.

It is not, I would argue, mere chance that Gratian and *Baptizato homine* use the same method to analyze the same patristic text, particularly when the patristic text in question does not seem to have circulated in the French schools until after Gratian. F is the only known pre-Gratian canonical collection or florilegium to transmit the passage from Gregory and furthermore the only one to do so

59. De pen. D.3 d.p.c.17 (ed. Friedberg, 1214, supported by Aa Fd): "Sed uerba diffinitionis non ad diuersa tempora sed ad idem tempus referuntur, uidelicet ut tempore quo deflet mala que commisit, non committat quod adhuc eum flere oporteat. Quod ex subsequentibus uerbis eiusdem auctoritatis datur intelligi, dum dicitur: 'Nam qui sic alia deplorat ut tamen alia committat, adhuc penitentiam agere aut ignorat aut dissimulat' [c.6]."

in the same fragmentation as Gratian and *Baptizato homine*.[60] Apart from Gratian and *Baptizato homine*, the *Summa sententiarum* appears to be the only contemporary work of scholastic theology that quotes or cites the passage from Gregory.[61] But the sentence collection *Deus itaque summe* was a formal source of the *Summa sententiarum*, and five of the six manuscripts that preserve *Deus itaque summe* transmit *Baptizato homine* as its tract on penance.[62] So there is reason to believe that the *Summa sententiarum*'s knowledge of this passage from Gregory was due to its familiarity with *Baptizato homine*.[63]

The other main reason to think that Gratian formulated d.p.c.17 in dependence on *Baptizato homine* is that he devotes the second half of distinction 3 to refuting the view that people can perform penance and receive forgiveness for one sin while simultaneously indulging in other sins. As already noted, *Baptizato homine* rejects an interpretation of the text in c.6 very close to the one given by Gratian in d.p.c.17 because, on Gregory's authority, it affirms that people can perform penance and receive forgiveness for one sin while persisting in other sins. Gratian does not allude to this problem in d.p.c.17. His decision to discuss this issue in the second half of distinction 3, however, suggests that he was aware of it and of the difficulty it posed for his interpretation of c.6 and similar authorities adduced in favor of the non-repeatability of penance.

Chapter 4 noted the puzzling structure of distinction 3 of *De peni-*

60. F119 (Florence, Biblioteca Medicea Laurenziana, Plut.V sin 7, fol. 80rb–va).

61. *Summa sententiarum* 6.12, PL 176, 149BC. The French schools before Gratian and the *Summa sententiarum* were, however, familiar with a text from Ambrose that Gratian cites at De pen. D.3 c.1 ("Penitentia est et mala preterita plangere et plangenda iterum non committere"), which overlaps in part with Gregory's text. See the references in Larson, *Master of Penance*, 139n6.

62. For detailed proof that the *Summa sententiarum* depends on a text like *Deus non habet* or its reworking *Deus itaque summe*, see Lotton, *Psychologie et morale*, 5:373–79; Heinrich Weisweiler, "Die Arbeitsweise der sogenannten *Sententiae Anselmi*: Ein Beitrag zum Entstehen der systematischen Werke der Theologie," *Scholastik* 34 (1959): 190–232. For evidence that the *Summa sententiarum* depends on *Deus itaque summe* in particular, see Wei, "A Twelfth-Century Treatise," 17–20. Regarding the tract on penance, see the manuscript descriptions in Wei, "The Sentence Collection *Deus non habet*," 12–18.

63. The use of *Baptizato homine* is even more likely if, as has been argued, the author of the *Summa sententiarum* was an Italian. See Gastaldelli, "La 'Summa sententiarum,'" 537–46.

tentia, which finds no parallel in the works of such French contemporaries as Abelard and Hugh.[64] *Baptizato homine* provides an explanation for this unusual design choice. Gratian was trying to correct what he regarded as *Baptizato homine*'s mistaken arguments. Textual parallels support this claim. *Baptizato homine* contains parallels to four of the five arguments or authorities that Gratian adduces in support of the view that people can perform penance and receive forgiveness for one sin while indulging in other sins. Gratian states in d.p.c.39 that those who defend this position base their claim on Nahum 1:9: "God will not judge the same [sin] twice." God, they assert, judges whomever a priest judges. Therefore, whoever is punished by a priest, will not be judged a second time by God. "But whom a priest judges, God judges, whose person [the priest] assumes in church. Therefore he who is punished by a priest for a sin, will not be judged again by God for the same sin."[65]

This same line of reasoning is found in *Baptizato homine*, although in a different context. In critiquing the view of those who assert that only those who will never sin again can truly perform penance, *Baptizato homine* considers the permissibility of being punished twice for the same crime. What happens to a murderer who performs all the works of satisfaction enjoined upon him by his confessor—including, let us suppose, fasting, alms, pilgrimage, and imprisonment—but later commits another sin, for instance, theft? If his penance was worthless, can God still punish him for his sin of murder? No, suggests *Baptizato homine*, because a priest has already punished him in the place of God, and no one ought to serve the same sentence twice.[66]

64. The closest parallel I have found is *Summa sententiarum* 6.13, PL 176, 151D, which discusses first the return of sins and then whether one can perform penance for just one of two mortal sins. But as mentioned, the *Summa sententiarum* may depend on *Baptizato homine*.

65. De pen. D.3 d.p.c.39 (ed. Friedberg, 1229, supported by Aa Fd): "Sed quem sacerdos iudicat Deus iudicat, cuius personam in ecclesia gerit. Qui ergo a sacerdote semel pro peccato punitur, non iterum pro eodem peccato a Deo iudicabitur." Larson, *Master of Penance*, 153, argues for the influence of the *Glossa ordinaria* to Lv 10:19 because the gloss employs an analogous phrase, "in persona ecclesie, cuius figuram gerit."

66. *Baptizato homine* §23, ed. Wei, 94.121–29: "Iterum, illi opponitur 'Inanis est penitentia etc.' Contigit quod commisit homicidium, subiuit sententiam sa-

In *Baptizato homine,* two further objections to the permissibility of double punishment then follow. The first of these continues the thought experiment with the murderer turned thief. If this criminal's first penance was worthless, reasons *Baptizato homine,* then so was his satisfaction. This person would therefore still be guilty of murder and theft and would have to perform satisfaction for both sins. Such a conclusion, however, notes *Baptizato homine,* contradicts the custom of the church, which never presumes to impose punishment twice for the same sin.[67] The other objection raised by *Baptizato homine* to the permissibility of being punished twice for the same sin is a text by Jerome. According to Jerome, if an infidel is killed while committing adultery, then, supposing that the punishment is equal to the sin, this person will not be punished further by God.[68] Gratian mentions both of these objections in d.p.c.41, although in reverse order (see table 5-1). His wording parallels the phrasing in *Baptizato homine.* In the allusion to Jerome, both d.p.c.41 and *Baptizato homine* employ the phrases *opponitur de Ieronimo*/*De Ieronimo etiam opponitur, quod si infidelis* (*fidelis* Aa) *adulterando interficeretur,* and *non amplius a Deo*/*amplius non puniretur.*

A comparison of the other objection (*Iterum, si illa ...*) yields more ambiguous results. On the one hand, Gratian introduces it rather suddenly. The word *illa* in d.p.c.41 is superfluous and seems to suggest that the if-clause continues an earlier train of thought. The passage appears to be wrenched from its original context, although Gra-

cerdotis, ieiunauit, elemosinam dedit, peregrinatus est, passus est carceres, omnibusque sibi iniunctis peractis, commisit furtum. Quid inde iudicandum est? Sed secundum hanc sententiam nichil ualuit, nec fuit penitentia. Sed uidetur deus iniustus si amplius punit, quia sacerdos uice dei puniuit, et de eodem nemo debet bis subire sententiam, 'quia non consurgit duplex tribulatio' (Nah 1:9)."

67. Ibid. §24, ed. Wei, 95.130–35: "Iterum, si illa non fuit satisfactio pro illo furto, ille homicidii et furti reus tenetur. Oportet igitur eum de utroque satisfacere. Sed nemo adeo insanit quod dicat eum iterum debere satisfacere, et huius rei argumentum consuetudo ecclesie est, que alicui de eodem bis imponere penam non presumit."

68. Ibid. §25, ed. Wei, 95.136–38: "De Ieronimo etiam opponitur, qui refert quod si infidelis adulterando interficeretur, si illa pena esset par peccato, quod de illo amplius non puniretur." The material source is Jerome, *Commentarius in Naum* 1:9, ed. Marcus Adriaen, CCSL 76A (Turnhout: Brepols, 1964), 534.271–80.

Table 5-1. Comparison of De pen. D.3 d.p.c.41 and *Baptizato homine*

De pen. D.3 d.p.c.41	*Baptizato homine* §25, §24
Item *opponitur de Ieronimo, qui* super Naum sentire uidetur *quod, si infidelis*[a] *adulterando interficeretur, de* adulterio *non amplius* a Deo *puniretur.*	*De Ieronimo* etiam *opponitur, qui* refert *quod si infidelis adulterando interficeretur,* si illa pena esset par peccato, quod *de* illo *amplius non puniretur.*
[a]fidelis *Aa*	
Item, si illa satisfactio non fuit, quam in adulterio uiuens pro homicidio obtulit, cum adulterii eum penituerit, utriusque penitentia ei imponenda erit[a]; quod a ratione alienum ecclesiastica probatur consuetudine, que pro eodem peccato (nisi reiteratum fuerit) nulli bis penitentiam imponit.	Iterum, si illa non fuit satisfactio pro illo furto, ille homicidii et furti reus tenetur. Oportet igitur eum de utroque satisfacere. Sed nemo adeo insanit quod dicit eum iterum debere satisfacere et huius rei argumentum consuetudo ecclesie est, que alicui de eodem bis imponere penam non presumit.
[a]erat *Fd*[2]	

Note: Left-hand column is from ed. Friedberg, 1224, supported by Aa Fd. Right-hand column is from *Baptizato homine* §§24–25, ed. Wei, 95.130–38.

tian has modified it so that all the internal references are consistent. In place of a murderer turned thief, Gratian speaks of a person who performed penance for murder while continuing to live in adultery. *Baptizato homine*, on the other hand, presents this objection as a continuation of the immediately preceding thought experiment. The word *illa* in §24 points to the story of the murderer turned thief set forth in §23. As preserved in the manuscripts, however, §24 is not unproblematic, since it mistakenly states that the original satisfaction was performed for theft rather than for murder.

There is one final indication that Gratian may have drawn upon *Baptizato homine* in the composition of d.p.c.39–d.p.c.41: a variant in c.40. This canon contains the authority from Gregory quoted in *Baptizato homine* §18 and alluded to again in §34 in support of the view that people can perform penance for one sin while continuing to indulge in other sins. It is found in only one of Gratian's known formal sources: the sentences on penance preserved in F, where it appears as F102 (fol. 78vb) (see table 5-2).

Unlike many of the other sentences preserved in this codex, F102 is not preserved in any other manuscript. This is unfortunate because F contains poor readings. A comparison of F102 with *De peni-*

Table 5-2. Comparison of F102, De pen. D.3 c.40, and *Baptizato homine*

F102 (fol. 78vb)	De pen. D.3 c.40	*Baptizato homine* §18
	'Pluit Dominus[a] super unam ciuitatem et super alteram non pluit, et eandem ciuitatem ex parte compluit et[b] ex parte aridam relinquit.'	'Pluit Dominus super unam de ciuitatibus etcetera.'
Cum ille qui proximum odit ab aliis se uitiis corrigit *atque emendare contendit,* una eademque ciuitas ex parte compluitur et ex parte remanet arida, quia sunt quidam qui alia uitia resecant, in aliis grauiter perdurant.	Cum ille qui proximum odit ab aliis uitiis se corrigit, una eademque ciuitas ex parte compluitur et ex parte arida manet, quia sunt[c] qui cum[d] uitia quedam resecant, in aliis grauiter perdurant[e].	Cum ille qui proximum odit ab aliis uitiis se corrigit, una eademque ciuitas ex parte compluitur et ex parte arida manet, quia sunt qui cum quedam uitia resecant, in aliis grauiter perdurant.
	[a]*post* ciuitatem *Aa* [b]*om. Aa* [c]*add.* quidam *Aa* [d]quedam uitia *Aa* [e]pergrauiter durant *Fd[ac]*	

Note: Center column is from ed. Friedberg, 1224, supported by Aa Fd. Right-hand column is from *Baptizato homine,* ed. Wei, 93.93–97.

tentia and *Baptizato homine* nevertheless uncovers one important corruption common to all three: the reading *Cum ille qui proximum odit* rather than *Cum uero et ipse proximus qui audit.*[69] It also reveals one significant variant that *De penitentia* and *Baptizato homine* share *vis-à-vis* F102: the omission of the phrase *atque emendare contendit.*

These variants, shown in table 5-2, suggest that Gratian took c.40 not from the sentences on penance preserved in F, but rather from *Baptizato homine.* Gratian does not seem to have taken any other canons from *Baptizato homine.* It would have been natural for him to do so in this one instance, however, since he seems to have used *Baptizato homine* as a quarry for arguments in favor of the view that people can perform penance for one sin while continuing to indulge in other sins.

Gratian concludes distinction 3 by explaining the aforementioned arguments and authorities. Nahum 1:9 ("God will not judge the

69. Gregorius Magnus, *Homiliae in Ezechielem* 1.10.23, ed. Marcus Adriaen, CCSL 142 (Turnhout: Brepols, 1971), 156.409.

same [sin] twice"), he argues, does not show that every sin which God punishes with a temporal punishment in this life will not be punished further in the hereafter. Otherwise, every wicked person would wish to be struck dead by God and thus, by a brief and momentary punishment, avoid eternal torment. Instead, Gratian says, Nahum refers only to those who change their behavior as a result of punishment. For those who become more evil, present sufferings are simply the prelude to eternal torment.[70]

The objection from Jerome about the infidel apprehended in adultery, on the other hand, Gratian dismisses through the quotation and examination of the actual passage (c.44). Read in its entirety and in context, the passage does not, as *Baptizato homine* claims, affirm that an adulterer sentenced to death in this life will not be punished in the next. Instead, it teaches that minor sins will be punished by brief and temporal punishments, whereas major sins will be punished by long and eternal ones.[71]

Similarly, Gratian argues, the passage from Gregory (c.40) does not in fact deal with pardon for a crime but rather its detestation. When a sinner performs penance for just one of many sins, the Lord is said to "rain down" on him in part not because he has already received forgiveness from God, but because he has begun to detest his sins. Detestation of sin is likened to rain because through it grace is instilled into a sinner's heart, so that by it he may come to true penance or, at the very least, merit lesser punishment from God.[72]

The remaining objection shared with *Baptizato homine*, that satisfaction would have to be repeated if one were unable to perform penance for one of many sins, Gratian answers with a distinction borrowed from the theology of baptism and first elaborated by Augustine.[73] As with baptism received in bad faith (*ficte*), which be-

70. De pen. D.3 d.p.c.42.

71. De pen. D.3 d.p.c.43.

72. De pen. D.3 d.p.c.44.

73. Cf. Larson, "The Influence of the School of Laon," 224–27, who argues that Gratian's direct source for this idea was Anselm of Laon's *sententiae*, perhaps by means of oral transmission. Larson bases her argument on the claim that "the one person with whom he shared the specific idea that a sacrament can be carried out at one time and its effect can come to realization at a later time upon demonstration of faith (or true repentance) was Anselm of Laon" (227).

comes an occasion for grace when the one baptized begins to possess true faith, so too penance performed for just one of many sins becomes fruitful when a sinner later repents and performs penance for his other transgressions. Thus, although one does not receive forgiveness from God when one performs penance for only one of many sins, the penance that one performs is not worthless and does not need to be repeated. For when one finally does perform penance for one's other transgressions, one will receive the due reward for the first penance, that is, remission of sin.[74] It is in this sense in particular, says Gratian, that we should understand various authorities (cc.45, 46) about God's always rewarding good deeds, although these can also refer to God's bestowal of temporal rewards and the reduction of one's sufferings in hell.[75] God is so good and just that he rewards our false penances when we finally perform true penance.

The Return of Sins

Distinction 4 of *De penitentia* argues that the punishment due for forgiven sins returns when one later commits another serious sin. Gratian does not explain why he thought this question worthy of investigation—aside from the fact that it is one possible corollary of

---

Yet, as she herself acknowledges in a footnote, this statement is untrue. *Summa sententiarum* 5.5, PL 176, 130B–131B, expresses the same idea, as does the treatise on baptism *Deinceps querendum est cuiusmodi genus purgationis*, which circulated together with the sentence collection *Deus itaque summe*. Additional testimonies could no doubt be found if one were to comb the published and unpublished texts. Anselm, the *Summa sententiarum*, and *Deinceps querendum est* all probably took the idea directly from Augustine, whom they cite. The section of *De baptismo contra Donatistas* in which Augustine affirms this view circulated widely in the twelfth century, most notably through its incorporation into the *Sententiae magistri A.* (no. 506 in Maas, *Liber sententiarum*, 317; Florence, Biblioteca Medicea Laurenziana, Plut. V sin. 7, fol. 41ra).

74. De pen. D.3 d.p.c.44 §2, quoted in chapter 4, p. 134n84.

75. De pen. D.3 d.p.c.46 (ed. Friedberg, 1227, supported by Aa Fd): "Quamquam memoria bonorum ad presentem remunerationem possit referri, sicut Gregorius in omelia de diuite et Lazaro scribit." De pen. D.3 d.p.c.48 (ed. Friedberg, 1228, supported by Aa Fd): "Potest etiam referri memoria bonorum ad mitiorem penam habendam, ut bona que inter multa mala fiunt non proficiant ad presentis uel future uite premium obtinendum, sed ad tolerabilius extremi iudicii supplicium subeundum."

the view that penance cannot be repeated. But parallels with *Augustinus in libro vite* and *Baptizato homine* suggest that at least one goal was to respond to objections that contemporaries raised against his preferred view, that forgiven sins return. One of the main works to which he was responding may have been *Baptizato homine*, which expresses a preference for the view that forgiven sins do not return and dismisses the possibility that the return of sins could accord with divine justice.

Baptizato homine considers the return of sins in connection with the problem of the repeatability of penance. As discussed above, *Baptizato homine* considers three positions, the first and third of which affirm that forgiven sins return.[76] In support of the view that sins return, defenders of the first position point to Psalm 108:14: "May the iniquity of his fathers be remembered in the sight of the Lord, and let not the sin of his mother be blotted out," and Gregory the Great's commentary on Matthew 18:32: "and that which we believed to be remitted through penance is strictly demanded of us."[77] Both authorities seem to suggest that God sometimes punishes previously forgiven sins—Psalm 108:14 parental sins, Matthew 18:32 personal sins. But, *Baptizato homine* argues, these biblical passages do not in fact support this doctrine, at least not if one accepts the first position's premises, namely that after one performs penance, one cannot sin criminally, and if one does sin criminally, then one's previous penance was not real. For according to the first position, one's previously forgiven sins only have the appearance of being remitted; in fact, they never really are remitted. Yet if this is the case, then it is difficult to see how sins can really be said to return.[78]

76. *Baptizato homine* §17, ed. Wei, 93.84–87: "Est iterum in hac sententia quod dimissa redeunt iuxta illud: 'In memoriam redeat iniquitas patrum'; et super illum locum 'serue nequam': 'et quod dimissum per penitentiam credebamus a nobis districte exigitur.'" Ibid. §41, ed. Wei, 99.245–47: "Sunt autem alii qui concedunt similiter quod post peractam penitentiam aliquis peccat, sed si peccat, id quod dimissum erat per penitentiam statim redit."

77. Gregory the Great, *Dialogi* 4.62.2, ed. Adalbert de Vogüé, *Dialogues*, 3 vols. (Paris: Éditions du Cerf, 1978–80), 3:204.21–206.24.

78. *Baptizato homine* §26, ed. Wei, 95.139–46: "Opponitur quoque ad hoc quod dictum est: 'peccata redeunt, et quod dimissum esse per penitentiam credebamus exigitur.' Queritur namque quid sit hoc dicere: 'peccatum est dimissum;

Furthermore, *Baptizato homine* argues, the return of sins also contradicts Matthew 18:32–33: "Wicked servant, I forgave you all your debt because you besought me." According to Matthew, God really and truly did remit the unforgiving servant's debt. The only way for defenders of the first position to explain away this passage, *Baptizato homine* argues, is to say that God only appeared to forgive the servant. But such a solution would eliminate any difference between the Lord and the unforgiving servant. Just as the unforgiving servant chose not to forgive his fellow servant, so too would the Lord have only pretended to forgive the unforgiving servant.[79]

The final objection that *Baptizato homine* levels against the return of sins as presented by defenders of the first position is an excerpt from Prosper of Aquitaine's second *Responsio ad capitula Gallorum*.[80] Prosper concedes that those who end their lives apart from Christ will be punished eternally. Nevertheless, he appears to deny that they will be punished for their remitted sins, whether actual or original.

Because it belongs to the second and preferred position in *Baptizato homine*, the non-return of sins finds considerably more favor with the treatise's author.[81] The one objection it raises against this view is an authority which states that "sins return and that which was remitted through penance is demanded [of us]." Yet, says *Baptizato homine*, the words of Prosper easily explain away this text. According to Prosper, forgiven sins do not return, and one will not be punished

---

peccatum redit.' Si autem dimissum uidebatur, sic opponitur. Cum dimissum uidebatur, uel erat dimissum uel non erat. Sed si non erat dimissum, quomodo redit? Si autem erat dimissum, quomodo et quare redit? Et quid est hoc: 'peccatum erat dimissum'?"

79. Ibid. §27, ed. Wei, 95.147–96.153: "Amplius, cum dicat 'uidebatur quidem sed non erat dimissum,' quomodo exponitur hoc: 'Serue nequam, omne debitum dimisi tibi quoniam rogasti me. Nonne oportuit te misereri conseruo tuo, sicut et ego tui misertus sum'? An dicent 'sicut tui misertus sum,' id est sicut uidebar dimisisse? Si autem aliter intelligitur, dicant et dent differentiam inter dominum et seruum."

80. Ibid. §29, ed. Wei, 96.162–66: "Postremo, ex auctoritate opponitur Prosperi in responsionibus: 'Qui recedit a Christo et alienus a gratia finit hanc uitam, quid nisi in perditionem uadit?' Sed non in id quod remissum est recidit, nec in originali peccato damnabitur qui tamen ea morte afficitur, que ei per dimissa debebatur." Gratian quotes the same text at De pen. D.4 c.14.

81. *Baptizato homine* §30, ed. Wei, 96.167–71.

for any sins for which one undergoes sufficient punishment in this life, even if one dies in sin.[82]

Only at the very end of the treatise, in presenting its third position, does *Baptizato homine* mention yet another possible way to defend the return of sins.

And thus do they expound the proposition "sin returns," that is, that someone will be punished for a sin, for which he was not worthy of being punished. For at one time it was remitted in such a way that if he had died, God would not have punished him. For it was remitted truly and without any condition. But as soon as he sins, it returns. However, if it is asked how this occurs, they ascribe it to God's justice. By what justice this occurs, however, they say they are ignorant.[83]

The treatise does not seem to consider this position very viable because it does not provide any authorities or arguments in its favor. Indeed, the closing sentences suggest that the author of *Baptizato homine* found the position incoherent. Its supporters invoke God's justice, but are unable to explain how the return of sins can possibly be just.

Read in light of *Baptizato homine*, particularly its assessment of the third position, distinction 4 of *De penitentia* can be seen as an attempt to prove the rationality and justice of the return of sins. Distinction 4 begins by listing the authorities that seem to support the return of sins. Like both *Augustinus in libro vite* and *Baptizato homine*, Gratian considers together authorities for the return of personal sins and the return of parental sins. Gratian quotes Psalm 108:14 and Matthew 18:32—the same biblical passages as *Baptizato homine*—in support of

82. Ibid. §38, ed. Wei, 99.222–30: "Nunc opponatur ad id quod dictum est: 'peccata non redeunt.' Dicit auctoritas: 'peccata redeunt et quod dimissum erat per penitentiam exigitur.' Iste oppositiones soluuntur secundum predictam auctoritatem Prosperi. Et est summa huius sententie, ut breuiter dicatur, quod dimissa peccata non redeunt et pro quibuscumque peccatis aliquis penam pertulit secundum quantitatem peccatorum etiam si in peccato moriatur, quod de illis amplius non punietur. Nec tamen negatur quin aliqui hic et in futuro puniendi sint."

83. Ibid. §41, ed. Wei, 99.247–100.253: "Et sic exponunt hanc propositionem 'peccatum redit,' id est aliquis pro peccato puniendus est, pro quo commisso quandoque non erat dignus puniri. Quandoque enim sic fuit dimissum quod si moreretur, deus non puniret. Uere enim et sine omni conditione erat dimissum. Sed statim ut peccat, redit. Si autem queritur quomodo hoc fiat, iustitie dei hoc ascribunt; qua autem iustitia fiat, hoc se ignorare dicunt."

the return of sins, as well as texts by or attributed to Augustine (cc.1, 3, 4, 7), Hrabanus Maurus (c.1 §1), Gregory (c.2), and Bede (cc.5, 6). Some of these authorities assert that God will mete out to sinners the punishment due for original and/or inherited sins previously remitted in baptism, while others assert that God will mete out to sinners the punishment due for previously remitted actual sins.

In d.p.c.7 Gratian then writes:

> However, of those who follow this sentence, some say that sins which return are remitted according to justice, but not according to prescience, just as the names of the disciples who later fell away were written in the book of life on account of justice, which they used to serve, but not according to prescience, which did not hold them in the number of those who were to be saved.[84]

Commenting on this passage, the decretist Huguccio claimed that Gratian had introduced the distinction between justice and prescience simply because he wanted an excuse to talk about divine foreknowledge and predestination.[85] But a comparison with *Baptizato homine* suggests that he introduced the distinction in earnest, to neutralize objections to his interpretation of the return of sins.

Gratian believes that the end of c.8 clearly supports the idea that God sometimes remits sins according to justice but not according to prescience. However, the beginning of the authority, he says, seems to provide support for what seems—but in the end will turn out not—to be a different view, that in baptism and penance God remits sins so completely that, were a person to die immediately afterward, he or she would be saved.[86] This latter formulation of the return of

84. De pen. D.4 d.p.c.7.

85. Huguccio, *Summa decretorum ad* De pen. D.4 d.p.c.7 v. *Eorum* (*Horum* Aa Fd Friedb.) *uero* (Paris, BNF, lat. 15387, fol. 167rb): "Assignat Magister quandam differentiam inter eos qui dicunt peccata dimissa redire. Quidam enim eorum dicunt quod peccata reditura dimittuntur secundum iustitiam et non secundum prescientiam. Alii eorum dicunt quod omnino et ex toto dimittuntur. Modicum ualet hec differentia, sed uoluit Gratianus habere occasionem tractandi de prescientia siue de predestinatione Dei."

86. De pen. D.4 d.p.c.8 (ed. Friedberg, 1232, supported by Aa Fd): "Finis huius auctoritatis eorum sententie concordat qui peccata dicunt remitti secundum iustitiam, non secundum prescientiam.... Alii uero, quamvis fateantur peccata redire, tamen seu per baptisma seu per penitentiam asserunt omnino peccata re-

sins is the one described in *Baptizato homine*. The *alii* mentioned in that treatise assert that forgiven sins which return are "at one time ... remitted in such a way that if he had died, God would not have punished him. For it was remitted truly and without any condition. But as soon as he sins, it returns."[87]

Baptizato homine describes proponents of this formulation of the return of sins as being unable to provide a rational explanation for their position and simply ascribing everything to God's justice.[88] Gratian proves the treatise incorrect by showing how *Baptizato homine*'s formulation is identical to the formulation of the return of sins that relies upon the distinction between God's justice and prescience. Those who believe that sins return, he explains, must believe both that some sins are remitted according to justice and not prescience and that baptism and penance so completely remit sin that, were a person to die immediately afterward, he or she would be saved.[89]

Gratian, moreover, goes on specifically to refute the main authority on the return of sins that *Baptizato homine* had used to defend its preferred position, the excerpt from Prosper mentioned above. Those who say that remitted sins do not return, Gratian writes, attempt to prove their view through the authority of Gregory and Prosper.[90] In refuting these proof texts, however, Gratian ignores the text by Gregory (c.13), which *Baptizato homine* does not discuss, and chooses instead to focus on the text by Prosper (c.14) that had served as the chief authority against the return of sins in *Baptizato homine*.

> The end of this authority [namely, c.14, the excerpt from Prosper] appears to contradict the beginning. For the return of sins or being damned in original sin is nothing other than receiving the punishment due for a sin

mitti, et plena fide accedentem ad lauacrum renasci non aqua tantum sed etiam Spiritu sancto, et si postea peccaturus sit, deinde penitentem et si aliquando recasurus sit, tamen tempore sue penitentie ita perfecte expiatum affirmant ut, si tunc moreretur, salutem inueniret eternam. Quorum sententie eiusdem auctoritatis principium consentit."

87. *Baptizato homine* §41, ed. Wei, 99.248–100.250.

88. Ibid., ed. Wei, 100.251–53.

89. See the overview provided in chapter 4, esp. pp. 136–43.

90. De pen. D.4 d.p.c.12 (ed. Friedberg, 1235, supported by Aa Fd): "Qui autem dicunt quod peccata dimissa non redeant, auctoritate Gregorii et Prosperi sententiam suam affirmare conantur."

after its remission. Proponents of this position, however, determine the contrary authorities thus: remitted sins are said to return because anyone who returns to the vomit [of sin] after having received remission will be punished all the more harshly, so much the more that he, having abused God's benignity, has shown himself ungrateful for the remission of his [sins].[91]

Gratian's refutation bears many similarities to the corresponding passage in *Baptizato homine*.[92] Not only does it, like *Baptizato homine*, echo 2 Peter 2:22 in its reference to vomit (*ad uomitum redierit/canis ad uomitum*), but it also attributes to proponents of the non-return of sins the same justification for their position. Sins are said to return not because they in fact return, but because the sinner is punished even more harshly for later sins.

Conclusion

Italy in the twelfth century is not known for being a center of theological activity. None of its cathedral schools ever achieved the renown of the schools of northern France, nor did any Abelard or John of Salisbury commemorate the life of its masters. But twelfth-century Italy was not a theological wasteland. It had its own fair share of masters and students, who, like their more famous northern French compeers, both engaged in theological debate and recorded their opinions in writing.

91. De pen. D.4 d.p.c.14 (ed. Friedberg, 1236, supported by Aa Fd): "Finis huius auctoritatis principio contraire uidetur. Neque enim aliud est peccata dimissa redire uel in originali peccato dampnari, quam penam peccato debitam post eiusdem remissionem excipere. Auctoritates uero sibi contrarias, assertores huius sententie ita determinant: peccata dimissa redire dicuntur, quia quisquis post acceptam remissionem ad uomitum redierit tanto grauius punietur, quanto magis benignitate Dei abusus singulorum remissioni accepte ingratus extitit. Verum illa sententia fauorabilior uidetur, quia pluribus roboratur auctoritatibus et euidentiori ratione firmatur."

92. *Baptizato homine* §34, ed. Wei, 97.194–98.201: "Si iterum opponitur: 'penitens ad peccatum reuersus, canis ad uomitum,' sic respondeatur: canis dum cibo deprimitur, uomit et leuigatur, sed resumens iterum grauatur. Similiter peccator. Deponit quidem peccatum penitendo, sed iterum peccando grauatur. Non tamen de eodem. Non enim idem homicidium uel periurium potest committere. Sed tamen ita grauatur de posteriori, sicut grauabatur de priori, et grauius etiam puniendus."

Gratian, this chapter has tried to show, was one of these masters and his work, particularly his penitential theology, should be interpreted in light of contemporary Italian theological works. The debates recorded in these writings suggest that Gratian's own interest in penitential theology was rooted in contemporary controversies and that *De penitentia* is at least in part a work of criticism and correction. The core of *De penitentia* engages with issues debated in contemporary sentence collections of probable Italian origin, such as *Ut autem hoc evidenter* and *Baptizato homine*, which may have been among Gratian's formal sources. It employs many of the same proof texts and arguments as these works, but uses them to defend diametrically opposed positions. Like *Principium et causa* and works dependent on it, *Ut autem hoc evidenter* argues that those who possess charity can never lose it, that only the predestined can possess charity, and that those who possess charity can sin without losing it. Gratian, however, explicitly rejects all three of these theses in distinction 2 of *De penitentia*. Together with the related treatise *Augustinus in libro vite*, *Baptizato homine* suggests that people can perform penance fruitfully for just one of many sins and that forgiven sins do not return. But these views did not find favor with Gratian, who rejects them explicitly and indeed may have structured distinctions 3 and 4 of *De penitentia* to refute arguments articulated in *Baptizato homine*. For Gratian, penitential theology and critical theology were closely intertwined.

6

From Penitential Theology to the Canon Law of Magic

No matter how well written or skillfully argued, a work falls short if it fails to find an audience. This chapter explores one strategy that Gratian appears to have adopted to address this problem and its rather surprising consequence. Gratian, I propose, attempted to disseminate his critique of contemporary scholastic penitential theology—which, chapter 5 argued, he sets forth in *De penitentia*—by incorporating it into his textbook on canon law, the *Decretum*. In the process of doing so, he was led to include and contribute to the systematization of the canon law of magic and superstition. These topics had received great attention in earlier penitentials and canonical collections composed in border regions like Germany, perhaps because they were intended for recently Christianized peoples, but had receded in prominence in some areas by the eleventh and twelfth centuries.[1] Gratian played an important role in ensuring that magic and superstition continued to attract the attention of jurists and confessors as well as in providing a new framework for their analysis.

1. Adriaan H. Gaastra, "Between Liturgy and Canon Law: A Study of Books of Confession and Penance" (PhD diss., University of Utrecht, 2007), 165: "The indifference towards pagan superstitions or food taboos indicates that these topics were no longer considered relevant in the eleventh and twelfth centuries."

The medieval church inherited its belief in the existence of magic, as well as a mistrust for its powers, from the ancient world. Both Greeks and Romans often consulted astrologers, diviners, oracles, soothsayers, and other practitioners of magic, even though such scholars also developed laws to limit and/or outlaw such persons.[2] Among the books of the Old Testament, Exodus prescribes the death penalty for sorcerers (*maleficos*), while Leviticus forbids the consultation of magicians (*magos*) and diviners (*ariolos*).[3] The New Testament mentions magic more rarely but typically in a negative light, with the notable exception of the magi from the east, who Matthew tells us visited and worshipped the baby Jesus in Bethlehem. Few readers of the Bible find Elymas, the magician and false prophet who opposed the apostle Paul, or Simon Magus, the magician who tried to buy the Holy Spirit, to be very sympathetic characters.[4] The latter, in particular, became reviled in later Christian tradition as a hypocrite and heresiarch, the inventor of simony.[5]

Augustine of Hippo was the first Christian thinker to formulate a comprehensive theory explaining why magic was wrong. Magicians, he taught, possess no special power of their own, but accomplish all that they accomplish through the help of demons. Words, gestures, and objects used in magical rites are signs and sacrifices offered to demons, imploring them and informing them of their human suppliant's will. At its heart, then, all magic is idolatry and demon worship. Good magic is a contradiction in terms, and no true Christian can practice magic.[6]

Augustine's critique of magic won widespread acceptance among

2. See Fritz Graf, *Magic in the Ancient World*, trans. Franklin Philip (Cambridge, Mass.: Harvard University Press, 1997); J. B. Rives, "Magic in Roman Law: The Reconstruction of a Crime," *Classical Antiquity* 22 (2003): 313–39; Georg Luck, *Arcana Mundi: Magic and the Occult in the Greek and Roman Worlds; A Collection of Ancient Texts*, 2nd ed. (Baltimore, Md.: Johns Hopkins University Press, 2006).

3. Ex 22:18: "maleficos non patieris uiuere"; Lv 19:31: "ne declinetis ad magos nec ab ariolis aliquid sciscitemini ut polluamini per eos; ego Dominus Deus uester."

4. Acts 8:9–24, 13:6–12.

5. See Alberto Ferreiro, *Simon Magus in Patristic, Medieval, and Early Modern Traditions* (Leiden: Brill, 2005).

6. Augustine, *De doctrina christiana* 2.19.29–24.37, ed. Joseph Martin, CCSL 32 (Turnhout: Brepols, 1962), 53–60; Hersperger, *Kirche, Magie und "Aberglaube,"* 167–71.

Christian thinkers and quickly became the standard Catholic view of the matter. Yet because magic was such a pervasive part of late antique and early medieval society, magical practices persisted even after the conversion of the Romans and barbarians to Christianity.[7] Canons from early medieval councils and tariffs in early medieval penitentials testify to the persistence of pre-Christian magical rites among the inhabitants of northern and western Europe, as well as to the adaption of Christian rites and symbols to magical ends. The German abbot Regino of Prüm thought that contemporary abuses were numerous and serious enough to merit including, and probably forging, a variety of canons on magic in his *Libri duo de synodalibus causis et disciplinis ecclesiasticis*.[8] His canonical collection is the first to group together material on magic thematically. Writing a century later in the same general region, Burchard of Worms concurred on the relevance of this material for the clergy, who needed the guidance of these canons in ministering to and disciplining the faithful. Burchard incorporated Regino's canons on magic almost wholesale into his *Decretum* and supplemented them with a number of new texts.[9] In addition, he reorganized and systematized this material, taking care to clarify the scriptural principles on which the rulings were based and to harmonize the punishments they prescribed.[10] Burchard is not usually thought of as a jurist, yet, as Greta Austin has shown, he was a systematic thinker and his *Decretum* marks an important step in the growth of legal reflection.[11]

7. Valerie Flint, *The Rise of Magic in Early Medieval Europe* (Princeton, N.J.: Princeton University Press, 1991).

8. On Regino's concern with contemporary abuses, *Das Sendhandbuch des Regino von Prüm = Reginonis Prumiensis Libri duo de synodalibus causis et disciplinis ecclesiasticis*, ed. and trans. Wilfried Hartmann (Darmstadt: Wissenschaftliche Buchgesellschaft, 2004), 21–22: "Illud etiam adiciendum, quod multa flagitiorum genera hoc pessimo tempore in ecclesia et perpetrata sunt et perpetrantur, quae priscis temporibus inaudita, quia non facta, et ideo non scripta et fixis sententiis damnata, quae modernis patrum regulis et damnata sunt et quotidie damnantur." The canons dealing with magic are canons 354–78 of book 2. On Regino's canonical collection, see Kéry, *Canonical Collections of the Early Middle Ages*, 128–33; Fowler-Magerl, *Clavis*, 77–79.

9. Austin, *Shaping Church Law*, 265–76. For a guide to the literature, see Kéry, *Canonical Collections*, 133–55; Fowler-Magerl, *Clavis*, 85–90.

10. Austin, *Shaping Church Law*, 174–79.

11. Ibid., esp. 2–4.

Gratian, of course, represents an even more advanced and critical stage in the development of canon law, including the canon law of magic. Although he nowhere provides a comprehensive treatment of magic, he does draw attention to and examine it in two of his *causae*. *Causa* 26 concerns a priest who refuses to stop practicing divination, while *Causa* 33 deals with a man suffering from magically induced impotence. In connection with the first of these *causae*, Gratian examines five questions regarding divination and two regarding penance. In connection with the second, he examines one question on magically induced impotence and one on penance (which, however, corresponds to an entire treatise on penance, the tract *De penitentia*), as well as three questions relating to marriage. *Causa* 26 contributed to the systematization of the canon law of magic by shifting the focus away from the amount of penance due for any specific act of magic to more theoretical problems about magic, such as its definition, sinfulness, divisions, and the way in which it should be punished. Although this section of the *Decretum* attracted little attention from Gratian's twelfth- and thirteenth-century commentators, it played an important role in treatments of magic from the fourteenth century onwards, when the growth of learned magic and the emergence of witchcraft allegations stimulated intense legal analysis of this topic.[12] In addition, the placement of this *causa* near *Causae* 23 and 24 encouraged later commentators to think of these *causae* as a unit, the so-called *causae hereticorum*, and thus to place magic in a new category, that of heresy, rather than simply viewing it as a form of idolatry, as Augustine had taught.[13] *Causa* 33 advanced the systematization of the canon law of magic by posing explicitly the question of the relationship between magically induced impotence and natural im-

12. Edward Peters, *The Magician, the Witch, and the Law* (Philadelphia: University of Pennsylvania Press, 1978), 15.

13. See, e.g., Rufinus, *Summa decretorum* ad C.26 pr., ed. Singer, 423, and Johannes Faventinus, *Summa decretorum* ad C.26 pr. (Vat. Borgh. 71, fol. 138rb), who copies Rufinus almost verbatim: "Postquam interposuit necessarium tractatum de priuilegiis ecclesiarum, redit agere de hereticis: sortilegium enim et auguratio similisque superstitio (augurium et his similia *Faventinus*), de quibus hic agitur, heresis species sunt (species est heresis *Faventinus*), in eis utique, qui fidem Christi receperunt (susceperunt *Faventinus*)."

potence.[14] In addition, through its proximity to *De penitentia*, it also stimulated reflection on the role of intention in the punishment of magical crimes.[15]

This chapter proposes—in an admittedly speculative but I hope not unjustified fashion—that Gratian's interest in penitential theology affected his handling of the canon law of magic and thus contributed indirectly to its systematization. More specifically, this chapter argues that Gratian's desire to incorporate his theological treatise on penance, *De penitentia*, into his *Decretum* was the main reason why he decided to deal with the subject of magic at all. Gratian's treatment of magically induced impotence is brief and not particularly sophisticated. He broaches this subject in *Causa* 33, it seems, mainly because it provides him with an excuse for considering confession and penance. One of Gratian's formal sources explicitly recommends confession as a cure for magically induced impotence. Gratian appears to have latched onto this detail and made it a central element of *Causa* 33 not because he thought it the best way to cure an embarrassing preternatural ailment, but rather because he was looking for a way to integrate *De penitentia* into the *causa* structure of the *Decretum*.

Gratian's reasons for inserting a discussion of divination are harder to discern, but likewise may have been connected to *De penitentia*. Gratian perhaps composed questions 6 and 7 of *Causa* 26, which discuss aspects of penance not dealt with in that tract, to supplement the treatment of penance found in *De penitentia*. Desire to integrate these questions into the *causa* structure of the *Decretum* may have led Gratian to combine them with material on divination, including a

14. See esp. Catherine Rider, "Between Theology and Popular Practice: Medieval Canonists on Magic and Impotence," in *Boundaries of the Law: Geography, Gender, and Jurisdiction in Medieval and Early Modern Europe*, ed. Anthony Mussen (Aldershot: Ashgate, 2005), 53–66.

15. The redactor of the second recension was the earliest of Gratian's readers to explore this subject. See the second-recension addition De pen. D.1 c.20 (ed. Friedberg, 1163), which is actually a dictum and not a canon: "Cogitatio non meretur penam lege ciuili, cum suis terminis contenta est. Discernuntur tamen a maleficiis ea, que de iure effectum desiderant. In his enim non nisi animi iudicium consideratur." The first Bolognese gloss apparatus *Ordinaturus Magister* comments approvingly to the word *maleficiis* (Mi = Munich, Bayerische Staatsbibliothek, Clm 27337, fol. 189v), "In maleficiis uoluntas spectatur non exitus uel effectus."

canon infamous among historians of witchcraft and the witch crazes, the canon *Episcopi*, thereby producing *Causa* 26.[16] Since Gratian probably composed *Causa* 26 after he had already finished composing *Causa* 33, *Causa* 33 could have served as a model for *Causa* 26, inspiring Gratian to combine material on magic and penance in a single causa yet again.

Impotence, Confession, and the Creation of *Causa* 33

Causa 33 begins with one of the most entertaining and bizarre stories found in Gratian's *Decretum*.

A man rendered impotent by magic (*maleficiis*) finds himself cuckolded and then abandoned by his wife, who runs off and publicly marries her seducer. In response, the man confesses the [unspecified] crime he has committed—[not to a priest but] to God alone—thereby obtaining release from his impotence. He seeks his wife, and she comes back to him. So that he may have more time for prayer and receive the eucharist worthily, he takes a vow of continence. His wife, however, refuses her assent. It is asked: [First,] whether a woman can obtain a separation from her husband on account of impotence? Second, whether after the separation she can marry someone with whom she has previously committed fornication [that is, adultery]? Third, whether a crime can be wiped away by confession of the heart alone? Fourth, if one may render the marriage debt during times meant for prayer? Fifth, whether a man can take a vow of continence without his wife's consent, or whether he can obtain her consent by threats?[17]

16. Gratian includes the canon *Episcopi* as C.26 q.5 c.12. On the contribution of this canon to medieval and early modern understandings of witchcraft, see Jeffrey Burton Russell, *Witchcraft in the Middle Ages* (Ithaca, N.Y.: Cornell University Press, 1972), 75–80.

17. C.33 pr. (ed. Werckmeister, 488): "Quidam (uir *add. Aa*[pc] *Friedb. Werck.*) maleficiis impeditus uxori sue debitum reddere non poterat. Alius interim clanculo eam corrupit; a uiro suo separata corruptori suo publice nubit; crimen quod admiserat corde tantum Deo confitetur; redditur huic facultas cognoscendi eam: repetit uxorem suam; qua recepta, ut expeditius uacaret orationi et ad carnes agni purus accederet, continentiam se seruaturum promisit; uxor uero consensum non adhibuit. Queritur an propter impossibilitatem coeundi a uiro suo aliqua sit separanda? Secundo, an post separationem ei nubere ualeat cum quo prius fornicata est? Tertio, si sola confessione cordis crimen possit deleri? Quarto, si tempore orationis quis ualeat reddere coniugii debitum? Quinto, an uir sine consensu uxoris continenti-

Although the term *causa* might lead one to expect otherwise, this case statement bears little resemblance to an actual legal dispute or court case. Not only are the issues raised by the case statement diverse and only tenuously related, the story as a whole is also clearly imaginary. Blaming male impotence on magic (*maleficium*) seems to have been fairly common in medieval Europe, and seduction, adultery, and even bigamy are known to have occurred frequently during this time period.[18] It is hard to believe, however, that any of Gratian's contemporaries could have been so unlucky as to experience each and every single one of these marital misfortunes, or that, after finally recovering his potency and becoming reconciled with his wife, a man suffering from these afflictions would decide that he no longer had any interest in sex and then take a vow of continence.

Modern scholars have often praised Gratian's *causae* for their believability and close connection to medieval legal practice. According to John T. Noonan, for instance, "only a lawyer could have designed the hypotheticals of Part II, made and savored the legal distinctions of the dicta, and shown as much interest in rules and process as in doctrine."[19] R. W. Southern remarks that "Nearly two-thirds of the whole work—its whole central core—takes the form of generally imaginary, but sometimes evidently real, situations at every level of magnitude, which give rise to astonishingly complicated disputes in a hierarchy of ecclesiastical courts of law."[20] And in Frederick Paxton's view, *Causa* 13, which examines a dispute between two churches over tithes and burial rights, presents "one of the most vivid examples of legal argument in the *Decretum*.... The mind and experience of a lawyer clearly lie behind the narrative at the core of Gratian's thirteenth case."[21]

am uouere possit uel si minis et (uel *Friedb. Werck.*) terroribus licentiam uouendi ab ea extorquere ualeat?"

18. On magically induced impotence, see Catherine Rider, *Magic and Impotence in the Middle Ages* (Oxford: Oxford University Press, 2006). On adultery, see James A. Brundage, *Law, Sex, and Christian Society in Medieval Europe* (Chicago: University of Chicago Press, 1987), 207–9.

19. Noonan, "Gratian Slept Here," 145–72.

20. Southern, *Scholastic Humanism*, 1:288–89.

21. Paxton, "Gratian's Thirteenth Case and the Composition of the *Decretum*," 123 and 128.

In the judgment of these lawyers and historians, Gratian's *causae* possess the same qualities as the hypothetical cases used in modern legal education. In modern law schools, students study hypothetical cases in order to explore the principles underlying legal scenarios, as well as to gain a better understanding of the consequences of legal rules and how they work in practice. Hypothetical cases are analytical tools, which professors use to teach students legal reasoning. Gratian seems to have designed the realistic case statements in the *Decretum* with this same purpose in mind: he thought they would help his students get a better grasp of the principles and consequences of ecclesiastical laws.

As John Noël Dillon has emphasized, however, only a small number of Gratian's case statements in fact resemble conceivable legal disputes. For the majority of Gratian's *causae*, including *Causa* 33, the case statements are simply imaginary stories. They "consist of the blunt narration of a series of generally unlawful actions; these, in turn, concern loosely related legal issues."[22] In their diffuse and idiosyncratic nature, they differ from not only the hypothetical cases employed in modern legal education, but also the ones characteristic of medieval civilian and later canonistic *quaestiones disputatae*.[23] In the *Decretum*'s unrealistic *causae*, the case statement is primarily an organizational rather than an analytical tool. Its main task is not to aid the comprehension of legal principles and their consequences, but rather to introduce topics of canon law for consideration. In other words, Gratian designed the case statements of the *Decretum*'s clearly fictitious *causae* not to shed greater light on some legal principle or other or to test his students' abilities to spot legal issues, but rather

22. John Noël Dillon, "Case Statements (Themata) and the Composition of Gratian's Cases," *ZRG KA* 92 (2006): 306–36, at 308.

23. In contrast to civilian and later canonistic *quaestiones disputatae*, some of the earliest canonistic representatives of the genre, which date to a decade or two after Gratian, follow Gratian in being more diffuse and unrealistic. See Gérard Fransen, "Les questions disputées dans les facultés de droit," in *Les questions disputées et les questions quodlibétiques dans les facultés de théologie, de droit et de médecine*, ed. Bernardo C. Bazàn et al., Typologie des Sources du Moyen Âge Occidental 44–45 (Turnhout: Brepols, 1985), 223–77, esp. 245.

simply to provide an excuse for treating a variety of legal issues as a group within the same *causa*.[24]

This frequent use of *causae* as an organizational rather than an analytical tool becomes particularly clear when one compares and contrasts the relationship between the case statement and questions in realistic *causae* with their relationship in unrealistic *causae*. In realistic *causae*, consideration of real-life problems, like disagreements between churches over tithes or between bishops and monasteries over the control of parish churches, prompted Gratian to explore issues key to resolving these disputes. As with hypothetical cases considered in modern-day law schools, the scenario described in case statements of this sort preceded and informed the formulation of the accompanying questions. In clearly fictitious *causae* like *Causa* 33, however, formulation of the questions preceded the creation of the case statements. Gratian did not first dream up the fantastic case statement of *Causa* 33, meditate upon its legal significance, and then conclude that the story raised five particularly challenging legal questions. Instead, he knew in advance what questions he wanted to discuss in the *causa* and then, without any regard for realism, crafted a case statement that would allow him to treat each one in turn.

In *Causa* 33, the case statement is nothing more than an entertaining story that provides Gratian with an excuse to group together questions on diverse and unrelated issues. Scholars have often argued that question 3, which is devoted to confession and in fact corresponds to an entire treatise on penitential theology, *De penitentia*, is out of place and for that reason must be a late addition to the *Decretum*, even though they have also often held, somewhat contradictorily, that the original form of *Causa* 33 probably included a highly abbreviated question 3 consisting of only a few canons on penance.[25] Question 3 alone has nothing to do with marriage, the general topic of not only the other four questions in *Causa* 33, but also the nine surrounding *cau-*

24. By spotting legal issues, I mean to refer to that staple of law school final exams, the "issue spotter."

25. See, e.g., Jacqueline Rambaud, "L'étude des manuscrits du Décret de Gratien conservés en France," *Studia Gratiana* 1 (1953): 119–45, at 130 and 131; Rambaud, "Le legs," 82–90; Chodorow, *Christian Political Theory*, 13; Gaudemet, "Le débat," 52 and 58; Brundage, *Medieval Canon Law*, 191.

sae (*Causae* 27–32 and 34–36).[26] Yet aside from touching in some way or other on marriage, no common theme unites the other four questions in *Causa* 33 either. From a jurisprudential viewpoint, there is no reason for treating together impotence, vows of continence, times permissible for sexual relations, and the permissibility of marrying one's former accomplice in adultery. Although Gratian discusses all of these questions in the same *causa*, his treatment of these issues is in fact unrelated, both to one another and to issues explored in *De penitentia*. The four questions on marriage and the question on confession appear together in *Causa* 33 for one reason and one reason only: Gratian decided to craft a case statement raising all five issues.

Crafting the Case Statement

There are several possible explanations as to why Gratian decided to treat confession together with questions pertaining to marriage in *Causa* 33. The material on confession may have simply been an afterthought. Gratian, it could be argued, originally intended *Causa* 33 to deal solely with marriage, but later decided to insert a treatise on penance, which he turned into the *causa*'s third question. Also conceivable is that Gratian for some reason originally intended for *Causa* 33 to include a short treatment of confession, but not a full-blown treatise on penance (*De penitentia*). The expansion of an originally short question on confession into the treatise on penance found in the first-recension *Decretum*, one could argue, happened only later in the redactional process. Here I will advance yet another view. Based on an analysis of the case statement and its relationship to the questions in the *causa*, as well as the results of chapter 5 concerning Gratian's interest in penance, I will propose that Gratian did not insert a discussion of penance into a pre-existing and independently-conceived *Causa* 33, but rather that he created *Causa* 33 in order to incorporate a largely pre-existing and independent tract on penance into the *Decre-*

26. For an overview of the first-recension version of the *causae* on marriage, see Jean Werckmeister, "Les deux versions du *De matrimonio* de Gratien," *RDC* 48 (1998): 301–16; Werckmeister, *Décret de Gratien: Causes 27 à 36; Le Mariage* = *RDC* 58–59 (2011).

tum.[27] Gratian had material on penance, namely *De penitentia*, that he wanted to include in his textbook. Probably because the earliest stages of the *Decretum* consisted solely of *causae*, he decided not to append this material as a separate treatise, but rather to integrate it into the *Decretum* through the creation of a new and highly contrived *causa* centering on magically induced impotence.[28] Thus was *Causa* 33 born.

The case statement to *Causa* 33 consists of four main units. In the first unit, Gratian tells us that the protagonist suffers from magically induced impotence. In the second unit, we learn of the wife's seduction and marriage to her seducer. In the third unit, the protagonist confesses his sin to God, is cured of his impotence, and recovers his wife. In the fourth and final unit, the protagonist takes a vow of continence against his wife's wishes so that he may be able to devote more time to prayer and to receive the eucharist worthily.

Parallels with C.27 q.2 suggest that the first and fourth units belong to the very original form of the case statement. This question examines the problem posed by girls who have been betrothed but wish to renounce their fiancés and marry someone else.[29] In coming to his solution, Gratian considers various arguments for and against the view that people who have been betrothed are already married, including arguments derived from the canon law of impotence and religious vows, which are the subjects of the first and fourth units of the case statement to *Causa* 33. Early medieval law did not dis-

27. I am not the first to suggest that *De penitentia* was originally an independent treatise. See, e.g., Hödl, *Die Geschichte*, 164: "Es sprechen gewichtige Gründe dafür, daß der Bußtraktat des *Decretum Gratiani* ursprünglich selbständig war und nachträglich in das Dekret aufgenommen wurde. Die äußere Sonderstellung des Traktates im *Decretum* als q. 3 C 33 de poenitentia weist auf die ursprüngliche Selbständigkeit hin [There are weighty grounds for thinking that the penitential tract of Gratian's *Decretum* was originally independent and incorporated into the *Decretum* only subsequently. The external placement of the tract in the *Decretum* as *quaestio* 3 of *Causa* 33 is an indication of its original independence]."

28. A number of scholars have suggested that the *Decretum* originated with the *causae*. This is, for example, the assumption underlying much of the literature on Sg. See chapter 1. For an example from an opponent of Larrainzar's hypothesis, see Dillon, "Case Statements," esp. 325–28.

29. C.27 q.2 d.a.c.1 (ed. Werckmeister, 134): "Sequitur secunda questio qua queritur an puelle alteri desponsate possint renuntiare priori conditioni et transferre sua uota ad alium. Hic primum uidendum est an sit coniugium inter eos? Secundo, an possint ab inuicem discedere?"

tinguish clearly between betrothal and marriage, and regulations dealing with betrothed couples sometimes suggested that they had already entered into an indissoluble bond. Canons dealing with impotence and vows of continence, Gratian argues, prove otherwise. Impotence and vows of continence bear no direct relationship to each other, but both show that betrothal and marriage are distinct and separate.

Gratian's first main argument in C.27 q.2 against the view that people who are betrothed are already married rests on differences in rules governing sexual relations and entrance into religious life. According to the apostle Paul in 1 Corinthians 7:3–5, a wife must consent to sexual relations with her husband and a husband to sexual relations with his wife whenever the other spouse so desires. The only exception is when both spouses agree to temporary continence so that they may devote more time to prayer. For this reason, a man cannot enter the religious life without his wife's consent, nor can a wife without her husband's. Religious are forbidden to engage in sexual relations, whereas spouses must "pay the marriage debt" unless both agree otherwise.[30] But, as Gratian points out, those who have been betrothed may take a vow of continence without their fiancé or fiancée's knowledge and even enter religious life without their future spouse's consent. Consequently, he concludes, betrothal and marriage cannot be identical.[31]

Differences in rules concerning natural frigidity provide Gratian with the other main argument in C.27 q.2 against the view that

30. C.27 q.2 d.p.c.18 (ed. Werckmeister, 156): "Item Apostolus precipit ut uxor reddat debitum uiro et uir uxori, nisi forte ex consensu ad tempus ut expeditius uacent orationi. Vnde datur intelligi quod sine consensu alterius non licet alteri uacare orationi. Item propositum melioris uite uir sumere non potest sine consensu uxoris et e conuerso."

31. C.27 q.2 d.p.c.26 (ed. Werckmeister, 166–68): "Ecce quod coniugati sine consensu alterius continentiam profiteri non possunt. Sponsi uero, etiam inconsultis quas sibi desponsauerunt, exemplis et auctoritate probantur continentiam posse seruare.... patet quod sponsi non exquisito consensu suarum sponsarum continentiam profiteri ualent." C.27 q.2 d.p.c.28 (ed. Werckmeister, 170): "Cum ergo coniugatorum continentia nisi ex amborum consensu Deo offerri non ualeat; cum uir sui corporis potestatem non habeat sed mulier, sponse autem monasterium possint eligere et sponsi non exquisito consensu sponsarum propositum melioris uite assumere ualeant: patet quod inter sponsum et sponsam coniugium non est."

those who have been betrothed are already married. When impotence occurs after a marriage has already been consummated, the spouses must remain together. When impotence prevents the consummation of a marriage, however, the woman is free to leave her spouse and remarry. Since marriage is indissoluble, argues Gratian, the man and woman in this latter scenario were never really husband and wife.[32]

C.27 q.2 helps explain why Gratian decided to discuss impotence and vows of continence together in *Causa* 33—the canons concerning impotence and vows of continence help prove that betrothal is distinct from marriage. C.27 q.2 does not, however, provide any insight into why Gratian chose to broach the problem of magically induced impotence in particular, nor why he thought it fitting to treat adultery and confession in *Causa* 33 as well. The case statement's literary sources, however, shed light on Gratian's thought process. Gratian appears to have drawn most of the details for the case statement of *Causa* 33 from just three canons: two taken from the *Panormia* and one taken from the *Tripartita*. Two of these canons were among Gratian's formal sources for *Causa* 33, while the third is found immediately after a group of canons that Gratian took from the *Panormia* and used to create C.33 q.1.

Panormia 6.117 appears to have provided Gratian with the main outlines of his hypothetical case in *Causa* 33, most notably, magically

32. C.27 q.2 d.p.c.28 §§1–3 (ed. Werckmeister, 170): "Item cum secundum Augustinum illa mulier non pertineat ad matrimonium cum qua docetur non fuisse commixtio sexus. Item secundum Leonem illa non pertinet ad matrimonium in qua docetur non fuisse nuptiale misterium: apparet quod inter sponsum et sponsam coniugium non est. Item Nicolaus papa precepit de his qui ab aduersariis excecantur aut membris detruncantur, ut ob hanc infirmitatem talium coniugia non soluantur. De his autem qui causa frigiditatis uxoribus debitum reddere non possunt, statuit Gregorius papa ut uterque eorum septima manu propinquorum tactis sacrosanctis reliquiis iureiurando dicat quod numquam permixtione carnis coniuncti una caro effecti fuissent. Tunc mulier secundas nuptias poterit contrahere; uir autem qui frigide nature est maneat sine spe coniugii." C.27 q.2 d.p.c.29 (ed. Werckmeister, 172–74): "Ecce impossibilitas coeundi, si post carnalem copulam inuenta fuerit in aliquo, non soluit coniugium. Si uero ante carnalem copulam deprehensa fuerit, liberum facit mulieri alium uirum accipere. Vnde apparet illos non fuisse coniuges; alioquin non liceret eis ab inuicem discedere, excepta causa fornicationis; et sic discedentes oportet manere innuptos aut sibi inuicem reconciliari."

induced impotence, confession to God, separation on account of impotence, remarriage, and the original husband being reconciled with his wife. Gratian certainly knew this text since the first recension includes it as C.33 q.1 c.4. The canon, known after its opening words as *Si per sortiarias*, is an extract from a letter of Archbishop Hincmar of Reims, written toward the very end of 860, to Archbishops Rudolf of Bourges and Frotar of Bordeaux, together with all the bishops of Aquitaine concerning Count Stephen of Auvergne's attempt to break off his betrothal to the daughter of another Aquitanian nobleman, Count Raymond.[33] An important ecclesiastic and one of the foremost jurists of the Carolingian era, Hincmar received numerous petitions for spiritual and legal advice. His surviving letters deal extensively with contemporary problems and lawsuits, from mundane property disputes to such high-profile cases as King Lothar II's attempt to divorce his wife Theutberga.[34] For the purposes of this chapter, the exact details of the salacious dispute between Stephen and Raymond, as well as Hincmar's opinion about how it could be resolved, are irrelevant. What matters instead are that Hincmar in the course of his letter broaches the problem of magically induced impotence and that his musings on this subject entered the canonical tradition as the canon *Si per sortiarias*.

In *Si per sortiarias*, Hincmar advises those rendered impotent by magic to confess their sins to God and a priest and to render satisfaction to God through tears, prayers, alms, and fasting.[35] Hincmar's un-

33. Hincmar of Reims, *De nuptiis Stephani et filiae Regimundi Comitis*, ed. Ernst Perels, *Epistolae Karolini aevi (VI): Hincmari archiepiscopi Remensis epistolae* 136, MGH Epp. 8.1 (Berlin: MGH, 1939), 87–107. For an analysis of this marriage dispute, see Philip Lyndon Reynolds, *Marriage in the Western Church: The Christianization of Marriage During the Patristic and Early Medieval Periods* (Leiden: Brill, 1994), 354–61.

34. For a recent, stimulating analysis of Hincmar's discussion of the proceedings against Theutberga, see Abigail Firey, "The Protection of Privacy: Secrets and Silence," chap. 2 of *A Contrite Heart: Prosecution and Redemption in the Carolingian Empire* (Leiden: Brill, 2009), 9–60.

35. *Panormia* 6.117: "Si per sortiarias atque maleficas, occulto, sed nunquam vel nusquam iniusto Dei iudicio permittente et diabolo preparante, concubitus non sequitur, hortandi sunt quibus ista eveniunt ut corde contrito et spiritu humiliato Deo et sacerdoti de omnibus peccatis suis puram confessionem faciant, et profusis lacrymis ac largioribus elemosinis et orationibus atque ieiuniis domi-

articulated assumption here seems to be that magically induced impotence is in some ways a punishment for sin. If people led holy and pure lives, God would not permit them to suffer the effects of magic. Confession and performing penance are thus key means to curing magically induced impotence. Hincmar also recommends that those suffering magically induced impotence try exorcism and other medicines of the church. If, says Hincmar, these means fail and the husband remains impotent, then the husband and wife can be separated and the wife can remarry. After the wife remarries, however, says Hincmar, she can never return to her original husband, even should he be cured of his impotence.

A second canon, *Panormia* 6.120, seems to have inspired Gratian to spice up his narrative with the addition of a seduction story. "If a man marries a woman and is unable to sleep with her, and his brother secretly (*clanculo*) corrupts her and she becomes pregnant, let them [the husband and wife] be separated. With due account being taken of their fragility, however, let mercy be granted to [let them live] a marriage only in God [that is, chastely]."[36] The *Panormia* reproduces the text of the canon in the considerably altered form found in Burchard's *Decretum*.[37] Although the *Panormia* correctly attributes this canon to the Council of Tribur (895), it follows Burchard in erroneously identifying the text as the council's third canon rather than its fifth judgment.[38] As in the case statement, the situation described in

no satisfaciant, et per exorcismos ac cetera medicine ecclesiastice munia, ministri ecclesie tales quantum annuerit Dominus qui Abimelech ac domum eius Abrahe orationibus sanavit, sanare procurent. Qui forte si sanari non potuerint, separari valebunt. Sed postquam alias nuptias expetierint, illis in carne viventibus quibus iuncte fuerint, prioribus quos reliquerant, etiam si possibilitas concumbendi eis reddita fuerit, reconciliari nequibunt."

36. *Panormia* 6.120: "Vir si duxerit uxorem, concumbere cum ea non valens, et frater eius clanculo eam vitiaverit et gravidam reddiderit, separentur. Considerata autem imbecillitate misericordia eis impertiatur ad coniugium tantum in Domino."

37. Burchard, *Decretum* 9.43, ed. Gerard Fransen and Theo Kölzer, *Decretorum libri XX* (Cologne, 1548; reprinted Aalen: Scientia Verlag, 1992), 128ra. On Burchard's alteration of his sources, see Austin, *Shaping Church Law*, esp. chap. 11: "Making Sense of Burchard's Textual Alterations."

38. *Iudicia Concilii Triburiensis* 5, ed. Alfred Boretius and Victor Krause, *Capitularia regum Francorum*, MGH Capit. 2 (Hanover: MGH, 1897), 207.

the canon concerns an impotent man who is cuckolded in secret. Both the case statement and the canon use the word *clanculo* to describe the seducer's actions. Although Gratian does not cite it in *Causa* 33, he must have been familiar with the canon, since it appears immediately after a series of canons that he used in composing C.33 q.1. Moreover, the first recension includes the original, pre-Burchard version of this canon as C.27 q.2 c.31.[39]

A third canon, *Tripartita* 3.15.79 (= *Panormia* 6.85), probably informed Gratian's treatment of the last part of the case statement: the discussion of spouses and vows of chastity. This canon, found in the first recension at C.33 q.5 c.2, contains an extract from a letter of Pope Alexander II to Landulf of Corsica. In the letter, Alexander admonishes Landulf for having entered a monastery while gravely ill and of having extorted his wife's consent to the matter through intimidation and threats of killing her (*minis et terroribus eam occidendi*). This same phrase, "intimidation and threats" (*minis et terroribus*), appears in the case statement of *Causa* 33. Alexander tells Landulf that one has to enter the monastic life freely, not out of fear. He also explains that spouses require each other's consent before they can enter religious life.[40]

The original form of *Causa* 33 must have included at least questions 1 and 5, since in composing the case statement Gratian drew

39. The formal source of C.27 q.2 c.31 seems to have been *Tripartita* 3.16.29, which is the only one of Gratian's normal formal sources to include this version of the canon.

40. JL 3497 = *Tripartita* 3.15.79: "Notificasti te mortetenus infirmatum et peccatorum tuorum recordatione et terrore ualde pauefactum, anxie quesisse monachum fieri, et a tua uxore minis et terroribus eam occidendi ad hoc licentiam extorsisse, et sic te monachicam uestem sine abbate sumpsisse, et monasterium petiisse. Postea uero cum sanus factus esses, . . . utpote penitens deuictus domum remeasse, et post multos dies quorundam sapientium consilio ad iam dicte mulieris cubile redisse. Nunc autem si tibi tua uxore uti liceat, nostrum requiris consilium. Si ita denique est ut tuus nuntius narrat, non uidetur nobis rationabiliter neque sana mente id factum, quoniam cum omni homini ad monachicam uitam tendenti legaliter, sancte, et iuste sit peragendum, tu contra leges minaciter et uiolenter a tua uxore partim terrore mortis, partim tue infirmitatis doloribus exanimatus deuia sequutus, nulla ut dicitur licentia accepta recessisti, et monasterium petiisti. Non enim uiolentia sed ex pari uoluntate et consensu . . . hoc fieri debet, neque uir in monasterium recipiendus est, nisi uxor illius femineum monasterium elegerit, aut professa continentiam habitum cum festinatione mutauerit."

upon canons included in each question. In the case statement, however, the narrative element that connects the issue examined in question 1 (impotence) to the issue examined in question 5 (vows of continence) is confession. Without confession, the case statement would have had to end early, with the wife's marriage to her seducer. Only confession enables Gratian to move the plot forward.

Gratian's case statements are extremely sparse. Each detail that Gratian brings up plays a role in the accompanying questions. If the original form of the case statement to *Causa* 33 mentioned confession, then the original form of *Causa* 33 must have included a question dealing with this subject as well. The fact that Gratian discusses penance in a *causa* otherwise concerned with marriage thus cannot be cited as evidence that *De penitentia* is an interpolation or a late addition to the *Decretum*. Instead, the very presence of a question on penance amidst a group of questions otherwise concerned with issues pertaining to marriage suggests that Gratian believed penance to be an important topic and raises the possibility that his primary purpose in composing *Causa* 33 was to provide a means for integrating material on penance into the rest of the *Decretum*.

Motivation and Inspiration

In *Si per sortiarias*, Hincmar suggests several different remedies for magically induced impotence. Although he mentions confession, he does not lay particular weight on this option. Why, then, does Gratian single out this detail for inclusion in the case statement of *Causa* 33? The answer, I would like to suggest, has to do with the way in which Gratian came up with the idea for *Causa* 33. *Causa* 33 did not originate with the first question on magically induced impotence, but rather with the third question on penance, that is, *De penitentia*. Prior to coming across *Si per sortiarias*, Gratian already had material on penance that he wanted to incorporate into the *Decretum*. The detail about confession in *Si per sortiarias* caught his eye not because medieval people regularly thought of confession as a means for curing magically induced impotence, but rather because he was already on the lookout for ways to create a case statement involving penance.

Two considerations support this hypothesis. First, no other twelfth-century canonist or theologian draws attention to confession as a cure for magically induced impotence. All theological and canonistic reflection on magically induced impotence in the period prior to and immediately after Gratian derives from *Si per sortiarias*. Ivo of Chartres appears to have been the one responsible for rediscovering this text and bringing it to the attention of contemporaries. Thanks to its incorporation into the Ivonian *Decretum* in the period 1093–95, the canon achieved a fairly wide circulation in twelfth-century canonical collections and florilegia.[41] After Gratian incorporated it into his *Decretum* and Peter Lombard into his *Four Books of Sentences*, the circulation of *Si per sortiarias* increased even further.[42]

Of authors writing before or around the same time as Gratian, only the anonymous marriage treatises associated with the school of Laon specifically address the problem of magically induced impotence, which they discuss in dependence on Hincmar's text. Two of the earliest treatises—*In primis hominibus* and *Cum omnia sacramenta*—reproduce an abbreviated form of *Si per sortiarias* but do not comment on Hincmar's suggestion that couples suffering from magically induced impotence should confess their sins.[43] Another three treatises paraphrase Hincmar rather than quote him verbatim. They list

41. Ivonian *Decretum* 8.194. On Ivo's *Decretum*, see Rolker, *Canon Law*; Kéry, *Canonical Collections*, 250–53; Fowler-Magerl, *Clavis*, 193–98. According to *Clavis canonum*, five pre-Gratian canonical collections aside from the Ivonian *Decretum* contain *Si per sortiarias*: *Panormia* 6.117, *Tripartita* 3.15.69, *Collection in 10 Parts* 7.24.2.6, *Collection in Nine Books* (Arch. S. Pietro C. 118) 8.1.127, and *Collectio Ambrosiana II* 108. To these one can add item 150 of the marriage tract of the *Sententiae magistri A*. See Heinrich J. F. Reinhardt, *Die Ehelehre der Schule des Anselm von Laon: Eine theologie- und kirchenrechtsgeschichtliche Untersuchung zu den Ehetexten der frühen Pariser Schule des 12. Jahrhunderts*, BGPTM n.F. 14 (Münster: Aschendorff, 1974), 217.1–11.

42. See Rider, *Magic and Impotence*, 58–67; Rider, "Between Theology and Popular Practice." Peter Lombard incorporated *Si per sortiarias* into his textbook at *Sententiae in IV libris distinctae* 4.34.3, ed. Ignatius Brady, 3rd ed. (Rome: Grottaferrata, 1971–81), 2:465.

43. Bernd Matecki, ed., *Der Traktat In primis hominibus: Eine theologie- und kirchenrechtsgeschichtliche Untersuchung zu einem Ehetext der Schule von Laon aus dem 12. Jahrhundert*, Adnotationes in Ius Canonicum 20 (Frankfurt am Main: Peter Lang, 2001), 31*.3–12; *Cum omnia sacramenta*, ed. Franz Bliemetzrieder, *Anselms von Laon Systematische Sentenzen*, BGPM 18.2–3 (Münster i. W.: Aschendorff, 1919), 129–51, at 141.

prayer, fasting, vigils, and almsgiving as ways to cure magically induced impotence, but omit confession.[44] Yet another treatise discusses the problem of magically induced impotence, but does not comment at all on ways to cure it.[45]

Gratian's commentators, the decretists, likewise fail to develop Hincmar's suggestion that confession can cure magically induced impotence. As remedies for magically induced impotence, for instance, Paucapalea suggests prayers, alms, and sacrifices offered by a priest, but not confession.[46] Rufinus reproduces this same list with the addition of fasting, while Stephen of Tournai simply proposes exorcisms and prayers.[47] Roland of Bologna and Simon of Bisignano, on the other hand, ignore the problem of how one can remedy magically induced impotence entirely, devoting attention only to the legal aspects of frigidity and *maleficium*.[48]

To my knowledge, only one writer prior to the thirteenth century—aside from Hincmar and Gratian—may even possibly mention

44. *Decretum Dei fuit*, ed. Weisweiler, *Das Schrifttum*, 361–79, at 373.4–9; Friedrich Stegmüller, ed., "*Sententiae Berolinenses*: Eine neugefundene Sentenzensammlung aus der Schule des Anselm von Laon," *Recherches de théologie ancienne et médiévale* [hereafter "*RTAM*"] 11 (1939): 33–61, at 59.35–60.3; *Coniugium est secundum Isidorum*, ed. Franz Bliemetzrieder, "Théologie et théologiens de l'école épiscopale de Paris avant Pierre Lombard," *RTAM* 3 (1931): 273–91, at 280.121–27.

45. *Sententiae Atrebatenses*, ed. Lottin, *Psychologie et morale*, 437.96–101.

46. Paucapalea, *Summa decretorum* ad C.33 q.1, ed. Johann Friedrich von Schulte, *Die Summa des Paucapalea über das Decretum Gratiani* (Giessen: E. Roth, 1890), 130: "De his auctoritate Higmarii ostenditur, quod post multas orationes ad deum fusas et eleemosynas pauperibus datas sacrificiaque pro eis a sacerdote oblata, si sanari nequeunt, separari valebunt."

47. Rufinus, *Summa* ad C.33 q.1, ed. Singer, 497: "Si vero impossibilitas conveniendi ex arte provenit maleficii, tunc interpositis orationibus, ieiuniis, helimosinis, sacrificiis aliquanto tempore, si postea concubitus non sequitur, separabuntur." Stephan of Tournai, *Summa decretorum* ad C.33 q.1, ed. Johann Friedrich von Schulte, *Die Summa des Stephanus Tornacensis über das Decretum Gratiani* (Giessen: E. Roth, 1891), 245: "Si autem ex maleficiis, cum exorcismis et orationibus debent sanari."

48. Roland, *Sententiae*, ed. Ambrosius M. Gietl, *Die Sentenzen Rolands, nachmals Papstes Alexander III* (Freiburg im Breisgau: Herder, 1891; reprinted in Amsterdam: RODOPI, 1969), 282; Simon of Bisignano, *Summa decretorum* ad C.33 q.1 c.4, ed. Pierre V. Aimone, *Summa in Decretum Simonis Bisinianensis, Monumenta Iuris Canonici, series A: Corpus Glossatorum* [hereafter "MIC.A"] 8 (Vatican City: BAV, 2014), 465.45–466.65.

confession as a cure for magically induced impotence. The eleventh-century scholar Constantine the African discusses the problem of magically induced impotence in his translation of the Arabic medical encyclopedia the *Pantegni.*[49] As remedies, he suggests mainly magical and folkloric practices, such as sprinkling the bile of a black dog around a bewitched couple's house. Only as a last resort does he recommend confession and other ecclesiastical remedies.

But if the above methods do not work because the couple's sins are hanging over them, they should go to a priest or bishop and confess. And if no remedy is found, after they have confessed, they should take communion from the bishop or a devout priest on the day of the Resurrection or the Ascension of the Lord, or Pentecost. When they have taken the body and blood of Christ, the bride and groom should give each other the kiss of peace. When they have received the blessing from the bishop or priest, the bishop or priest should give them this verse of the prophet, written on a slip of parchment: "The voice of the Lord is upon the waters" etc (Psalm 29:3). Then they should go home and abstain from intercourse for three days and nights, and afterwards do the deed, that is, have intercourse. And thus all diabolical actions are destroyed.[50]

This paragraph concerning ecclesiastical remedies for magically induced impotence, however, may not be authentic, since it differs in tone from the rest of the *Pantegni* and is absent from a number of the manuscripts. While an erroneous exemplar could explain the omission of this passage from so many manuscripts, it is also possible that the passage is a later interpolation. All the extant manuscripts containing this section of the *Pantegni* date to the early thirteenth century or later.[51] Rather than being evidence that late eleventh-century medical writers viewed confession as a remedy for magically induced impotence, the passage may in fact simply testify to the great influence exercised by *Si per sortiarias* after its incorporation into Gratian's *Decretum* and Peter Lombard's *Four Books of Sentences.*

49. See Rider, *Magic and Impotence,* 45–51, for a discussion of Constantine's views; 67–71 for a discussion of their limited influence on later medical literature; and 215–28 for an edition and translation of the relevant section of the *Pantegni* dealing with magically induced impotence.

50. Constantine the African, *Pantegni,* "Practica," book 8, chap. 29. Translated in Rider, *Magic and Impotence,* 225; emphasis added.

51. Rider, *Magic and Impotence,* 48–49.

The second indication that Gratian's primary motivation in creating *Causa* 33 was to integrate pre-existing material on penance into the *Decretum* is the great amount of space he devotes to penance. In Fd, the only manuscript to preserve an uninterpolated version of the first-recension *Causa* 33, *De penitentia* occupies more than eleven folios.[52] In contrast, the other four questions of *Causa* 33 take up less than two folios.[53] Although modern scholars have frequently taken the disproportionate length of *De penitentia* as a sign that it is a later interpolation, no manuscript or internal evidence exists to support this view for the first-recension *De penitentia*. A better explanation for the disparity in length, I would contend, is not that Gratian greatly expanded an originally compact C.33 q.3, but rather that he added other questions to an originally lengthy treatment of penance. In coming up with the idea for *Causa* 33, Gratian did not begin with questions on marriage and then move from there to questions on penance. Rather he began with material on penance and moved from there to marriage.

The Testimony of C.33 q.2

Discrepancies between the announced theme of C.33 q.2 and the material actually treated in this question provide further evidence for the centrality of penance to Gratian's conception of *Causa* 33. When Gratian wrote the case statement to *Causa* 33, he already knew what he wanted to discuss in the *causa*. He did not compose the case statement arbitrarily, but rather designed it in such a way that he would have a reason for examining certain predetermined questions. The protagonist in the case statement suffers from preternaturally caused erectile dysfunction because Gratian wanted *Causa* 33 to include a discussion of magically induced impotence (C.33 q.1). The protagonist's wife commits adultery and marries her seducer because Gratian wanted the *causa* to explore the problems posed by the marriage of adulterous lovers (C.33 q.2). Confession to God cures the protagonist's illness because Gratian wanted the *causa* to include a treatment of penance (C.33 q.3). The protagonist decides to abstain from

52. Fd, fols. 88rb–99va.
53. Fd, fols. 87rb–88rb and 99vb–100rb.

sexual relations with his wife and spend more time praying because Gratian wanted the *causa* to examine the permissibility of engaging in sexual relations during times of prayer (C.33 q.4), as well as the permissibility of taking vows of continence without spousal consent (C.33 q.5).

For questions 1 and 3–5 of *Causa* 33, what Gratian ends up producing in the first recension (and remains unchanged in later versions of his text) corresponds to his initial plans as set forth in the case statement. Only for C.33 q.2 does what Gratian produces in the first recension differ markedly from what he initially proposes. Gratian begins this question by stating that there is no reason for him to examine the marriage of adulterous lovers. An earlier section of the *Decretum*, he says, already proves that women can marry men with whom they have previously committed "fornication," that is, adultery. For this reason, he will devote C.33 q.2 to a different question: whether a man who has separated from his wife without demonstrating a sufficient cause and obtaining an ecclesiastical judgment should be forced to return to her.

> Above, it was proven that a woman can marry someone with whom she has previously fornicated. For her husband is dead to her. From the time when she was separated from him by ecclesiastical judgment, she was freed from his law. Whence according to the apostle she should marry whom she wills, as long as it is in the Lord. But it is asked whether one who has separated from his wife without an ecclesiastical judgment and without having demonstrated any cause for separation should be forced to return to her.[54]

Two factors seem to have contributed to Gratian's decision to alter C.33 q.2. First, by the time he finally sat down to write the question, he no longer had any reason to discuss the marriage of adulterous lovers there. It is difficult to determine the relative order in which Gratian composed the various sections of the *Decretum*. The sharp con-

54. C.33 q.2 d.a.c.1 (ed. Werckmeister, 498): "Quod autem ei cum quo prius fornicata fuerat post separationem nubere possit, superius probatum est. Mortuus est enim sibi uir eius. Ex quo iudicio ecclesie ab eo separata ab eius lege soluta est. Vnde iuxta Apostolum nubat cui uult, tantum in Domino. Sed queritur si sine ecclesiastico iudicio nulla causa discidii rationabiliter probata ab ea discessisset, an esset cogendus redire ad eam."

trast between what Gratian initially proposes to examine in C.33 q.2 and what he actually ends up examining, however, strongly suggests that he wrote question 2 later than the rest of the *causa*, most probably after he had already written *Causa* 31. *Causa* 31 describes a man who corrupts someone else's wife. After the cuckolded husband dies, the adulterer marries the widow. He then swears to give his new wife's daughter to a certain person in marriage, but she refuses her assent and the father marries her to another person. The first suitor, however, demands that the daughter be handed over to him. Gratian raises three questions: First, can a woman who has been polluted by adultery be taken in marriage? Second, can a girl be married to someone against her will? Third, after she has been betrothed, can she marry someone else?[55]

Like *Causa* 33, *Causa* 31 is a *causa* where Gratian knew what questions he wanted to discuss prior to composing the case statement. Although the case statement is not particularly fantastic, the questions it raises do not bear any particularly strong relation to one another. From a jurisprudential perspective, there is no reason why Gratian should discuss together the marriage of adulterers, the marrying off of daughters against their will, and the breaking of betrothals. The case statement provides the sole reason for treating all three questions in the same *causa*.

The allusion in C.33 q.2 d.a.c.1 (*Quod ... superius probatum est*) to an earlier section of the *Decretum* in which it is proven that adulterous lovers can marry each other must be a reference to C.31 q.1. This latter question attempts to resolve the apparent contradiction between a canon falsely attributed to Pope Leo, which forbids adulterous lovers to enter into marriage, and excerpts from the writings of Augustine, who appears to permit such marriages explicitly.[56] After introducing a

55. C.31 pr. (ed. Werckmeister, 326): "Vxorem cuiusdam alius construprauit; eo mortuo adulter adulteram sibi in uxorem accepit; filiam ex ea susceptam cuidam in coniugem se daturum iurauit; illa assensum non prebuit; deinde pater alii eam tradidit; a primo reposcitur. Queritur an possit duci in coniugium que prius est polluta per adulterium? Secundo, an filia sit tradenda inuita alicui? Tertio, an post patris sponsionem illa possit nubere alii?"

56. C.31 q.1 c.1 (ed. Werckmeister, 326): "Nullus ducat in matrimonium quam prius polluit adulterio." The text is really taken from Council of Tribur (895), c.51,

number of distinctions, Gratian comes to the conclusion that it is indeed permissible for a widowed adulteress to marry her former lover. In only one instance does Gratian, following earlier canonical tradition, forbid such marriages. If a man causes the death of his lover's husband or if he promises his lover that he will marry her after her husband's death, then, says Gratian, he cannot marry her. Otherwise, he can marry her, but only after performing penance.[57]

The reference to C.31 q.1 in the initial dictum of C.33 q.2 shows that by the time Gratian began to compose C.33 q.2, he had already said all that needed to be said about the marriage of adulterous lovers in this earlier question. Since C.31 q.1 caused Gratian to change the entire topic of C.33 q.2, he must have written C.31 q.1 prior to C.33 q.2. The phrase *superius probatum est* in the initial dictum, moreover, suggests that by the time he began to compose C.33 q.2, he had also come up with the case statement and other questions to *Causa* 31 and decided to place this new *causa* before *Causa* 33. The case statement of *Causa* 33, however, probably predates the composition of C.31 q.1. If it did not, then Gratian would not have had any reason for including details about adultery in the case statement or for originally proposing to examine the permissibility of marriage between adulterous lovers. These features make sense only if they are the relic of an earlier compositional stage, a time when Gratian was still contemplating treating this problem in *Causa* 33 rather than *Causa* 31.

The second reason why Gratian appears to have changed the topic of C.33 q.2 is that he wanted to create a smoother transition from the discussion of impotence in C.33 q.1 to the discussion of penance

---

ed. Boretius and Krause, MGH Capit. 2, 241. C.31 q.1 c.2 (ed. Werckmeister, 328): "Denique mortuo eo cum quo fuit uerum conubium fieri potest coniugium cum qua precessit adulterium. Item in libro de bono coniugali: Posse sane fieri licitas nuptias ex personis illicite coniunctis, honesto placito subsequente, manifestum est." The material sources are Augustine, *De nuptiis et concupiscentia* 1.11, ed. Carol Urba and Joseph Zycha, CSEL 42 (Vienna: F. Tempsky, 1902), 223.18–20, and Augustine, *De bono coniugali* 14.17, ed. Joseph Zycha, CSEL 41 (Vienna: F. Tempsky, 1900), 209.15–16.

57. C.31 q.1 cc.3–5. C.31 q.1 d.p.c.3 (ed. Werckmeister, 330): "Hic subaudiendum est nisi post peractam penitentiam et si nihil in morte uiri machinatus fuerit uel si uiuente uiro fidem adultere non dedit, sumpturum eam sibi in coniugem si uiro eius superuiueret."

in C.33 q.3.[58] The Latin canonical tradition was unanimous in teaching that husbands could not dismiss their wives without an ecclesiastical judgment. Gratian appears to have broached this issue in his eventual version of C.33 q.2 mainly, or perhaps even solely, because it provides him with an excuse to discuss penance. In the first recension, Gratian devotes just one canon to the problem of husbands dismissing their wives on their own initiative, without an ecclesiastical judgment (c.1). The rest of the question examines whether husbands can kill their own wives (d.p.c.4–c.6, c.8–d.p.c.9), why the canons teach that penitents should return to their former state after seven years of penance (d.p.c.10–d.p.c.11), and whether those who have performed penance can marry or engage in marital relations with their spouses (d.p.c.11 §1, cc.13, 14, 19). Gratian's general conclusion is, unsurprisingly, that husbands cannot kill their wives. If a wife is guilty of adultery, then she should perform penance for seven years, at the end of which time her husband may dismiss her, if he should so desire. However, if a husband should kill his wife, then he must remain unwed for the rest of his life, unless it is feared that, because of his youth, he will probably fall into incontinence.[59] The canons generally prohibit penitents from returning to secular affairs or engaging in marriage. Nevertheless, because the fear of dissolving a marriage or of later sexual incontinence can cause sinners to delay or neglect to undertake penance, other canons permit penitents to remain married if they are already married or to enter into marriage if not yet married.[60]

58. This link was already noted by the *Glossa ordinaria* to De pen. D.1 d.a.c.1 v. *Vtrum* (Rome, 1582), col. 2184: "quia mentionem fecerat Grat. de penitentia supra e. q.2 Admonere [C.33 q.2 c.8], ideo hic tractat de ea."

59. C.33 q.2 d.p.c.9 (ed. Werckmeister, 514): "In premissis auctoritatibus quique prohibentur adulteras coniuges suas occidere; sed post septem annorum penitentiam permittitur eis illas dimittere. Si autem illas interfecerint, iubentur sine spe coniugii perpetuo manere, nisi forte propter lapsum iuuenilis incontinentie ad matrimonia contrahenda eis misericordia impendatur."

60. C.33 q.2 d.p.c.11 §1 (ed. Werckmeister, 518): "De penitentibus quoque queritur an eis generaliter post penitentiam peractam coniugia concedantur? Generaliter enim canonica auctoritate penitentes prohibentur ad secularem militiam redire uel matrimonia contrahere." C.33 q.2 d.p.c.12 (ed. Werckmeister, 518): "Sed quia timore soluendi coniugii nonnulli ad penitentiam accedere differunt, uel propter lapsum adolescentie, quem formidant, penitentie remedium su-

Overall, the canons in C.33 q.2 are straightforward and unproblematic, and they elicit little commentary from Gratian. His treatment in this section neither breaks new legal ground, nor contributes to a better understanding of the hypothetical "case" described at the beginning of *Causa* 33.[61] This material does, however, provide Gratian with an excuse to broach the topic of penance prior to C.33 q.3, thereby providing a smoother transition from C.33 q.1 to C.33 q.3. The presence of this material thus provides yet more evidence that C.33 q.3 was neither a later interpolation, nor in the beginning just a highly abbreviated *quaestio*. Gratian did not insert a discussion of penance into *Causa* 33 at a late date or on a mere whim. Rather, a discussion of penance lies at the very heart of *Causa* 33 and explains the presence of the other questions, from the first question on magically induced impotence to the last question on vows of continence.

Divination, Penance, and the Creation of *Causa* 26

Similar considerations suggest the influence of *De penitentia* in the creation of *Causa* 26. C.33 q.1 and C.26 qq.1–5 have many thematic connections, as do C.33 q.3 and C.26 qq.6–7. C.33 q.1 and C.26 qq.1–5 are the only two sections of the *Decretum* to deal with magic. Although far from a complete treatment, they form the classical loci for later canonistic reflection on the subject.[62] C.33 q.3 and C.26 qq.6–7, on the other hand, are two of the three main sections of the *Decretum* that treat penance.[63] C.33 q.3 focuses on confession and issues of penitential theology, whereas C.26 qq.6–7 deal with reconciliation and the assigning of penance.

Gratian's questions on magic rarely or never mention penance, and his questions on penance rarely or never mention magic. Perhaps for this reason, Gratian's medieval and modern commentators have

---

scipere negligunt, auctoritate canonica permittitur eis uel contracta matrimonia retinere uel alia contrahere." These two dicta are contiguous in the first recension; c.12 was added only in the second recension.

61. For a somewhat different assessment in a different context, see Peter Landau, "Ehetrennung als Strafe," *ZRG KA* 81 (1995): 148–88, at 176–78.

62. See Hersperger, *Kirche, Magie und "Aberglaube."*

63. The other main section is D.50.

never drawn attention to the fact that the only two *causae* in the *Decretum* to deal with magic both also deal with penance. Is this parallel between *Causa* 26 and *Causa* 33 a simple coincidence? Or is it rather another example of *De penitentia*'s influence on the structure and contents of the *Decretum*? Here I will explore the latter possibility.

Case Statement

Like *Causa* 33, *Causa* 26 begins with an entertaining story.

> A certain priest is convicted before the bishop of being a soothsayer and fortune-teller. Censured by the bishop, he [nevertheless] refuses to cease [engaging in these magical practices]. He is excommunicated. But on his deathbed he is reconciled by a certain priest without consulting the bishop. Penance is assigned to him according to the quantity of time established by the canons. First, it is asked what soothsayers are? Second, whether being a soothsayer is a sin? Third, from whom did divination take its origin? Fourth, what are the types of divination? Fifth, whether soothsayers and fortune-tellers must be excommunicated if they refuse to stop? Sixth, whether one excommunicated by a bishop can be reconciled by a priest without consulting the bishop? Seventh, whether penance should be assigned to the dying according to the quantity of time?[64]

The individual elements of the case statement seem realistic. Numerous medieval sources report or allege the existence of cleric-magicians. The *Life of Pope Sergius* (687–701) in the *Liber Pontificalis*, for instance, recounts how Paschal, the archdeacon of the Roman church, was deposed for practicing incantations and soothsaying.[65] Gerbert of Aurillac, who reigned as Pope Sylvester II from 999–1003, was reputed to be a sorcerer.[66] And John of Salisbury relates how, as a youth, he

64. C.26 pr. (ed. Friedberg, 1019–20, supported by Aa Fd): "Quidam sacerdos sortilegus esse et diuinus conuincitur apud episcopum; correptus ab episcopo noluit cessare; excommunicatur; tandem agens in extremis reconciliatur a quodam sacerdote episcopo inconsulto; indicitur sibi penitentia sub quantitate temporis prefixa canonibus. Primum queritur, qui sint sortilegi? Secundo, an sit peccatum esse sortilegum? Tertio, a quibus genus diuinationis sumpsit exordium? Quarto, quot sint genera diuinationis? Quinto, an sortilegi uel diuini sint excommunicandi, si cessare noluerint? Sexto, an excommunicatus ab episcopo possit reconciliari a presbitero, illo inconsulto? Septimo, si morientibus est indicenda penitentia sub quantitate temporis?"

65. The relevant section was excerpted and incorporated into *Panormia* 8.82.

66. Peters, *Magician*, 28.

was apprenticed to a soothsayer-priest.[67] Clerics in the central Middle Ages, moreover, belonged to the relatively small class of literate persons who could draw upon and use the body of learned magic inherited from antiquity. Thanks to the translation movement from Greek and Arabic, the learned tradition of magic was beginning to experience a revival during Gratian's lifetime.[68] The fortune-telling and soothsaying priest described by Gratian thus may have had a contemporary counterpart.

Nevertheless, the questions which Gratian raises suggest that the scenario described in the case statement does not correspond to an actual legal dispute or court case, but rather that it, like the case statement of *Causa* 33, is imaginary.[69] As with *Causa* 33, *Causa* 26 groups together questions dealing with diverse and legally unrelated issues. Questions 1–5 define divination and explain why it is sinful, whereas questions 6 and 7 deal with two issues of penitential discipline: whether priests can reconcile those excommunicated by a bishop and whether confessors should mete out penances to the dying in accordance with the times stipulated in the canons. All of these questions relate in some way to the scenario described in the case statement. Jurisprudentially, however, questions 1–5 are unrelated to questions 6 and 7. The problems of penitential discipline examined in these latter two questions are not specific to any particular type of sin. Can a priest reconcile someone excommunicated by a bishop? Must a confessor assign penances to the dying in accordance with the canons? Understanding the nature of divination and the reasons for its sinfulness contributes nothing to answering these two questions. Although

67. John of Salisbury, *Policraticus* 1.12, ed. K. S. B. Keats-Rohan, CCCM 118 (Turnhout: Brepols, 1993); Peters, *Magician*, 47–48.

68. On the translation movement, see Marie-Thérèse d'Alverny, "Translations and Translators," in *Renaissance and Renewal in the Twelfth Century*, ed. Robert Benson and Giles Constable (Cambridge, Mass.: Harvard University Press, 1982), 421–62.

69. Cf. Pier Virginio Aimone Braida, "Gratian, the Decretists, and Astrology," in *Proceedings of the Tenth International Congress of Medieval Canon Law*, ed. Kenneth Pennington, Stanley Chodorow, and Keith H. Kendall, MIC.C 11 (Vatican City: BAV, 2001), 817–39, at 822, who asserts that "Gratian based *Causa* 26 ... on an actual case in which a priest was denounced to his bishop for being a 'sortilegus et diuinus.'"

Gratian uses a story about divination to introduce questions 6 and 7, he develops and resolves them without reference to this sin. Admittedly, Gratian tacks six canons dealing with magic and superstitious practices to the end of question 7. However, he provides no commentary for these canons and does not attempt to relate these canons to the actual topic of question 7. Aside from these canons, nothing in his treatment of questions 6 and 7 relates to or presupposes the material discussed in questions 1–5. Questions 6 and 7 would fit equally well in a *causa* dealing with homicide, arson, treason, adultery, or some other grave sin.

A similar argument can be made concerning the relationship between questions 6 and 7. Although both questions deal with penance, they are unrelated to each other jurisprudentially. Knowing that priests can reconcile those excommunicated by bishops in cases of extreme necessity does not provide any insight into whether confessors should mete out penances to the dying in accordance with the canons, nor does knowledge about the length of penances which one should assign to the dying assist in determining whether priests can reconcile those excommunicated by bishops. By including questions dealing with these two jurisprudentially distinct issues in the same *causa*, Gratian betrays yet again his interest in the *causa* as an organizational rather than an analytical tool. Gratian, I would like to suggest, did not create the questions in *Causa* 26 to illuminate the scenario sketched out in the case statement. Rather, he created the case statement to provide an excuse for examining the *causa*'s seven questions.

From Penitential Theology to the Reconciliation of Excommunicates

The idea for C.26 qq.6–7 may have come to Gratian either during or after the composition of *De penitentia*, for C.26 qq.6–7 and *De penitentia* draw on the same formal sources and even cite several of the same authorities. In the first recension, C.26 qq.6–7 consist of thirteen canons (see table 6-1): five come from the *Tripartita*, three from the 3L, and six from the *Polycarpus*. Of the five from the *Tripartita*, three come from the same title (*Tripartita* 3.28) that provided Gratian with

De pen. D.1 c.90. Similarly, 3L 3.19, the title from which he took C.26 q.6 cc.13–14, was one of Gratian's main formal sources for distinctions 1 and 7 of *De penitentia*. It provided him with not only De pen. D.1 c.61–87, but also De pen. D.7 c.2 and c.5.[70]

Since *Tripartita* 3.28 and 3L 3.19 are both devoted to penance, it is unsurprising that Gratian would have drawn upon them in composing C.26 qq.6–7. It is surprising, however, that he does not exploit *Polycarpus* 6.19, the corresponding title on penance in the *Polycarpus*, since he draws upon the *Polycarpus* for the last six canons of C.26 q.7 (cc.13–16, 16a, 18; c.17 is a second-recension addition).[71] This failure to make use of *Polycarpus* 6.19, I would like to suggest, is a sign that Gratian composed C.26 qq.6–7 in at least two stages. In an initial stage, Gratian attempted to supplement lacunae in *De penitentia*'s treatment of penance by drawing upon formal sources used in its composition, that is, the *Tripartita* and 3L. Since he found these two sources sufficient for his purposes, he did not bother drawing upon sources not used in the composition of *De penitentia*, such as the *Polycarpus*. In a second stage, he tried to supplement *Causa* 26's discussion of magic by tacking on canons from the *Polycarpus*. The lack of any transition between C.26 q.7 c.1, which deals with penance, and the six canons from the *Polycarpus*, which deal with magic, raises the possibility that he did not originally intend to place them at the end of C.26 q.7, but that for some reason he never got around to integrating them into C.26 qq.1–5.[72] (C.26 q.7 cc.2–12 are second recension additions.)

An examination of the dicta of C.26 q.6 also reveals points of contact with *De penitentia*. The central argument of this question is that, in cases of necessity, priests do not need the permission of the bishop to reconcile penitents whom the bishop has excommunicated. Like

70. Wei, "Law and Religion in Gratian's *Decretum*," 162–77; Wei, "A Reconsideration of St. Gall," 148–53.

71. C.26 q.7 c.16a was removed in the second recension.

72. Cf. Larson, *Master of Penance*, 260, who suggests that the six canons on magic at the end of C.26 q.7 were placed there "to remind one of the specific *causa* at hand, a priest excommunicated for refusing to stop practicing sorcery or divination." She sees evidence for her suggestion in C.26 q.7 c.16a, which is the only one of the six canons to mention penance.

earlier canonists, Gratian does not distinguish clearly between true excommunication and public penance, what later canonists would eventually term major and minor excommunication, respectively. Major excommunication was a sanction imposed on those unwilling to repent, while minor excommunication/public penance was a disciplinary measure imposed on those who were willing to amend their lives or unable to fight back. The two penalties involved differing degrees of exclusion from Christian worship and society, but both were supposed to end in a rite of reconciliation.[73] The canons that Gratian quotes thus sometimes mention excommunication, at other times penance, but he treats them all as relevant to the problem at hand, which he resolves not by distinguishing between two types of excommunication, but rather by distinguishing between two types of reconciliation: public and private. Priests, he writes, cannot publicly reconcile those whom the bishop has excommunicated, that is, they cannot receive in a public ceremony before the door of the church and in mass those whom the bishop has excommunicated. At the bishop's command, however, they can reconcile in private those performing penance for secret sins (*occultis peccatis*) as well as those on the verge of death (*in extremis*).[74] To justify this latter claim, Gratian introduces a number of arguments based on scripture and

73. On the development of a gradual distinction between major and minor excommunication, see Artur Michael Landgraf, "Grundlagen für ein Verständnis der Busslehre der Früh- und Hochscholastik," *Zeitschrift für katholische Theologie* 51 (1927): 161–93; Landgraf, "Sünde und Trennung von der Kirche in der Frühscholastik," *Scholastik* 5 (1930): 210–47; François Russo, "Pénitence et excommunication: Étude historique sur les rapports entre la théologie et le droit canonique dans le domaine pénitentiel du IXe au XIIIe siècle," *Recherches de science religieuse* 33 (1946): 257–79 and 431–51, esp. 437–51; Peter Huizing, "Doctrina decretistarum de variis speciebus excommunicationis," *Gregorianum* 33 (1952): 499–530; Josephus Zeliauskas, *De excommunicatione vitiata apud glossatores (1140–1350)* (Zurich: Pas-Verlag, 1967), 16–20.

74. C.26 q.6 d.p.c.3 (ed. Friedberg, 1037, supported by Aa Fd): "Ecce, quod ab episcopo excommunicatus per sacerdotem reconciliari non potest. Sed notandum est quod reconciliatio alia est publica, alia priuata. Publica reconciliatio est, quando penitentes ante ecclesie ingressum publice representantur et per impositionem manus episcopalis ecclesie publice reconciliantur. Hec sacerdotibus uidentur (uidetur sacerdotibus *Friedb.*) esse prohibita. Vnde circa finem illius capituli non simpliciter prohibentur penitentes reconciliare, sed in publica missa. Priuata uero reconciliatio est, quando de occultis peccatis penitentes uel in extre-

Table 6-1. The Formal Sources of C.26 qq.6–7

First recension	*Tripartita*	3L	*Polycarpus*
C.26 q.6 c.1	**2.19.2**		
C.26 q.6 c.4	**3.28.8**		6.19.5
C.26 q.6 c.5	**2.19.3**		
C.26 q.6 c.12	**3.28.10**		8.1.10
C.26 q.6 c.13		**3.19.14**	8.1.2
C.26 q.6 c.14		**3.19.2**	
C.26 q.7 c.1	**3.28.7**		
C.26 q.7 c.13			**6.11.4**
C.26 q.7 c.14			**6.11.5**
C.26 q.7 c.15			**6.11.7**
C.26 q.7 c.16			**6.11.12**
C.26 q.7 c.16a			**6.11.19**
C.26 q.7 c.18			**6.11.20**

Note: Bold face indicates Gratian's probable formal sources.

the Pseudo-Augustinian *De vera et falsa penitentia*. He asks rhetorically:

But if the sinner is menaced by the necessity of death and the bishop is so far removed that the priest cannot consult him, will penance be denied to the dying? And will the gift of reconciliation be denied the penitent whom, when converted, God grants pardon according to (Ezek 33:12): "In whatever hour the sinner is converted" etc. and moreover (Zec 1:3): "Turn to me with your whole heart and I will turn to you" etc.? Will the church neglect to reconcile [such a one] to herself? Will the church disdain to absolve externally one whom God has already revived internally? Will the bishop's absence damn him whom the grace of the divine presence illuminates through the bath of regeneration? Those who are dying are aided even by laymen if priests are absent. Why, then, should one be incapable of being helped by the gift of reconciliation if the bishop should happen to be absent? If, according to Augustine, someone near death who confesses to an associate his depraved crime becomes worthy of pardon

mis agentes ad gratiam reconciliationis accedunt. Hec reconciliatio potest fieri per sacerdotem." See also C.26 q.6 d.p.c.11, quoted in the following note.

on account of his desire for a priest, why should one who does not refuse to confess his guilt to a priest similarly not be worthy of reconciliation on account of his desire for the bishop?[75]

Significantly, both of the biblical quotations as well as the sentence of Pseudo-Augustine alluded to in the dictum are found in distinction 1 of *De penitentia*.[76] Of course, Gratian's source for the first biblical quotation could also have been C.26 q.6 c.13, which quotes that passage as well. But *De penitentia* is the only part of the *Decretum* that contains the two remaining texts. These points of contact between C.26 qq.6–7 and *De penitentia* are a possible indication that Gratian formulated C.26 qq.6–7 in dependence on and possibly to supplement *De penitentia*'s treatment of penance.

Divination, Maleficium, and Magic

Why did Gratian decide to combine questions on penitential discipline with questions relating to divination? After all, as mentioned above, questions dealing with some other grave sin would have worked equally well. One possibility is that Gratian just happened to have a particular interest in the casting of lots. The use of lots and re-

75. C.26 q.6 d.p.c.11 (ed. Friedberg, 1039, supported by Aa Fd): "Ecce, quod episcopo precipiente penitentes de occultis peccatis, siue in periculo constituti per presbiterum possunt reconciliari. Sed si necessitate mortis peccator urguetur, et episcopus ita remotus est, quod presbiter eum consulere non possit, negabitur penitentia morienti? et beneficium reconciliationis non prestabitur penitenti, quem conuersum Deus recipit ad ueniam, iuxta illud: 'In quacumque hora peccator conuersus fuerit' etc. et item: 'Conuertimini ad me (in toto corde uestro *add Friedb.*), et ego conuertar ad uos,' ecclesia sibi reconciliare negliget? quem intus Deus suscitauit, ecclesia foris absoluere contempnet? dampnabit absentia episcopi quem gratia diuine presentie illustrat per lauacrum regenerationis? Morituris succurritur etiam a laicis, si presbiteri defuerint. Cur ergo beneficio reconciliationis per presbiterum eis subueniri (subueniri ei *Friedb.*) non poterit, si contigerit episcopum deesse (esse *Fd*[1], abesse *Aa*)? si secundum Augustinum qui agens in extremis confitetur socio turpitudinem criminis fit dignus uenia ex desiderio sacerdotis, cur non similiter sit dignus reconciliatione ex desiderio episcopi qui sacerdoti non negat maculam sui reatus?"

76. De pen. D.1 d.p.c.32, c.34, d.p.c.87, c.88. Compare the following section of De pen. D.1 c.88 (ed. Friedberg, 1188, supported by Aa Fd) with the end of C.26 q.6 d.p.c.11: "Et si ille cui confitebitur, potestatem soluendi non habeat, tamen fit dignus uenia ex desiderio sacerdotis, qui ei confitetur (confitetur socio *Friedb.*) turpitudinem criminis."

lated forms of divination was certainly important in the medieval era. Moreover, the canons dealing with the subject were contradictory. As Gratian states at the beginning of C.26 q.2, numerous examples from the Bible seem to show that divination is neither sinful nor superstitious. When God punished the entire people of Israel for a crime committed by Achar, the Lord commanded Joshua to uncover the culprit through the casting of lots (Jos 7). Similarly, when Jonathan had broken the fast ordered by his father, the king, Saul uncovered his guilt through the casting of lots (1 Sm 14). The Bible also reports the use of lots in connection with or by Jonah (Jon 1), Zechariah (Lk 1), and Peter (Acts 1), and a canon by Augustine specifically states that "lots are not evil."[77] Yet, as Gratian also points out, other authorities explicitly forbid the use of lots. Canons by Augustine, Bede, and Jerome all teach that Christians should not engage in any form of divination, regardless of biblical precedents to the contrary (cc.2–4).

Another possibility is that the idea came from some text that Gratian stumbled across in the course of working on the *Decretum*. Perhaps he was inspired by C.2 q.8 c.3. The end of this first-recension canon mentions as an afterthought that those who consult diviners and magicians (*sortilegos magosque*) should not be allowed to make accusations in court. Or perhaps his work on *Causa* 23, which deals with violence and war, made him aware of the many legal issues

77. C.26 q.2 d.a.c.1 (ed. Friedberg, 1020, supported by Aa Fd): "Quod autem sortes exquirere peccatum non sit, exemplis et auctoritate (auctoritatibus *Friedb.*) probatur. Cum enim Achar (Achan *Friedb.*) de anathemate furtim subripuisset et ob eius peccatum populus cesus apud Ayn hostibus terga dedisset, precepit Dominus Iosue, ut sortibus exquireret, quo peccante populus in manibus hostium cadere meruerat. Iosue preceptum accipiens misit sortes, primum super tribus, deinde super familias, demum super personas, et ita cecidit sors super Achar (Achan *Friedb.*). Saul quoque, cum pugnans contra Philisteos iurasset, se interfecturum quicumque ante solis occasum de populo comederet, sorte deprehendit Ionathan filium suum mel comedisse, quod sceptro acceperat, quem cum morti tradere uellet, populo supplicante reuocauit sententiam. Ionas quoque, cum a facie Domini fugeret, a nautis sorte deprehensus in mari deiectus, et a ceto est absorptus. De Zacharia etiam legitur quod sorte exiit, ut incensum poneret. Mathias uero similiter a beato Petro sorte in apostolatum et Iude succesor eligitur. Quod ergo tantorum exemplis probatur, patet malum non esse." C.26 q.2 c.1 (ed. Friedberg, 1020, supported by Aa Fd): "Sors non est aliquid mali, sed res in humana dubietate diuinam indicans uoluntatem."

involving divination. Gratian took many of the canons in *Causa* 23 from book 8 of the *Panormia*, which was also Gratian's main formal source for questions 2 and 5 of *Causa* 26. In fact, in the *Panormia* the canons on magic appear immediately after the canons on violence.

Given the lack of clear literary sources for the case statement to *Causa* 26, we can only speculate. My hypothesis is that *Causa* 26 combines questions on magic and penance because Gratian deliberately modeled the *causa* after *Causa* 33. Canonical collections generally did not employ "magic" as an overarching term to describe rites and practices (supposedly) capable of harnessing supernatural powers. Instead, they simply grouped together canons dealing with various forms of magic without using any one particular word to describe their contents. The rubric to book 10 of Burchard's *Decretum*, for instance, simply enumerates the various types of magic and their practitioners: *de incantatoribus, de auguribus, divinis, sortilegis et variis illusionibus diaboli ... deque singulorum poenitentia.*[78] The rubric to book 11 of Ivo's *Decretum*, which treats the same material, is almost identical: *Hec pars continet de incantatoribus, de auguribus, de divinis, de sortilegis, de sortiariis et variis illusionibus diaboli et de singulorum penitentia.* Yet specific canons did explicitly connect divination and magic, as well as *maleficium* and magic. Three canons in the first recension of Gratian's *Decretum* explicitly link divination to magic, while one canon connects *maleficium* and magic.[79] Thus even though Gratian does not explicitly connect C.33 q.1 to C.26 qq.1–5, it seems possible that he, like modern scholars, would have recognized that their subject matter was related and that this similarity could have influenced his design of *Causa* 26.

The Views of the Decretists

Gratian's medieval commentators attempt to make sense of *Causa* 33 by interpreting it in light of the *causae* on marriage. Taking their

78. Burchard, *Decretum* 10.tit., ed. Fransen and Kölzer, 133r.

79. C.26 q.5 c.2 (ed. Friedberg, 1027); C.26 q.5 c.5 (ed. Friedberg, 1028); C.26 q.5 c.12 (ed. Friedberg, 1030–31). C.26 q.5 c.14 (ed. Friedberg, 1032, supported by Aa Fd): "Nec mirum de magorum prestigiis, quorum in tantum prodiere maleficiorum artes."

cue from the prominence of magically induced impotence in the case statement, as well as the *causa*'s placement in the midst of nine other *causae* on marriage, they advance a number of conflicting yet closely related explanations for the presence of *Causa* 33 in the *Decretum*. According to Paucapalea, Gratian inserted *Causa* 33 into the *Decretum* because it had become standard by his day to investigate whether magically induced impotence was a valid reason for obtaining a separation.

> [Gratian] had said in the preceding *causa* that a man whose wife has been corrupted by infirmity and is unable to render the [marriage] debt may take another [woman] in marriage. Moreover, because some [men] impeded by magically induced impotence are unable to render the debt to [their] wives, it has become customary to ask whether they should be separated, [and] he subjoins a *causa* in which he shows that such [couples] can be separated.[80]

Rufinus, on the other hand, asserts that Gratian inserted *Causa* 33 into the *Decretum* in order to demonstrate that women could sometimes remarry before their husbands' deaths.

> It has been said above in the seventh question [of *Causa* 32] that, while one spouse lives, the other cannot be joined to another. But because she who has been delivered to [her husband's] house, although not yet known [carnally], is said to have been made a bride by this transport, lest it appear that even [a wife of this sort] can in no case marry another while her husband lives, [Gratian] therefore appends a *causa* concerning those suffering from frigidity and magically induced impotence, showing how their wives are able to accept others [in marriage] even while [their husbands] live.[81]

80. Paucapalea, *Summa* ad C.33 pr., ed. Schulte, 130: "Dixerat in praecedenti causa, quod vir, cuius uxor infirmitate corrupta debitum non valens reddere, licite poterat alteram ducere. Ceterum quia nonnulli maleficio impediti nequeunt quidem debitum reddere uxori, utrum sint separandi, solet quaeri, causam subnectit, in qua tales separari posse ostendit."

81. Rufinus, *Summa* ad C.33 pr., ed. Singer, 496: "Dictum fuerat superius in VII. questione quod altero coniuge vivente alius alii copulari non potest. Sed quoniam que in domum traducta est, licet nondum cognita, ex ipsa ductione dicitur coniunx effecta, ne videretur et hec viro vivente in nullo casu posse alteri nubere, ideo subnectit aliam causam de frigidis et maleficiis impeditis, ostendens quomodo ipsis viventibus uxores eorum valent alios accipere." Although Rufinus was an adherent of the *copula* theory of marriage formation, here he invokes the *traditio* theory, according to which marriage rests on the delivery of the wife to the husband. On the *traditio* theory, see Brundage, *Law, Sex, and Christian Society*, 266–67.

Stephen of Tournai provides yet a third explanation for the presence of *Causa* 33 in the *Decretum*. According to Stephen, Gratian inserted *Causa* 33 because he wanted to explain the differences in how the church deals with sexual infirmity in men and women.

It was shown in the preceding *causa* [that is, *Causa* 32] that a wife cannot be set aside on account of infirmity or languor. But because infirmity sometimes impedes a husband from rendering the marriage debt, which happens sometimes by magic, sometimes because of the frigidity of nature, [Gratian] subjoins a *causa* in which it is asked whether those suffering from magically induced impotence or frigidity should be separated from their wives.[82]

Common to each of these different and conflicting interpretations is the mistaken belief that magically induced impotence is the *raison d'être* of *Causa* 33. Failing to consider *Causa* 33 as a whole, these decretists end up uncovering not the reasons why Gratian originally composed *Causa* 33, but rather the reasons why, in hindsight, his decision to place *Causa* 33 after *Causa* 32 makes some jurisprudential sense.

Approaching *Causa* 33 on its own terms rather than in relationship to the other *causae* on marriage, this chapter has tried to show, reveals a completely different and, I would argue, more accurate way of understanding the genesis of *Causa* 33, one that recognizes the centrality of penance. Gratian's primary purpose in composing *Causa* 33 was not to discuss questions relating to marriage, but rather to integrate largely pre-existing material on penance into the *Decretum*. Gratian already had material on penance that he wanted to insert into the *Decretum* prior to beginning work on the rest of the *causa*. He crafted the case statement in the way that he did because he needed an excuse for incorporating this material into the *Decretum*. Particular details in the canonistic tradition concerning impotence and vows of continence—most notably Hincmar of Reims's advice that couples suffering from magically induced impotence should confess their sins to both God and a priest—led Gratian to treat these issues together in

82. Stephan of Tournai, *Summa* ad C.33 pr., ed. Schulte, 245: "Ostensum est in superiori C., propter infirmitatem vel languorem uxorem non posse dimitti. Sed quia quandoque infirmitas reddendi debiti maritum impedit, quae contingit aliquando maleficiis, aliquando ex naturae frigiditate, subiungit causam, in qua quaeritur, an maleficiis impediti vel frigidi sint ab uxoribus separandi?"

a single *causa* along with questions pertaining to penance. These other issues, however, were not Gratian's main focus; from beginning to end, his focus was penance. The considerations raised by Rufinus and Stephen may explain why Gratian placed *Causa* 33 after *Causa* 32: C.33 q.1 deals with what could be regarded as exceptions to cases discussed in C.32 q.7. As explanations for why Gratian composed *Causa* 33, however, they fall short.

If the brevity of Gratian's discussion is an accurate indication, he took little interest in the problem of magically induced impotence. C.33 q.1 deals mainly with impotence in general. When Gratian finally broaches the topic of magically induced impotence at the end of the question, all he does is note the contradiction between what Hincmar states in c.4 and what Pseudo-Gregory states in c.2. "For there [in c.2], after he recovers his potency, she is ordered to separate from the second man she married and return to the first. Here [in c.4], however, she cannot be reconciled with her first [husband] while the one she married second lives."[83] Gratian makes no effort, however, to reconcile these differences or otherwise to explore the problems posed by magically induced impotence. His reticence on this matter suggests that, had it not been for his desire to integrate *De penitentia* into the *causa* structure of the *Decretum*, he might never have inserted this canon into his textbook. The prominence of magic in *Causa* 33—as well as its subsequent development by later theologians and canonists—is thus to a large extent a historical accident. The main reason why magic appears in this *causa* is not because Gratian found magically induced impotence important or because he was trying to make his textbook as comprehensive as possible, but rather because he was looking for an interesting way to integrate material on penance into the *causa* format.

There is less evidence concerning the genesis of the other locus of the canonistic treatment of magic, *Causa* 26. Gratian's medieval commentators interpret this *causa* in light of the immediately preceding

83. C.33 q.1 d.p.c.4 (ed. Werckmeister, 496): "Sed in hoc uidetur contrarius premisso capitulo Gregorii. Ibi enim post possibilitatem redditam iubetur separari ab eo cui secundo nupserat et redire ad primum. Hic autem uiuente eo cui secundo copulata fuerat, primo reconciliari non poterit."

causae. Connecting *Causa* 26 to *Causa* 25, which deals with the privileges of churches and priests, Paucapalea asserts that the purpose of *Causa* 26 is to show priests that they cannot usurp episcopal functions and prerogatives with impunity.

[Gratian] said above that the privileges of churches and priests should remain inviolate and unsullied for all time. But lest priests usurp with impunity the functions of bishops, whose power as respects the sacerdotal dignity is common with the priest, he subjoins the case of a priest who reconciles another priest censured by the bishop, without consulting the same bishop, and in this did not fear to usurp pontifical [prerogatives].[84]

Rufinus, in contrast, connects *Causa* 26 with *Causae* 23 and 24 on heretics. "After [Gratian] interposed a necessary tract on the privileges of churches, he returns to treating of heretics: for the casting of lots and augury and similar superstitions, which are treated here, are a species of heresy, at any rate in those who have received the faith of Christ."[85]

The evidence considered in this chapter suggests a different explanation for how and why *Causa* 26 came about, one that acknowledges its thematic and literary connections to *Causa* 33 and *De penitentia*. Wanting to supplement his treatment of penance in *De penitentia*, Gratian, I suggest, decided to pattern *Causa* 26 after *Causa* 33 by once again combining questions on penance and questions on magic. Because his treatment is more detailed, it seems less plausible that Gratian's interest in penance was the main cause of his decision to include questions on divination in the *Decretum* as it seems to have been for the question on magically induced impotence. Nevertheless, his interest in penance and experience with *De penitentia* may well have been one of the prime factors behind the composition of that *causa*.

84. Paucapalea, *Summa* ad C.26 pr., ed. Schulte, 107–8: "Dixerat superius, quod privilegia ecclesiarum et sacerdotum inviolata et intemerata cunctis debent manere temporibus. Sed ne episcoporum officia, quorum potestas quantum ad sacerdotum attinet dignitatem, cum presbyterio est communis, ipsi presbyteri impune usurparent, casum subnectit cuiusdam sacerdotis, qui alium sacerdotem ab episcopo notatum eodem inconsulto in extremis reconciliavit, et in hoc pontificalia usurpare non timuit."

85. Rufinus, *Summa* ad C.26 pr.

Conclusion

The preceding pages have proposed that Gratian's interest in penitential theology affected his treatment of canon law in a rather startling and unexpected way—by inspiring him to treat magically induced impotence (C.33 q.1) and divination (C.26 qq.1–5) in the first recension of his *Decretum*. Gratian, chapter 5 argued, disagreed with some contemporary views on penance and compiled the core of *De penitentia* to criticize and correct them. To disseminate his critique, this chapter suggested, Gratian decided to integrate his own treatise on penance into the first recension of the *Decretum*, which he did by creating a *causa* uniting magic and penance. Literary and textual analysis suggested the following chronology in the genesis of *Causa* 33: first, the composition of (most of) *De penitentia*; second, the composition of the case statement to *Causa* 33; third, the composition of C.31 q.1; and fourth, the composition of C.33 q.2. For an unknown reason, I suggested, Gratian adapted this basic blueprint to *Causa* 26, which likewise unites magic and penance. Penance may not have been a form of magic, as older Protestant controversialists argued, but, at least for Gratian, penance certainly seems to have stimulated interest in its canon law.

Part 3

Gratian, a Theologian of the Sacraments and Liturgy?

7

Gratian, a Sacramental Theologian?

Modern assessments of Gratian the sacramental theologian have changed dramatically over the past century. While scholars still recognize the importance of the *Decretum* to the development of sacramental theology, many doubt that Gratian himself had much to do with it. The tract *De consecratione,* the primary locus of material on the sacraments in the *Decretum,* played a crucial role in Rudolph Sohm's argument that the sacraments are central to the *Decretum.*[1] And the tract was a major source for later sacramental theologians, particularly Peter Lombard in his *Four Books of Sentences.*[2] But, as first Jacqueline Rambaud's manuscript studies and later Anders Winroth's discovery of the first recension show, *De consecratione* is a later addition to the *Decretum,* one that probably does not stem from Gratian himself.[3] John Van Engen defended Gratian's authorship of *De*

1. Sohm, *Das altkatholische Kirchenrecht.* Major critiques of Sohm include: Ulrich Stutz, "Review of Sohm, *Das altkatholische Kirchenrecht,*" *ZRG KA* 8 (1918): 238–46; Franz Gillmann, "Einteilung und System des Gratianischen Dekrets nach den alten Dekretglossatoren bis Johannes Teutonicus einschliesslich," *AKKR* 106 (1926): 472–574.

2. Marcia L. Colish, *Peter Lombard,* 2 vols. (Leiden: Brill, 1994), 1:89: "Peter goes a long way toward incorporating the work of Gratian into his sacramental theology."

3. See the overview of the two recensions in chapter 1, pp. 24–26; Winroth, *The Making of Gratian's Decretum.*

consecratione because he regarded the tract as a "complete treatise on the sacraments" and because *De consecratione*, in his judgment, reflected the interests of not only the speculative theologian, but also the "practical" one, that is, the canonist.[4] But if, as Winroth has argued, the two recensions have different authors, then neither reason adduced by Van Engen provides particularly cogent support for Gratian's authorship of *De consecratione*. And without *De consecratione*, it is unclear to what extent the first recension deals with sacramental theology or Gratian qualifies as a sacramental theologian.

This chapter reassesses Gratian the sacramental theologian on the basis of the first recension. Part 2 of this book argued that Gratian was a penitential theologian. This chapter will argue that he was a theologian of the other sacraments (with the exception of marriage) to only a limited extent.[5] Not only does Gratian devote relatively little space to the sacraments in the first recension, but the topics that he does consider are more legal than theological in nature, that is, they are topics that the later schools judged to be more the preserve of jurists than theologians. The redactor of the second recension may have been a sacramental theologian; the author of the first recension was largely not.

This chapter consists of two sections. The first section provides an overview of the sacraments in canon law prior to Gratian. It shows that sacramental law and theology occupied a prominent place in the major canonical collections that circulated in the early twelfth century, including Gratian's major formal sources. The second section then looks at what Gratian chose to include on the sacraments in the first recension and demonstrates that they leave out much of the sacramental theology that was present in the canon law of his day. The first recension explores the validity of sacraments adminis-

4. John Van Engen, "Observations on 'De consecratione,'" in *Proceedings of the Sixth International Congress of Medieval Canon Law*, ed. Stephan Kuttner and Kenneth Pennington, MIC.C 7 (Vatican City: BAV, 1985), 309–20, quotation at 312.

5. Gratian appears to have regarded penance as a sacrament. See C.1 q.1 d.p.c.42 (ed. Friedberg, 375, supported by Aa Bc Fd P): "Non est enim de hoc sacramento [i.e., ordination] ut de ceteris; cetera enim uel ad culpas abluendas dantur, ut baptismus et penitentia." In contrast, there is no evidence that Gratian regarded marriage as a sacrament.

tered by unworthy priests and heretics, their proper minister, their recipients, and one of their effects, spiritual affinity. But the first recension leaves out many major topics, above all eucharistic theology.

The Sacraments in Pre-Gratian Canon Law

Modern Catholic doctrine recognizes only seven rites as sacraments: baptism, confirmation, the eucharist, penance, extreme unction, holy orders, and matrimony.[6] Pre-Gratian theology and canon law, in contrast, defined the sacraments both more broadly and more restrictively.[7] On the one hand, authors frequently used the term "sacrament" to denote any sacred sign.[8] Hugh of St. Victor, for instance, applies the term to such diverse rites and objects as the sprinkling of holy water, reception of ashes, benediction of palms and branches, Easter candles, and the sign of the cross, as well as the theological virtue of faith.[9] On the other hand, other authors, most notably Isidore of Seville, restricted the term "sacrament" to just baptism, confirmation, and the eucharist.[10]

Individual sacraments were frequent subjects of canonical legislation from the patristic era onward. For instance, already with the

6. See, e.g., book 4, part 1 of the *Code of Canon Law: Latin-English Edition* (Washington, D.C.: Canon Law Society of America, 1983), which treats only these seven rites as sacraments.

7. Damien van den Eynde, "Les définitions des sacrements pendant la première période de la théologie scolastique (1050–1235)," *Antonianum* 24 (1949): 183–228 and 439–88; Josef Finkenzeller, *Handbuch der Dogmengeschichte* 4.1: *Die Lehre von den Sakramenten im allgemeinen: Von der Schrift bis zur Scholastik* (Freiburg: Herder, 1980).

8. Finkenzeller, *Lehre von den Sakramenten*, 119.

9. Hugh of St. Victor, *De sacramentis* 2.9.1 and 1.10.9, PL 175, 471D–478B and 341C–344A.

10. Isidore of Seville, *Etymologiarum sive Originum libri xx* 6.19.39, ed. W. M. Lindsay, 2 vols. (Oxford: Oxford University Press, 1911): "Sacramentum est in aliqua celebratione, cum res gesta ita fit ut aliquid significare intellegatur, quod sancte accipiendum est. Sunt autem sacramenta baptismum et chrisma, corpus et sanguinis [Domini]." For other authors who accepted this narrow definition of the sacraments, see Nicholas M. Haring, "The Interaction Between Canon Law and Sacramental Theology in the Twelfth Century," in *Proceedings of the Fourth International Congress of Medieval Canon Law*, ed. Stephan Kuttner, MIC.C 5 (Vatican City: BAV, 1976), 483–93, at 484.

Council of Neocaesarea (315) there appear canons on baptism, holy orders, and marriage.[11] The First Council of Nicaea (325) issued canons dealing with the qualifications of the clergy and the eucharist.[12] And the Council of Sardica (343) promulgated numerous canons pertaining to ordination.[13]

Later councils and popes continued this legislative activity, which increased particularly during the Carolingian period.[14] As part of his efforts to reform the Frankish church, Charlemagne issued numerous decrees on the sacraments, including its liturgy, as well as on cultic practices more generally.[15] These canons dealt mainly with sacramental law rather than sacramental theology. They were commands concerning how the sacraments should be performed or received rather than expositions of the meaning and significance of the sacraments.

The papal reform movement of the eleventh century and the Berengar Controversy ushered in a new era in sacramental canon law.[16] The reform movement, often referred to as the Gregorian Reform, sought to stamp out various abuses among the clergy. The reformers focused principally on nicolaitism (clerical concubinage) and simony—the buying and selling of church offices or, more generally, of any spiritual thing—but later also turned their attention to the lay investiture of ecclesiastical offices.[17] The Berengar Controversy, on the other hand, was a theological controversy about the nature

11. Council of Neocaesarea, ed. Cuthbert Hamilton Turner, *Ecclesiae Occidentalis Monumenta iuris antiquissima* 2.1 (Oxford: Clarendon Press, 1907), 12–15.

12. Council of Nicaea, cc.2, 4, 13, and 18, ed. Giuseppe Alberigo et al., *Conciliorum oecumenicorum generaliumque decreta: Editio critica* 1: *The Oecumenical Councils from Nicaea I to Nicaea II (325–787)*, Corpus Christianorum (Turnhout: Brepols, 2006), 20–22, 27, and 29–30. For English translations, see *Decrees*, ed. Tanner, 1:6, 7, 12, and 14–15.

13. Hamilton Hess, *The Early Development of Canon Law and the Council of Serdica*, 2nd ed. (Oxford: Oxford University Press, 2002), which updates his *The Canons of the Council of Sardica, A.D. 343: A Landmark in the Early Development of Canon Law* (Oxford: Oxford University Press, 1958).

14. For a general introduction to the period, see Roger E. Reynolds, "The Organisation, Law, and Liturgy of the Western Church, 700–900," in *The New Cambridge Medieval History* 2: *c. 700–c. 900*, ed. Rosamond McKitterick (Cambridge: Cambridge University Press, 1995), 587–621.

15. See the overview of the history of liturgical law in chapter 8, pp. 249–53.

16. See Munier, *Les sources patristiques*, 59–62.

17. For an introduction to the reform, see Uta-Renate Blumenthal, "The Pa-

of the eucharist. Berengar of Tours was a French master who taught that, through the words of consecration, bread and wine become the body and blood of Christ, but without ceasing to be bread and wine. In the late 1040s and 1050s and again in the 1070s, scholars and councils condemned and repudiated Berengar's teachings. The eucharist, they taught, is more than just a sign of Christ's body and blood; it actually is his body and blood and only his body and blood.[18]

One of the main consequences of both the papal reform movement and the Berengar Controversy was the large-scale incorporation of patristic texts, particularly texts on the sacraments, into the canonical tradition and a corresponding sacramentalization and theologization of canon law. In justifying their positions on such issues as the validity of sacraments administered by heretics and the nature of the eucharist, actors on both sides of the papal reform movement and Berengar Controversy appealed to the Church Fathers. The texts that they marshalled often made their way into not only polemical works, but also canonical collections. Ivo of Chartres contributed the most to this canonical reception of patristic texts.[19] Based at least in part on the writings produced during the Berengar Controversy, Ivo compiled a collection of mainly patristic texts on the eucharist, which he later incorporated into book 2 of his *Decretum*.[20] Together

---

pacy, 1024–1122," in *The New Cambridge Medieval History* 4.2: *c. 1024–c.1198*, ed. David Luscombe and Jonathan Riley-Smith (Cambridge: Cambridge University Press, 2004), 8–37; Kathleen G. Cushing, *Reform and Papacy in the Eleventh Century: Spirituality and Social Change* (Manchester: Manchester University Press, 2005).

18. On the Berengar Controversy, see Jean de Montclos, *Lanfranc et Bérenger: La controverse eucharistique au XIe siècle* (Leuven: Spicilegium Sacrum Lovaniense, 1971); Charles M. Radding and Francis Newton, *Theology, Rhetoric, and Politics in the Eucharistic Controversy, 1078–1079: Alberic of Monte Cassino against Berengar of Tours* (New York: Columbia University Press, 2003). On early scholastic eucharistic theology, see Gary Macy, *Theologies of the Eucharist in the Early Scholastic Period: A Study of the Salvific Function of the Sacrament According to Theologians, c. 1080–c. 1220* (Oxford: Oxford University Press, 1984).

19. Munier, *Les sources patristiques*, esp. 39–40 and 54; Peter Landau, "Wandel und Kontinuität im kanonischen Recht bei Gratian," in *Sozialer Wandel im Mittelalter: Wahrnehmungsformen, Erklärungsmuster, Regelungsmechanismen*, ed. Jürgen Miethke and Klaus Schreiner (Sigmaringen: J. Thorbecke, 1994), 215–33, at 221.

20. Christof Rolker, "The Earliest Work of Ivo of Chartres: The Case of Ivo's Eucharist Florilegium and the Canon Law Collections Attributed to Him," *ZRG KA* 124 (2007): 109–27; Rolker, *Canon Law*, 139–40.

with other material on the sacraments that he had gathered, these authorities made their way into many subsequent canonical collections, most notably the Pseudo-Ivonian *Panormia* and the second recension of Gratian's *Decretum*.[21]

Almost all major canonical collections after Ivo, including Gratian's main formal sources, contain a significant number of patristic texts and, as a result, also deal extensively with the sacraments.[22] In particular, the first two titles of Collection B of the *Tripartita*—that is, *Tripartita* 3, which is an abbreviation of Ivo's *Decretum*—deal with baptism and the sacraments.[23] Book 1 of the *Panormia* includes numerous canons on baptism, confirmation, the eucharist, and the mass.[24] Book 3 of the *Polycarpus* contains titles on the eucharist and baptism and confirmation.[25] And the 3L has titles on baptism and confirmation and the eucharist.[26]

The Sacraments in the First Recension

Of all the sacramental topics addressed in the canonical tradition, the first recension considers just four relating to the five ecclesiastical rites (baptism, confirmation, the eucharist, extreme unction, and orders) that, together with penance and marriage, came to be recognized as sacraments: their validity, their minister, their recipients, and one of their effects, spiritual affinity. Insofar as the first two topics really concern the sacrament of orders, later theologians and canonists judged them to be more the preserve of canon law than theology,

21. See Munier, *Les sources patristiques*, 40–41.

22. On Gratian's main formal sources, see the discussion in chapter 1, pp. 20–24.

23. *Tripartita* 3.1: "De baptismo"; 3.2: "De sacramentis."

24. *Panormia* 1: "De fide. De diversis heresibus. De sacramento fidei, id est baptismate, et ministerio baptizandorum et consecrandorum et consignandorum et consignatorum et de observatione singulorum, et quid conferat baptisma, quid confirmatio. De sacramento corporis et sanguinis Domini. De missa et sanctitate aliorum sacramentorum."

25. *Polycarpus* 3.9: "De corpore Domini sacrorumque custodia"; 3.10: "De baptismo et impositione manus."

26. 3L 1.15.tit., ed. Joseph Motta, *Collectio canonum trium librorum*, 2 vols., MIC.B 8/I-II (Vatican City: BAV, 2005–8), 2:46: "De baptismo et manus impositione"; App. 23.tit., ed. Motta, 2:308: "De obseruantia sacrificii."

while the last topic, spiritual affinity, was a topic for both theologians and canonists.[27]

Sacramental Validity

Of all questions pertaining to the sacraments (aside from penance and marriage), Gratian devotes the greatest amount of space to the issue of sacramental validity. Gratian elaborates this topic mainly in *Causa* 1 in connection with the topic of simony. Simony and the validity of sacraments administered by simoniacs had been subjects of heated debate ever since the papal reform movement of the mid-eleventh century. In their efforts to combat simony, radical reformers such as Humbert of Silva Candida denied the validity of sacraments administered by not only simoniacally ordained clergy, but also clergy ordained by simoniacs without simony, *gratis*.[28] For these rigorists, distinguishing between the dogmatic validity of a sacrament and its spiritual efficacy made no sense and only muddied the underlying issue. No one can give to another what he himself does not possess, and simoniacs, being heretics, do not possess the Holy Spirit. Simoniacs are thus unable to confer grace on others through any of their sacraments. According to the rigorists, not only are simoniacs unable to transmit the sacrament of orders to others, but they are also unable to validly administer any of the other sacraments, such as baptism, confirmation, or the eucharist.[29]

This extreme view never appears to have had more than a small number of adherents.[30] Instead, not only anti-reformers, but also most

27. See pp. 10–12 in the introduction to this book.

28. On the origins and development of simony, see Anton Leinz, *Die Simonie: Eine kanonistische Studie* (Freiburg im Breisgau: Herder, 1902); N. A. Weber, *A History of Simony in the Christian Church to 814* (Baltimore: J. H. Furst, 1909); R. A. Ryder, *Simony: An Historical Synopsis and Commentary* (Washington, D.C.: The Catholic University of America Press, 1931); Hans Meier-Welcker, "Die Simonie im frühen Mittelalter," *Zeitschrift für Kirchengeschichte* 64 (1952–53): 61–93; Joseph Weitzel, *Begriff und Erscheinungsformen der Simonie bei Gratian und den Dekretisten* (Munich: M. Hueber, 1967).

29. Carl Mirbt, *Die Publizistik im Zeitalter Gregors VII.* (Leipzig: Hinrichs, 1894), 378–86; Louis Saltet, *Les réordinations: Étude sur le sacrement de l'ordre* (Paris: V. Lecoffre, 1907).

30. John Gilchrist, "*Simoniaca haeresis* and the Problem of Orders from Leo IX to

reform-minded clergy affirmed the working of the sacraments independently of the minister's merits. Alger of Liège provides one notable example. In his *Liber de misericordia et iustitia,* which was the main source for Gratian's discussion of simony, Alger attempts to shed light on the dogmatic validity of ordinations administered by unworthy ministers by examining not only the canons dealing with this specific subject, but also canons dealing with the validity of baptisms and masses performed by such persons.[31] Based on these texts, Alger concludes that the dogmatic validity of a sacrament depends entirely on observation of the correct form and is independent of the minister's merits or demerits. According to Alger, subjective factors play a role only as regards the efficacy of a valid sacrament. Sacraments administered by ministers within the church are efficacious only when received worthily, while those administered by ministers outside the church are never efficacious, regardless of the recipient's moral status. Like most of the reformers, Alger regarded simony as a heresy and thus rejected the spiritual efficacy of sacraments, including baptism, administered by simoniacs even when performed *gratis.* But unlike many of his contemporaries, Alger regarded nicolaitism as a mere disciplinary problem and hence argued that it was possible to receive the sacraments of married priests fruitfully.[32]

Gratian comes to somewhat different conclusions in his own examination of the problem of sacramental validity. Like Alger, Gratian agrees that sacraments performed within the unity of the Catholic church work independently of the minister's merits. The dogmatic validity of Catholic sacraments depends solely on observance of the correct form and is unaffected by a minister's merits or demerits, even though the moral status of the recipient determines their efficacy or lack thereof. Yet while Alger simultaneously affirms the general validity of heretical sacraments and denies their general ability to communicate grace, Gratian is unwilling to make such broad gen-

Gratian," in *Proceedings of the Second International Congress of Medieval Canon Law,* ed. Stephan Kuttner and J. Joseph Ryan, MIC.C 3 (Vatican City: BAV, 1965), 209–35.

31. Kretzschmar, *Alger von Lüttichs Traktat,* 141–54.

32. Ibid., 48–55.

eralizations. Instead, his position on these issues differs from sacrament to sacrament.[33]

Gratian is most objectivist and Augustinian in his teaching on baptism.[34] As a sacrament of necessity, baptism can be efficaciously received from any sort of minister whatsoever.[35] Those who are baptized by schismatics or heretics, he argues, do not obtain the virtue or effect of the sacrament, that is, the remission of sins, so long as they remain in communion with them.[36] If one does not share in the schism or heresy, however, and the baptism is performed according to the form of the church, then the baptism is immediately efficacious.[37] In fact, Gratian teaches, one can receive baptism efficaciously even from a pagan.[38]

For the most part, however, Gratian is unwilling to make similar concessions concerning the other sacraments, although his statements here are contradictory.[39] As Adam Zirkel persuasively dem-

33. In general, I follow the interpretation of Adam Zirkel, *"Executio potestatis": Zur Lehre Gratians von der geistlichen Gewalt,* Münchener theologische Studien, 3. Kanonistische Abteilung 33 (St. Ottilien: Eos Verlag, 1975). Since C.1 q.1 differs little between the two recensions, Zirkel's careful and painstaking analysis of Gratian's views remains mostly valid.

34. Ibid., 54–56.

35. Ibid., 47, points out that, despite speaking of sacraments of necessity in the plural, Gratian in fact seems to conceive of only baptism as a sacrament of necessity.

36. C.1 q.1 d.p.c.53 (ed. Friedberg, 379, supported by Aa Bc Fd): "Alii formam ecclesie in baptizando seruant. Sed dum ab eis baptizantur, qui in heresi uel scismate eis communicant, sacramentum quidem baptismi ab eis accipiunt, uirtutem uero non sequuntur (consequuntur *Friedb.*), quam sine fide nullus consequi potest. Vnde de Domino dicitur, quod in patria sua non poterat facere signum propter incredulitatem eorum."

37. C.1 q.1 d.p.c.57 (ed. Friedberg, 380, supported by Aa Bc Fd): "Nemo in heresi uel scismate constitutus intelligendum (intelligendus *Friedb.*) est. Ceterum, si cum fidei integritate et animi puritate de manu hereticorum aliquis in forma ecclesie baptisma acceperit, tunc impletur illud Augustini: 'Per lapideum canalem aqua transit ad areolas.' Et iterum (item *Aa Bc*): 'Spiritualis uirtus sacramenti' etc."

38. C.1 q.1 d.p.c.58 (ed. Friedberg, 380, supported by Aa Bc Fd): "Ecce quando ab hereticis baptisma (datur *add. Aa*) cum sua uirtute accipitur, cuius tam necessaria ministratio (amministratio *Friedb.*) est, ut nec etiam a paganis datum possit reiterari."

39. C.24 q.1 d.p.c.39 (ed. Lenherr, 53.5–10): "Baptisma namque siue ab heretico siue etiam a laico ministratum fuerit, dummodo in unitate catholice fidei

onstrated around forty years ago, Gratian sometimes affirms the dogmatic validity of the eucharist, ordination, and other sacraments celebrated by heretics, rejecting only their spiritual efficacy, while at other times he denies both their dogmatic validity and their efficacy. Many but not all the affirmations of dogmatic validity occur in dicta copied from Alger, whereas all but one of the denials appear in passages that Gratian himself composed.[40] Gratian's inconsistency on this point, however, is not simply due to his reliance on Alger, but stems at least in part from the ambiguity of the distinction that Gratian introduces between power (*officium, potestas*) and execution (*effectus, executio*). Later canon law would distinguish between the sacramental power of orders, conferred in ordination, which grants the one ordained the ability to celebrate the sacraments, and the non-sacramental power of jurisdiction, conferred by delegation from a superior, which grants the delegate the authority to judge or command those within a certain geographic area and which is also necessary for the exercise of certain sacramental functions. The power of orders imprints an indelible character on the one ordained. It can never be lost, although it cannot be legitimately exercised without the proper grant of jurisdiction. The power of jurisdiction, in contrast, imprints no indelible character and may be delegated even to a layperson.[41]

Gratian's distinction between power and execution is more fluid and imprecise than the later distinction between orders and jurisdiction. In certain passages, Gratian interprets execution in the same way that later canonists interpret jurisdiction: as a necessary prerequisite for the *legitimate* exercise of sacramental power. But in other passages Gratian interprets execution in another sense: as a neces-

---

accipiatur, non carebit effectu. Alia uero sacramenta, ut sacri corporis et sanguinis Domini, excommunicationis uel reconciliationis, si ab heretico uel catholico non sacerdote ministrentur, uel nullum uel letalem habebunt effectum."

40. Zirkel, *Executio potestatis*, esp. the summary of his findings at 154–60.

41. On this distinction and its development, see Raoul Naz, *Dictionnaire de droit canonique*, 7 vols. (Paris: Letouzey, 1935–65), 6:1148–50, s.v. "Ordre en droit occidental"; Charles Lefebvre, ibid., 7:77–108, s.v. "Pouvoirs de l'église"; John Joseph Ryan, *The Separation of "Ordo" and "Iurisdictio" in Its Structural-Doctrinal Development and Ecclesiological Significance: A Dogmatic-Historical Contribution Towards the Renewal of Canon Law* (PhD diss., Universität Münster, 1972).

sary prerequisite for the *valid* exercise of sacramental power. Later theologians and canonists would eliminate this ambiguity. Gratian himself perhaps never actually perceived it.

The Minister

Gratian devotes only a small amount of space to the question of who can administer the sacraments, dealing with the minister of ordination in the most detail. In the first recension, D.23 reproduces a series of canons from the pseudonymous Fourth Council of Carthage detailing how ordinations into each grade of the ecclesiastical hierarchy should be performed.[42] The canons describing the ordinations into major orders (bishop, priest, deacon) all mention the bishop as the minister.[43] Later on, Gratian explicitly acknowledges that the proper minister of holy orders is the bishop. A bishop is to be ordained by the other bishops of the province.[44] Priests and other ministers, on the other hand, should be ordained by their own bishop.[45]

Gratian treats the question of who should administer the other sacraments much more briefly. The priest is the proper minister of the eucharist as well as of baptism. But other persons, including children and pagans, can validly administer baptism as well.[46] The proper minister of confirmation, on the other hand, is just the bishop. In his absence, however, an ordinary priest may also perform the sacrament.[47]

42. In reality, the fictitious Fourth Council of Carthage was the canonical collection known as the *Statuta ecclesiae antiqua* (ca. 476–85), ed. Charles Munier, *Les Statuta ecclesiae antiqua: Édition—Études critiques* (Paris: Presses Universitaires de France, 1960).

43. D.23 cc.7, 8, 11 (ed. Friedberg, 82 and 83). The material source for these canons is the Fourth Council of Carthage, cc.2–4, in *Concilia Africae*, ed. Munier, 344 = *Statuta ecclesiae antiqua*, cc.90–92, ed. Munier, 96.

44. D.65 d.p.c.8 (ed. Friedberg, 252, supported by Aa Bc Fd P): "His auctoritatibus datur intelligi quod episcopi a comprouincialibus suis debent ordinari."

45. D.67 d.a.c.1 (ed. Friedberg, 253, supported by Aa Bc Fd P): "Presbiteri uero et corepiscopi ab uno episcopo ordinari possunt." D.70 d.a.c.1 (ed. Friedberg, 256, supported by Aa Bc Fd P): "Ab episcopis alterius ciuitatis clericus ordinari non poterit."

46. C.1 q.1 d.p.c.58 (ed. Friedberg, 380).

47. JE 1298 = D.95 c.1 (ed. Friedberg, 331, supported by Aa Bc Fd P): "Peruenit quoque ad nos quosdam scandalizatos fuisse quod presbiteros crismate tan-

The Recipient

Gratian goes into detail only about who should be the recipient of the sacrament of orders. Following the catalog of qualities listed by the apostle Paul in 1 Timothy 3:2–7 and Titus 1:7–9, though as interpreted by the *Glossa ordinaria* to the Bible, Gratian declares that candidates for bishop should be free from grave sin, have been married at most once since their baptism, sober in drink, prudent, that is, learned both in letters and secular administration, virtuous, graceful and appropriately dressed, hospitable, pure in both morals and speech, not gluttonous, slow to anger, not litigious, that is, not prone to argument, not avaricious, that is, not a usurer/money-lender, and mature in the faith rather than a neophyte.[48] In addition, those who are not truly penitent, those who have performed public penance, public officials, public litigants, slaves or serfs who have not obtained their master's permission, those with a serious physical defect, the sons of priests, and religious without the consent of their abbot should, as a rule, be excluded.[49] But these prohibitions can be dispensed with when there is an appropriate cause.[50]

One Effect of Baptism and Confirmation: Spiritual Affinity

The only effect of a sacrament that Gratian devotes any significant attention to in the first recension is spiritual affinity. This mari-

---

gere eos qui baptizati sunt prohibuimus. Et nos quidem secundum ueterem usum nostre ecclesie fecimus. Sed si omnino hac de re aliqui contristantur, ubi episcopi desunt, ut presbiteri etiam in frontibus baptizatos crismate tangere debeant, concedimus." On the interpretation of this decretal from Gregory the Great, see Franz Gillmann, *Zur Lehre der Scholastik vom Spender der Firmung und des Weihesakraments* (Paderborn: Schöningh, 1920).

48. D.25 d.p.c.3 §1 (ed. Friedberg, 92); D.26 d.a.c.1; D.35 d.a.c.1 §1 (ed. Friedberg, 130); D.36 d.a.c.1; D.40 d.a.c.1; D.41 d.a.c.1; D.42 d.a.c.1 (ed. Friedberg, 151); D.43 d.a.c.1 (ed. Friedberg, 153); D.44 d.a.c.1 (ed. Friedberg, 156); D.45 d.a.c.1 (ed. Friedberg, 160); D.46 d.a.c.1 (ed. Friedberg, 167); D.47 d.a.c.1 (ed. Friedberg, 169); D.48 d.a.c.1 (ed. Friedberg, 174). See also pp. 61–62.

49. D.51 d.a.c.1 (ed. Friedberg, 203); D.54 d.a.c.1 (ed. Friedberg, 206); D.55 d.a.c.1 (ed. Friedberg, 215); D.56 d.a.c.1 (ed. Friedberg, 219); D.58 d.a.c.1 (ed. Friedberg, 224).

50. D.61 d.p.c.8 §2 (ed. Friedberg, 230, supported by Aa Bc Fd P): "Sed sciendum est quod ecclesiastice prohibitiones proprias habent causas, quibus cessantibus cessant et ipse."

tal impediment appears to have grown out of late antique customary mores and practices. In the fifth and sixth centuries, baptismal sponsorship created close social ties between sponsor (godparent) and sponsored (godchild). Participants viewed and treated each other as family and like family were therefore forbidden from intermarrying. First in the Byzantine East, but from the eighth century onward also in the Latin West, legislators issued laws and canons prohibiting various forms of marital union between those connected by bonds of spiritual kinship, for instance, between godparent and godchild, between godparent and parent of the godchild, and between the child of a godparent and a godchild. Other legislation ordered the separation of spouses who served as sponsors for their own children, or forbade such separation when done deliberately to achieve a divorce.[51]

As it took shape in the decades immediately preceding Gratian, canon law recognized two main sources and three main types of spiritual affinity. The main sources of spiritual affinity were baptism and confirmation. Performing these sacraments, receiving these sacraments, or serving as a sponsor in these sacraments created bonds of spiritual affinity that restricted one's possible marriage partners. In the terminology of the later canonists, the main types of spiritual affinity were paternity, compaternity, and fraternity. Paternity refers to situations involving a spiritual parent and a spiritual child, such as that created by a godparent and godchild; compaternity to situations involving a spiritual parent or the spiritual parent's spouse and the biological or adoptive parent of the spiritual child or that parent's spouse; and fraternity to situations involving the spiritual parent's biological or adoptive children and the godchild or the godchild's siblings. These types of affinity could be anterior, and thus impediments to, marriage, or they could be supervening, that is, they could arise between an already married couple.[52]

51. Joseph H. Lynch, "Spiritual Kinship and Sexual Prohibitions in Early Medieval Europe," in *Proceedings of the Sixth International Congress of Medieval Canon Law*, ed. Kuttner and Pennington, 271–88; Rudolf Weigand, "Die Ausdehnung der Ehehindernisse der Verwandschaft," *ZRG KA* 80 (1994): 1–17, at 8–16; Enrique de León, *La "cognatio spiritualis" según Graciano* (Milan: Giuffrè, 1996), 13–67.

52. On these pre-Gratian developments, see De León, *Cognatio spiritualis*, 70–104.

The first recension examines three issues pertaining to spiritual affinity.[53] C.30 q.1 examines what later canon law would term supervening spiritual affinity. Can a husband who becomes a spiritual father to his biological child henceforth engage in conjugal relations with his wife, or vice versa?[54] Gratian's answer in the first recension is extremely clear. He cites two canons ordering separation in this situation (cc.1–2) and five canons commanding spouses to remain together (cc.3–7), followed by the closing dictum (d.p.c.10) containing Gratian's own position: regardless of whether a spouse contracts it accidentally or deliberately, supervening spiritual affinity provides no grounds for annulling a marriage.[55]

C.30 q.3 investigates what later canon law would call spiritual fraternity. Are godchildren or adopted children permitted to marry the biological children of their godparents/adopters?[56] The first recension cites just two canons in response (cc.1–2), both of which forbid such marriages.[57]

Finally, C.30 q.4 examines what later canon law would call spiritual compaternity. Canon law since the Carolingian period clearly affirmed that godparents were not allowed to marry the parents of

53. While all five *quaestiones* in C.30 deal with marriage, only C.30 qq.1, 3, and 4 touch upon spiritual affinity.

54. C.30 q.1 d.a.c.1 (ed. Werckmeister, 275): "Quod autem proprium filium in spiritualem sibi transferens sue uxori debitum reddere non ualeat, ratione et auctoritate probatur. Nulla enim auctoritate permittitur ut quis commatri sue carnaliter copuletur."

55. C.30 q.1 d.p.c.10 (ed. Werckmeister, 288): "His itaque auctoritatibus apparet quod siue proprium siue tantummodo uiri filium mulier de sacro fonte susceperit, non ideo a uiro suo est separanda. Quod et de uiro similiter oportet intellegi."

56. C.30 q.3 d.a.c.1 (ed. Werckmeister, 292): "Quod autem spirituales uel adoptiui filii naturalibus copulari non possint Nicolaus papa respondens ad consulta Bulgarorum testatur ita dicens."

57. A third canon (c.5) added to the question in the second recension, was already present in the first recension, but attached to the end of C.30 q.4 c.5. The two canons are in fact parts of the same decretal of Paschal II, JL 6436, and were transmitted as a unit in earlier canonical collections, including the *Polycarpus* and 3L, either of which could have been Gratian's formal source. On the transmission of JL 6436, see Uta-Renate Blumenthal, "Decrees and Decretals of Pope Paschal II in Twelfth-Century Canonical Collections," *BMCL* 10 (1980): 15–30, at 19–20, reprinted in her *Papal Reform and Canon Law in the 11th and 12th Centuries*, Variorum Collected Studies Series CS618 (Aldershot: Ashgate, 1998), no. XII.

their godchildren. But did the same apply to a godparent's spouse? And what of a godchild's step-parent? The first recension focuses on an extreme limit case. Is a man (A) permitted to marry his wife's (B) godchild's (C) father's (D) wife (E), after both his own wife (E) and the father (D) of the godchild (C) in question pass away? The wife (B) cannot marry the father (D) of the godchild (C) because they are *compatres*, that is, parents of the same child (C). One is a spiritual parent (B); the other is a biological one (D). But to what extent did such an impediment pass to those made one flesh with B and D, namely A and E?[58]

In the first recension, Gratian cites two canons (cc.1–2) that he alleges forbid and two canons that he claims permit (cc.4–5) marriage in this case, though in fact none of the authorities he cites addresses this exact fact pattern. The first canon, a decretal of Pope Nicholas I, forbids a man from marrying two *commatres*, that is, a woman and her godchild's mother. The reason given for the prohibition, which Gratian takes over in revised form in d.p.c.5, is that by becoming one with his wife in marriage, a man acquires her bonds of spiritual affinity. Hence his wife's *commater* is also his own *commater*, and marriages between a man and his *commater* are forbidden.[59] The second canon similarly forbids a man from having sexual relations with two *commatres*.[60] But c.4 permits a man to marry his godchild's father's wife, as long as she is not his *commater*—in the context of this can-

58. C.30 q.4 d.a.c.1 (ed. Werckmeister, 300): "Relictam uero compatris uxoris sue nullus in coniugem ducere potest."

59. JE 2849 = C.30 q.4 c.1 (ed. Werckmeister, 300): "Sciscitatur a nobis sanctitas uestra si aliquis homo duas commatres habere ualeat unam post alteram. In quo meminisse debet scriptum esse: 'Erunt duo in carne una.' Itaque cum constet quia uir et mulier una caro per conubium efficiuntur, restat nimirum uirum compatrem constitui illi mulieri cuius matrimonio assumpta uxor commater esse uidebatur et idcirco liquet uirum illi femine non posse iungi in copula que commater eius erat, cum qua idem fuerat una caro effectus."

60. C.30 q.4 c.2 (ed. Werckmeister, 300): "Si pater et filius aut duo fratres cum una muliere aut si cum matre et filia aut cum duabus sororibus, aut cum duabus commatribus aliquis concubuerit, secundum antiquam et humaniorem diffinitionem octo annis peniteat." The *Decretum* misattributes the canon to the Council of Chalcedon. The material source appears to be a penitential. See *Poenitentiale Valicellanum III*, ed. Friedrich Wilhelm Wasserschleben, *Die Bußordnungen der abendländischen Kirche* (Halle, 1851), 682–83.

on the biological mother of his godchild.[61] And c.5 permits a man to marry his wife's *commater*.[62] Gratian resolves these difficulties by invoking a principle adumbrated but not explicitly formulated in c.1, which would become extremely important in later centuries.[63] Becoming one flesh, that is, engaging in sexual relations, Gratian declares, transmits spiritual affinity from one person to another. Canons that forbid a man from marrying his wife's *commater* apply in those instances when a man has had sex with his wife after a bond of spiritual affinity has arisen. Canons that permit such marriages refer to those instances when the bond of spiritual affinity has not been transmitted from one spouse to the other.[64]

Gratian's Omissions

Two omissions in the first recension's treatment of the sacraments are particularly noteworthy. First, Gratian does not explore theoretical questions concerning orders, baptism, confirmation, and the eucharist. In particular, he does not address the nature of Christ's presence in the eucharist. As *De penitentia* shows, Gratian had no qualms about exploring the more theoretical aspects of sacramental theology on other occasions, when he wanted to. But Gratian did not do

61. C.30 q.4 c.4 (ed. Werckmeister, 302): "Qui spiritualem compatrem habet cuius filium de lauacro sacri fontis accepit et eius uxor commater non est, liceat ei defuncto compatre suo eius uiduam ducere in uxorem si nullam habet consanguinitatis propinquitatem. Quid enim? Numquid non possunt coniungi quos nulla propinquitas carnalis uel nulla generatio secernit spiritualis?" The material source is Council of Tribur (895), c.47, ed. Boretius and Krause, *Capitularia regum Francorum*, 240.

62. JL 6436 = C.30 q.4 c.5 (ed. Werckmeister, 302): "Post uxoris obitum cum commatre uxoris uiri superstitis coniugio copulari nulla uidetur ratio uel auctoritas prohibere. Neque enim cognationi carnis cognatio spiritus comparatur neque per carnis unionem ad unionem spiritus pertransitur." On the transmission of this decretal, see Blumenthal, "Decrees and Decretals of Pope Paschal II," 19–20.

63. De León, *Cognatio spiritualis*, 279–88.

64. C.30 q.4 d.p.c.5 (ed. Werckmeister, 304): "Notandum uero est quod aliud est commatrem alicuius cognoscere atque aliud derelictam ab aliquo commatrem alicuius fieri. Auctoritas illa Nicolai pape et Calcedonensis sinodi illum prohibet commatris sue uxoris matrimonio copulari qui uxori sue debitum reddidit postquam illius commater extitit. Illa uero auctoritas Triburiensis concilii illos permittit matrimonio copulari cuius uxor post quam a uiro suo derelinquitur illius commater efficitur nec post compaternitatem a uiro suo cognoscitur."

so for the other sacraments, perhaps, I would suggest, because he saw no need to. For instance, since Berengar's condemnation, everyone agreed that in consecration the bread and wine truly become the body and blood of Christ. They just differed in their explanations as to why this transformation mattered.[65] Chapter 5 argued that Gratian composed the core of *De penitentia* largely to critique and correct contemporary theological positions that he regarded as erroneous. He may not have done the same for the other sacraments, including the eucharist, because the controversies there did not have the same contemporary importance or urgency.

The second omission in Gratian's treatment of the sacraments concerns a topic that would draw the interest of many later canonists: the liturgy. Gratian's discussion of sacramental validity, the minister of the sacraments, recipient of the sacraments, and effects of the sacraments certainly offered him the occasion to explore the liturgy of the sacraments as well as more general questions of liturgical theology, if he had wished to do so. But he did not. Why he did not will be investigated in chapter 8.

Conclusion

The sacraments occupied a prominent place in the canonical tradition prior to Gratian and, as a result of the large-scale incorporation of patristic texts caused by the papal reform movement and Berengar Controversy, were particularly well represented in most of Gratian's main formal sources. Nevertheless, the first recension treats only a limited number of issues relating to sacramental law or sacramental theology. It devotes a significant amount of attention to the problem of sacramental validity and the conditions under which spiritual affinity arises, but little to no space to the ministers of these sacraments, their recipients (except in the case of orders), or their other effects. The first recension also leaves out material on eucharistic

65. See Macy, *Theologies of the Eucharist*, who finds in all the theologians he studies agreement on the real presence of Christ in the eucharist, but different interpretations of why the eucharist matters.

theology and the liturgy. Omission of material on eucharistic theology and other more theoretical issues concerning the sacraments, this chapter suggested, was due to the fact that the debates no longer had the same importance or urgency as contemporary debates on penance. In contrast, the omission of material on the liturgy, chapter 8 will propose, has different roots and is related both to Gratian's views on custom and to his vision of what the *Decretum* should be.

8

Gratian, a Liturgist?

Chapter 7 considered Gratian's theology of the sacraments aside from penance, which was treated earlier in this book, and marriage, which he does not seem to have classified as a sacrament. The purpose was to consider the extent to which Gratian can be deemed a sacramental theologian and, in addition, to provide a positive sketch of what the first recension says on the sacraments. The present chapter attempts to shed light on one of the omissions revealed by that exercise: Gratian's neglect of the liturgy. Despite the prominence of the liturgy in the canonical collections and canon law of the eleventh and early twelfth centuries, the first recension omits not only liturgical theology, but even liturgical law. Almost every section addressing the liturgy in the *Decretum* was added only in the second recension.

This chapter proposes that the contrasting treatment of the liturgy (and, to a lesser extent, the sacraments) in the two recensions reflects contrasting visions of what the *Decretum* should be: an analytical concord of discordant canons, or a comprehensive compilation of canon law? Gratian sought to make the first recension the former, a *Concordia*, and thus had no qualms about omitting the liturgy from his textbook. The redactor of the second recension, in contrast, wanted to produce a comprehensive compilation of canon law and thus took great pains to fill the lacunae in Gratian's work.[1] His efforts took two forms. In the distinctions and *causae,* additions on the liturgy appear as scattered digressions. In *De consecratione,* in contrast, they form part of a lengthier, more coherent tract on ecclesiastical rites. These contrasting visions for the *Decretum,* I furthermore suggest, may have been related to contrasting visions of what the discipline of canon law should encompass.

This chapter consists of four sections. The first section provides an overview of the development of the canon law of the liturgy up to Gratian's day. It shows that material on the liturgy, particularly liturgical law, occupied a prominent place in the major canonical collections that circulated in the early twelfth century, including Gratian's major formal sources. For this reason, I argue, Gratian's neglect of the liturgy could not have been accidental; rather, it must have been deliberate. The second and third sections then examine the way in which the second recension responded to Gratian's neglect of the liturgy, namely, through the haphazard insertion of canons on the liturgy throughout the distinctions and *causae* and the compilation of *De consecratione.* While the manner in which the distinctions and *causae* incorporate material on the liturgy differs from the manner in which *De consecratione* incorporates such material, both parts of the *Decretum* evince the same desire to make Gratian's textbook more comprehensive and both draw on the same formal sources to realize this shared aim. For these and other reasons, I argue, the same person or group of persons was probably responsible for both expanding the distinctions and *causae,* on the one hand, and compiling *De consecratione,* on the other, and this person or group of persons was not

1. There is no necessary incompatability between analysis and comprehensive coverage. But in practice an emphasis on one can lead to the neglect of the other. What I mean to emphasize by my terminology is that Gratian privileged analysis over comprehensive coverage and, perhaps for that reason, chose not to cover certain canon law topics where there were fewer contradictions in the canons. The redactor of the second recension, in contrast, privileged comprehensive coverage over analysis. For that reason, he had no qualms about adding many canons and topics with only a minimal amount of analysis or sometimes even no analysis whatsoever. In many places, the goal of the redactor was simply to incorporate relevant texts into the second recension of the *Decretum,* not to analyze them.

Gratian. Finally, the fourth section explores possible explanations for why Gratian chose largely to ignore the liturgy in the first recension. The answer, I propose, is rooted in Gratian's interest in discordant canons and attitude towards local customs. Gratian wanted to produce an analytical concord of discordant canons pertaining to the law of the universal church. However, little conflict existed on many liturgical questions and local custom governed many other aspects of the liturgy.

Liturgy in Canon Law before Gratian

Texts dealing with the liturgy only gradually came to constitute a significant part of the canonical tradition. Prior to the Carolingian period, local custom rather than universal or particular legislation determined most aspects of the liturgy. While standard liturgical formulas and broad families of rites had emerged by the fourth and fifth centuries, liturgical books differed greatly from region to region and often from church to church. Liturgists felt free to and often did modify the contents of sacramentaries, ordinals, pontificals, and other liturgical books, whether by altering existing texts or by composing entirely new ones.[2] Moreover, while councils and popes began to issue an increasing number of decrees on liturgical matters in the fourth and fifth centuries, they tended to focus on when, where, who, and with what the liturgy should be celebrated rather than on how or in what order individual components of the liturgy should be performed. Patristic and early medieval legislation rarely regulated the mechanics of individual rites or attempted to impose liturgical uniformity over particular dioceses and regions.[3] Instead, Church Fathers and ecclesiastical lawmakers generally concerned themselves with the events leading up to and the circumstances surrounding liturgical ceremonies, for instance, the catechumenate, the conditions that candidates

2. Cyrille Vogel, *Introduction aux sources de l'histoire du culte chrétien au moyen âge*, rev. ed. (Spoleto: Centro italiano di studi sull'alto Medioevo, 1975), 20–31.

3. For some examples, see Paul Hinschius, *System des katholischen Kirchenrechts mit besonderer Rücksicht auf Deutschland*, 6 vols. (Berlin: I. Guttentag, 1869–97; reprinted in Graz: Akademische Druck- u. Verlagsanstalt, 1959), 4:6–7.

for baptism have to fulfill, the time when and the place where baptism should take place, and the minister of baptism; the places where mass can be said, the consecration of these places, the activities that can take place within them, and their decoration; the observance of Sunday, the date of Easter, the practice of fasting, and the liturgical calendar; and attendance at mass on Sundays and during feast days, fasting before mass, the frequency with which the eucharist should be received, the elements to be used for the eucharist, the necessary conditions for communicating, and the proper minister of the eucharist.[4]

It was not until the Carolingian period that the mechanics of the liturgy became an object of major concern for legislators and canonists.[5] As part of his efforts to reform the Frankish church, Charlemagne issued numerous decrees on liturgical practice. Councils held during his reign prescribed the adoption of Roman practices concerning baptism, liturgical chant, the kiss of peace, and the recitation of the names of the dead during mass, as well as the observation of the four Roman feasts of the Virgin (Purification, Conception, Assumption, and Nativity), Ash Wednesday, Holy Week, Rogations, and even clerical footwear.[6] The forgeries that circulated under the name of Pseudo-Isidore were even more important for the later canon law of the liturgy.[7] Because the biographies in the *Liber pontificalis* provide the template for much of the *False Decretals* and the *Liber Pontificalis* devotes especial attention to each pontiff's ceremonial and cultic activities, the *False Decretals* repeatedly return to the subject of liturgical practices and ceremonies.[8] To give just a few examples from the earliest decretals,

4. Jean Gaudemet, *L'Église dans l'empire romain (IVe–Ve siècles)*, Histoire du Droit et des Institutions de l'Église en Occident 3 (Paris: Sirey, 1958), 55–70, 653–65, and 681–85.

5. For a general introduction to the period, see Roger E. Reynolds, "The Organisation, Law, and Liturgy of the Western Church, 700–900," in *The New Cambridge Medieval History* 2, ed. McKitterick, 587–621.

6. Cyrille Vogel, "La reforme cultuelle sous Pépin le Bréf et sous Charlemagne (deuxième moitié du VIIIe siècle et premier quart du IXe siècle)," in *Die karolingische Renaissance*, ed. Erna Patzelt (Graz: Akademische Druck- u. Verlagsanstalt, 1965), 173–242, at 214–18.

7. On Pseudo-Isidore, see the overview in chapter 2, pp. 45–48.

8. I would like to thank Eric Knibbs for pointing this out to me. On the *Liber*

Pseudo-Clement outlines the baptismal process and the benefits of baptism; Pseudo-Anacletus stipulates the number of participants who should be present when a priest or bishop celebrates mass; Pseudo-Alexander explains why water and wine must be mixed together in the celebration of the eucharist; and Pseudo-Telesphorus lays down rules concerning fasting, the time when mass should be celebrated, and the Gloria.[9] The *False Decretals* thus deal with both liturgical theology and liturgical law, but engage in liturgical theology largely as an aid to justifying the liturgical regulations that they create.

Through their incorporation into canonical collections, late patristic and Carolingian texts on the liturgy achieved a wide circulation, thereby becoming the foundation for the canon law of the liturgy. While the eleventh-century reformers also enacted legislation on the liturgy, their contribution was quantitatively much smaller.[10] In supplementing the lacunae in the canon law of the liturgy, canonists of the reform period turned more readily to the works of the Church Fathers and such Carolingian liturgists as Hrabanus Maurus than to contemporary canons and decretals.

Almost all major eleventh- and early twelfth-century canonical collections devote significant space to the liturgy. Texts on the liturgy were most prominent in the *Collection in Five Books* and its numerous derivatives, which circulated mainly in southern Italy.[11] But texts on

Pontificalis, see Louis Duchesne, *Le Liber pontificalis: Texte, introduction, et commentaire*, 2nd ed., 3 vols. (Paris: E. Thorin, 1955–57).

9. JK †12 and †13 = Pseudo-Clement, *Epistolae* 3.62 and 4.79, ed. Hinschius, *Decretales Pseudo-Isidorianae*, 54 and 64; JK †2 = Pseudo-Anacletus, *Epistolae* 1.9–10, ed. Hinschius, 70; JK †24 = Pseudo-Alexander, *Epistolae* 1.9, ed. Hinschius, 99; JK †34 = Pseudo-Telesphorus, *Epistolae* 1.1–3, ed. Hinschius, 109–11.

10. On liturgical law during this period, see Reinhard Elze, "Gregor VII. und die römische Liturgie," *Studi Gregoriani* 13 (1989): 179–88; H. E. J. Cowdrey, "Pope Gregory VII (1073–85) and the Liturgy," *The Journal of Theological Studies*, n.s. 55 (2004): 55–83.

11. Mario Fornassari, ed., *Collectio canonum in V libris (Lib. I–III)*, CCCM 6 (Turnhout: Brepols, 1970); Roger E. Reynolds, "The South-Italian Canon Law *Collection in Five Books* and Its Derivatives: New Evidence on Its Origins, Diffusion, and Use," *Mediaeval Studies* 52 (1990): 278–95, reprinted in his *Law and Liturgy in the Latin Church, 5th–12th Centuries*, Variorum Collected Studies Series CS457 (Aldershot: Variorum, 1994), no. XIV. For a guide to the literature, see Kéry, *Canonical Collections of the Early Middle Ages*, 157–60; Fowler-Magerl, *Clavis*, 82–85.

the liturgy also occupied a significant part of more widely diffused works. Burchard, for instance, devotes book 3 of his *Decretum* to the canon law of churches, book 4 to baptism and confirmation, book 5 to the eucharist, and book 13 to fasting and the church calendar.[12] And texts on the liturgy also features prominently in Gratian's main formal sources.[13] Anselm of Lucca devotes book 5 of his canonical collection to the "ordinations of the church and their law and status" and book 9 to the sacraments.[14] The first five titles of Collection B of the *Tripartita*, that is, *Tripartita* 3, deal with baptism, the sacraments, ecclesiastical goods, the observation of days, and fasting.[15] Book 1 of the *Panormia* includes numerous canons on baptism, confirmation, the eucharist, and the mass, while book 2 contains canons on the constitution of the church, the offerings of the faithful, church consecration, priests and their churches, tithes, asylum, sacrilege, the alienation and return of ecclesiastical goods, and fasting.[16] Book 3 of the *Polycarpus* contains titles on churches and basilicas, the foundation of churches and monasteries, the consecration of churches, the reconsecration of churches, images and pictures in churches, the cult of the saints, the eucharist, baptism and confirmation, ecclesiastical customs, celebration of Easter, the order of celebrating mass, ecclesiastical rites, and fasting.[17] And the 3L has titles on the necessity of

12. See Burchard, *Decretum* 3.tit., 4.tit., 5.tit., and 13.tit., ed. Gerard Fransen and Theo Kölzer, *Decretorum libri XX* (Cologne, 1548; reprinted in Aalen: Scientia Verlag, 1992), 57r, 83r, 94r, and 158r.

13. On Gratian's main formal sources, see pp. 20–24.

14. See Anselm's collection 5.tit. and 9.tit. ed. Friedrich Thaner, *Anselmi episcopi Lucensis collectio canonum: Una cum collectione minore* (Innsbruck: Wagner, 1906–15; reprinted in Aalen: Scientia Verlag, 1960), 231 and 459.

15. *Tripartita* 3.1–5.

16. *Panormia* 1 and 2.

17. *Polycarpus* 3.1.tit.: "Quid sit ecclesia quidve basilica"; 3.2.tit.: "De institutione ecclesiarum et monasteriorum"; 3.4.tit.: "De consecratione ecclesiarum"; 3.5.tit.: "De ecclesiis reconsecrandis"; 3.6.tit.: "De restauratione ecclesiarum"; 3.7.tit.: "De imaginibus et picturis ecclesiarum"; 3.8.tit.: "An loca vel honores sanctorum retinentibus aliquid addant"; 3.9.tit.: "De corpore Domini sacrorumque custodia"; 3.10.tit.: "De baptismo et impositione manus"; 3.16.tit.: "De observatione ecclesiasticorum"; 3.17.tit.: "De celebratione sancti pasche"; 3.18.tit.: "De constitutione et ordinatione offitii celebrandi in ecclesia"; 3.24.tit.: "De ritibus ecclesiasticis"; 3.25.tit.: "De observatione XLme atque ieiunii"; 3.26.tit.: "De ieiunii et abstinentie discretione."

papal approval for the consecration of new churches, the celebration of mass, baptism and confirmation, fasting, images, the eucharist, and feast days.[18]

Given the abundance of material relating to the liturgy, particularly liturgical law, in each of Gratian's main formal sources—Anselm's collection, the *Tripartita*, the *Panormia*, the *Polycarpus*, and the 3L—the almost complete absence of such material in the first recension cannot have been due to Gratian's ignorance of the relevant provisions, but rather must have been deliberate. For reasons that will be explored below, Gratian chose to leave the liturgy out of the *Decretum*. The presence of the canon law of the liturgy in the *Decretum*'s vulgate form stems not from Gratian, but rather from the redactor of the second recension.

Canon Law of the Liturgy in the Two Recensions

A comparison of the two recensions brings out Gratian's stark indifference toward the canon law of the liturgy. Gratian and the redactor of the second recension had access to all the same major formal sources, but Gratian passed over most texts relating to the liturgy, whereas the redactor of the second recension went out of his way to add them to Gratian's work.

Liturgical Vestments

Liturgical vestments provide one notable example of the contrasting stances of the first and second recensions to the liturgy.[19] The first recension devotes several dicta and one canon to the question of how clerics are supposed to dress in going about their everyday

18. 3L 1.15.tit., ed. Joseph Motta, *Collectio canonum trium librorum*, 2 vols., MIC.B 8/I-II (Vatican City: BAV, 2005–8), 1:68: "De nouis ecclesiis auctoritate apostolica consecrandis"; 2.10.tit., ed. Motta, 1:204: "Vt episcopus sacrificans testes habeat et de missarum celebratione"; 3.7.tit., ed. Motta, 2:46: "De baptismo et manus impositione"; 3.8.tit., ed. Motta, 2:73: "De ieiunio"; App. 5.tit., ed. Motta, 2:278: "De cruce et imagine"; App. 23.tit., ed. Motta, 2:308: "De obseruantia sacrificii"; App. 33.tit., ed. Motta, 2:327: "De obseruatione diei festi."

19. On liturgical vestments, see Pierre Salmon, *Étude sur les insignes du pontife dans le rit romain: Histoire et liturgie* (Rome: Officium Libri Catholici, 1955); Janet Mayo, *A History of Ecclesiastical Dress* (New York: Holmes and Meier, 1984).

activities. D.41 teaches that clerics should not wear bright or dirty clothes, while C.21 q.4 stresses that clerics may not wear bright garments.[20] The entire first recension, however, includes only a single canon concerning vestments worn during the celebration of the liturgy: D.100 c.1, a conciliar canon that Gratian misattributes to Pope Pelagius, which stipulates that archbishops, primates, and patriarchs obtain the pallium within three months of their consecration.[21] Gratian's reason for introducing this canon into the first recension, moreover, has nothing to do with a concern for the proper use of liturgical garments. As the preceding dictum makes clear, Gratian quotes this text to show that patriarchs, primates, and archbishops are not permitted to ordain bishops prior to receiving the pallium.[22] While the cited canon does not explicitly state that reception of the pallium is a prerequisite for the performance of episcopal ordination, it implies that this is the case when it states that the failure of metropolitans to petition for receipt of the pallium has resulted in bishoprics being left destitute.[23]

20. D.41 d.a.c.1, quoted in chapter 2, p. 64. C.21 q.4 d.a.c.1 (ed. Friedberg, 857, supported by Aa Fd): "Quod uero fulgidis uel (et *Friedb.*) claris uestibus eis ornari non liceat, in septima Sinodo iubetur, in qua sic statutum est." C.21 q.4 c.1 rubr. (ed. Friedberg, 857): "Corripiantur clerici, qui in unguentis et claris uestibus et fulgidis lasciuiunt." C.21 q.4 c.1 rubr. (Aa Fd): "Fulgidis et claris uestibus clericus ornari non debet." The material source of C.21 q.4 c.1 is the Second Council of Nicaea, c.16, ed. Giuseppe Alberigo et al., *Conciliorum oecumenicorum generaliumque decreta: Editio critica* 1: *The Oecumenical Councils from Nicaea I to Nicaea II (325–787)*, Corpus Christianorum (Turnhout: Brepols, 2006), 336–37. For an English translation of the Nicene canon, see *Decrees*, ed. Tanner, 1:150–51.

21. D.100 c.1 rubr. (ed. Friedberg, 352, supported by Aa): "Infra tres menses fidem suam exponere et pallium postulare a Romana ecclesia quisque metropolitanus studeat." The material source is Council of Rome (875), c.2, ed. Friedrich Maasen, "Eine römische Synode aus der Zeit von 871 bis 878," *Sitzungsberichte der kaiserlichen Akademie der Wissenschaften, Philosophisch-historische Classe* 91 (1878): 773–92, at 781–82.

22. D.100 d.a.c.1 (ed. Friedberg, 351–52, supported by Aa Bc Fd²): "Episcopos autem ordinare ante pallium acceptum nec archiepiscopo, nec primati, nec patriarche licet, quod ex auctoritate Pelagii Pape (licet minus euidenter) datur intelligi."

23. D.100 c.1 (ed. Friedberg, 352, supported by Aa Bc Fd²): "Quoniam quidam metropolitanorum fidem suam secundum priscam consuetudinem sancte sedi apostolice exponere detrectantes usum pallii neque expetunt, neque percipiunt, ac per hoc episcoporum consecratio uiduatis ecclesiis non sine periculo protelatur, placuit, ut quisquis metropolitanus ultra tres menses consecrationis sue ad

In contrast to Gratian, the redactor of the second recension devotes considerable attention to not only the pallium, but also other liturgical vestments. The most extensive additions on liturgical vestments, D.100 cc.2–11 (minus the *paleae* c.3 and c.7), provide further details on the requirements for receiving the pallium, its use, and its benefits.[24] The pallium, these additions make clear, is only given to one whose merits make him worthy of its reception.[25] The one receiving the pallium must make a profession of faith prior to its reception.[26] He can only wear the pallium in church during the celebration of mass.[27] And with the reception of the pallium the ecclesiastic in question should both receive confirmation of his church's old privileges and obtain the use of new ones.[28]

---

fidem suam exponendam palliumque suscipiendum ad apostolicam sedem non miserit, commissa sibi careat dignitate, sitque licentia metropolitanis aliis, post secundam et tertiam commonitionem uiduatis ecclesiis cum consilio Romani Pontificis ordinando episcopum (episcopo *Fd*[2]) subuenire."

24. On the pallium, see José Martí Bonet, *Roma y las iglesias particulares en la concesión del palio a los obispos y arzobispos de Occidente: Año 513–1143* (Barcelona: Facultad de Teología de Barcelona, Editorial Herder, 1976); Steven A. Schoenig, "The Papacy and the Use and Understanding of the Pallium from the Carolingians to the Early Twelfth Century" (PhD diss., Columbia University, 2009).

25. JE 1491 = D.100 c.2 rubr. (ed. Friedberg, 352): "Honor pallii non detur nisi meritis exigentibus et fortiter postulanti." D.100 d.p.c.3 (ed. Friedberg, 353): "Causarum uero merita accipienda sunt, ut et is, qui postulat, mereatur accipere et fidei sue professionem prius iuramento confirmet et apostolicis decretis atque sinodalibus statutis se obediturum nichilminus caueat."

26. JE 2989 = D.100 c.4 rubr. (ed. Friedberg, 353): "Nisi post consuetam fidei professionem pallium dari non debet." JE 1748 = D.100 c.5: "Qui pallium desiderat accipere, prius illicita a se amouere promittat."

27. JE 1374 = D.100 c.6 (ed. Friedberg, 353): "Nonnisi ad missarum solempnia archiepiscopo uti pallio licet [rubr.]. Pallium tibi transmisimus, quo fraternitas tua intra ecclesiam ad sola missarum solempnia utatur." JE 1259 = D.100 c.8 (ed. Friedberg, 354): "Illud, frater karrissime, tibi non putamus ignotum, quod prope de nullo metropolitano in quibuslibet mundi partibus sit auditum, extra missarum tempus usum sibi pallii uendicasse."

28. D.100 d.p.c.8 (ed. Friedberg, 354): "Priuilegia quoque semper cum usu pallii debent concedi." JE 1751 = D.100 c.9 (ed. Friedberg, 354): "Rationis ordo omnino nos admonet ut cum usu pallii aliqua largiri priuilegia debeamus." JE 1161 = D.100 c.10 rubr. (ed. Friedberg, 355): "Vsus pallii conceditur et antiqua priuilegia innouantur." JE 1387 = D.100 c.11 (ed. Friedberg, 355): "cui pallium nos direxisse cognoscite atque cuncta priuilegia concessisse, que predecessores nostri eius predecessoribus contulerunt."

Other texts added in the second recension stress the necessity of obtaining papal permission before certain liturgical vestments may be worn. D.23 d.p.c.9–c.10, for instance, require bishops and deacons to obtain papal approval before they wear the dalmatic, while D.93 d.p.c.20–c.22 demand papal approval before deacons wear sandals and before any cleric wears the maniple.[29] But the majority of second-recension additions on liturgical vestments deal not with papal permission for their use but rather with when and how they should be worn. A dictum added to D.23 states that priests should wear a stole when they celebrate mass, a claim the second recension backs up with a canon from the Third Council of Braga (675).[30] The canon stipulates under pain of excommunication that priests wear a stole when they celebrate mass or receive the eucharist. Just as they wear a stole on both shoulders when they are ordained, so too must they do so for the celebration or reception of the eucharist.[31] The stole receives even further attention somewhat later on in D.25. Priests, the second recension states, should wear a stole over both shoulders, deacons over only their left.[32] A canon from the Fourth Council of Toledo (633) provides the symbolic and theological justi-

29. D.23 d.p.c.9 (ed. Friedberg, 82): "Dalmaticis autem nec episcopis, nec diaconibus absque apostolica licentia uti permittitur." D.93 d.p.c.20 (ed. Friedberg, 325): "Compagis uero calciari absque apostolici licentia diaconibus non permittitur, sicut nec mapulis uti absque eiusdem auctoritate quibuslibet clericis conceditur."

30. D.23 d.p.c.8 (ed. Friedberg, 82): "Sicut autem in die ordinationis sue sacerdos orario utroque humero ambitur, ita tempore consecrationis eodem orario instanter uti debet." Third Council of Braga, c.3, ed. Vives, *Concilios Visigóticos e Hispano-Romanos*, 374–75.

31. D.23 c.9 (ed. Friedberg, 82): "Ecclesiastica institutione prefixum nouimus ut omnis sacerdos, cum ordinatur, orario utroque humero ambiatur.... Qua ergo ratione tempore sacrificii non assumit, quod se in sacramento accepisse non dubitat? Proinde modis omnibus conuenit, ut, quod quisque percepit in consecratione honoris, hoc retineat et in oblatione uel perceptione sue salutis; scilicet, ut cum sacerdos ad solempnia missarum accedit, aut per se Deo sacrificium oblaturus, aut sacramentum corporis et sanguinis Domini nostri Iesu Christi sumpturus, non aliter quam orario utroque humero circumseptus, sicut et tempore ordinationis sue dignoscitur consecratus, ita ut de uno eodemque orario ceruicem pariter et utrumque humerum premens signum in suo pectore preparet crucis."

32. D.25 d.p.c.2 (ed. Friedberg, 92): "Sacerdos quoque utrumque humerum orario ambit; diaconus uero sinistrum tantum, ut ad ministerium expeditus discurrat."

fication for this regulation.[33] Deacons need to wear a stole over their left shoulder in honor of the fact that they pray or preach, but they need to keep their right shoulder free so that they will be unencumbered when assisting the priest in his duties.[34] Other canons added to D.23 forbid doorkeepers, lectors, and psalmists/cantors from wearing stoles.[35]

The alb is the subject of a canon added to D.93. In the first recension, D.93 c.19 consists solely of canons 39 and 40 from the so-called Fourth Council of Carthage, which command deacons to sit wherever the priest may command them to sit and to respond when questioned by a priest.[36] The second recension expands D.93 c.19 by appending one sentence corresponding to canon 41 from this same pseudo-council. This extra sentence/canon from the Fourth Council of Carthage commands deacons to wear the alb only during the oblation and readings.[37]

Consecrated Vessels

Another aspect of the liturgy largely neglected in the first recension but given great attention in the second recension is the law regulating the use and handling of consecrated vessels. In the first

33. Fourth Council of Toledo, c.40, ed. Vives, 206, is the material source for D.25 c.3 (ed. Friedberg, 92).

34. D.25 c.3 (ed. Friedberg, 92): "Vnum orarium oportet, Leuitam gestare in sinistro humero, propter quod orat, id est predicat; dexteram autem partem oportet habere liberam, ut expeditus ad ministerium sacerdotale discurrat."

35. D.23 c.27 (ed. Friedberg, 86): "Ministrum non oportet orariis uti, nec ostia derelinquere." D.23 c.28 (ed. Friedberg, 87): "Non oportet lectores atque psalmistas orariis uti, et sic legere aut psallere." The material source for these two canons is Council of Laodicea, cc.22–23, ed. Turner, *Ecclesiae Occidentalis Monumenta iuris antiquissima* 2.3 (Oxford: Clarendon Press, 1939), 361–63.

36. On the fictitious Fourth Council of Carthage, see chapter 7, p. 239. Fourth Council of Carthage, cc.39–40, ed. Charles Munier, *Concilia Africae a. 345–a. 525*, CCSL 149 (Turnhout: Brepols, 1974), 348 = *Statuta ecclesiae antiqua*, cc.59 and 61, ed. Munier, *Les Statuta ecclesiae antiqua*, 90. D.93 c.19 (first recension) (ed. Friedberg, 325, supported by Aa Bc Fd P): "Diaconus sedeat iubente presbitero quolibet loco. Item diaconus in conuentu presbiterorum interrogatus loquatur."

37. D.93 c.19 (added in second recension) (ed. Friedberg, 325): "Alba uero tantum tempore oblationis et lectionis utatur." The material source for this addition is Fourth Council of Carthage, c.41, ed. Munier, 348 = *Statuta ecclesiae antiqua*, c.60, ed. Munier, 90.

recension, Gratian touches upon this subject in his discussion of simony and the alienation of church property. C.1 q.3 d.p.c.11–c.12 declare that consecrated objects may not be bought or sold.[38] They belong to a series of texts forbidding the sale of ecclesiastical property, most of which focus on land, benefices, and tithes. C.12 q.2, on the other hand, investigates whether those who have been given church property thereby acquire legal ownership of it.[39] In the first recension, the question focuses on incomes, oblations, tithes, and landed possessions, but also includes two canons that explicitly mention consecrated objects.[40]

The second recension greatly expands the number of texts dealing with the alienation of consecrated objects.[41] Consecrated objects, additions to C.12 q.2 make clear, belong to God and should thus be returned to him if usurped by private individuals, but may be alienated if the purpose is to redeem captives.[42] Additions to C.14 q.6, on the other hand, address the issue of the return of consecrated objects. In the first recension, this question consists of but a single dictum and canon that focus on whether usurers are able to perform legitimate penance without restoring their ill-gotten gains. The second recension adds a dictum and an excerpt from a letter of Gregory to ad-

38. C.1 q.3 d.p.c.11–c.12 (ed. Friedberg, 417, supported by Aa Bc Fd P): "Item ex epistola Vrbani pape [inscr.]. Que ex consecratione proueniunt in suum ius ui uel munere nemo conuertat [rubr.]. Res ecclesie que (uel *add. Friedb.*) ex consecratione proueniunt, in suum ius uel ui uel aliquo munere aliquem conuertere non debere docens sanctus Vrbanus ait: Quisquis res ecclesiasticas que Dei dona sunt, quoniam a Deo fidelibus et a fidelibus Deo donantur, queque ab eodem gratis accipiuntur et ideo gratis dari debent propter sua lucra uendit uel emit, cum eodem Simone donum Dei pecunia possideri existimat." Friedberg's layout is misleading. C.1 q.3 d.p.c.11–c.12 is really a single canon taken from 3L 2.9.24, ed. Motta, 1:198, that reproduces Placidus of Nonantula, *Liber de honore ecclesiae* 52, ed. Lotkar von Heinemann and Ernst Sackur, MGH LdL 2 (Hanover: MGH, 1892), 566–639, at 589. The papal letter quoted therein is JL 5743 by Pope Urban II.

39. C.12 q.2 d.a.c.1 (ed. Friedberg, 687, supported by Aa Bc Fd P): "Nunc queritur, si sacerdotes aliqua de rebus ecclesie dedisse noscuntur, an his, qui eas acceperunt, aliqua firmitate constabunt?"

40. C.12 q.2 c.13 (ed. Friedberg, 690) and c.70 (ed. Friedberg, 710).

41. C.12 q.2 cc.2, 3, 10, 14, and d.p.c.16–c.17 (ed. Friedberg, 687–92).

42. C.12 q.2 cc.2, 3, 10 (ed. Friedberg, 687–89). JK 1481 = C.12 q.2 c.14 rubr. (ed. Friedberg, 691): "Pro redemptione captiuorum uasa sacra non prohibentur alienari."

dress the issue of returning ill-gotten objects that have subsequently been consecrated. In such an instance, the redactor of the second recension teaches, the object itself should not be returned. Instead, its equivalent in value should be restored.[43]

The most extensive additions on consecrated objects in the second recension, however, deal not with their alienation or return but rather with their handling and use. In the first recension, D.23 considers, in descending order, ordination into the grades of the ecclesiastical hierarchy. After c.20 on the psalmist, the distinction moves directly to c.24 on the consecration of virgins and then to c.33 on the benediction given to married people. In the second recension, however, the redactor inserts a series of canons on sacred vessels and vestments as well as on some miscellaneous liturgical matters between c.24 and c.33. Pseudo-Isidore furnishes one regulation prohibiting consecrated virgins and nuns from touching altar cloths and consecrated vessels or from censing altars, while patristic and early medieval councils are the sources for the other prohibitions: c.26 prohibiting subdeacons from entering the sacristy and touching sacred vessels; cc.27–28 forbidding doorkeepers, lectors, and psalmists from wearing stoles; c.29 forbidding women from teaching men and laymen from teaching in the presence of clerics unless called upon to do so; c.30 forbidding unconsecrated ministers from entering the sacristy and touching consecrated vessels; c.31 forbidding lectors and others from carrying sacred vessels unless they have been ordained subdeacon by a bishop; and c.32 forbidding all from touching sacred vessels in the sacristy except subdeacons and acolytes.[44]

43. C.14 q.6 d.p.c.1 (ed. Friedberg, 743): "Si uero rem alienam quis consecrauerit, non eandem, sed estimationem eius restituere debet."

44. D.23 d.p.c.24 (ed. Friedberg, 85–86): "Vasa sacrata et uestimenta altaris mulieres Deo dedicate contingere et incensum circa altaria deferre prohibentur." D.23 c.25 (ed. Friedberg, 86): "Sacratas Deo feminas uel monachas sacra uasa uel sacratas pallas penes uos contingere, et incensum circa altaria deferre, perlatum est ad apostolicam sedem: que omnia uituperatione et reprehensione plena esse, nulli recte sapientium dubium est. Quapropter huius sancte sedis auctoritate hec omnia uobis resecare funditus, quanto citius poteritis, censemus. Et ne pestis hec latius diuulgetur, per omnes prouincias abstergi citissime mandamus." The material source is JK †61 = Pseudo-Soter, *Epistolae* 2.3, ed. Hinschius, 124. D.23 c.26 (ed. Friedberg, 86): "Non oportet subdiaconos licentiam habere in sec-

Consecration, Use, and Immunity of Churches

In the first recension, Gratian deals extensively with property rights over ecclesiastical buildings, but is largely silent about their cultic aspects, mentioning these in only three places. First, Gratian includes one canon forbidding bishops from demanding payment for church consecration in his discussion of simony in C.1 q.1.[45] The reference to church consecration occurs in passing, and though Gratian mentions it in the rubric to the canon, he does not draw attention to it in any of his dicta.[46]

The second reference to church consecration in the first recension occurs in C.1 q.2, which deals with the problem of simoniacal entry into the religious life.[47] C.1 q.2 c.1, taken from the Second Coun-

---

retarium siue sacrarium (quod Greci diaconium appellant) ingredi, et contingere uasa dominica." The material source is Council of Laodicea, c.21, ed. Turner, 361. D.23 cc.27 and 28 are quoted above, p. 257n35. D.23 c.29 (ed. Friedberg, 86): "Mulier, quamuis docta et sancta, uiros in conuentu docere non presumat. Laicus autem presentibus clericis (nisi ipsis rogantibus) docere non audeat." The material source is really Fourth Council of Carthage, c.99, ed. Munier, 352 = *Statuta ecclesiae antiqua*, c.37, ed. Munier, 86. D.23 c.30 (ed. Friedberg, 86): "Non oportet insacratos ministros licentiam habere in secretarium (quod Greci diaconium appellant) ingredi, et contingere uasa dominica." The material source is Council of Agde (506), c.66, ed. Charles Munier, *Concilia Galliae a. 314–a. 506*, CCSL 148 (Turnhout: Brepols, 1963), 228. D.23 c.31 (ed. Friedberg, 87): "Non liceat cuilibet ex lectoribus sacra altaris uasa portare, nec aliis, nisi his, qui ab episcopo subdiaconi fuerint ordinati." The material source is First Council of Braga, c.10, ed. Vives, 73. D.23 c.32 (ed. Friedberg, 87): "Non liceat quemlibet ministeria tangere, nisi subdiacono aut acolito, in secretario uasa dominica." The material source is Martin of Braga, *Capitula*, c.41, ed. C. W. Barlow, *Martini episcopi Bracarensis opera omnia* (New Haven, Conn.: Yale University Press, 1950), 135.

45. C.1 q.1 c.106 (ed. Friedberg, 400, supported by Aa Bc Fd P): "Statuimus, ut sicut pro dedicandis basilicis et dandis ordinibus nichil accipiendum est, ita etiam pro balsamo siue pro luminaribus emendis nichil presbiteri crisma accepturi dent. Episcopi itaque de facultatibus ecclesie balsamum emant, et luminaria singuli in ecclesiis suis." The material source is Council of Châlons, c.16, ed. Albert Werminghoff, *Concilia aevi Karolini*, MGH Conc. 2.1 (Hanover: MGH, 1906), 277.

46. C.1 q.1 c.106 rubr. (ed. Friedberg, 400, supported by Aa Bc Fd P): "Nec (Non debet *Aa*) pro dedicandis basilicis uel (nec *Friedb.*) pro ceteris sacramentis conferendis aliquid exigi debet (*om. Aa*)."

47. On this topic, see Joseph H. Lynch, *Simoniacal Entry into Religious Life from 1000 to 1260: A Social, Economic, and Legal Study* (Columbus: Ohio State University Press, 1976).

cil of Braga (572), forbids bishops from demanding payment when they consecrate a church, but permits them to accept voluntary offerings.[48] The canon has no immediate relationship to the question examined in the *causa*, and Gratian does not refer to it explicitly in the dicta. But the canon does agree with the solution proposed by Gratian at the beginning of the question. Demanding payment for entry to the religious life, Gratian notes, is a form of simony, so religious houses may not make payment of a set fee a condition for entry. It is not simoniacal, however, for those who wish to enter a religious house to offer gifts of their own volition. Such freely given gifts are perfectly fitting and acceptable.[49]

The third reference to church consecration in the first recension occurs in C.16 q.2. The first of the so-called *causae monachorum*, *Causa* 16 considers a series of questions on the relationship between monasteries and the diocesan bishop. Can monks take on pastoral functions like the celebration of mass for the laity, the administration of penance, and baptism? If they can and a bishop permits monks to possess a chapel, do the monks also possess the right to appoint the chapel's pastor, or does this right remain reserved to the bishop? Can rights to a church be acquired by prescription? If a church can acquire another church by prescription, does the same hold true of monasteries? In other words, can a monastery acquire a church by prescription? Can the owner of land on which a chapel is built claim the chapel as his own property? Can an archpriest or bishop claim by his own authority rather than a judicial sentence a chapel that he believes belongs

48. C.1 q.2 c.1 (ed. Friedberg, 407–8, supported by Aa Bc Fd P): "Placuit ut quotiens ab aliquo fidelium ad consecrandas ecclesias episcopi inuitantur, non quasi ex debito munus aliquod a fundatore requirant; sed si ipse quidem aliquid ex suo uoto obtulerit, non respuatur, si uero aut paupertas illum aut necessitas retinet, nichil exigatur ab illo." The material source is Second Council of Braga, c.5, ed. Vives, 83.

49. C.1 q.2 d.a.c.1 (ed. Friedberg, 407, supported by Aa Bc Fd P): "Sequitur secunda questio qua queritur an pro ingressu monasterii pecunia sit exigenda uel exacta persoluenda? Hoc utrumque licite (licitum *Bc P*) fieri, utriusque testamenti serie comprobatur.... Hinc liquido apparet quod ingressuri monasterium sua debent offerre rectoribus, nec aliter sunt recipiendi, nisi sua obtulerint. Sed aliud est sua sponte offerre, aliud exacta persoluere.... Non ergo his auctoritatibus permittitur rectoribus ab ingressuris aliquid exigere, sed sponte oblata suscipere, quia illud dampnabile est, hoc uero minime."

to his church, or by doing so does he lose the right to repossession? Can an abbot with the consent of the bishop and clergy hold a chapel donated to his monastery by laymen?[50] In the midst of answering these questions, Gratian touches upon church consecration.[51] He cites two canons at the end of C.16 q.2 that seem to suggest that newly constructed churches belong to the bishop in whose diocese they are constructed rather than to the person responsible for financing the construction. C.16 q.2 c.8, a canon from the First Council of Orange (441), declares that a bishop who constructs a church in another bishop's diocese is not allowed to consecrate it. That right, rather, belongs to the bishop in whose diocese the church has been built.[52] C.16

50. C.16 pr. (ed. Friedberg, 761, supported by Aa Fd): "Quidam abbas habebat parrochitanam ecclesiam; instituit ibi monachum, ut officium populo celebraret; possedit eam per quadraginta (lx. *Aa Fd*) annos sine aliqua interpellatione; tandem querela aduersus abbatem mouetur a clericis baptismalis ecclesie, in cuius diocesi parrochitana ecclesia illa consistebat. Hic primum queritur, utrum monachis liceat officia populis celebrare, penitentiam dare et baptizare? Secundo, si contigerit eos capellam (capellas *Friedb.*) habere episcopali beneficio, an ab eis sint instituende, an ab episcopis? Tertio, an iura ecclesiarum prescriptione tollantur? Quarto, si ecclesia aduersus ecclesiam prescribat, an etiam monasterium aduersus ecclesiam prescribere possit? Quinto, si capellam in suo territorio edificatam iure territorii sibi uendicare ualeat? Sexto, si archipresbiter uel episcopus sua auctoritate, non iudiciaria sententia capellam illam inrepserit, an cadat a causa, ut ecclesia, cui presidet, non ultra habeat ius reposcendi quod suus pastor illicite usurpauit? Septimo queritur, si laici capellam (illam *add. Fd² Friedb.*) tenebant (ut quibusdam moris est) et in manibus abbatis eam refutauerint (refutauerunt *Aa Fd*), et ordinandam tradiderint (tradiderunt *Aa Fd*), an consensu episcopi et clericorum abbas possit eam tenere?"

51. C.16 q.2 d.p.c.7 = C.16 q.5 d.a.c.1 (ed. Friedberg, 787, supported by Aa Fd): "Tales etsi ius territorii habeant, tamen (*om. Aa*) potestatem gubernandi populum et spiritualia ministrandi non habent. Quod etiam de episcopo intelligendum est." This dictum raises an objection to church consecration based on the distinction between a right to a territory and the power to govern the people and administer spiritualia there. On the peculiar numbering of this section of the *Decretum*, see the note of the Correctores Romani reproduced by Friedberg (ibid.).

52. C.16 q.2 c.8 = C.16 q.5 c.1 (ed. Friedberg, 787, supported by Aa Fd): "Episcopus qui in alterius diocesi ecclesiam edificat, eius consecrationem sibi uendicare non audeat [rubr.]. Si quis episcoporum in aliene ciuitatis territorio pro quacumque suorum oportunitate ecclesiam edificare disponit, non presumat dedicationem, que illius est, in cuius territorio ecclesia assurgit (surgit *Fd*). Edificatori uero episcopo hec gratia reseruetur, ut quos desiderat clericos in re sua ordinari ipsos ordinet, in cuius territorium est." In the second recension, the canon continues for another three lines. The material source is Council of Orange, c.9, ed. Munier, 80–81.

q.2 c.9, on the other hand, a canon from the Fourth Council of Toledo (633), declares that possession of a church does not destroy *conventus*, what the decretists interpreted as the diocesan bishop's spiritual authority over the people who attend the church.[53] The closing dictum, however, ignores church consecration, focusing instead on the problem of possession. Both the builder and the bishop in whose territory a church is constructed have rights over the church. The builder owns the church, but the bishop has the right to appoint the pastor, though only with the consent of the builder.[54]

These brief and only passing mentions of church consecration in the first recension contrast with the considerably longer and more explicit consideration of both this and other aspects of the canon law of ecclesiastical buildings found in the second recension.[55] The additions C.1 q.1 d.p.c.124–c.125, for instance, condemn those who make payments to prevent a church from being consecrated, while the addition C.16 q.2 c.10 reiterates the prohibition, found in C.16 q.2 c.8, of a bishop consecrating a church that he has constructed in

53. C.16 q.2 c.9 = C.16 q.5 c.2 (ed. Friedberg, 788, supported by Aa Fd): "Basilice nouiter condite ad episcopum pertinent cuius conuentus esse constiterit [rubr.]. Possessio teritorii conuentum non adimit, ideoque noue basilice que condite fuerint, ad eum proculdubio pertinebunt episcopum, cuius conuentus esse constiterit." The material source is Fourth Council of Toledo, c.35, ed. Vives, 205. On the spiritual authority of the bishop see, e.g., Rufinus, *Summa decretorum* ad C.16 q.2 c.9 v. *non adimit conventum*, ed. Singer, 358: "i.e. populum ad ecclesiam illam convenientem, quasi: licet sua sit ecclesia quantum ad possessionem, non tamen suus est populus, qui ad ecclesiam convenit, immo episcopi Bononiensis, qui habet potestatem eum spiritualiter regendi, condemnandi et absolvendi."

54. C.16 q.2 d.p.c.10 = C.16 q.5 d.p.c.3 (ed. Friedberg, 788, supported by Aa Fd): "Quod de iure ordinandi, non possidendi intelligendum est. His auctoritatibus facile perpendi potest, quod siue abbates siue episcopi in suis castellis uel uillis ecclesias edificauerint, non omnino (*om. Friedb.*) ideo episcopo in cuius diocesi fuerint, conuentus adimitur, et ideo sacerdotes iuxta illud Vrbani et Nicolai in eis nonnisi per episcopos, cum consensu tamen et electione edificantium ordinari possunt."

55. For an overview of these subjects, see Didier Méhu, "*Historiae* et *imagines* de la consécration de l'église au moyen âge," in *Mises en scène et mémoires de la consécration de l'église dans l'occident médiéval*, ed. Didier Méhu, Collection d'Études Médiévales de Nice 7 (Turnhout: Brepols, 2007), 15–48; Peter Landau, "Traditionen des Kirchenasyls," in *Asyl am heiligen Ort*, ed. Klaus Barwig and Dieter R. Bauer (Ostfildern: Schwabenverlag, 1994), 47–61; Martin Siebold, *Das Asylrecht der römischen Kirche mit besonderer Berücksichtigung seiner Entwicklung auf germanischen Boden* (Münster: Helios-Verlag, 1930).

another bishop's diocese.[56] More significantly and interestingly, additions to D.68 address the reconsecration of churches. D.68 examines whether those who have been ordained by consecrators who are later shown not to have been bishops should be reordained. The issue was controversial because ordination to the same grade in the ecclesiastical hierarchy was supposed to be unrepeatable. In resolving this problem, the first recension argues that a person who has been ordained by someone who is later shown not to have been a bishop was in fact never truly ordained and hence receives consecration for the first time when the rite of ordination is repeated and, furthermore, that a person the validity of whose consecration is in doubt, yet who has in fact been validly ordained, is merely reanointed when the rite is performed again, not reordained. The solution, Gratian maintains, is the same as for a person whose baptism is in doubt. When such a person is baptized anew, he or she receives the grace of baptism only if he or she was not already validly baptized previously.[57]

The redactor of the second recension's contribution to this issue was to argue that the same practice is observed in the consecration of

56. C.1 q.1 d.p.c.124 (ed. Friedberg, 405): "Qui autem pecuniam accipiunt, ut ordinandis sacros ordines non tribuant, uel ut canonice electioni assensum non prebeant, aut ecclesias edificandis uel consecrandis lapidem benedictum uel consecrationem subtrahant, multis argumentis accepte pecunie rei et infames esse probantur." JE 6606 = C.1 q.1 c.125 (ed. Friedberg, 406): "Sacrilegi sunt iudicandi qui ecclesias non permittunt regulariter ordinari [rubr.]. Sunt quidam qui uel uiolentia uel fauore non permittunt ecclesias regulariter ordinari. Hos etiam decernimus ut sacrilegos iudicandos." JE 1884 = C.16 q.2 c.10 rubr. (ed. Friedberg, 788): "Edificatori episcopo in diocesi alterius ecclesiam consecrare non licet."

57. D.68 d.p.c.2 (ed. Friedberg, 254, supported by Aa Bc Fd P): "Quod ergo consecratus in eodem ordine iterum consecrari prohibetur, de eo intelligendum est, qui consecratus est ab illo, quem certum erat ius consecrandi habere. Qui autem ab illo consecratur, quem non constat ius consecrandi habuisse, iterum consecrandus est, quia si ille ius consecrandi non habuit (habuerit *Friedb.*), iste ex olei effusione nichil consecrationis accepit. Et quia in ipso ordine consecratus non erat, nunc quasi primum ad consecrationem ueniens ab episcopo sacerdotalem benedictionem et consecrationem consequitur. Si autem ius consecrandi habuit (habuerit *Friedb.*), in prima unctione consecutus est consecrationem; in secunda uero non reiteratur consecratio, sed sola unctio, sicut de quo dubium est, an sit baptizatus, an non, debet baptizari; qui (quod *Aa Fd*) si prius baptizatus non fuerat, consequitur gratiam baptismi, si autem baptizatus erat, nichil accipit in secunda unctione, nec pertinet hoc ad reiterationem baptismi, sed ad cautelam salutis."

churches, a claim he supports with a canon attributed to the Council of Nicaea.[58] The canon is not found in any known pre-Gratian canonical collection, being instead a twelfth-century forgery.[59] In all likelihood, the forger was not the redactor of the second recension. The redactor cites the pseudo-Nicene canon to justify the reconsecration of churches in special circumstances. But, at least according to Peter Landau, the person who forged the canon probably did so to combat the prevalent practice of reconsecrating churches consecrated by simoniacs. Since the days of Pseudo-Isidore and particularly during the Investiture Controversy, legislators and canonists had generally maintained that churches consecrated by heretics, of which simoniacs were considered a subgroup, had to be reconsecrated. They did not attribute efficacy independent of the minister's merits to church consecration, but rather made its working dependent on the subjective state of the consecrator. The author of the pseudo-Nicene canon on church reconsecration attempted to combat this view by likening church consecration to baptism. Just as there is a general prohibition on rebaptism, so too is there a general prohibition on the reconsecration of churches. A church is validly consecrated so long as the person who performs the consecration has faith in the Trinity. Any other personal failings of the consecrator are irrelevant, and a consecrated church stays validly consecrated so long as it is not desecrated by burning, the shedding of blood, or sexual pollution.

58. D.68 d.p.c.2, last sentence, which was added only in the second recension (ed. Friedberg, 254): "Hoc etiam de ecclesiis consecrandis similiter obseruandum est." D.68 c.3 (ed. Friedberg, 254): "Vnde in Niceno Concilio [inscr.]. Non debet iterum consecrari ecclesia semel consecrata [rubr.]. Ecclesiis Deo consecratis non debet iterum consecratio adhiberi, nisi aut ab igne exuste, aut sanguinis effusione, aut cuiuscumque semine pollute fuerint: quia sicut infans a qualicumque sacerdote in nomine Patris et Filii et Spiritus sancti semel baptizatus, non debet iterum baptizari, ita nec locus Deo dicatus iterum consecrandus est, nisi propter eas causas, quas superius nominauimus, si tamen fidem sancte Trinitatis tenuerunt, qui eum consecrauerunt." The canon is cited again at De cons. D.1 c.20.

59. Here and for the rest of the paragraph I summarize the analysis of Peter Landau, "Das Verbot der Wiederholung einer Kirchweihe in der Geschichte des kanonischen Rechts: Ein Beitrag zur Entwicklung des Sakramentenrechts," in *Studia in Honorem eminentissimi Cardinalis Alphonsi M. Stickler*, ed. R. J. Castillo Lara, Studia et textus historiae iuris canonici 7 (Rome: LAS, 1992), 225–40, at 225–34.

Other second-recension additions deal with the use and immunity of church buildings. In the first recension, D.42 simply affirms that bishops must show hospitality to others, particularly the poor and widows, for instance, by providing them with food.[60] A dictum and two canons added to D.42 in the second recension, however, qualify this prescription by explaining that, as a rule, such hospitality should not take place in church.[61] Eating and reclining in church are forbidden, except in cases of necessity, to help out travelers, and even then the ordinary populace should be prevented from attending such meals as much as possible.[62]

Additions to C.17 q.4, in contrast, deal with asylum. This question investigates whether the possessions of a monk who leaves the monastery without the abbot's position should be returned to him.[63] To shed light on this problem, the first recension includes a number of canons on the alienation of ecclesiastical property.[64] The second recension adds numerous canons on the right to asylum.[65] Whoever re-

60. D.42 d.a.c.1 (ed. Friedberg, 151, supported by Aa Bc Fd P): "Hospitalem uero sacerdotem esse oportet." D.42 c.1 (ed. Friedberg, 151, supported by Aa Bc Fd P): "Si quis despicit eos, qui fideliter agapas, id est conuiuia, pauperum exhibent et propter honorem Domini conuocant fratres, et noluerit communicare huiuscemodi uocationibus, paruipendens quod geritur, anathema sit." D.42 d.p.c.1 (ed. Friedberg, 151, supported by Aa Bc Fd P): "Hinc etiam Iohannes Euangelista in epistola sua quendam Diotrepem excommunicat, qui nec pauperes recipiebat, et recipientes de ecclesia eiciebat." The material source of D.42 c.1 is Council of Gangra, c.11, ed. Turner, *Ecclesiae Occidentalis Monumenta iuris antiquissima* 2.2 (Oxford: Clarendon Press, 1913), 197–98.

61. D.42 d.p.c.2 (ed. Friedberg, 152): "Sed licet ipsa conuiuia despicienda non sint, nec tamen in ecclesiis celebrari, nec clericos ad ea conuocatos partes sibi ex eis tollere oportet."

62. D.42 c.4 (ed. Friedberg, 152): "Non oportet in basilicis seu in ecclesiis agapen facere et intus manducare, uel accubitus sternere." The material source is Council of Laodicea, c.28, ed. Turner, 367. On attending such meals, see D.42 c.5 (ed. Friedberg, 152): "Nulli episcopi uel clerici in ecclesia conuiuentur, nisi forte transeuntes hospitiorum necessitate illic reficiantur. Populi etiam ab huiusmodi conuiuiis quantum fieri potest prohibeantur." The material source is *Breviarium Hipponense*, c.29, ed. Munier, 41.

63. C.17 q.4 d.a.c.1 (ed. Friedberg, 815, supported by Aa Fd): "Si autem sine licentia abbatis de monasterio discesserit, queritur utrum sua sint ei reddenda an non?"

64. C.17 q.4 cc.1, 4, 5, 39, and 40 (ed. Friedberg, 815–16 and 826).

65. C.17 q.4 cc.6–11, c.20, d.p.c.20, d.p.c.29, and d.p.c.31–c.36 (ed. Friedberg,

moves by force someone who has sought asylum in a church is guilty of sacrilege and if convicted of the crime can suffer capital punishment.[66] Even masters are not allowed to remove their slaves by force, until and unless they have sworn an oath not to harm them.[67]

Fasting and the Liturgical Calendar

In the first recension, Gratian briefly mentions two canons on fasting to illustrate the importance of reception for the validity of laws. Laws are instituted when they are promulgated, but they can be abrogated by contrary usage. Gratian provides two concrete examples: a Pseudo-Isidorian forgery attributed to Pope Telesphorus and a decretal of Gregory the Great. Both decretals command clerics to abstain from meat and other delicacies for the whole of Quinquagesima, that is, the seven weeks before Easter. Yet, Gratian notes, neither decretal possesses binding force any more. The general failure to fast from the start of Quinquagesima has abrogated these canons.[68]

The second recension deals with fasting in much greater detail. It inserts two canons by Pseudo-Telesphorus, whose decrees on fast-

816–18, 819–20, and 822–25). Another second-recension addition on asylum is D.87 c.6 (ed. Friedberg, 305).

66. C.17 q.4 d.p.c.29 (ed. Friedberg, 822): "Qui autem de ecclesia ui aliquem exemerit, uel in ipsa ecclesia, uel loco, uel cultui, sacerdotibus et ministris aliquid iniurie importauerit, ad instar publici criminis et lese maiestatis accusabitur et conuictus siue confessus capitali sententia a rectoribus prouincie ferietur."

67. C.17 q.4 d.p.c.31 (ed. Friedberg, 823): "Verum ne reuerentia religionis dominos suo iure fraudaret, si famuli ad ecclesie septa confugientes inde nequaquam abstrahantur, sacris canonibus est institutum, ut prestito a domino sacramento impunitatis, ei etiam reddatur inuitus."

68. D.4 d.p.c.3 (ed. Friedberg, 6): "Leges instituuntur, cum promulgantur, firmantur, cum moribus utentium approbantur. Sicut enim moribus utentium in contrarium nonnulle leges hodie abrogate sunt, ita moribus utentium ipse leges confirmantur. Vnde illud Thelesphori pape (quo decreuit, ut clerici generaliter a quinquagesima a carnibus et deliciis ieiunent) quia moribus utentium approbatum non est, aliter agentes transgressionis reos non arguit." D.4 d.p.c.6 (ed. Friedberg, 7, supported by Aa Bc P): "Hec etsi legibus constituta sunt, tamen quia communi usu approbata non sunt, se non obseruantes transgressionis (reos *add. Friedb.*) non arguunt; alioquin his non obedientes proprio priuarentur honore, cum illi, qui sacris nesciunt obedire canonibus, penitus officio iubeantur carere suscepto; nisi forte quis dicat, hec non decernendo esse statuta, sed exhortando conscripta. Decretum uero necessitatem facit, exhortatio autem liberam uoluntatem excitat."

ing the first recension mentions but does not quote, into D.4.[69] And it also adds D.76 d.a.c.1–c.11, a long series of texts that try to make sense of the contradictory regulations on the seasons of fasting. While the later canonical tradition agreed that there were four official seasons of fasting, councils, popes, and Church Fathers disagreed on how to reckon them. Some canons state that the four seasons of fasting occur in March, June, September, and December, whereas others describe them as corresponding to Lent, the period after Pentecost, the seventh month, and the tenth month.[70] Some canons, moreover, appear to forbid fasting during the period leading up to Pentecost, while other canons permit it.[71] The second recension gathers these contradictory canons, taken mainly from 3L 3.8, which also served as the formal source for De cons. D.5 cc.16–31, and resolves them by introducing two distinctions.[72] First, it argues,

69. D.4 cc.4–5 (ed. Friedberg, 6).

70. An example of the former type of canon is D.76 c.2 (ed. Friedberg, 267): "Constituimus, ut quatuor tempora anni ab omnibus hominibus cum ieiunio obseruentur, id est in Martio, in hebdomada prima; in Iunio, secunda; in septembri, tertia; in decembri, quarta." The material source is Council of Mainz (813), c.34, ed. Albert Werminghoff, *Concilia aevi Karolini*, MGH Conc. 2.1 (Hanover: MGH, 1906), 269. An example of the latter type of canon is D.76 c.6 (ed. Friedberg, 269): "Siquidem ieiunium uernum in quadragesima, estiuum in pentecosten, autumpnale in mense septimo, hiemale in hoc, qui est decimus, celebremus." The material source is Leo the Great, *Tractatus septem et nonaginta* 19.2, ed. Antoine Chavasse, CCSL 138 (Turnhout: Brepols, 1973), 77.26–36.

71. D.76 c.8 (ed. Friedberg, 270): "Scire debet sanctitas uestra: 'Per hos quinquaginta dies nobis est iugis et continuata festiuitas, ita ut hoc omni tempore neque ad obseruandum indicamus ieiunia, neque ad exorandum Deum genibus succedamus.'" The material source for lines 1–13 in Friedberg's edition is Maximus of Turin, *Sermones* 44.1–2, ed. Almut Mutzenbecher, *Sermonum collectio antiqua, nonnullis sermonibus extravagantibus adiectis*, CCSL 23 (Turnhout: Brepols, 1962), 178.1–6, 12–18, and 22–23. The material source for the remainder of the text is Ambrose, *De apologia prophetae David* 8.42, ed. Karl Schenkl, CSEL 32.2 (Vienna: F. Tempsky, 1887), 325.12–16. On the latter type of canon, see D.76 c.10 (ed. Friedberg, 271): "Post pasca usque ad pentecosten, licet traditio ecclesiarum abstinentie rigorem prandiis relaxauerit, tamen si quis monachorum uel clericorum ieiunare cupit, non sunt prohibendi, quia et Antonius et Paulus et ceteri Patres antiqui etiam in his diebus in heremo leguntur abstinuisse, neque soluisse abstinentiam, nisi tantum die dominico." The material source is Isidore of Seville, *De ecclesiasticis officiis* 1.43(42).2, ed. Christopher M. Lawson, CCSL 113 (Turnhout: Brepols, 1989), 48.10–15.

72. See Joseph Motta, "Tabula synoptica" to *Collectio canonum trium librorum*, 2

the canons sometimes calculate the months according to the Jewish method, sometimes according to the Latin one, but the Latin method is to be preferred.[73] Second, while it is not fitting for the church to command fasting during the fifty days between Easter and Pentecost, one can fast during this period on one's own if one chooses to. There is no absolute prohibition on fasting between Easter and Pentecost.[74]

All the other second-recension additions relating to the liturgical calendar deal with prohibited activities. Since the sixth century, councils, popes, and theologians had consistently promoted Sunday as a day of rest, later doing the same for feast days and times of fasting.[75] Gratian does not include any of these general prohibitions in the first recension, but he does devote attention to one aspect of this prohibition, explored in C.15 q.4, namely whether priests and bishops can hear litigation on Sundays.[76] The first recension cites just one canon on this topic, taken from the Council of Tarragona (516), which forbids ecclesiastics from hearing court cases then.[77] The second recension expands C.15 q.4 with two other canons. One, a forgery from the Pseudo-Isidorian *Capitula Angilrami*, simply reiterates the prohibition of ecclesiastics hearing court cases on Sunday.[78] The

vols., MIC.B 8/I-II (Vatican City: BAV, 2005–8), 2:455–56. Motta considers 3L to be the probable formal source for D.76 cc.1, 4, 5, 6, and 10. He considers an unknown common source the probable formal source for D.76 cc.2, 3, and 7.

73. D.76 d.p.c.6 (ed. Friedberg, 269): "Primum uero mensem, quartum, septimum, et decimum non Ebreorum ratione debemus accipere, sed nostra. Primus enim mensis apud illos est Aprilis, quartus Iulius, septimus October, decimus Ianuarius."

74. D.76 d.p.c.8 (ed. Friedberg, 270): "Necessario ergo ecclesia constituit ut post diem pentecostes ieiunia celebrentur. Sed quod in illis quinquagesima diebus ieiunandum esse negatur, ex obseruantie necessitate intelligitur." D.76 d.p.c.9 (ed. Friedberg, 271): "Obseruantia uero similis quod ad factum, non quod ad necessitatem."

75. For an overview, see Hubert Schiepek, *Der Sonntag und kirchlich gebotene Feiertage nach kirchlichem und weltlichem Recht,* Adnotationes in Ius Canonicum 27 (Frankfurt am Main: Peter Lang, 2003), 186–215.

76. C.15 q.4 d.a.c.1 (ed. Friedberg, 752–53): "Quod uero die dominico nec episcopo, nec presbitero causam uentilare aliquam liceat, in Terraconensi Concilio prohibetur, in quo sic statutum est."

77. C.15 q.4 c.1 rubr. (ed. Friedberg, 753): "Ministri ecclesie die dominico causas uentilare non debent." The material source is Council of Tarragona, c.4, ed. Vives, 35.

78. C.15 q.4 c.3 (ed. Friedberg, 753): "Nullus episcopus uel infra positus die

other, a canon from the Council of Erfurt (932), is broader. It prohibits all court cases, not just ecclesiastical ones, on not only Sundays, but also feast days and during the four seasons of fasting.[79]

Additions to C.22 q.5 and C.33 q.4 address related prohibitions. C.22 q.5 examines whether a person who forces another to commit perjury is himself guilty of perjury.[80] In the first recension, the question focuses largely on the stated topic. But the second recension adds a notable digression, forbidding the taking of oaths from Septuagesima through the octave of Easter, from Advent to the octave of Epiphany and during the four periods of fasting, major feast days, Sundays, and rogation days.[81] C.33 q.4, on the other hand, examines whether it is permissible to engage in conjugal relations during times of prayer.[82] Gratian's answer in the first recension is yes, unless both spouses agree to refrain from sexual relations.[83] The redactor of the second recension does not modify Gratian's argument, but he does

---

dominico causas iudicare presumat." The material source is *Capitula Angilramni*, c.7, ed. Schon, *Die Capitula Angilramni*, 156.

79. C.15 q.4 c.2 (ed. Friedberg, 753): "Placita secularia dominicis diebus uel aliis precipuis festis, seu etiam in his diebus in quibus legitima ieiunia celebrantur, secundum canonicam institutionem minime decreuimus fieri." The material source is Council of Erfurt (932), c.2, ed. Ernst-Dieter Hehl, *Die Konzilien Deutschlands und Reichsitaliens 916–1001* 1: *916–960*, MGH Conc. 6.1 (Hanover: MGH, 1987), 108.

80. C.22 q.5 d.a.c.1 (ed. Friedberg, 882–83): "Quod autem quinto loco queritur, si licitum esset quod archidiaconus iurauerat, an episcopus esset reus periurii, qui ad peierandum archidiaconum cogebat?"

81. C.22 q.5 d.p.c.16 (ed. Friedberg, 887): "Preterea sunt quedam tempora quibus iurare prohibemur." C.22 q.5 c.17 (ed. Friedberg, 887): "Decreuit sancta sinodus ut a septuagesima usque in octauam pasce et ab aduentu Domini usque in octauam epiphanie, nec non et in ieiuniis quatuor temporum et in letaniis maioribus et in diebus dominicis et in diebus rogationum (nisi de concordia et pacificatione) nullus super sacra euangelia iurare presumat."

82. C.33 pr. (ed. Werckmeister, 488): "Quarto, si tempore orationis quis ualeat reddere coniugii debitum?"

83. C.33 q.4 d.p.c.11 (ed. Werckmeister, 540): "Hec autem seruanda sunt si uxor consensum adhibere uoluerit; ceterum sine eius consensu nec causa orationis continentia seruari debet. Vnde Augustinus in libro de adulterinis coniugiis." C.33 q.4 c.12 (ed. Werckmeister, 540): "Nisi ex consensu communi orationi coniuges uacare non possunt [rubr.]. Apostolus nec ad tempus ut uacent orationi, nisi ex consensu uoluit coniuges inuicem carnali fraudari debito." The material source is Augustine, *De adulterinis coniugiis* 1.2, ed. Joseph Zycha, CSEL 41 (Vienna: F. Tempsky, 1900), 348.25–27.

interrupt it by introducing a series of texts prohibiting weddings during the seasons of fasting.[84] Since he never refutes these canons, the redactor of the second recension probably wanted to present them as having continued binding force.

Confirmation and the Celebration of the Eucharist

Desire to integrate the liturgy into Gratian's textbook is also evident in the second-recension additions on confirmation and the eucharist. As discussed in chapter 7, Gratian in the first recension considers these sacraments mainly and most extensively in connection with the crime of simony and the marital impediment of spiritual affinity. For this reason, the first recension deals at great length with the relationship between these sacraments and criminal or marital law, but treats their liturgical aspects only in passing or not at all. The second recension, in contrast, discusses these sacraments not only insofar as they relate to criminal and marital law, but also as they pertain to the church's liturgical and sacramental life.

The issue of when and how priests may use chrism provides one example of this new attention to the liturgical aspects of the sacraments. In the first recension, D.95 includes only one liturgical regulation. Citing Gregory the Great, Gratian states that, if no bishops are present, priests are permitted to anoint those who have been baptized with chrism, that is, priests may perform confirmation in the absence of bishops.[85] Gratian's reason for introducing this canon, he tells us, is to demonstrate that the preceding canons, which order priests to obey bishops, should not be understood as saying that priests are forbidden from performing the sacraments when bishops are present, but rather as affirming a filial relationship between the

84. C.33 q.4 d.p.c.7–c.11. C.33 q.4 d.p.c.7 (ed. Werckmeister, 538): "Hinc etiam in diebus abstinentie nuptie celebrari prohibentur."

85. JE 1298 = D.95 c.1 (ed. Friedberg, 331): "Vbi episcopi desunt, baptizatos in frontibus presbiteri crismate tangant [rubr.]. Peruenit quoque ad nos quosdam scandalizatos fuisse quod presbiteros crismate tangere eos qui baptizati sunt prohibuimus. Et nos quidem secundum ueterem usum nostre ecclesie fecimus. Sed si omnino hac de re aliqui contristantur, ubi episcopi desunt, ut presbiteri etiam in frontibus baptizatos crismate tangere debeant, concedimus." On the interpretation of this canon, see Gillmann, *Zur Lehre der Scholastik*.

two. Priests should obey bishops as sons obey their fathers.[86] Priests are inferior to bishops hierarchically, but not as regards sacramental power. For priests and bishops are the same; the difference between the two grades of the ecclesiastical hierarchy is merely the result of custom.[87] Priests, after all, are able to administer confirmation.[88] And they may teach when bishops are present.[89]

The redactor of the second recension was by no means uninterested in episcopal and presbyteral collegiality, since he appended a number of canons on the subject to the end of D.95.[90] But what seems to have interested him most about this section of the *Decretum* was the mention of chrism, since he inserted not only canons but also dicta on the subject.[91] These additions make two new points. First, bishops can use the same consecrated oil for anointing the sick that they use for confirmation.[92] In other words, chrism may be used in the sacra-

86. D.95 d.a.c.1 (ed. Friedberg, 331, supported by Aa Bc Fd P): "Quod autem sacerdotes supra iubentur episcopis tamquam subditi obedire, non ita intelligendum est, quasi non liceat eis baptizatos crismate tangere uel (baptizatos ... uel *om. Friedb.*) presentibus episcopis sacra misteria celebrare, sicut episcopali supercilio quidam ab his uolebant presbiteros prohibere, sed quia presbiteri pontificibus, tamquam filii parentibus, debent obedire. (Baptizatos etiam crismate eis tangere conceditur *add. Friedb.*)"

87. D.95 c.5 rubr. (ed. Friedberg, 332, supported by Aa Bc Fd P): "Presbiter idem est qui et episcopus ac sola consuetudine presbiteris episcopi presunt." The material source is Jerome, *Commentarius in epistulam Pauli Apostoli ad Titum*, ed. Federica Bucchi, CCSL 77C (Turnhout: Brepols, 2003), 14.244–51 and 15.283–86. On the development of this idea up to Gratian's day, see Roger E. Reynolds, "Patristic 'Presbyterianism' in the Early Medieval Theology of Sacred Orders," *Mediaeval Studies* 45 (1983): 311–42, reprinted in his *Clerics in the Early Middle Ages: Hierarchy and Image*, Variorum Collected Studies Series CS669 (Aldershot: Ashgate, 1999), no. V.

88. D.95 c.1, quoted in chapter 7, p. 271n85.

89. D.95 c.6 rubr. (ed. Friedberg, 333, supported by Aa Bc Fd P): "Coram episcopis presbiteris docere licet (liceat *Fd P*)." The material source is Pseudo-Jerome, *De septem ordinibus ecclesiae*, ed. Athanasius Walter Kalff (Wurzburg, 1938), 46.14–15, 47.8–48.2, 50.3–51.1, 51.6–15, 52.9–53.3, 55.2–6, and 56.3–57.3. On *De septem ordinibus ecclesiae*, see Roger E. Reynolds, "The Pseudo-Hieronymian 'De septem ordinibus ecclesiae': Notes on Its Origins, Abridgments, and Use in Early Medieval Canonical Collections," *Revue Bénédictine* 80 (1970): 238–52, reprinted in his *Clerical Orders in the Early Middle Ages: Duties and Ordination*, Variorum Collected Studies Series CS670 (Aldershot: Ashgate, 1999), no. I.

90. D.95 cc.8–11 (ed. Friedberg, 334–35). D.95 c.12 is a later *palea*.

91. D.95 d.p.c.1–c.4 (ed. Friedberg, 331–32).

92. D.95 d.p.c.2 §1 (ed. Friedberg, 332): "Sed queritur, an episcopis liceat eo-

ment of extreme unction. Second, priests should obtain chrism from their own bishops each year before Easter.[93]

Numerous other additions in the second recension deal with the mass. Additions to D.6, for instance, broach the previously unasked question whether those who have suffered nocturnal pollution should abstain from receiving the eucharist or, if they are priests, from saying mass.[94] The redactor of the second recension's answer, based on a letter of Gregory the Great, is that it depends. If the nocturnal pollution is simply the result of an abundance of bodily fluids or bodily infirmity, then there is no need to abstain from receiving communion or celebrating mass afterward. If the cause of the nocturnal pollution was overeating or having drunk too much the night before and there are others who can celebrate mass, then it would be better for the priest in question to refrain. But if the nocturnal pollution was due to lascivious thoughts that the person entertained prior to going to sleep, then he is guilty of a serious sin and, it is implied but not stated, should abstain from communion and the celebration of mass.[95]

---

dem oleo ungere infirmos? uel si inpenitentibus huiuscemodi unctio sit concedenda?" JK 311 = D.95 c.3 rubr. (ed. Friedberg, 332): "Oleo sanctificato non prohibetur episcopus tangere infirmos."

93. D.95 d.p.c.3 (ed. Friedberg, 332): "Crisma uero a suis episcopis ad baptismi sanctificationem presbiteri petant. Vnde in Cartaginensi Concilio IV." D.95 c.4 (ed. Friedberg, 332): "Presbiteri, qui per dioceses ecclesias regunt, non a quibuslibet episcopis, sed a suis, nec per iuniorem clericum, sed omni anno aut per se ipsos, aut per illum, qui sacrarium tenet, ante pasce solempnitatem crisma petant." The material source is Fourth Council of Carthage, c.36, ed. Munier, 347 = *Statuta ecclesiae antiqua*, c.87, ed. Munier, 94.

94. D.6 d.a.c.1 (ed. Friedberg, 9): "Quia uero de nature superfluitate sermo cepit haberi, queritur an post illusionem que per somnium accidere solet, corpus Domini quilibet accipere ualeat, uel si sacerdos sit, sacra misteria celebrare."

95. JE 1843 = D.6 c.1 (ed. Friedberg, 9–10): "Sed est in eadem illusione necessaria ualde discretio, qua subtiliter pensare debeat, ex qua re accidat menti dormientis. Aliquando enim ex crapula, aliquando ex nature sue superfluitate aut infirmitate, aliquando ex cogitatione contingit pollutio. Et quidem cum ex nature superfluitate uel infirmitate euenerit, omnimodo hec illusio non est timenda, quia hanc animus nesciens pertulisse magis dolendus est, quam fecisse. Cum uero ultra modum appetitus gule in sumendis alimentis rapitur, atque idcirco humorum receptacula grauantur, habet exinde animus aliquem reatum, non tamen usque ad prohibitionem sacri misterii percipiendi, uel missarum sollempnia celebrandi, cum fortasse aut dies festus exigit, aut exhibere ministerium pro eo, quod sacerdos alius deest, ipsa necessitas compellit. Nam si adsunt alii, qui implere ministerium ualeant, illusio per crapulam facta a perceptione sacri mis-

Psalmody features in second-recension additions to D.12 and D.92. In D.12, which examines the authority of custom, Gratian concludes that customs of the universal church or long-standing customs that do not contradict the canons should be observed, but that recent and local customs should be abolished when it is opportune to do so.[96] The redactor of the second recension found it apposite to append to the end of Gratian's discussion examples of what he felt were such local customs in need of elimination, namely, the psalmodic practices described in D.12 c.13 and c.14. The first text is a canon from the Eleventh Council of Toledo commanding all churches in a province to adopt the psalmody used in the metropolitan church.[97] The second text, a canon from the First Council of Braga, declares that the same psalmody should be observed for matins and vespers.[98] Additions to D.92, on the other hand, present instructions on how psalmody should be performed. D.92 d.a.c.1–c.1 assert that God must be praised more by the

terii prohibere non debet, sed ab immolatione sacri misterii, ut arbitror, abstinere debet humiliter, si tamen dormientem turpi imaginatione non concusserit. Nam sunt quibus ita plerumque illusio nascitur, ut eorum animus etiam in somno corporis positus turpibus imaginationibus non fedetur. Qua in re unum ibi ostenditur, ipsa mens rea non tunc uel in suo iudicio libera cum se etsi in dormientis corpore nichil meminit uidisse, tamen in uigiliis corporis meminit se in ingluuiem cecidisse. Sin uero ex turpi cogitatione uigilantis oritur illusio in mente dormientis, patet animo reatus suus."

96. D.12 d.p.c.11 (ed. Friedberg, 30): "Hoc autem de consuetudine illa intelligendum est, que uel uniuersalis ecclesie usu, uel temporis prolixitate roboratur. Ceterum, si pro uarietate temporum uel animorum uarie consuetudines introducantur, inuenta opportunitate, resecande sunt potius quam obseruande."

97. D.12 c.13 (ed. Friedberg, 30–31): "placuit sancto concilio, ut metropolitane sedis auctoritate coacti uniuscuiusque prouincie ciues rectoresque ecclesiarum unum eundemque in psallendo teneant modum, quem metropolitana in sede cognouerint institutum, nec aliqua diuersitate cuiusque ordinis uel officii a metropolitana se patiantur sede disiungi.... Abbatibus sane indultis officiis, que iuxta uoluntatem sui episcopi regulariter illis implenda sunt, cetera officia publica, id est uesperam, matutinum, siue missam, aliter quam in principali ecclesia celebrare non liceat.... Sub ista ergo regula discipline non solum metropolitanus totius sue prouincie pontifices uel sacerdotes adstringat, sed etiam ceteri episcopi subiectos sibi ecclesiarum rectores obtemperare institutionibus cogant." The material source is Eleventh Council of Toledo, c.3, ed. Vives, 356–57.

98. D.12 c.14 (ed. Friedberg, 31): "Placuit omnibus communi consensu, ut unus atque idem psallendi ordo in matutinis uel uespertinis officiis teneatur, et non diuerse ac priuate, neque monasteriorum consuetudines cum ecclesiastica regula sint permixte." The material source is First Council of Braga, c.1, ed. Vives, 71.

heart than by the voice, while D.92 d.p.c.1–c.2 forbid deacons from serving as cantors, lest they neglect their other liturgical duties.[99]

A second-recension addition to D.70 deals with the prefaces used for mass. In the first recension, this distinction simply notes that the Council of Chalcedon forbids clerics from being ordained without a title, that is, ordained without a designated church that he will serve and from which he will receive financial and material support.[100] The second recension inserts an additional canon on this subject taken from the Council of Piacenza (1095).[101] Perhaps as an afterthought, the second recension then notes that this same council added a tenth preface to the nine ancient prefaces to the mass and gives the text of the new preface in full.[102]

99. D.92 d.a.c.1 (ed. Friedberg, 317): "Cum autem ad ecclesiam uenerint, corde magis quam uoce Deo cantandum meminerint." D.92 c.1 rubr. (ed. Friedberg, 317): "Corde non uoce Deum laudare debemus." The material source is Jerome, *Commentarius in epistulam Pauli Apostoli ad Ephesios* 5:19, PL 26, 528. D.92 d.p.c.1 (ed. Friedberg, 317): "Ab officio autem cantandi et psallendi diaconi inueniuntur excepti, ne, dum uocis modulationi student altaris ministeria negligant." D.92 c.2 (ed. Friedberg, 317–18): "Cantandi officium sibi diacones non usurpent [rubr.]. In sancta ecclesia Romana dudum consuetudo est ualde reprehensibilis exorta, ut quidam ad sacri altaris ministerium cantores eligantur, et in diaconatus ordine constituti modulationi uocis inseruiant, quos ad predicationis officium et elemosinarum studium uacare congruebat. Vnde fit plerumque ut in sacro ministerio, dum blanda uox queritur, congrua uita negligatur, et cantor minister Deum moribus stimulet, cum populum uocibus delectet. Qua de re presenti decreto constituo, ut in sede hac sacri altaris ministri cantare non debeant, solumque euangelice lectionis officium inter missarum solempnia exsoluant; psalmos uero ac reliquas lectiones censeo per subdiaconos uel, si necessitas exigit, per minores ordines exhiberi." The material source is a canon promulgated at the July 5, 595, Roman synod held under Gregory the Great. *Gregorii I papae Registrum epistolarum*, ed. Paul Ewald and Ludwig Hartmann, MGH Epp. 1 (Berlin: MGH, 1891), 1:363.4–14.

100. D.70 d.a.c.1 (ed. Friedberg, 256, supported by Aa Bc Fd P): "Ab episcopis alterius ciuitatis clericus ordinari non poterit, nec etiam a proprio absolute ordinandus est: absoluta autem ordinatio Calcedonensi Concilio prohibetur et uacuam habere manus impositionem precipitur; in quo sic statutum est."

101. D.70 c.2 (ed. Friedberg, 257): "Sanctorum canonum statutis consona sanctientes decernimus, ut sine titulo facta ordinatio irrita habeatur, et in qua ecclesia quilibet titulatus est, in ea perpetuo perseueret." The material source is Council of Piacenza, c.15, ed. Robert Somerville, *Pope Urban II's Council of Piacenza* (Oxford: Oxford University Press, 2011), 97–98.

102. D.70 d.p.c.2 (ed. Friedberg, 257): "In eodem etiam concilio antiquis nouem prefationibus decima addita est, que ita se habet: 'Equum et salutare, que et unigenitum tuum Spiritus sancti obumbratione concepit, et uirginitatis glo-

Yet another interesting second-recension addition on the mass occurs in C.7 q.1. In the first recension, this question focuses on determining whether a living bishop may be assigned a co- or auxiliary bishop.[103] To this end, Gratian considers various canons on the legitimacy of replacing an old or sick bishop, the possibility of assigning a bishop a helper, and the problem of episcopal translation.[104] In the second recension, the redactor maintains the same basic framework, but introduces one notable digression. What should be done when a priest begins but then is unable to finish saying mass?[105] His answer, based on two canons from Visigothic church councils, is that one of the other clergy in attendance should take his place and finish what he started. Canon law prescribes that everyone saying mass should have at least one other priest in attendance. If some illness overcomes the celebrant, the other priest should take over.[106]

---

ria permanente lumen eternum mundo effudit, Iesum Christum Dominum nostrum.'" On this Marian preface, see Somerville, *Pope Urban II's Council of Piacenza,* 115 and the literature cited therein.

103. C.7 pr. (ed. Friedberg, 566): "Hic primum queritur utrum uiuente episcopo alius possit in ecclesia eadem ordinari?"

104. For an analysis, see Sommar, "Gratian's *Causa VII,*" 78–96, at 83–85.

105. C.7 q.1 d.p.c.14 (ed. Friedberg, 573): "Ne autem huiuscemodi passionibus sacerdotibus subito occupatis ceptum officium inexpletum remaneat, institutum est, ut sacerdos, siue psallens, siue sacrificans, alios secum habeat, qui, si huiusmodi casus interuenerit, inchoata misteria perficere ualeant."

106. C.7 q.1 c.15 (ed. Friedberg, 573): "nobis uerendum est et cauendum, ne horis illis atque temporibus quibus Domino psallitur uel sacrificatur, unicuique diuinis officiis singulariter insistenti perniciosa passio uel quelibet corporis ualitudo occurat, que aut corpus subito obrui faciat, aut mentem alienatione uel terrore confundat. Huiusmodi ergo casibus precauentes necessarium duximus instituere, habeat quisquis ille canens Deo atque sacrificans post se uicini solaminis adiutorem, ut si aliquo casu ille, qui officia impleturus accedit, turbatus fuerit uel ad terram elisus, a tergo semper habeat qui eius uicem exequatur intrepidus." The material source is Eleventh Council of Toledo, c.14, ed. Vives, 366. C.7 q.1 c.16 (ed. Friedberg, 573–74): "Nichil contra ordinis statutum temeritatis ausu presumatur, neque illa que summa ueneratione censentur, ulla presumptione soluantur, cum ad hoc tantum fieri iussa sunt, ne interrupta noscantur, ne languoris prouentu robore salutis natura priuetur.... Censuimus ergo conuenire, ut cum a sacerdotibus missarum tempore sancta misteria consecrantur, si egritudinis accidat cuiuslibet euentus, quo ceptum nequeat consecrationis explere ministerium, sit liberum episcopo uel presbitero alteri consecrationem exequi cepti officii." The second recension misattributes the canon to the Eighth Council of Toledo. In fact, the material source is Seventh Council of Toledo, c.2, ed. Vives, 253.

The Tract *De consecratione*

Perhaps because the piecemeal addition of liturgical regulations to Gratian's textbook was too slow, cumbersome, and unsystematic, the redactor of the second recension—or another one of Gratian's early readers—ended up appending an entire tract on the liturgy and sacraments, *De consecratione,* to the end of the *Decretum.* In this section, I examine two aspects of *De consecratione* that link it with the redactor of the distinctions and *causae* rather than with Gratian, the author of the first recension: first, the overlapping chronology of the revised distinctions and *causae,* on the one hand, and *De consecratione,* on the other hand; and second, the thematic similarities between *De consecratione* and the rest of the second recension.

Chronology of the Second Recension and *De consecratione*

The chronology of the second recension links *De consecratione* closely to the revised distinctions and *causae,* certainly more closely than to the first recension. For though *De consecratione* was probably appended to the *Decretum* only after the revised distinctions and *causae* had been completed and published, work on *De consecratione* may have already been underway during the genesis of the second recension and the tract was probably added to the *Decretum* by the early 1150s and certainly had been added already by 1158.

The primary evidence for the view that the revised distinctions and *causae* were originally published separately, without *De consecratione,* comes from the two earliest known introductions to the *Decretum,* known after their incipits as *Hoc opus inscribitur* and *In prima parte agitur,* respectively. Neither introduction mentions *De consecratione.* Yet whereas *Hoc opus inscribitur* appears to have been composed for the first recension, *In prima parte agitur* was certainly composed for the second recension.[107] *In prima parte agitur* refers to numerous sec-

107. On these abbreviations, see Carlos Larrainzar, "Notas sobre las introducciones *In prima parte agitur* y *Hoc opus inscribitur,*" in *Medieval Church Law,* ed. Müller and Sommar, 134–53; Larrainzar, "El resumen de C.37 del *Decretum Gratiani,*" in *Mélanges en l'honneur d'Anne Lefebvre-Teillard,* ed. Bernard d'Alteroche et al. (Paris: Éditions Panthéon-Assas, 2009), 639–64. See also José-Miguel Viejo-

tions not found in Gratian's original textbook. To give but a few examples from the additions on the liturgy, this introduction notes that the distinctions discuss the times when fasting should be observed, the times when an archbishop can wear the pallium, and the renewal of ancient privileges upon the conferral of the pallium.[108] In addition, *In prima parte agitur* states that the *causae* discuss the payment of bribes to prevent the construction or consecration of churches, finishing a mass begun by another priest, the right to asylum, the times when oaths are forbidden, and the prohibition of weddings during times of fasting.[109] As discussed above, however, all of these topics were added only in the second recension.

Although the addition of *De consecratione* to the *Decretum* probably postdates the publication of the revised distinctions and *causae*, work on *De consecratione* may have begun before this time, since a dictum in what is probably the earliest section of *De consecratione*, De cons. D.1 d.p.c.50, seems to reference the first rather than the second recension. This dictum cites D.75 c.4 and c.7 and D.76 c.12 to show that mass should be celebrated around vespers during the four seasons of fasting and at the beginning of the night on Saturdays.[110]

Ximénez, "La versión original de C.29 del Decreto de Graciano," *Ius ecclesiae* 11 (1998): 149–85, at 177–78.

108. For the relevant text of *In prima parte agitur*, see Larrainzar, "Notas," 152–53. The noted subjects are discussed in the following second-recension additions: D.76 d.a.c.1–c.11; D.100 cc.6 and 8; and D.100 d.p.c.8–c.11.

109. *In prima parte agitur* to C.1 q.1 (Bc, fol. 2ra): "Similiter symoniaci probantur qui peccunie [*sic*] interuentu ordinandi sacros ordines non tribuunt, canonice electioni assensum non prebent, ecclesiis edificandis uel consecrandis lapidem benedictum uel consecrationem subtrahant" (corresponding to C.1 q.1 d.p.c.124–c.125); to C.7 q.1 (Bc, fol. 4vb–5ra): "ubi etiam prohibentur sacerdotes soli diuina misteria celebrare ut si forte humanitus eis aliquid acciderit per astantes consacerdotes inchoata misteria perficiantur" (corresponding to C.7 q.1 d.p.c.14–c.16); to C.17 q.4 (Bc, fol. 8va): "et quomodo confugientes ad ecclesiam non sunt uiolenter abstrahendi uel quando exire cogendi ostenditur" (corresponding to C.17 q.4 cc.6–11, c.20, d.p.c.20, d.p.c.29, d.p.c.31–c.36); to C.22 q.5 (Bc, fol. 10rb): "quibus etiam temporibus iurare prohibemur" (corresponding to C.22 q.5 d.p.c.16–c.17); to C.33 q.4 (Bc, fol. 15ra): "Ibidem etiam ostenditur quod non liceat alicui coniugali operi tempore orationis uacare, nec in diebus abstinentie nuptias celebrare" (corresponding to C.33 q.4 d.p.c.7–c.11).

110. De cons. D.1 d.p.c.50 (ed. Friedberg, 1307): "In ieiuniis etiam quatuor temporum circa uespertinas horas, in sabbato uero sancto circa noctis initium missarum solempnia sunt celebranda. Vnde Leo episcopus: 'Quod a patribus nostris' [D.75 c.4]. Item Gelasius: 'Ordinationes presbiterorum' [D.75 c.7]. Item Pe-

These canons are not contiguous in the second recension, but they form an unbroken series in the first recension. Their citation in De cons. D.1 d.p.c.50 may indicate that *De consecratione* was begun before DD.75–76 were expanded with material on the liturgy. The most extensive set of additions to these two distinctions, D.76 d.a.c.1–c.11, deals with fasting and may have been added around the same time as work was begun on distinction 5 of *De consecratione*. Both sections treat the same general topic, fasting, and take their canons from the same main formal source, 3L 3.8.[111]

Work on *De consecratione* did not come to an end, however, until after the redactor of the second recension had begun revising the distinctions and *causae* or perhaps not until after he had already completed the revision process. Two sections of *De consecratione* demonstrate knowledge of second-recension additions to the distinctions and *causae*. De cons. D.1 c.20, which contains the pseudonymous Nicene canon on church reconsecration discussed above, is a doublet of the addition D.68 c.3.[112] The text of these doublets is not entirely identical, but the only two variants are minor enough for both doublets to derive from the same formal source or for one doublet to derive from the other. Distinction 4 of *De consecratione*, on the other hand, refers explicitly to an addition to the *causae* on marriage added in the second recension. After quoting a canon forbidding women to baptize, *De consecratione* notes that it does not apply in cases of necessity, "whence Urban II's [decretal] 'Super quibus consuluit' cited above in the tract on marriage, in the section on spiritual affinity."[113] The text referred to is C.30 q.3 c.4, a decretal of Pope Urban II to Vitalus of Brescia, which was added only in the second recension.[114]

---

lagius: 'Dilectionis tue rescripta' [D.76 c.12]. Require in tractatu ordinandorum."

111. See the analytical tables in Joseph Motta, ed., *Collectio canonum trium librorum: Parts altera (Liber III et Appendix)*, MIC.B 8/II (Vatican City: BAV, 2008), 455–56.

112. See the discussion of church reconsecration above pp. 264–65.

113. De cons. D.4 c.20 (ed. Friedberg, 1367): "Mulier, quamuis docta et sancta, baptizare aliquos uel uiros docere in conuentu, non presumat." The material source is a combination of Fourth Council of Carthage, cc.99 and 100, ed. Munier, 352 = *Statuta ecclesiae antiqua*, cc.37 and 41, ed. Munier, 86. De cons. D.4 d.p.c.20 (ed. Friedberg, 1367): "Nisi necessitate cogente. Vnde Vrbanus II: 'Super quibus consuluit' etc., ut supra in tractatu coniugii, ubi de compatribus agitur."

114. JL 5741 = C.30 q.3 c.4 (ed. de León, 159–60): "Vnde Urbanus secundus

The earliest firm *terminus ante quem* for the finished *De consecratione* is given by Peter Lombard's *Four Books of Sentences*, which was completed in 1155–58.[115] But use of *De consecratione* by the earliest decretists and abbreviators of the *Decretum* suggests that *De consecratione* was compiled considerably earlier and that it in fact dates to only shortly after the publication of the revised distinctions and *causae*. Paucapalea, whose *summa* dates to sometime between 1146 and the early 1150s, comments on *De consecratione*.[116] And *De consecratione* appears in condensed form in *Quoniam egestas*, perhaps the oldest abbreviation of Gratian's textbook, which likely dates to around 1150 as well.[117]

Thematic Similarities

In addition to the chronological links between *De consecratione* and the rest of the second recension, there is a thematic link as well. Both *De consecratione* and the revised distinctions and *causae* evince a strong interest in the liturgy. Gratian's medieval and modern readers have generally argued that *De consecratione* differs from the rest of the *Decretum* in not only form, but also function. Aside from some cross-references, the tract lacks dicta. And its contents have often struck readers as more sacramental than the rest of the second recension. Indeed, according to many interpreters, the concept of sacrament is key to understanding *De consecratione*. The oldest such interpretation dates back to the second half of the twelfth century. Expanding a classifi-

---

scribit Vitali presbitero Brixiensi dicens: 'Super quibus consuluit nos tua dilectio hoc uidetur nobis ex sententia respondendum ut et baptismus sit si instante necessitate femina puerum in nomine Trinitatis baptizauerit et quod spiritualium parentum filii uel filie ante uel post compaternitatem genite possunt legitime coniungi preter illam personam qua compatres sunt effecti.'"

115. See the discussion of the *Decretum*'s dating in chapter 1, pp. 24–26.

116. Ed. Schulte, *Die Summa des Paucapalea*, 144–46. On the date of Paucapalea's *summa*, see Rudolf Weigand, "Frühe Kanonisten und ihre Karriere in der Kirche," *ZRG KA* 76 (1990): 135–55, at 136.

117. Rudolf Weigand, "Die Dekretabbreviatio 'Quoniam egestas' und ihre Glossen," in *Fides et ius*, ed. Winfried Aymans (Regensburg: Friedrich Pustet, 1991), 249–65; Weigand, "The Transmontane Decretists," in *The History of Medieval Canon Law in the Classical Period, 1140–1234*, ed. Hartmann and Pennington, 174–210, at 175–76. Since most of Sg is based on the first rather than the second recension and Sg does not include *De consecratione*, the abbreviation/transformation of the *Decretum* found in Sg may predate *Quoniam egestas*.

cation developed by Hugh of St. Victor, Rufinus and (following him) decretists all the way up to Huguccio assert that *De consecratione* is a treatise on four types of sacraments: "salutary" sacraments, by which salvation is acquired; "ministratory" sacraments, which are exercised in the divine office; "veneratory" sacraments, which are performed to commemorate a sacred thing; and "preparatory" sacraments, which assist in the celebration of the other sacraments.[118] Distinction 1 of *De consecratione*, they claim, deals with preparatory sacraments, distinctions 2 and 4 with salutary ones, distinction 3 with veneratory sacraments, and distinction 5 with ministratory ones.[119]

In modern times, Rudolph Sohm has argued that Gratian structured the entire *Decretum*—with the exception of DD.1–20 on the sources of church law—around the "old catholic" sacraments, that

118. On the origins of this classification in the writings of Hugh of St. Victor, see Ghellinck, *Le mouvement théologique du XIIe siècle*, 537–47.

119. Rufinus, *Summa* ad De cons., ed. Singer, 537–38: "sacramentorum species quadriformiter propagatur. Alia enim sunt salutaria, alia ministratoria, alia veneratoria, alia preparatoria. Salutaria sunt quibus salus acquiritur, ut baptismus, eucharistia et confirmatio. Ministratoria: que in officiorum ministeriis exercentur, ut missarum laudes et cetera diurna vel nocturna officia clericorum vigiliis sedulo deputata. Veneratoria: que per certa anni tempora in alicuius rei sacre memoriam venerabiliter exercentur, ut sunt dominice festivitates, scil. conceptio Salvatoris, nativitas, theophania, ypapanti, passio, resurrectio, ascensio, pentecoste et sanctorum anniversarie celebrationes. Preparatoria: que omnibus prefatis sacramentis celebrandis preparantur, ut clericorum, ecclesiarum, ecclesiasticorum vasorum et omnium ecclesie utensilium libanimumque consecratio. Et prima quidem et ultima proprie sunt sacramenta: quando sanctificantur, sanctificant. Primis namque sacramentis persone, ultimis persone et res sanctificantur. Et quia sacramenta, ideo irreiterabilia.... Duo autem media significantius dicuntur sacramentalia, sacramentis scil. adiuncta et de eis pendentia. Omnium itaque ecclesiasticarum causarum ab extra pulsantium rumoribus complacatis iam quasi internis meditationibus ludens huius voluminis auctor misteriorum profundam soliditatem evolvit et dividit, quinque distinctionibus universam tractatus seriem comprehendens. In quarum prima agit de sacramentis preparatoriis; in secunda et quarta de salutaribus dicit, quippe in secunda de sacrificio altaris, in quarta de lavacro baptismatis; in tertia de veneratoriis; in quinta de ministratoriis tangit, subiungens de ieiuniis. Terminato labore operis gloriosi in duobus capitulis de fide integra Spiritus sancti, ut opus gratum Gratiani gratia divina esse perfectum omnibus legentibus innotescat. Et quoniam ceterorum sacramentorum locus est ecclesia—non enim rite nisi in ecclesia consecrata conficiuntur sacramenta—, ideo prius de ecclesiarum dedicatione, quasi de priori naturaliter sacramento edisserit." The later decretists simply repeat Rufinus's views.

is, visible forms of invisible grace that stem not from the essence, ability, or indelible character of an individual Christian or priest, but rather from the essence, ability, and power of the church, which is present in the gathering of the individual Christian community. In Sohm's view, DD.21–101 and *Causae* 1–26 deal with ordination, *Causae* 27–36 with marriage, *De penitentia* with penance, and *De consecratione* with the remaining old catholic sacraments.[120]

Finally, John Van Engen has suggested that *De consecratione* reflects a traditional understanding of sacraments as referring, strictly speaking, to just baptism, confirmation, and the eucharist. Gratian's practical orientation accounts for the many canons dealing with church consecration, sacred objects, the mass, the liturgical calendar, and fasting, as well as the order in which they and the material on the sacraments appear in *De consecratione*. The lack of dicta, apparent disregard for contradictions between canons, and the disorder of some sections, on the other hand, are probable signs that Gratian never got around to finishing *De consecratione*.[121]

Ingenious as these explanations are, a comparison with earlier canonical collections suggests a much more mundane explanation for *De consecratione*'s structure and one that does not separate the tract from the rest of the second recension. The arrangement of *De consecratione* has nothing to do with any exalted theory of the sacraments or special understanding of how the sacraments should fit into the larger framework of canon law and doctrine, but rather reflects the structure of earlier, non-Ivonian canonical collections. In many respects, *De consecratione* follows a model established by Burchard of Worms, though as altered and reworked by Italian canonical collections of the late eleventh and early twelfth centuries. Late antique and early medieval conciliar legislation, papal decretals, and canonical collections had dealt for the most part only with administrative, disciplinary, and procedural issues. While they did not ignore the sacraments, they focused far more attention on the ecclesiasti-

120. Sohm, *Das altkatholische Kirchenrecht*, esp. 19–51.

121. John Van Engen, "Observations on 'De consecratione,'" in *Proceedings of the Sixth International Congress of Medieval Canon Law*, ed. Kuttner and Pennington, 309–20.

cal hierarchy, church property, clerical and lay behavior, and court procedure. With the transition from chronologically to systematically arranged canonical collections, compilers began both to introduce more material on the sacraments into the canonical tradition and to arrange the existing material into books and titles. Burchard's contribution to this development was of the utmost importance. While he did not introduce many new texts on baptism, confirmation, and the eucharist into the canonical tradition, what he did do was just as important: systematically arrange existing regulations and connect them to the liturgy.[122] Burchard devotes book 3 of his *Decretum* to churches, ecclesiastical property, and sacred objects, book 4 to baptism and confirmation, and book 5 to the eucharist.[123]

In considering the canon law of the sacraments, modern scholars have rightly stressed the importance of Ivo of Chartres. Inspired at least in part by the Berengar Controversy over the eucharist, Ivo introduced numerous patristic texts on the sacraments into the canonical tradition. He placed these newly canonized authorities at the beginning of his *Decretum*, devoting book 1 to the Catholic faith, baptism, and confirmation and book 2 to the eucharist and mass.[124] Burchard and the eleventh-century reformers had begun their canonical collections with texts on the Roman primacy. Ivo's arrangement was a deliberate departure from this tradition, one which found many imitators, most notably Collection B of the *Tripartita*, that is, book 3 of the *Tripartita*, and the Pseudo-Ivonian *Panormia*.

In producing *De consecratione*, however, the redactor of the second recension looked not to any of these French sources with their emphasis on the sacraments as such, but rather to Italian canonical collections that, like Burchard, prefaced their treatment of the sacraments with sections on churches and the liturgy.[125] Anselm of Lucca, for instance, devotes book 5 of his canonical collection (Recension

122. On the new texts, see the tables in Hoffman and Pokorny, *Das Dekret des Bischofs Burchard von Worms*, 199–205.

123. See the overview of the history of liturgical law above pp. 249–53.

124. See Charles Munier, *Les sources patristiques*, 39–40; Rolker, "The Earliest Work of Ivo of Chartres," 109–27; Rolker, *Canon Law*, esp. 182–83.

125. For more specific references to the material discussed in this paragraph, see pp. 252–53.

A) to church consecration and property and book 9 to the eucharist, baptism, and confirmation. Book 9 opens with canons on the eucharist (cc.1–10) and then treats baptism and confirmation (cc.11–27), before closing with canons on heretical and schismatic sacraments and the sacraments of the wicked (cc.28–49). Gregory of San Grisogono's *Polycarpus* similarly deals with churches, the liturgy, and sacred objects before treating the eucharist, baptism, and confirmation. The titles of the third book deal to a great extent with the material treated by *De consecratione* and in the same order: "On the consecration of churches" (3.4); "On reconsecrating churches" (3.5); "On the restoration of churches" (3.6); "On images and pictures in churches" (3.7); "Whether the places or honors of the saints add anything" (3.8); "On the body of the Lord and the guarding of sacred objects" (3.9); "On baptism and the imposition of hands" (3.10); "On ecclesiastical rites" (3.24); "On the observation of Quadragesima and fasting" (3.25); "On discretion in fasting and abstinence" (3.26); and "On discretion in fasting and eating" (3.27). The same is true of the 3L. Title 8 of book 2 deals with the consecration of churches, church rites, and their sacraments, while title 7 of book 3 deals with baptism and confirmation and title 8 of book 3 with fasting.

De consecratione contains a great deal of material on the sacraments, but they were not its exclusive or arguably even predominant focus. The liturgy, particularly liturgical law, claims just as—if not more—important a place and seems furthermore to have attracted greater attention from the tract's compiler. For whereas the compiler copied much of his sacramental material from the *Panormia* and the *Sententiae magistri A.*, leaving the canons in largely the same order, he generally took the canons on the liturgy from a variety of different formal sources, which he greatly rearranged.[126]

Distinction 1 provides a particularly clear example of the great attention devoted to the liturgy. The compiler took the canons in this distinction from each of the *Decretum*'s five normal formal sources,

126. On the sacramental material, see Rambaud, "Le legs," 91–93; Landau, "Gratian und die Sententiae Magistri A.," 311–26, at 316–19, reprinted in Landau, *Kanones und Dekretalen*, 161*–76*, with retractations at 474*–75*, at 166*–69*.

which he ordered in a fairly systematic fashion. The distinction progresses logically from church consecration (cc.1–38), to consecrated vestments and vessels (cc.39–46), to the celebration of the mass (cc.47–73). And each section in the distinction provides a relatively clear exposition of its topic. The first two canons, which comprise a single text in the manuscripts, provide arguments from the Old Testament for the necessity of church consecration, while the third canon declares that all church consecrations should be accompanied by mass. New churches can be dedicated only with the approval of the pope (cc.4–8) or local bishop (c.9) and never out of avarice (c.10). Church consecration is important because mass can only be celebrated in consecrated places (cc.11–15), and a church's dedication should be commemorated annually (cc.16–17). Several canons treat the problem of when a church should be rededicated (cc.18–24) as well as the consecration of altars (cc.25–32). The apparent digression of cc.27–29, which forbid the consecration of churches or the celebration of mass in cemeteries, was probably occasioned by the inclusion of c.26, which stipulates that altars must contain relics. The compiler, we can conjecture, included cc.27–29 to make clear the difference between the relics of saints and the remains of ordinary, sinful individuals. The remaining canons in this opening section forbid the celebration of mass in private chapels (cc.33–35) and address questions pertaining to the deconsecration of churches (cc.36–38).

After treating church consecration, distinction 1 next sets forth regulations concerning sacred vestments and vessels, treating in turn how they are to be disposed of (c.39), who should handle them (cc.40–44), and what they should be made of (cc.45–46). The compiler appears to have dealt with these issues in this order rather than in the more logical reverse order because of the immediately preceding canons (cc.36–38), which treat the deconsecration of a church. For the compiler, c.39 provided a better way to transition to the subject of sacred vestments and vessels than cc.45–46, which deal with the material to be used for the chalice, patena, and altar cloths.

The final section of distinction 1, which treats the mass, is more loosely structured, but far from disorganized. For the most part, it deals first with matters pertaining to clergy and then with matters relevant to laypersons. The distinction covers the apostolic origins of the rite for celebrating mass (c.47), the time of day when mass should be celebrated (cc.48–51), private masses (c.52), the number of masses priests may celebrate in a day (c.53), the singing of hymns and the Gloria (cc.54–56), the behavior of clerics during mass (c.57), the number of clergy aside from the celebrant who should be in attendance (cc.59–61), the behavior of laypersons (cc.62–70), the prefaces of the mass (cc.71–72), and prayers for the living and the dead (c.73).

Distinction 3 and the middle and end of distinction 5 are less well organized than distinction 1, but likewise demonstrate the compiler's great attention to the liturgy. The chronologically ordered Collection A of the *Tripartita*, that is, books 1–2 of the *Tripartita*, was the source for almost all of the canons in distinction 3, which rearranges the material into several thematic units pertaining to the liturgical calendar: Quadragesima (cc.6–9), times of fasting (cc.11–16), Maundy Thursday (cc.17–18), the feast of the discovery of the true cross (c.19), Easter (cc.21–26), and the use of images (cc.27–29). The 3L and both collections A and B of the *Tripartita*, on the other hand, were the formal sources for De cons. D.5 cc.16–38/40. The compiler took cc.16–31 largely unchanged from 3L 3.8, reproducing the canons in the same order as his formal source and only omitting four canons not included elsewhere in *De consecratione* or the rest of the *Decretum*. But he was less mechanical in compiling the remaining canons. Collections A and B of the *Tripartita* provided him with the text of cc.32–40, but not their order or arrangement, both of which differ substantially. The compiler's purpose in introducing these canons is somewhat puzzling, since, with the exception of c.32, they do not discuss fasting explicitly.[127] But he perhaps intended them to provide more explicit ordinances concerning how Christians should observe the "great and general fast" discussed in c.25, which emphasizes that fasting is not just about abstaining from food, but also involves abstaining from sin.[128] With the

127. Cf. Van Engen, "Observations," 318: "It is nevertheless difficult, if not indeed impossible, to discover in D.3 and D.5 cc.13–38/40 any underlying theme or argument."

128. De cons. D.5 c.25 (ed. Friedberg, 1418): "Ieiunium autem magnum et

exception of cc.39–40, which concern the Holy Spirit, all of the canons deriving from the *Tripartita* deal with Christian behavior and morality. They are arranged in descending order of spiritual perfection, treating first monks (cc.32, 33), then canons (c.34), priests (c.35), clerics (c.36), clerics and laypersons (c.37), and lastly women (c.38).

Finally, it should be pointed out that the liturgical aspects of the sacraments receive greater attention in *De consecratione* than do their theology. The opening section of distinction 2, for instance, which deals with liturgical aspects of the eucharist, derives from just three sources—the *Tripartita, Panormia,* and the 3L—but has been substantially rearranged to provide a more logical and thematically coherent exposition than the rest of the distinction, which deals with eucharistic theology. The distinction begins with the elements necessary for the eucharistic sacrifice (cc.1–7) and then includes a canon on the incomparable value of the eucharist (c.8). Perhaps because c.8 mentions that the eucharist should be offered by one with a pure conscience, the distinction next inserts a canon explaining when to grant the kiss of peace (c.9). Most of the remaining canons in this part of the distinction deal with who, when, and how the eucharist should be received and handled. Ministers must always communicate after they perform the consecration (cc.10–12), while laypersons can communicate as often as they like (cc.13–14, 17–18, 20) unless they have been excommunicated (c.15), but at least three times a year (cc.16, 19) and only if they have abstained from conjugal relations beforehand (c.21). Only clerics should handle the body of Christ (c.23). Those who communicate unworthily sin in doing so (cc.24–25), as do those who mishandle the eucharist, for instance, by spilling the sacred blood (c.27), vomiting up the host (c.28), or committing the eucharist to laymen or women (c.29). Laypersons should not enter while mass is being celebrated (c.30), and mass should be celebrated according to the usage of the metropolitan church (c.31).

The remainder of distinction 2 is considerably less polished. The

---

generale est abstinere ab iniquitatibus et ab illicitis uoluptatibus seculi, quod est perfectum ieiunium." The material source is Augustine, *In Iohannis evangelium tractatus* 17.4–5, ed. Radbod Willems, CCSL 36 (Turnhout: Brepols, 1954), 172.21–23, 28–34, 37–44, and 1–5.

compiler took most of cc.32–97 from the *Panormia, Sententiae magistri A.*, and Peter Abelard's *Sic et non* or a closely related collection. For the most part, the compiler simply reproduced the canons from these sources in the same order, making use first of the *Panormia* and then supplementing the material with additional texts found in the *Sententiae magistri A.* and the *Sic et non.* The one major change that the compiler introduced was to place *Panormia* 1.130–32 at the beginning of this sequence. *Panormia* 1.130–31 (= De cons. D.2 cc.32–33) define the notions of sacrament and sign, while *Panormia* 1.132 applies these concepts to the eucharist. Almost all the remaining canons deal in some way with the spiritual meaning and significance of the eucharist. Other than that, however, they lack any real order or development.

Distinction 4 is perhaps the most poorly organized distinction in *De consecratione.* Most of the canons are taken over unchanged and in the same order from four collections: the *Tripartita, Panormia,* 3L, and *Sententiae magistri A.* In many respects, the distinction is simply a *Quellenblock* collection, that is, a canonical collection that reproduces its formal sources in blocks. Due to the fact that these formal sources, with the exception of Collection A of the *Tripartita,* were systematically arranged collections, however, the subsections of distinction 4 are fairly well structured. But the distinction as a whole is both meandering and repetitive. It returns again and again to many of the same topics, for instance, the baptism of children (cc.7, 33, 74, 76, 130, 138, 139, 142, 144); the sacrament's proper minister, operation independent of the minister's merits, and administration by heretics or schismatics (cc.19–21, 23–27, 36, 39–41, 43–51); its form (cc.28–32, 38, 52, 78–86); and the use and consecration of chrism (cc.87, 88, 90, 119–26). While the distinction deals with many theological topics, especially original sin and grace, it dwells in particular on the liturgical aspects of baptism, for instance, the times when the sacrament should be administered (cc.11–18), the catechumenate and baptismal ceremony (cc.54–70), and godparents (cc.100–105), as well as such already mentioned topics as the form of baptism and the use and consecration of chrism.

To conclude this section: *De consecratione* deals with both the sacraments and the liturgy, but devotes especial attention to the liturgy and displays more interest in liturgical law than in liturgical theology. Like the revised distinctions and *causae*, then, a particular aim of *De consecratione* was probably to supplement the *Decretum*'s coverage of the liturgy.

Controversy and Custom

Gratian himself provides no explanation for his omission of texts on the liturgy, so any attempt at explaining his decision must, in the end, be speculative. In this final section of the chapter, I would like to suggest two possibilities. First, while Gratian, the author of the first recension, clearly sought to provide comprehensive coverage of some areas of canon law, at other times, such as in his treatment of penitential theology, he focused only on disputed or controversial issues. The omission of texts on the liturgy from the first recension, I propose, may be related to the general lack of controversy concerning liturgical matters in the Italy of his day.

Second, I would like to suggest, Gratian's reserve toward the liturgy may have been related to his ideas on custom as a source of law. In the *Tractatus de legibus*, Gratian distinguishes between three main categories of law: natural law, constitution, and custom. Custom occupies the lowest place. Not only does it lack binding force when it contradicts natural law, but it also gives way before contrary written constitutions. Moreover, if a custom is local and of only recent origin, it should be eliminated once the circumstances that led to its introduction have changed.[129] Gratian quotes a text by Augustine to explain why.

I think that, when it is suitable, one may abrogate without hesitation those things that are not encompassed by the authority of sacred Scrip-

129. D.11 d.p.c.4 (ed. Friedberg, 24, supported by Aa Bc P): "Cum uero nec sacris canonibus nec humanis legibus consuetudo obuiare monstratur, inconcussa (incontrouersia *P*) seruanda est." D.12 d.p.c.11 (ed. Friedberg, 30, supported by Aa Bc P): "Hoc autem de consuetudine illa intelligendum est, que uel uniuersalis ecclesie usu, uel temporis prolixitate roboratur. Ceterum, si pro uarietate temporum uel animorum uarie consuetudines introducantur, inuenta opportunitate, resecande sunt potius quam obseruande."

ture, found established in episcopal councils, or confirmed by the custom of the universal Church and that vary so much according to the different habits of various places that the purpose of the men who instituted them can be discovered only with great difficulty or not at all. For, even if they are not contrary to the faith, they oppress the very religion that God's mercy freed from servile burdens so that it could employ brief clear rites of praise. But today even the condition of the Jews is more tolerable since, although they do not acknowledge the age of freedom, they are subject only to the rites of the Law and not to human impositions.[130]

The plethora of local observances, Augustine argues, is a great burden, one more onerous than the Jewish ceremonial law from which Jesus came to liberate the faithful.

Two aspects of Gratian's treatment of law have possible links to his exclusion of texts on the liturgy from the first recension. First, all the concrete examples of customs mentioned in the canons he cites are liturgical. Basil in D.11 c.5 explicitly mentions the following customs that he says should be observed without fail: the sign of the cross, the prayers during the liturgy of the eucharist, praying toward the east, anointing the baptismal font with oil, anointing thrice with oil those who are to be baptized, and interrogating those about to be baptized whether they are willing to renounce Satan and his angels.[131] And Augustine in D.12 c.11 explicitly mentions the annual celebration of Easter, the Ascension, and Pentecost as universal customs that should always be kept, while he identifies regulations con-

130. D.12 c.12 (ed. Friedberg, 30, supported by Aa Bc P). English translation taken from Gratian, *Treatise on Laws*, 47. The material source is Augustine, *Epistulae* 55.35, ed. Klaus D. Daur, CCSL 31 (Turnhout: Brepols, 2004), 263.746–58.

131. D.11 c.5 (ed. Friedberg, 24–25, supported by Aa Bc P): "Que enim (ut inde ordiamur) scriptura salutifere crucis signaculo fideles docuit insigniri? uel que (que uel *tr. Bc P*, que per *Aa*^{ac}) trifariam digesta super panem et calicem prolixe orationis uel consecrationis uerba commendauit? Nam non modo, quod in euangelio continetur uel ab Apostolo insertum secretis dicimus, sed et alia plura adicimus magnam quasi uim commendantia misteriis. Que orientem uersus nos orare litterarum forma docuit? Benedicimus fontem baptismatis oleo unctionis. Huc accedit, quod ter oleo inungimus quos baptizamus, uerbis abrenuntiare satane et (*om. Friedb.*) angelis eius informamus. Vnde et (*om. Friedb.*) hec et alia in hunc modum non pauca, nisi tacita ac mistica traditione a Patribus ecclesiastico more ac reuerentiori diligentia sunt in ministeriis obseruata (magis *add. Aa*$^{post\ silentio}$ *Friedb.*) silentio, quam publicata scripto?" The material source is Basil, *De spiritu sancto* 27.66, PG 32, 188.

cerning fasting and the reception of the eucharist as local customs that are indifferent and can legitimately vary from place to place.[132]

The second aspect of Gratian's treatment of law that may be linked to his exclusion of the canon law of the liturgy from the first recension is his emphasis on the importance of popular reception to the validity of law. In D.4, he recognizes that non-observance abrogates written law. To have legal force, written law must be not only promulgated by legislators, but also approved by the actions of those who are supposed to be subject to it. If such approval is withheld, then written law loses its force.[133]

Both medieval and modern scholars have often commented on the apparent contradiction between D.4, with its emphasis on popular reception, regarded as a form of custom, and DD.11–12, which subordinates custom to written law.[134] The most popular solution among the decretists was to make abrogation through non-observance/contrary custom dependent on express or tacit papal consent.[135] Gratian himself, however, would no doubt have objected to this interpretation, both because he distinguished between usage and custom

132. D.12 c.11 (ed. Friedberg, 29–30, supported by Aa Bc P): "Illa autem, que non scripta, sed tradita custodimus, que quidem toto orbe terrarum (terrarum orbe *tr. Friedb.*) obseruantur, datur intelligi uel ab ipsis apostolis, uel plenariis conciliis, quorum est in ecclesia saluberrima auctoritas, commendata atque statuta retineri: sicut id quod Domini passio et resurrectio et ascensio in celum, aduentus Spiritus sancti anniuersaria solemnitate celebratur: et si quid aliud tale occurrerit quod seruetur ab uniuersis, quacumque se diffundit, ecclesia. Alia uero, que per loca terrarum regionesque uariantur, sicuti est quod alii ieiunant sabbatum, alii non: alii (uero *add. Friedb.*) cotidie communicant corpori et sanguini Domini, alii certis diebus accipiunt: et si quid aliud huiusmodi animaduerti potest, totum hoc genus rerum liberas habet obseruationes; quod enim neque contra fidem, neque contra bonos mores esse conuincitur, indifferenter (est *add. Aa*) habendum, et pro eorum, inter quos uiuitur societate seruandum est." The material source is Augustine, *Epistulae* 54.1, ed. Daur, CCSL 31, 226.17–228.50.

133. D.4 d.p.c.3, quoted on p. 267n68.

134. Luigi de Luca, "L'accettazione popolare della legge canonica nel pensiero di Graziano e dei suoi interpreti," *Studia Gratiana* 3 (1955): 193–276, provides the most detailed examination.

135. Jean Gaudemet, "La coutume en droit canonique," *RDC* 38 (1988): 224–51, at 241–49; Udo Wolter, "Die 'consuetudo' im kanonischen Recht bis zum Ende des 13. Jahrhunderts," in *Gewohnheitsrecht und Rechtsgewohnheiten im Mittelalter*, ed. Gerhard Dilcher et al., Schriften zur eropäischen Verfassungsgeschichte 6 (Berlin: Duncker and Humblot, 1992), 87–116, at 103–16.

and because he believed non-observance or contrary usage could abrogate at least certain laws even without papal consent. A comparison of D.4 and DD.11–12 demonstrates the correctness of this first claim. Gratian uses the word *mores* in D.4 to describe the observance or non-observance of written law—in other words, popular usage—while he employs the word *consuetudo* in DD.11–12 to describe those practices that should be observed when they do not contradict written law and eliminated when they do contradict it. Conceptually, usage and custom are distinct. Usage, which is generally regarded as a necessary precondition for the creation of custom, refers to the actual behavior of a group.[136] Custom, on the other hand, refers to a normative practice.

A consideration of the examples introduced in D.4, on the other hand, demonstrates Gratian's belief that contrary usage can abrogate written law despite the lack of papal consent. This distinction discusses decretals of Pseudo-Telesphorus and Pseudo-Gregory, both of which command clerics to abstain from meat and other delicacies for the whole of Quinquagesima (the seven weeks before Easter), rather than just for Quadragesima (the six weeks before Easter).[137] According to Gratian, neither decretal possesses legal force in his day. The general failure to fast from the start of Quinquagesima has abrogated these decrees, for clerics are not and cannot be punished for not fasting during Quinquagesima. While one might claim that later popes consented to the abrogation of these decretals, the same cannot be said for Pseudo-Telesphorus and Pseudo-Gregory. For Gratian, then, abrogation undoubtedly resulted from clerical resistance to the new fasting regulations rather than from the tacit consent of the pontiffs whose commands were being resisted. While Gratian concedes that a possible alternative explanation for the non-binding character of

136. The doctrine of Georg Friedrich Puchta (1798–1846), of course, constitutes an exception, since customary law depends solely on the belief of the legal community, not on actual usage. See Peter Landau, *Grundlagen und Geschichte des evangelischen Kirchenrechts und des Staatskirchenrechts* (Tübingen: Mohr Siebeck, 2008), 57.

137. On Pseudo-Telesphorus, see JK †34 = D.4 c.4. On Pseudo-Gregory, see JE †1987 = D.4 c.6 rubr. (ed. Friedberg, 6, supported by Aa Bc): "A quinquagesima ieiunandi propositum sumant, quos ecclesiastici gradus dignitas exornat."

the decretals of Pseudo-Telesphorus and Pseudo-Gregory is that they were merely intended to recommend fasting from the start of Quinquagesima, not command it, he himself seems to have given more credence to the first interpretation.[138]

Gratian's remarks on custom and popular reception, I propose, offer a possible explanation for why he omitted most texts pertaining to the liturgy from the first recension. Many liturgical practices were examples of regional rather than universal customs. Because Gratian was interested in setting forth the law of the universal church, he may have found many of the liturgical rules and regulations contained in his formal sources inappropriate for inclusion in his textbook. Many of the liturgical canons contained in Gratian's sources, moreover, had long fallen into desuetude, if they had ever been observed at all. For instance, a canon from the Council of Laodicea (ca. 343–81) added in the second recension forbids subdeacons from entering the sacristy and touching the sacred vessels.[139] Commenting on this text, the decretist Rufinus notes that it describes the custom of some larger churches, which assign special places to priests and deacons. When solemn offices are celebrated, those in minor orders cannot enter the places reserved to those in major orders, nor are subdeacons allowed to touch the vessels used for mass.[140]

A decretal of Gregory the Great added to the *Decretum* in the second recension provides another example of the local character of the liturgical regulations that Gratian omitted. Gregory insists that bishops and deacons must obtain papal permission before they can wear the dalmatic.[141] As Rufinus notes in his commentary to the preceding dictum, however, this regulation applied only in the ancient

138. D.4 d.p.c.6, quoted above p. 267n68.

139. D.23 c.26.

140. Rufinus, *Summa* ad D.23 c.26 v. *Non oportet*, ed. Singer, 55–56: "Hoc dicit iuxta quarundam magnarum ecclesiarum consuetudinem, ubi in officiis propria sunt loca sacerdotis, diaconis; et sacerdotis locus dicitur presbiterium, diaconi vero appellatur diaconium. Quando ergo sollempnia officia celebrantur, non licet minoribus ordinibus loca illa introgredi, nec licet subdiaconibus ipsis *conting. uasa domin.*, ubi est corpus et sanguis Domini, ad offerendum sacerdoti: quod quidem diacono solummodo competit."

141. JE 1748 = D.23 c.10 rubr. (ed. Friedberg, 82): "Absque apostolica licentia dalmaticis neque episcopis neque diaconibus uti licet."

church.[142] Rufinus does not explain why the decree no longer is in force, though the reason is clear enough. Later bishops and deacons failed to observe the practice.

A decretal of Pope Innocent I permitting bishops to perform extreme unction using chrism provides a final example.[143] Rufinus expresses his amazement at this canon, which was added in the second recension, because according to the custom of the church pure oil should be used.[144] He advances three possible explanations for the conflict between Innocent and contemporary ecclesiastical custom. First, the decretal by Innocent may have been abrogated later on. Alternatively, it may be speaking of the custom unique to only some churches. A final possibility is that it refers to a uniquely episcopal privilege. Priests are not allowed to use chrism when anointing the sick, but bishops are so allowed on account of their exceptional dignity.[145]

While Gratian devotes much attention to explaining contradictions between various written laws, he generally does not bother noting and explaining conflicts between written laws and local custom. On occasion, of course, he does invoke local custom to explain why certain canons conflict with each other.[146] But such appeals are unusual. On the whole and in practice, he seems to have cared more about written law. Gratian's general disinterest in local custom may therefore stand behind his general exclusion of the canon law of the liturgy from the first recension of the *Decretum*.

142. Rufinus, *Summa* ad D.23 d.p.c.9 v. *Dalmaticis autem*, ed. Singer, 54: "Hoc secundum antiqua tempora dicit, quando nulli ecclesie nisi ex speciali permissu Romane sedis uti dalmatici licebat; nunc autem quicumque diaconus ordinatur, suo loco et tempore vestiri dalmatica non prohibetur."

143. D.95 c.3.

144. On the various types of consecrated oil and their distinguishing features, see Philipp Hofmeister, *Die heiligen Öle in der morgen- und abendländischen Kirche: Eine kirchenrechtlich-liturgische Abhandlung* (Würzburg: Augustinus-Verlag, 1948), 18–24.

145. Rufinus, *Summa* ad D.95 c.3 v. *Illud ... tangere crismate*, ed. Singer, 190: "Mirum dicit, cum consuetudo ecclesie habeat, ut non crismate sed puro oleo perungatur infirmus. Sed aut huic derogatum est, aut secundum quarundam ecclesiarum morem loquitur. Aut forte si ceteris sacerdotibus egrum tangere crismate non liceat, episcopo tamen propter eius eximiam dignitatem permittitur."

146. One of the best known examples is the unrepeatability of solemn penance, which Gratian suggests is customary only in certain churches. See De pen. D.3 d.p.c.21 and De pen. D.3 d.p.c.49.

Conclusion

Even though the liturgy occupied a prominent place in the major canonical collections that circulated in the early twelfth century, Gratian chose to ignore the subject in the first recension of his *Decretum*. The redactor of the second recension responded to this neglect in two ways: first, the haphazard insertion of material on the liturgy throughout the distinctions and *causae*, and, second, the compilation of *De consecratione*. The shared aim in these sections of the second recension, as well as other links between them, suggests that the same person or group of persons was responsible for both expanding the distinctions and *causae*, on the one hand, and compiling *De consecratione*, on the other hand. The additions in the second recension and *De consecratione* deal with both liturgical theology and liturgical law, but particularly liturgical law. In contrast to Gratian, the redactor of the second recension could certainly be termed a liturgical lawyer. But even the redactor probably would not qualify as (much of) a liturgical theologian.

No definitive explanation can be given for why Gratian chose to ignore the liturgy in the first recension. I have suggested that the answer is rooted in Gratian's interest in discordant canons and attitude towards local custom. Gratian wanted to produce a textbook on the canon law of the universal church, with a focus on matters that were unclear or controversial. Dealing as it did above all with local custom, the liturgy may not have figured into his plans for what a canon law curriculum should embrace.

In the end, of course, the really significant question may be not why Gratian chose to omit liturgical law, but why the redactor of the second recension was determined to include it despite the fact that much of the content was local or inapplicable. I conclude this chapter with two suggestions. First, Marcia Colish has noted the reluctance of later "canonists to scrap legal precedents, however inapplicable they may [have become] to present realities.... Constitutionally, they were inclined to keep all the precedents on the books, however partially or intermittently they might seek to enforce them."[147] The

147. Marcia L. Colish, "Authority and Interpretation in Scholastic Theology," in Colish, *Studies in Scholasticism*, Variorum Collected Studies Series CS838 (Aldershot: Ashgate, 2006), no. II, at 2.

redactor of the second recension appears to have been a canonist in the same mold—more of a jurist than a theologian. Second, and relatedly, more so than the first recension, the second recension was intended to serve as a comprehensive compilation of canon law. The integration of liturgical law into the *Decretum* may thus reflect the redactor of the second recension's larger interest in supplementing the lacunae in Gratian's work. The lack of liturgical law, including sacramental liturgical law, was far from the only such lacuna, but it was one of the most striking.

Conclusion

Writing in the 1160s, the canonist Stephan of Tournai likened himself to a host who had invited two guests with very different tastes—the theologian and the legist—to a banquet. The legist, he feared, would regard his commentary as worthless if he attempted to treat matters pertaining to Roman legal science. The theologian, he thought, might do the same if he engaged in mystical exegesis. But as Stephan judged both theology and Roman law relevant to his endeavor, he asked his readers' indulgence so that the theologian might not lose the benefit of the laws, nor the legist the benefit of theological learning.[1]

Stephan demonstrates the growing awareness among medieval canonists of the hybrid nature of canon law and canonical jurisprudence as developed by Gratian and his immediate successors. Already in the later twelfth century, the influence of Roman law was beginning to win out.[2] Indeed, in hindsight, its triumph appears to have been inevitable. But in the 1160s, when Stephan was writing, it was far from clear where canon law was heading. Canon law was

1. Stephan of Tournai, *Prologus* to his *Summa decretorum*, ed. Herbert Kalb, *Studien zur Summa Stephans von Tournai: Ein Beitrag zur kanonistischen Wissenschaftsgeschichte des späten 12. Jahrhunderts* (Innsbruck: Wagner, 1983), 113–20, at 113.5–114.15. For an English translation, see Robert Somerville and Bruce C. Brasington, eds. and trans., *Prefaces to Canon Law Books in Latin Christianity: Selected Translations, 500–1245* (New Haven, Conn.: Yale University Press, 1998), 194–201, at 194. Kalb gives 1166–69 as the *summa*'s date of composition (*Studien*, 108–12).

2. See Pierre Legendre, *La pénétration du droit romain dans le droit canonique classique de Gratien à Innocent IV, 1140–1254* (Paris: Jouve, 1964).

still heavily indebted to theology, so much so that the decretist Rufinus could even state that canon law was a form of theology.[3]

This book explored one of the main reasons for the theological orientation of canon law in the twelfth century: Gratian's theological background and interests. During the twelfth century, neither theology nor canon law existed as an independent academic discipline. But the subjects that would develop into these disciplines did exist, and Gratian drew on both for the first recension of his *Decretum*. Gratian probably did not think of himself as a theologian. In his day, the term generally designated a person who studied the divine nature rather than scriptural learning or Christian doctrine more broadly.[4] By both later medieval and modern standards, however, he was a theologian, and his theology contributed to and shaped his jurisprudence.

Biblical learning was the first aspect of Gratian's theology that this book considered. In both theory and practice, chapter 2 showed, the Bible occupies a privileged place in Gratian's thought. Gratian's equation of the Bible with the natural law led him to treat scripture as the highest legal authority, but, at the same time, also forced him to develop doctrines and techniques for explaining biblical precepts and exempla that conflicted with his assessment of contemporary morality. Gratian's actual use of the Bible throughout the *Decretum* reflects these competing tendencies. On the one hand, Gratian cites the Bible extensively throughout the *Decretum*. On the other hand, only occasionally does he let the Bible trump other legal authorities. *Causae* 2–6 on procedural law, where Gratian uses the Bible to challenge and revise the prevailing canon law of his day, provides one of the most interesting and surprising exceptions. But, on the whole, the Bible's practical significance for the *Decretum* is due less to its having served as a direct source of law and more to its having provided Gratian with a starting point and framework for thinking about legal issues.

Penance was the second topic that this book considered and the other area where Gratian reveals himself to be a theologian. For

3. See Singer, "Einleitung" to *Die Summa decretorum des Rufinus*, lxvi n5.
4. See p. 3.

many decades, scholars suspected the highly theological tract *De penitentia* of being a later addition to the *Decretum*, one that probably did not stem from Gratian himself.[5] Anders Winroth's discovery of the first recension proved these suspicions to be unfounded. Gratian did indeed compose a treatise on penitential theology, which he then included in his textbook on canon law. His motivation for composing *De penitentia* appears to have been twofold. First, as detailed in chapters 3 and 4, Gratian, like many (particularly Italian) compilers of canonical collections before him, probably wanted to make sense of the dramatic changes in penitential practice and theology that had occurred since New Testament times and the contradictory canons that these changes had given rise to. Second, as argued in chapter 5, Gratian also appears to have had a critical, one might even say polemical, aim in composing *De penitentia*. He wrote at least the core of the treatise (distinctions 2–4) to critique and correct what he regarded as errors taught by contemporary masters and circulating in contemporary scholastic works, particularly in Italy. An accidental result of Gratian's interest in penitential theology, chapter 6 proposed, was the incorporation of material on the canon law of magic into the *Decretum*, as well as its further systematization and elaboration.

An unspoken but recurring theme of part 2 of this book was the need to adopt a broader approach to scholasticism than historians of canon law have generally taken to date. Since the late 1800s, historians of canon law have sought the link between the scholastics and Gratian in Peter Abelard's *Sic et non*.[6] Scholasticism's primary contribution to the development of canon law, it has been assumed, is the scholastic method for reconciling contradictory authorities that Abelard explicates in his treatise. One of the main arguments of this book has been that this traditional assumption is both wrong and misguided. Not only is there little evidence that the author of the first recension was familiar with either Abelard or his *Sic et non*, but the very

5. See the literature cited on p. 148n1.

6. I detailed this history in "Of Scholasticism and Canon Law: Narratives Old and New," a paper I gave at a workshop on New Discourses in Medieval Canon Law Research in Zurich (July 11–12, 2014), which will be published in expanded form in the conference volume.

attempt to make Gratian the disciple of famous masters is mistaken. The world of the twelfth century was a large one, and we should resist the temptation to make Gratian an acquaintance of other well-known thinkers just because they were well known. The *Decretum* reveals greater links to anonymous works associated with the school of Laon than to the writings of Abelard. And Gratian exploits these anonymous works in a variety of ways, which reveal both his sophistication and his independence from Anselm of Laon and his school.

The sacraments (aside from penance and marriage) and liturgy were the third and last topic that this book considered. Both the sacraments and the liturgy occupy a prominent place in Gratian's formal sources though, as chapters 7 and 8 demonstrated, the first recension largely ignores these topics. Despite his interest in penitential theology, Gratian was for the most part not a sacramental theologian and to even less of an extent a liturgical theologian. The first recension, in fact, ignores not only liturgical theology, but even liturgical law. The incorporation of the sacraments and liturgy into the *Decretum* was the work of the redactor of the second recension and the compiler of *De consecratione* (if he was a different person), who went to great lengths to incorporate material on both sacraments and liturgy into Gratian's textbook.

The shared interest in adding material on the sacraments and especially the liturgy to the *Decretum,* chapter 8 argued, suggests that the same person or group of people was responsible for revising the distinctions and *causae* in the second recension and compiling *De consecratione.* So too, I also argued, do textual links between the revised *causae* and distinctions, on the one hand, and *De consecratione,* on the other hand. While the second recension appears to have been published initially without *De consecratione* (sometime before 1150), the treatise was appended shortly afterward, probably by the early 1150s, definitely by 1158.[7]

Finally, the contrasting attention given to the sacraments and liturgy in the two recensions provides strong support for Winroth's thesis of two (or more) Gratians. Based above all on the contrasting use of Roman law in the two recensions, Winroth argued that

7. See pp. 277–80.

the two recensions have different authors. Where the first recension displays only a rudimentary knowledge of Roman law, the second recension displays a much more sophisticated grasp.[8] The contrasting attitude toward the sacraments and liturgy is another major difference, one that may well reflect fundamentally different visions of what the *Decretum* should be. For Gratian, the *Decretum* was primarily a *Concordia discordantium canonum*, a textbook designed to show students how to resolve real and apparent contradictions in the canons. For the redactor of the second recension, the *Decretum* was more a comprehensive collection of canon law. Of course, the contrasting attitudes toward the sacraments and liturgy may also reflect conflicting visions of what the emerging discipline of canon law should encompass. For Gratian, canon law was to be a discipline concerned primarily with the ecclesiastical hierarchy, church administration, and the internal forum. For the redactor of the second recension, Christian worship was also integral.

Regarding both the sacraments and the liturgy, then, it was Gratian who was more the radical, the redactor of the second recension who was more the conservative. Far from being the last great representative of Rudolph Sohm's old catholic sacramental law, Gratian tried to construct a new science of canon law on a theological but non-sacramental basis. This book began as a quest for Gratian the theologian. It ended with Gratian the jurist. That result should come as no surprise, as Gratian the theologian and Gratian the jurist were one and the same.

8. Winroth, *The Making of Gratian's Decretum*, 146–92.

Appendix

Augustinus in libro vite is extant in three manuscripts:

1. F = Florence, Biblioteca Medicea Laurenziana, Plut.V sin 7, fols. 76va–78rb.[1]
2. V = Vatican, Biblioteca Apostolica Vaticana, Vat. lat. 1350, fols. 56r–v (as items 48–53 of the appendix to the canonical *Collection in Fifty Books*).[2]
3. Z = Zurich, Zentralbibliothek, C 111 (390), fols. 101rb–102ra.[3]

Only F contains the treatise in its entirety. V contains just the beginning, while Z contains the beginning and middle. The text as preserved in V was probably copied from a manuscript of the *Sententiae magistri A.* that, like F and Z, contained additional texts on penance, since the immediately preceding items in V derive from the marriage tract of the *Sententiae magistri A.*[4] None of the manuscripts descends directly from any of the others.

The following edition of *Augustinus in libro uite* contains two apparatuses: an apparatus lectionum keyed to line numbers and an apparatus fontium keyed to footnotes.

1. For a description of the manuscript, see Maas, *Liber sententiarum*, 51–53; Wei, "*Deus non habet initium uel terminum*, 1–118, at 9 (under siglum Fp).

2. On the manuscript and canonical collection, see Roberto Bellini, "Un abrégé del Decreto di Burcardo di Worms: La collezione canonica in 20 libri (ms. Vat. lat. 1350)," *Apollinaris* 69 (1996): 119–95; Fowler-Magerl, *Clavis*, 179–80.

3. For a description of the manuscript, see Maas, *Liber sententiarum*, 49–51.

4. Items 32–47 of the appendix to the *Collection in Fifty Books* correspond to items 1–14, 27, 31, 32, 41, 62, 68, and 69 of the *Sententiae magistri A.*'s marriage tract. I follow the numbering in Reinhardt, *Die Ehelehre der Schule des Anselm von Laon*, 167–244.

[The Three Types of Penance]

Augustinus in libro uite doctus III. descripsit modos. Quorum primus est qui nouum hominem parturit donec per baptismum salutare fiat ablatio preteritorum peccatorum.

2 primus] prima Z 3 nouum] totum F baptismum] uel *male add.* F ablatio] oblatio F 4 peccatorum] *om.* Z

Secundus modus est cuius actio est subeunda per totam istam uitam qua in carne mortali degimus perpetua humilitate supplicationis, quia nemo uitam eternam incorruptibilem immortalemque desiderat, nisi eum uite huius temporalis, corruptibilis mortalisque peniteat. Ex cuius penitentie dolore erupit ille qui dixit: "Ve mihi quia peregrinatio mea longinqua facta est."[1] Sanctus etiam Iob non ait esse temptationem in hac uita, sed hanc uitam esse temptationem, dicens: "Numquid temptatio est uita humana super terram?"[2] Ideo miser homo tot mutationibus circumuallatus in hac uita superbire non debet, quamuis per baptismum iustificatus sit a prioribus peccatis, etiam si nichil committat, sed semper humilitatem seruare, que est disciplina Christiana.

Est tertius penitentie modus, cum de peccatis post baptismum perpetratis cordis contritio nos penitet. Non enim sic nascimur innouati per sanctificationem baptismi, ut ita statim deponamus carnis mortalitatem atque corruptionem, quemadmodum ibi deponimus preterita peccata. Et ideo fit illud quod quisque in se sentit, sicut ait Apostolus: "Corpus quod corrumpitur, aggrauat animam et deprimit terrena inhabitatio sensum multa cogitantem."[3] Ex hac tamen corruptione corporis quam ex peccato primi parentis patimur penam.

[Perfect Penance for Venial and Mortal Sins]

Dupliciter anima peccat post baptismum. Et quidem aut peccamus ex inuincibili necessitate et uenialiter, sicut est in potu et comestione, uerbo et risu ceterisque talibus de quibus quotiens cadimus, si totiens nos penitet et orationibus et elemosinis ea redimimus. Vere sunt ille penitentie et salubres. Vnde ait scriptura: "Iustus septies in die cadit et septies in die resurgit."[4] Que tamen si ultra modum coaceruamus, nos enecant et a complexu speciosi sponsi nos separant. Et enim ut massa ferri, sic nimio palearum onere aliquis potest opprimi.

Aut contra decalogum legis peccamus et criminose, ut in homicidio aut adulterio ceterisque talibus, de quibus dicitur: "Qui talia agunt regnum Dei

5 est$_1$] *om.* F actio est$_2$] actio F, actione Z (*male* actionē *legit*) istam uitam] ista V qua] qui Z **6** quia] et *praem.* V **7** immortalemque] immortalem V **7–8** huius uite eum *tr.* V **9** erupit] erumpit V **10–11** in — temptationem$_2$] *om. ob homoiotel.* Z **14** sed] *om.* F seruare] seruet F **16** Est] Item *praem. rubr.* Z tertius] tertium V modus penitentie *tr.* F **18** ita] istam F **20** in] *add. supra lin.* Z in se] *om.* V **21** inhabitatio] inhabitaturo V cogitantem multa *tr.* V **25** Et] E V quidem] quod Z **26** comestione] in *praem.* V **30** coaceruamus] coaceramur V enecant] necamus V **31** separant] separat V **33** et] *om.* F in] inter Z, *om.* F **34** ceterisque] -que *add. supra lin.* Z

1. Ps 119:5.
2. Job 7:1.
3. Ws 9:15.
4. Prov 24:16.

non possidebunt."[5] Quorum criminalium non, ut uenialium, plures penitentias perfectas et salubres agere ualemus, si plura committimus, ut approbat ipsius penitentie descriptio que ait: "Vera et perfecta penitentia est preterita mala flere et flenda iterum non committere."[6] Non effici potest ut aliquis peniteat perfecte fornicationis et sit adulter, aut furti et sit sacrilegus, aut homicidii et sit periurus. Vnde Gregorius: "Nec iam bona sunt opera que subortis prauis aliis operibus coinquinantur. Hinc per Salomonem dicitur: 'Qui in uno offenderit, multa bona perdet.' Hinc Iacobus dicit: 'Quicumque totam legem seruauerit, offendit autem in uno, factus est omnium reus.'"[7] Item Gregorius: "Quisquis uirtute aliqua pollere creditur, tunc ueraciter pollet, cum uitiis ex alia parte non subiacet. Nam si ex aliquo uitiis subditur, nec hoc est solidum, ubi stare putabatur. Vna itaque uirtus sine aliis aut omnino nulla est aut imperfecta."[8] Vnde Apostolus: "Modicum fermentum totam massam corrumpit."[9] Origenes etiam super Leuiticum ait: "In grauioribus criminibus semel tantum penitentie conceditur locus. Ista uero communia que frequenter incurrimus, semper penitentiam <recipiunt>, nec aliquando interciditur de huiusmodi commissis penitudinem gerere."[10] Ambrosius in libro penitentie prorsus eadem uerba Origenis aut actu aut casu ponit.[11] Igitur et aliis circumfultus rationibus, ut confiteor unum Deum, unam fidem, unum baptisma, sic confiteor unam ueram et perfectam penitentiam.

[Arguments for the Return of Sins]

Horum uerborum occasione quod non sit penitentia perfecta nisi una, audio quosdam sapientes potius subtiliter quam utiliter astruere quod si quis crimen commiserit et ex eo penituerit et iussione sacerdotis satisfecerit, si quando ut aliud crimen committat acciderit et absque penitentia eius obierit, eque in eternum et sine ulla penarum remissione de eo unde satisfecerit, ut ex eo unde non penituit punietur, sic argumentantes.

---

36 ualemus] ualeamus F **37** ipsius] temporis V est] *om.* Z **38** iterum] *om.* F **40** bona iam *tr.* Z **41** aliis prauis *tr.* F coinquinantur] inquinantur F **42** Hinc] huic Z dicit] ait F **44** Gregorius] *om.* Z **45** aliquo] aliqua V **46** est *om.* F **48** Origenes] Origes Z **50** penitentiam] penitet F <recipiunt> *correxi ex* Origen **50–51** nec — gerere *om.* Origen **51–178** Ambrosius — Explicit] *om.* V **51** commissis] commissi V **52** casu] causu F **56** penitentia] *add. supra lin.* Z **58** iussione] iussionem F **59** ut] *om.* Z **61** non] *om.* Z punietur] puniretur Z

---

5. Gal 5:21.

6. Cf. Pseudo-Ambrose, *Sermones Sancto Ambrosio hactenus ascripti* 25.1, PL 17, 655.

7. Gregory, *De moralia in Iob* 19.21.32, ed. Marcus Adriaen, CCSL 143A (Turnhout: Brepols, 1979), 982.7–11. The biblical quotations are Eccl 9:18 and Jam 2:10.

8. Gregory, *De moralia in Iob* 22.1.2, ed. Adriaen, CCSL 143, 1092.14–17 and 1093.34–35.

9. Gal 5:9.

10. Origen, *Homiliae in Leviticum* 15.2, ed. W. A. Baehrens, Die griechischen christlichen Schriftsteller der ersten drei Jahrhunderte 29 (Leipzig: Hinrichs, 1920), 489.19–22.

11. Cf. Ambrose, *De penitentia* 2.10.95–96, ed. Otto Faller, CSEL 73 (Vienna: F. Tempsky, 1955), 200.34–201.41.

[A1] Illa prioris criminis que dicta est penitentia aut est uera aut est falsa. Vera autem non est, quoniam futuri cautelam non habuerit. Ergo falsa. Sed falsam penitentiam penarum remissio non comitatur.

[A2] Item. Plurimorum criminum una fit penitentia tantum. Sed qui in uno crimine moritur, absque eius penitentia quantumcumque prius satisfecerit, unam penitentiam non habet. Ergo nulla. At ubi nulla est penitentia, nulla fit remissio.

[A3] Item afferunt euangelii auctoritatem, ubi habetur parabola de domino qui dimiserat omne debitum seruo suo, qui nolens dimittere debitum conserui sui, coactus reddere omne debitum quod dominus ei dimiserat usque ad ultimum quadrantem.[12] Quod significat si nos serui Dei qui dimisit nobis omnia peccata nostra, non dimiserimus fratri nostro peccanti in nobis, in districto illo examine tam de originalibus quam de actualibus usque ad minutum peccatum puniemur.

[A4] Addunt quoque illud quod Augustinus ait, scilicet quod quisque malus non solum sua, sed etiam parentum peccata luet, que per dilectionem fuerit imitatus.

[A5] Hec omnia Ezechielis auctoritate confirmant, qui dicit: "Si iustus peccauerit, omnium iustitiarum suarum obliuiscar."[13]

[Refutation of the Return of Sins]

His et aliis pluribus affirmant illam odibilem Dei seueritatem, ut si quis pluribus criminibus infectus sit et ex eis satisfecerit, sed in uno crimine inpenitens mortuus fuerit, eque ex omnibus penam sustinebit. Nos uero Deum pium, misericordem atque iustum credentes, sancte et religiose predicamus de quibuscumque criminibus pro modo peccati iussione sacerdotis homo in hoc mundo satisfecerit, ad quamcumque partem arbor ceciderit, de illis amplius non punietur. Nec obsunt tam pie sententie multiplices supradicte oppositiones iustitia defendente.

[Refutation of A1]

Nam uera est propositio que dicit falsam esse penitentiam ubi non est cautela de futuro. Sed falsa est assumptio que dicit: Sed remissio penarum non

---

65 Item] SItem F **69** parabola] *om.* Z **71–72** quod dominus ei dimiserat usque ad ultimum quadrantem *cancell. ante* seruo Z **74** districto] stricto Z **76–178** Addunt — Explicit] *om.* Z **91** propositio] prepositio F

---

12. Cf. Mt 18:23–34.
13. Ezek 18:24.

sequitur falsam penitentiam. A quocumque quidem remouetur una pars descriptionis, non illico et omnes partes remouentur. Veluti si cautelam de futuro remouetur ab aliquo necessario remouetur ab eodem et preteritorum fletus. Verbi gratia. Sanum esse dicamus qui preteritas egritudines curauit et futuris cautelam adhibuit. Si forte aliquis sanus ceterum curatis uulneribus uno superaddito moritur, concludat qui uult eum non ideo bene preterita curasse.

[Refutation of A2]

Iterum. Potest quis esse homicida et non adulter, adulter et non periurus. Si quis hoc mihi concedit, oportet ut credat aliquem homicidam posse penitere de adulterio et non periurio. Nec obest nobis illud "qui in uno legem offendit, omnium est reus" quod secundum unam sententiam sic intelligimus, qui uno crimine reus est ita perpetuo damnabilis est, sicut ille qui ex decalogo reus est.

Sed quod Gregorius ait, "nec bona sunt opera que malis inquinantur" et Salomon "qui in uno offendit multa bona perdit"[14] et quod non sit penitentia nisi una et si non una ergo nulla, hec tria una falce resecamus: quantum ad salutem uera sunt.

[Refutation of A3]

Oppositiones etiam euangelii quod seruus nolens dimittere conseruo suo dominus repetit omnia peccata, ita soluimus: Deus non puniet in seruo peccata que ipse puniuit, teste Augustino qui ait: "que tu punis, Deus non punit."[15] Sed de duritia quam habuit in conseruo, ita eterne puniet eum ac si nullum peccatum ei dimisisset nullumque bonum fecisset.

[Refutation of A4]

Iterum. Quod Deus minatur peccata parentum punire in tertiam et quartam generationem sane intelligendum est. Ipse enim ait: "Anima patris mea est et anima filii mea est."[16] Et alibi: "Quisque suum onus portabit."[17] Hinc intelligimus si quis bonus est, nec parentum peccata diligit, de peccatis parentum puniri non timet. Si uero per dilectionem imitatus fuerit parentum peccata, punietur ex eis. Quod non solum de peccatis parentum uerum est, sed etiam quorumcumque peccata diligimus, puniemur ex eis. Sed ideo apponitur in tertiam et quartam generationem. Quod si ita est, non uideo

---

95 necessario] non cessatio F

---

14. Eccl 9:18.
15. *Non inveni.*
16. Ezek 18:4.
17. Gal 6:5.

quid attineat ad hoc quod malus iterum debeat puniri de peccatis que ipsemet puniuit in se.

[Refutation of A5]

Iterum. Illud Ezechielis: "Si iustus peccauerit, omnes iustitias eius obliuiscar,"[18] sic intelligimus. Si iustus peccauerit criminaliter, omnis eius iustitia non prohibebit eum ab eterna ira.

[Proof of Author's Position]

Ita debilitatis eorum argumentis, iustitia cooperante, nos non detrahentes mortuis, nec inuidentes uiuis, Deum neque iniustum neque crudelem, neque malefidum credentes tenemus et firmiter credimus quod qui hic sua peccata punierit, ulterius inde non punietur. Magis hac magis ualet apud me illorum auctoritas qui Deum sue creature misericordem ubique predicant. Vnde Ieronimus super Aggeum prophetam: "Si quando uideris inter multa opera peccatorum facere quemquam aliqua que iusta sunt, non est tam iniustus Deus ut propter multa mala paucorum obliuiscatur bonorum."[19] Vnde alio: "Quecumque seminauerit homo, hec et metet."[20] Quod Gregorius euidenter exprimit cum dicit: "Nullum bonum irremuneratum, nullum malum inpunitum."[21] Si forte aduersarii inportune instent et dicant nullum esse bonum nisi quod ad salutem eternam ducat, confunditur exemplo ibidem apposito. Ait "nullum bonum irremuneratum, nullum malum inpunitum,"[22] sicut est euidens in obstetricibus que obstetricabant Hebreas in Egipto, que contra regium edictum timentes Deum commote pietate mares quos perimere iusserat seruabant. Quod cum rex impius percepisset querens quare hoc facerent, responderunt quod ipse non obseruarent mares, sed Hebrehe callide antequam uenirent ad eas parturiebant. Mentientes regi propter Dei timorem, quo in facto pie fuerunt atque impie, pie propter Dei timorem, impie propter mendacium.[23] Et ideo de mendacio punite, de pietate sunt remunerate, quia dedit eis Deus domos. Ecce remuneratum bonum, nec tale bonum quod duceret ad eternam salutem.

Iterum. Si alicuius penitentia quia imperfecta est, quoniam in futuro sibi non cauit, ideo omnimodo uana et nullius utilitatis reputanda est, nec eius

138 quemquam] quequam F 149 uenirent] conuenirent F^{ac}

18. Ezek 18:24.
19. Jerome, *Commentarius in Aggeum* 1:6, ed. Marcus Adriaen, CCSL 76A (Turnhout: Brepols, 1964), 720.244–47.
20. Gal 6:7.
21. Augustine, *Sermones ad fratres* 41, PL 40, 1315.
22. Ibid.
23. Ex 1:15–21.

satisfactio aliquod pondus aliquamue utilitatem conferre ualet. Sed imperfecte penitentie satisfactio quia de futuro sibi non cauit, multum tamen ponderis atque utilitatis habet, quia undecumque iuste pro quantitate satisfacimus quantumcumque deinceps criminose peccemus, de preteritis satisfactis, ulterius ecclesia satisfactionem iubere non presumit. Credimus ideo quod de satisfactis ulterius non puniemur. Quoniam que ecclesia hic ligat, ligata erunt, et que hic soluit, soluta erunt. Prodest igitur penitentia ideo imperfecta, quia de futuro sibi non cauit.

Nunc breuiter quid super hac sententia sentiam concludo sic. Venialium peccatorum assidue penitentie ueraces et salubres sunt. Criminalium in unoquoque una solum et perfecta est penitentia. Si aliquem tamen acciderit plura committere criminalia, que ex illis in hac uita ipse punit uel Deus punit, in futuro non punientur. Que aliquis hic <non> punit et Deus non punit, punientur in futuro. Et licet dicam que Deus punit hic non punientur in futuro, non propterea abnego quod pene quorumdam hic incipiant sed non hic finiantur. Id autem ago, quod Deus qui uerus est medicus pro quantitate peccati hic urit, secat, purgat, ulterius non secabit, non uret, non purgabit. Et si ea que Deus punit hic aliquando nobis ignorantibus non puniet in futuro, multo magis que nosmet punimus Deus non puniet. Sicut ait Ieronimus: "Non iudicabit Deus bis in idipsum, in tribulatione."[24] Rogo te dulcis amice, ut hec qualiacumque sint animo benigno accipias. Si qua meliora habes, mecum dulciter communices.

Explicit.

---

167 punit^{1}] ponit F^{ac} 168 <non> *scripsi* (*cf.* linn.124–26 et 173–74)   170 quod] que

---

24. Nah 1:9.

Bibliography

Manuscripts

Admont, Stiftsbibliothek, 23 and 43
Barcelona, Arxiu de la Corona d'Aragó, Santa María de Ripoll 78
Cologne, Dombibliothek, 7 and 25
Erfurt, Wissenschaftliche Allgemein-Bibliothek, Ampl. q.117
Florence, Biblioteca Medicea Laurenziana, Plut. V sin. 7
Florence, Biblioteca Nazionale Centrale, Conv. Soppr. A.1.402
London, British Library, Royal 9 A viii
Mantua, Biblioteca Comunale, 266 (C.l.4)
Munich, Bayerische Staatsbibliothek, Clm 2598, 4574, 5257a, 6231, 22272, 27337
Paris, BNF, lat. 3884 I-II, fol. 1, lat. 15387; nouvelles acquisitions latines 1761
St. Gall, Stiftsbibliothek, 673
Vatican, BAV, Vat. Borgh. 71; Vat. lat. 1345, 1348, 1350
Zurich, Zentralbibliothek, C 111 (390)

Printed Primary Sources

Bible

Biblia latina cum glossa ordinaria: Facsimile Reprint of the Editio princeps: Adolph Rusch of Strassburg 1480/81. Edited by Margaret T. Gibson and Karlfried Froehlich. 4 vols. Turnhout: Brepols, 1992.

Biblia sacra iuxta vulgatam versionem. Edited by Robert Weber. 4th ed. Stuttgart: Deutsche Bibelgesellschaft, 1994.

Glossa ordinaria in canticum canticorum. Edited by Mary Dove. CCCM 170. Turnhout: Brepols, 1997.

Councils and Capitularies

Capitula episcoporum 1. Edited by Peter Brommer. MGH Capit. episc. 1. Hanover: MGH, 1984.

Capitularia regum Francorum. Edited by Alfred Boretius and Victor Krause. MGH Capit. 2. Hanover: MGH, 1897.

Concilia aevi Karolini [742–814]. Edited by Albert Werminghoff. MGH Conc. 2.1. Hanover: MGH, 1906.

Concilia aevi Karolini [819–42]. Edited by Albert Werminghoff. MGH Conc. 2.2. Hanover: MGH, 1908.

Concilia Africae a. 345–a. 525. Edited by Charles Munier. CCSL 149. Turnhout: Brepols, 1974.

Concilia Galliae a. 314–a. 506. Edited by Charles Munier. CCSL 148. Turnhout: Brepols, 1963.

Concilia Galliae a. 511–a. 695. Edited by Charles de Clercq. CCSL 148A. Turnhout: Brepols, 1963.

Conciliorum oecumenicorum generaliumque decreta: Editio critica 1: *The Oecumenical Councils from Nicaea I to Nicaea II (325–787)*. Edited by Giuseppe Alberigo et al. Corpus Christianorum. Turnhout: Brepols, 2006.

Concilios Visigóticos e Hispano-Romanos. Edited by José Vives. Barcelona: Consejo Superiod de Investigaciones Científicas, Instituto Enrique Flórez, 1963.

Concilium Romanum [875]. Edited by Friedrich Maasen. "Eine römische Synode aus der Zeit von 871 bis 878." *Sitzungsberichte der kaiserlichen Akademie der Wissenschaften, Philosophisch-historische Classe* 91 (1878): 773–92, at 780–92.

Decrees of the Ecumenical Councils. Edited by Norman P. Tanner. 2 vols. London: Sheed and Ward, 1990.

Ecclesiae Occidentalis Monumenta iuris antiquissima 2.1–3. Edited by Cuthbert Hamilton Turner. Oxford: Clarendon Press, 1907–39.

Die Konzilien Deutschlands und Reichsitaliens 916–1001 1: *916–960*. Edited by Ernst-Dieter Hehl. MGH Conc. 6.1. Hanover: MGH, 1987.

Church Fathers and Ecclesiastical Writers

Abelard, Peter. *Capitula haeresum Petri Abaelardi*. Edited by E. M. Buytaert. CCCM 12. Turnhout: Brepols, 1969.

———. *Peter Abelard's Ethics*. Edited and translated by D. E. Luscombe. Oxford: Clarendon Press, 1971.

———. *Sententie Magistri Petri Abaelardi*. Edited by D. E. Luscombe. CCCM 14. Turnhout: Brepols, 2006.

———. *Sic et non: A Critical Edition*. Edited by Blanche B. Boyer and Richard McKeon. Chicago: University of Chicago Press, 1976.

Ambrose. *De apologia prophetae David*. Edited by Karl Schenkl. CSEL 32.2. Vienna: F. Tempsky, 1887.

———. *De penitentia*. Edited by Otto Faller. CSEL 73. Vienna: F. Tempsky, 1955.

———. *Expositio de psalmo CXVIII*. Edited by Michael Petschenig. CSEL 62. Vienna: F. Tempsky, 1913.

———. *Expositio evangelii secundum Lucam*. Edited by Marcus Adriaen. CCSL 14. Turnhout: Brepols, 1957.

Anselm of Laon. *Sententiae*. Edited by Lottin, *Psychologie et morale*, 5:19–142.

Augustine. *De adulterinis coniugiis*. Edited by Joseph Zycha. CSEL 41. Vienna: F. Tempsky, 1900.

———. *De bono coniugali*. Edited by Joseph Zycha. CSEL 41. Vienna: F. Tempsky, 1900.

———. *De correptione et gratia*. Edited by Georges Folliet. CSEL 92. Vienna: Verlag der österreichischen Akademie der Wissenschaften, 2000.

———. *De doctrina christiana*. Edited by Joseph Martin. CCSL 32. Turnhout: Brepols, 1962.

———. *De nuptiis et concupiscentia*. Edited by Carol Urba and Joseph Zycha. CSEL 42. Vienna: F. Tempsky, 1902.

———. *Epistulae*. Edited by Klaus D. Daur. CCSL 31–31B. Turnhout: Brepols, 2004–9.

———. *In Iohannis evangelium Tractatus CXXIV*. Edited by Radbod Willems. CCSL 36. Turnhout: Brepols, 1954.

———. *Sermones ad fratres*. PL 40, 1233–1358.

Basil. *De spiritu sancto*. PG 32, 67–218.

Bede. *In Lucae evangelium expositio*. Edited by David Hurst. CCSL 120. Turnhout: Brepols, 1960.

Bernold of Constance. *De excommunicatis vitandis, de reconciliatione lapsorum et de fontibus iuris ecclesiastici (Libellus X)*. Edited by Doris Stöckly. MGH Fontes iuris 15. Hanover: MGH, 2000.

Bonaventure. *Commentarium in quattuor libros Sententiarum*. Edited by Collegium S. Bonaventurae. S. Bonaventurae Opera omnia. 11 vols. Ad Claras Aquas (Quarracchi): Ex typographia Collegii S. Bonaventurae, 1882–1902.

Cassiodorus. *Expositio psalmorum*. Edited by Marcus Adriaen. CCSL 97–98. Turnhout: Brepols, 1958.

Gregory the Great. *Dialogi*. Edited by Adalbert de Vogüé. *Dialogues*. 3 vols. Paris: Éditions du Cerf, 1978–80.

———. *Gregorii I papae Registrum epistolarum*. Edited by Paul Ewald and Ludwig Hartmann. MGH Epp. 1. Berlin: MGH, 1891.

———. *Homiliae in euangelia*. Edited by Raymond Étaix. CCSL 141. Turnhout: Brepols, 1999.

———. *Homiliae in Ezechielem*. Edited by Marcus Adriaen. CCSL 142. Turnhout: Brepols, 1971.

———. *Moralia in Iob*. Edited by Marcus Adriaen. CCSL 143–143B. Turnhout: Brepols, 1979–85.

———. *Regula pastoralis*. Edited by Floribert Rommel. Sources Chrétiennes 381. Paris: Éditions du Cerf, 1992.

Hincmar of Reims. *Epistolae Karolini aevi (VI): Hincmari archiepiscopi Remensis epistolae*. Edited by Ernst Perels. MGH Epp. 8. Berlin: MGH, 1939.

Hugh of St. Victor. *De sacramentis*. PL 175, 173–618. In *Hugh of St. Victor on the Sacraments of the Christian Faith: De sacramentis*, translated by Roy J. Deferrari. Cambridge, Mass.: Medieval Academy of America, 1951.

Isidore of Seville. *Etymologiarum sive Originum libri xx*. 2 vols. Edited by W. M. Lindsay. Oxford: Oxford University Press, 1911.

———. *De ecclesiasticis officiis*. Edited by Christopher M. Lawson. CCSL 113. Turnhout: Brepols, 1989.

Jerome. *Commentarius in Aggeum*. Edited by Marcus Adriaen. CCSL 76A. Turnhout: Brepols, 1964.

———. *Commentarius in epistulam Pauli Apostoli ad Ephesios*. PL 26, 439–554.

———. *Commentarius in epistulam Pauli Apostoli ad Titum*. Edited by Federica Bucchi. CCSL 77C. Turnhout: Brepols, 2003.

———. *Commentarii in prophetas minores*. Edited by Marcus Adriaen. CCSL 76A. Turnhout: Brepols, 1964.

———. *Epistola adversus Iovinianum*. PL 23, 211–338.

John Chrysostom. *Homiliae in epistolam ad Hebreos*. PG 63, 10–456.

John of Salisbury. *Historia Pontificalis—Memoirs of the Papal Court*. Edited and translated by Marjorie Chibnall. London: Clarendon Press, 1956.

———. *Policraticus*. Edited by K. S. B. Keats-Rohan. CCCM 118. Turnhout: Brepols, 1993.

Leo the Great. *Tractatus septem et nonaginta*. Edited by Antoine Chavasse. CCSL 138. Turnhout: Brepols, 1973.

Liber Quare. Edited by Georg Polycarpus Götz. CCCM 60. Turnhout: Brepols, 1983.

Origen. *Homiliae in Leviticum*. Edited by W. A. Baehrens. Die griechischen christlichen Schriftsteller der ersten drei Jahrhunderte 29. Leipzig: Hinrichs, 1920.

Otto of Freising. *Gesta Friderici Imperatoris*. Edited by Georg Heinrich Pertz. MGH SS 20. Hanover: MGH, 1868.

Patrologiae Cursus Completus, Series Graeca. Edited by J.-P. Migne. 161 vols. Paris: Imprimerie Catholique, 1857–66.

Patrologiae Cursus Completus, Series Latina. Edited by J.-P. Migne. 217 vols. Paris: Imprimerie Catholique, 1841–55.

Peter Lombard. *Magistri Petri Lombardi Parisiensis episcopi sententiae in IV libris distinctae*. 3rd rev. ed. Edited by Ignatius Brady. Spicilegium Bonaventurianum 4. Grottaferrata: Editiones Collegii S. Bonaventurae ad Claras Aquas, 1971.

Peter of Poitiers. *Quinque libri sententiarum*. PL 211, 791–1280.

———. *Quinque libri sententiarum*. In *Sententiae Petri Pictaviensis*, edited by Philip S. Moore and Marthe Dulong. 2 vols. Notre Dame, Ind.: University of Notre Dame Press, 1940–50.

Peter the Chanter. *Summa de sacramentis et animae consiliis*. Edited by Jean-Albert Dugauquier. Louvain: Nauwelaerts, 1954–67.

Placidus of Nonantula. *Liber de honore ecclesiae*. Edited by Lotkar von Heinemann and Ernst Sackur. MGH LdL 2:566–639. Hanover: MGH, 1892.

Prosper of Aquitaine. *Pro Augustino Responsiones ad Capitula obiectionum gallorum calumniantium*. PL 51, 155–74.

Pseudo-Ambrose. *Sermones Sancto Ambrosio hactenus ascripti*. PL 17, 603–734.

Pseudo-Augustine. *De vera et falsa penitentia*. PL 40, 1113–30.

———. *Sermones supposititios*. PL 39, 1735–2354.

Pseudo-Jerome. *De septem ordinibus ecclesiae*. Edited by Athanasius Walter Kalff. Wurzburg: n.p., 1938.

Robert of Torigni. *The Chronicles of the Reigns of Stephen, Henry II, and Richard I 4: The Chronicle of Robert of Torigni*. Edited by Richard Howlett. Memorials of Great Britain and Ireland during the Middle Ages ["Rolls Series"] 82. London: Longman, 1889.

Roland of Bologna. *Die Sentenzen Rolands, nachmals Papstes Alexander III.* Edited by Ambrosius M. Gietl. Freiburg im Breisgau: Herder, 1891; reprinted in Amsterdam: RODOPI, 1969.

Diplomatic Documents

Gloria, Andrea, ed. *Codice diplomatico padovano.* Monumenti storici publicati dalla R. deputazione veneta di storia patria 1st ser., Documenti 4. Venice, 1879.

Laws and Codifications

Code of Canon Law: Latin-English Edition. Washington, D.C.: Canon Law Society of America, 1983.

Corpus iuris civilis. Edited by Theodore Mommsen et al. 3 vols. Berlin: Weidmann, 1872.

Canonical Collections and Canonistic Commentaries

Alger of Liège. *De misericordia et iustitia.* Edited by Kretzschmar, *Alger von Luttichs Traktat,* 187–375.

Anselm of Lucca. *Anselmi episcopi Lucensis collectio canonum: Una cum collectione minore.* Edited by Friedrich Thaner. Innsbruck: Wagner, 1906–15; reprinted in Aalen: Scientia, Verlag, 1960.

Burchard of Worms. *Decretorum libri XX.* Edited by Gerard Fransen and Theo Kölzer. Cologne, 1548; reprinted in Aalen: Scientia Verlag, 1992.

Collectio canonum in V libris (Lib. I–III). Edited by Mario Fornassari. CCCM 6. Turnhout: Brepols, 1970.

Collectio canonum trium librorum. Edited by Joseph Motta. 2 vols. MIC.B 8/I-II. Vatican City: BAV, 2005–8.

Gratian. *Corpus iuris canonici* 1: *Decretum magistri Gratiani.* Edited by Emil Friedberg. Leipzig: Veit, 1879; reprinted in Graz: Akademische Druck- u. Verlagsanstalt, 1959.

———. *Corpus iuris canonici emendatum et notis illustratum una cum glossis Gregorii XIII pont. max. iussu editum.* 3 parts in 4 vols. Rome, 1582.

———. *Décret de Gratien: Causes 27 à 36; Le Mariage.* Edited by Jean Werckmeister. *RDC* 58–59 (2011).

———. *The Treatise on Laws (Decretum DD. 1–20) with the Ordinary Gloss.* Translated by Augustine Thompson and James Gordley. Washington, D.C.: The Catholic University of America Press, 1993.

Gregory of San Grisogono. *Polycarpus.* Edited by Carl Erdmann. Unpublished typescript. http://www.mgh.de/datenbanken/kanonessammlung-polycarp/.

Ivo of Chartres. *Decretum.* https://ivo-of-chartres.github.io/decretum.html.

——— (Pseudo-). *Panormia.* https://ivo-of-chartres.github.io/panormia.html.

——— (Pseudo-). *Tripartita.* https://ivo-of-chartres.github.io/tripartita.html.

Liber canonum diversorum sanctorum patrum sive Collectio in CLXXXIII titulos digesta. Edited by Giuseppe Motta. Vatican City: BAV, 1988.

Martin of Braga. *Martini episcopi Bracarensis opera omnia*. Edited by C. W. Barlow. Papers and Monographs of the American Academy in Rome 12. New Haven, Conn.: Yale University Press, 1950.

Paucapalea. *Summa decretorum*. Edited by Johann Friedrich von Schulte. *Die Summa des Paucapalea über das Decretum Gratiani*. Giessen: E. Roth, 1890.

Peter of Blois. *Petri Blesensis opusculum de distinctionibus in canonum interpretatione adhibendis sive, ut auctor voluit, speculum iuris canonici*. Edited by Theophilus Augustus Reimarus. Berlin: Sumtibus G. Reimeri, 1887.

Poenitentiale Valicellanum III. Edited by Wasserschleben, *Die Bußordnungen der abendländischen Kirche*, 682–88.

Pseudo-Isidore. *Die Capitula Angilramni: Eine prozessrechtliche Fälschung Pseudoisidors*. Edited by Karl-Georg Schon. MGH Studien und Texte 39. Hanover: MGH, 2006.

———. *Decretales Pseudo-Isidorianae et Capitula Angilramni*. Edited by Paul Hinschius. Leipzig: B. Tauchnitz, 1863.

Regino of Prüm. *Das Sendhandbuch des Regino von Prüm = Reginonis Prumiensis Libri duo de synodalibus causis et disciplinis ecclesiasticis*. Edited and translated by Wilfried Hartmann. Darmstadt: Wissenschaftliche Buchgesellschaft, 2004.

Rufinus. *Die Summa decretorum des Rufinus*. Edited by Heinrich Singer. Paderborn: Schöningh, 1902.

Sicard of Cremona. *Summa decretorum* ad De cons. D.2. Edited by Kennedy, "The Moment of Consecration and the Elevation of the Host," 132.

Simon of Bisignano. *Summa in Decretum Simonis Bisinianensis*. Edited by Pierre V. Aimone. MIC.A 8. Vatican City: BAV, 2014.

Statuta ecclesiae antiqua. Edited by Charles Munier. *Les Statuta ecclesiae antiqua: Édition—Études critiques*. Paris: Presses Universitaires de France, 1960.

Stephan of Tournai. *Die Summa des Stephanus Tornacensis über das Decretum Gratiani*. Edited by Johann Friedrich von Schulte. Giessen: E. Roth, 1891.

———. "Prologue" to *Summa decretorum*. Edited by Kalb, *Studien*, 113–20.

The Summa Parisiensis on the Decretum Gratiani. Edited by Terence Patrick McLaughlin. Toronto: Pontifical Institute of Medieval Studies, 1952.

Sentence Collections (Anonymous)

Baptizato homine. Edited by Wei, "Penitential Theology," 89–100.

Coniugium est secundum Isidorum. Edited by Franz Bliemetzrieder. "Théologie et théologiens de l'école épiscopale de Paris avant Pierre Lombard." *RTAM* 3 (1931): 273–91.

Cum omnia sacramenta. Edited by Bliemetzrieder, *Anselms von Laon Systematische Sentenzen*, 129–51.

De conditione angelica et humana. Edited by Lefèvre, "Le *De conditione angelica et humana*," 256–75.

Decretum dei fuit. Edited by Weisweiler, *Das Schrifttum*, 361–79.

Deus itaque summe. Edited by Wei, "The Sentence Collection *Deus non habet*," 39–118.

Deus non habet. Edited by Wei, "The Sentence Collection *Deus non habet*," 39–118.

In primis hominibus. Edited by Bernd Matecki, *Der Traktat In primis hominibus: Eine theologie- und kirchenrechtsgeschichtliche Untersuchung zu einem Ehetext der Schule von Laon aus dem 12. Jahrhundert*. Adnotationes in Ius Canonicum 20. Frankfurt am Main: Peter Lang, 2001.

Principium et causa. Edited by Bliemetzrieder, *Anselms von Laon Systematische Sentenzen*, 47–106.

Sententiae Atrebatenses. Edited by Lottin, *Psychologie et morale*, 5:400–440.

Sententiae Berolinenses. Edited by Stegmüller, "*Sententiae Berolinenses*," 39–61.

Summa sententiarum. PL 176, 41–174.

Ut autem hoc evidenter. Edited by Wei, "A Twelfth-Century Treatise," 31–50.

Secondary Sources

Aimone Braida, Pier Virginio. "Gratian, the Decretists, and Astrology." In *Proceedings of the Tenth International Congress of Medieval Canon Law*, edited by Pennington et al., 817–39.

Alteroche, Bernard d', et al., eds. *Mélanges en l'honneur d'Anne Lefebvre-Teillard*. Paris: Éditions Panthéon-Assas, 2009.

Alverny, Marie-Thérèse d'. "Translations and Translators." In *Renaissance and Renewal*, edited by Benson and Constable, 421–62.

Anciaux, Paul. *La théologie du sacrement de pénitence au XIIe siècle*. Louvain: E. Nauwelaerts, 1949.

Andrée, Alexander. "Anselm of Laon Unveiled: The *Glosae super Iohannem* and the Origins of the *Glossa ordinaria* on the Bible." *Mediaeval Studies* 73 (2011): 217–60.

———. *Gilbertus Universalis: Glossa ordinaria in Lamentationes Ieremie prophete; Prothemata et Liber I; A Critical Edition with an Introduction and a Translation*. Stockholm: Almqvist and Wiksell International, 2005.

Artonne, André. "L'influence du Décret de Gratien sur les statuts synodaux." *Studia Gratiana* 2 (1954): 643–56.

Austin, Greta. *Shaping Church Law Around the Year 1000: The Decretum of Burchard of Worms*. Farnham: Ashgate, 2009.

Aymans, Winfried, ed. *Fides et ius*. Regensburg: Friedrich Pustet, 1991.

Bachrach, David. "Confession in the Regnum Francorum (742–900)." *Journal of Ecclesiastical History* 54 (2003): 3–22.

Backus, Irena, ed. *The Reception of the Church Fathers in the West* 1: *From the Carolingians to the Maurists*. Leiden: Brill, 1997.

Barwig, Klaus, and Dieter R. Bauer, eds. *Asyl am heiligen Ort*. Ostfildern: Schwabenverlag, 1994.

Basdevant-Gaudemet, Brigitte. *Église et autorités: Études d'histoire de droit canonique médiéval*. Limoges: Presses Universitaires de Limoges, 2006.

———. "Les sources de droit romain en matière de procédure dans le Décret de Gratien." In Basdevant-Gaudemet, *Église et autorités*, 213–51.

Bauer, Andreas, and Karl H. L. Welker, eds. *Europa und seine Regionen: 2000 Jahre Rechtsgeschichte*. Cologne: Böhlau, 2007.

Bazàn, Bernardo C., et al., eds. *Les questions disputées et les questions quodlibé-*

tiques dans les facultés de théologie, de droit et de médecine. Typologie des Sources du Moyen Âge Occidental 44–45. Turnhout: Brepols, 1985.

Bellini, Roberto. "Un abrégé del Decreto di Burcardo di Worms: La collezione canonica in 20 libri (ms. Vat. lat. 1350)." *Apollinaris* 69 (1996): 119–95.

Bellomo, Manlio. *The Common Legal Past of Europe, 1000–1800*. Translated by Lydia G. Cochrane. Washington, D.C.: The Catholic University of America Press, 1995.

Bellomo, Manlio, and Orazio Condorelli, eds. *Proceedings of the Eleventh International Congress of Medieval Canon Law*. MIC.C 12. Vatican City: BAV, 2006.

Benson, Robert, and Giles Constable, eds. *Renaissance and Renewal in the Twelfth Century*. Cambridge, Mass.: Harvard University Press, 1982.

Biller, Peter, and A. J. Minnis, eds. *Handling Sin: Confession in the Middle Ages*. Woodbridge: York Medieval Press, 1998.

Bliemetzrieder, Franz. *Anselms von Laon Systematische Sentenzen*. BGPM 18.2–3. Münster i. W.: Aschendorff, 1919.

Blomme, Robert. *La doctrine du péché dans les écoles théologiques de la première moitié du XIIe siècle*. Louvain: Publications Universitaires de Louvain, 1958.

Blumenthal, Uta-Renate. "Decrees and Decretals of Pope Paschal II in Twelfth-Century Canonical Collections." *BMCL* 10 (1980): 15–30. Reprinted in Blumenthal, *Papal Reform and Canon Law*, no. XII.

———. "The Papacy, 1024–1122." In *The New Cambridge Medieval History* 4.2: *c. 1024–c. 1198*, edited by Luscombe and Riley-Smith, 8–37.

———. *Papal Reform and Canon Law in the 11th and 12th Centuries*. Variorum Collected Studies Series CS618. Aldershot: Ashgate, 1998.

Bonet, José Martí. *Roma y las iglesias particulares en la concesión del palio a los obispos y arzobispos de Occidente: Año 513–1143*. Barcelona: Facultad de Teología de Barcelona, Editorial Herder, 1976.

Bras, Gabriel le. "Les Écritures dans le Décret de Gratien." *ZRG KA* 27 (1938): 47–80.

Bras, Gabriel le, Charles Lefebvre, and Jacqueline Rambaud, eds. *L'âge classique, 1140–1378: Sources et théories du droit*. Histoire du Droit et des Institutions de l'Église en Occident 7. Paris: Sirey, 1965.

Brasington, Bruce C., and Kathleen G. Cushing, eds. *Bishops, Texts and the Use of Canon Law around 1100: Essays in Honour of Martin Brett*. Aldershot: Ashgate, 2008.

Brown, Peter. "The Decline of the Empire of God: Amnesty, Penance, and the Afterlife from Late Antiquity to the Middle Ages." In *Last Things*, edited by Bynum and Freedman, 41–59.

Brundage, James A. *Law, Sex, and Christian Society in Medieval Europe*. Chicago: University of Chicago Press, 1987.

———. *Medieval Canon Law*. London: Longman, 1995.

Buchner, Jürgen. *Die Paleae im Dekret Gratians: Untersuchung ihrer Echtheit*. Rome: Pontificium Athenaeum Antonianum, 2000.

Bynum, Caroline Walker, and Paul Freedman, eds. *Last Things: Death and the Apocalypse in the Middle Ages*. Philadelphia: University of Pennsylvania Press, 2000.

Carpino, Francesco. *Il 'reditus peccatorum': Nelle collezioni canoniche e nei teologi fino ad Ugo da S. Vittore*. Rome: Istituto grafico tiberino, 1937.

Castillo Lara, R. J. *Studia in Honorem eminentissimi Cardinalis Alphonsi M. Stickler*. Studia et textus historiae iuris canonici 7. Rome: LAS, 1992.

Chodorow, Stanley. *Christian Political Theory and Church Politics in the Mid-Twelfth Century: The Ecclesiology of Gratian's Decretum*. Berkeley: University of California Press, 1972.

Colish, Marcia L. "Authority and Interpretation in Scholastic Theology." In Colish, *Studies in Scholasticism*, no. II.

———. *Peter Lombard*. 2 vols. Leiden: Brill, 1994.

———. *Studies in Scholasticism*. Variorum Collected Studies Series CS 838. Aldershot: Ashgate, 2006.

Condorelli, Orazio, ed. *"Panta rei": Studi dedicati a Manlio Bellomo*. 5 vols. Rome: Il Cigno Edizioni, 2004.

Congar, Yves. *A History of Theology*. Translated by Hunter Guthrie. New York: Doubleday, 1968.

Cooper, Kate, and Jeremy Gregory, eds. *Retribution, Repentance, and Reconciliation = Studies in Church History* 40 (2004).

Courtney, Francis. *Cardinal Robert Pullen: An English Theologian of the Twelfth Century*. Rome: Apud Aedes Universitatis Gregorianae, 1954.

Cowdrey, H. E. J. "Pope Gregory VII (1073–85) and the Liturgy." *The Journal of Theological Studies*, n.s. 55 (2004): 55–83.

Cubitt, Catherine. "Bishops, Priests and Penance in Late Saxon England." *Early Medieval Europe* 14 (2006): 41–63.

Cushing, Kathleen G. *Papacy and Law in the Gregorian Revolution: The Canonistic Work of Anselm of Lucca*. Oxford: Clarendon Press, 1998.

———. *Reform and Papacy in the Eleventh Century: Spirituality and Social Change*. Manchester: Manchester University Press, 2005.

Cushing, Kathleen G., and Richard F. Gyug, eds. *Ritual, Text and Law: Studies in Medieval Canon Law and Liturgy Presented to Roger E. Reynolds*. Aldershot: Ashgate, 2004.

De León, Enrique. *La "cognatio spiritualis" según Graciano*. Milan: Giuffrè, 1996.

Debil, A. "La première distinction du *De paenitentia* de Gratien." *Revue d'histoire ecclésiastique* 15 (1914): 251–73 and 442–55.

Delumeau, Jean. *Catholicism between Luther and Voltaire: A New View of the Counter-Reformation*. Translated by Jeremy Moiser. London: Burns and Oates, 1977.

Denifle, Heinrich. "Die Sentenzen Abaelards und die Bearbeitungen seiner Theologia vor Mitte des 12. Jhs." *Archiv für Literatur- und Kirchengeschichte des Mittelalters* 1 (1885): 402–624.

Dilcher, Gerhard, et al., eds. *Gewohnheitsrecht und Rechtsgewohnheiten im Mittelalter*. Schriften zur europäischen Verfassungsgeschichte 6. Berlin: Duncker and Humblot, 1992.

Dillon, John Noël. "Case Statements (Themata) and the Composition of Gratian's Cases." *ZRG KA* 92 (2006): 306–36.

Duggan, Charles. "Decretal Collections from Gratian's *Decretum* to the *Compila-*

tiones antiquae: The Making of the New Case Law." In *The History of Medieval Canon Law in the Classical Period*, edited by Hartmann and Pennington, 246–92.

Duchesne, Louis. *Le Liber pontificalis: Texte, introduction, et commentaire*. 2nd ed. 3 vols. Paris: E. Thorin, 1955–57.

Eichbauer, Melodie Harris. "St. Gall Stiftsbibliothek 673 and the Early Redactions of Gratian's *Decretum*." *BMCL* 27 (2007): 105–39.

Elze, Reinhard. "Gregor VII. und die römische Liturgie." *Studi Gregoriani* 13 (1989): 179–88.

Erdö, Peter, and Sz. Anzelm Szuromi, eds. *Proceedings of the Thirteenth International Congress of Medieval Canon Law*. MIC.C 14. Vatican City: BAV, 2010.

Ferreiro, Alberto. *Simon Magus in Patristic, Medieval, and Early Modern Traditions*. Leiden: Brill, 2005.

Finkenzeller, Josef. *Handbuch der Dogmengeschichte* 4.1: *Die Lehre von den Sakramenten im allgemeinen: Von der Schrift bis zur Scholastik*. Freiburg: Herder, 1980.

Firey, Abigail. *A Contrite Heart: Prosecution and Redemption in the Carolingian Empire*. Leiden: Brill, 2009.

———, ed. *A New History of Penance*. Leiden: Brill, 2008.

Flint, Valerie. *The Rise of Magic in Early Medieval Europe*. Princeton, N.J.: Princeton University Press, 1991.

Fontaine, Jacques, and Charles Pietri, eds. *Le monde latin antique et la bible*. Paris: Beauchesne, 1985.

Fournier, Paul. "Les collections attribuées à Yves de Chartres." *Bibliothèque de l'École de Chartres* 57 (1896): 645–98 and 58 (1897): 26–77, 293–326, 410–44, and 624–76. Reprinted in Fournier, *Mélanges*, 1:451–678.

———. *Mélanges de droit canonique*. Edited by Theo Kölzer. 2 vols. Aalen: Scientia Verlag, 1983.

Fournier, Paul, and Gabriel le Bras. *L'histoire des collections canoniques en Occident: Depuis les Fausses Décrétales jusqu'au Décrét de Gratien*. 2 vols. Paris: Sirey, 1931–32.

Fowler-Magerl, Linda. *Clavis canonum: Selected Canon Law Collections before 1140; Access with Data Processing*. MGH Hilfsmittel 21. Hanover: MGH, 2005.

———. "The Version of the *Collectio Caesaraugustana* in Barcelona, Archivo de la Corona de Aragón, MS San Cugat 63." In *Ritual, Text and Law*, edited by Cushing and Gyug, 269–80.

Fransen, Gérard. "Les questions disputées dans les facultés de droit." In *Les questions disputées et les questions quodlibétiques*, edited by Bazàn et al., 223–77.

Frantzen, Allen J. *The Literature of Penance in Anglo-Saxon England*. New Brunswick, N.J.: Rutgers University Press, 1983.

———. "The Significance of the Frankish Penitentials." *Journal of Ecclesiastical History* 30 (1979): 409–21.

Fuhrmann, Horst. *Einfluß und Verbreitung der pseudoisidorischen Fälschungen*. 3 vols. Schriften der MGH 24. Stuttgart: Hiersemann, 1973–74.

———. "The Pseudo-Isidorian Forgeries." In *Papal Letters in the Early Middle Ages*, edited by Jasper and Fuhrmann, 137–95.

Gaastra, Adriaan H. "Between Liturgy and Canon Law: A Study of Books of Confession and Penance." PhD diss., University of Utrecht, 2007.

———. "Penance and the Law: The Penitential Canons of the *Collection in Nine Books." Early Medieval Europe* 14 (2006): 85–102.

García y García, Antonio. "The Fourth Lateran Council and the Canonists." In *The History of Medieval Canon Law in the Classical Period*, edited by Hartmann and Pennington, 367–78.

Gastaldelli, Ferruccio, ed. *Scritti di letteratura, filologia e teologia medievali*. Spoleto: Centro italiano di studi sull'alto Medioevo, 2000.

———. "La 'Summa sententiarum' di Ottone da Lucca: Conclusione di un dibatto secolare." *Salesianum* 42 (1980): 537–46. Reprinted in *Scritti*, edited by Gastaldelli, 165–74.

Gaudemet, Jean. *L'Église dans l'empire romain (IV*e*–V*e *siècles)*. Histoire du Droit et des Institutions de l'Église en Occident 3. Paris: Sirey, 1958.

———. "La Bible dans les collections canoniques." In *La moyen âge et la Bible*, edited by Riché and Lobrichon, 327–69.

———. "La Bible dans les conciles (IVe–VIIe s.)." In *Le monde latin antique et la bible*, edited by Fontaine and Pietri, 289–310.

———. "La coutume en droit canonique." *RDC* 38 (1988): 224–51.

———. "Le débat sur la confession dans la Distinction I du 'de penitentia' (Décret de Gratien, C.33, q.3)." *ZRG KA* 71 (1985): 52–75.

———. "La doctrine des sources du droit dans le Décret de Gratien." *RDC* 1 (1950): 5–31. Reprinted in Gaudemet, *La formation du droit canonique médiéval*, no. VII.

———. *La formation du droit canonique et gouvernement de l'église de l'antiquité à l'âge classique: Recueil d'articles*. Strasbourg: Presses Universitaires de Strasbourg, 2008.

———. *La formation du droit canonique médiéval*. Variorum Collected Studies Series CS111. London: Variorum, 1980.

Genka, Tatsushi. "Gratians Umgang mit seinen Quellen in der C.15 q.1." In *"Panta rei,"* edited by Condorelli, 2:421–44.

———. "Hierarchie der Texte, Hierarchie der Autoritäten: Zur Hierarchie der Rechtsquellen bei Gratian." *ZRG KA* 95 (2009): 100–127.

———. "Zur textlichen Grundlage der Imputationslehre Gratians." *BMCL* 25 (2002–3): 40–81.

Germovnik, Franciscus. *Index biblicus ad Decretum Gratiani: Secundum editionem Aemilii Friedberg*. Lemont, Ill.: De Andreis Seminary, 1971.

Ghellinck, Joseph de. *Le mouvement théologique du XIIe siècle*. 2nd rev. ed. Bruges: Édition "De Tempel," 1948.

———. "La reviviscence des péchés pardonnés à l'époque de Pierre Lombard et de Gandulphe de Bologne." *Nouvelle revue théologique* 41 (1909): 400–408.

Gilchrist, John. "*Simoniaca haeresis* and the Problem of Orders from Leo IX to Gratian." In *Proceedings of the Second International Congress of Medieval Canon Law*, edited by Kuttner and Ryan, 209–35.

Gillmann, Franz. *Zur Lehre der Scholastik vom Spender der Firmung und des Weihesakraments*. Paderborn: Schöningh, 1920.

———. "Einteilung und System des Gratianischen Dekrets nach den alten Dekretglossatoren bis Johannes Teutonicus einschliesslich." *AKKR* 106 (1926): 472–574.

Giraud, Cédric. "Le recueil de sentences de l'école de Laon *Principium et causa*: Un cas de pluri-attribution." In *Parva pro magnis munera,* edited by Goullet, 245–69.

———. *Per verba magistri: Anselme de Laon et son école au XIIe siècle*. Turnhout: Brepols, 2010.

Golinelli, Paolo, ed. *Sant'Anselmo, Mantova e la lotta per le investiture*. Bologna: Pàtron, 1987.

Goering, Joseph. "The Scholastic Turn (1100–1500): Penitential Theology and Law in the Schools." In *A New History of Penance,* edited by Firey, 219–37.

Goering, Joseph, et al., eds. *Proceedings of the Fourteenth International Congress of Medieval Canon Law*. MIC.C 15. Vatican City: BAV (forthcoming).

Goullet, Monique, ed. *Parva pro magnis munera: Études de littérature tardo-antique et médiévale offertes à François Dolbeau par ses élèves*. Turnhout: Brepols, 2009.

Graf, Fritz. *Magic in the Ancient World*. Translated by Franklin Philip. Cambridge, Mass.: Harvard University Press, 1997.

Grebner, Gundula. "Lay Patronate in Bologna in the First Half of the 12th Century: Regular Canons, Notaries, and the *Decretum*." In *Europa und seine Regionen,* edited by Bauer and Welker, 107–22.

Gujer, Regula. *Concordia discordantium codicum manuscriptorum? Die Textentwicklung von 18 Handschriften anhand der D.16 des Decretum Gratiani*. Cologne: Böhlau, 2004.

Hamilton, Sarah. *The Practice of Penance, 900–1050*. Woodbridge: Royal Historical Society, 2001.

———. "Penance in the Age of Gregorian Reform." In *Retribution, Repentance, and Reconciliation,* edited by Cooper and Gregory, 47–73.

Haring, Nicholas M. "The Interaction Between Canon Law and Sacramental Theology in the Twelfth Century." In *Proceedings of the Fourth International Congress of Medieval Canon Law,* edited by Kuttner, 483–93.

Hartmann, Martina. "The Letter Collection of Abbot Wibald of Stablo and Corvey and the *Decretum Gratiani*." *BMCL* 29 (2011–12): 35–49.

Hartmann, Wilfried, ed. *Bischof Burchard von Worms 1000–1025*. Mainz: Selbstverlag der Gesellschaft für Mittelrheinische Kirchengeschichte, 2000.

Hartmann, Wilfried, and Gerhard Schmitz, eds. *Fortschritt durch Fälschungen? Ursprung, Gestalt und Wirkungen der pseudoisidorischen Fälschungen*. Hanover: Hahn, 2002.

Hartmann, Wilfried, and Kenneth Pennington, eds. *The History of Medieval Canon Law in the Classical Period, 1140–1234: From Gratian to the Decretals of Pope Gregory IX*. Washington, D.C.: The Catholic University of America Press, 2008.

Helmholz, Richard H. *The Spirit of Classical Canon Law*. Athens: University of Georgia Press, 1996.

Helmholz, Richard H., et al., eds. *Grundlagen des Rechts: Festschrift für Peter Landau zum 65. Geburtstag*. Paderborn: Schöningh, 2000.

Hersperger, Patrick. *Kirche, Magie und "Aberglaube": Superstitio in der Kanonistik des 12. und 13. Jahrhunderts*. Cologne: Böhlau, 2009.

Hess, Hamilton. *The Canons of the Council of Sardica, A.D. 343: A Landmark in the Early Development of Canon Law*. Oxford: Oxford University Press, 1958.

———. *The Early Development of Canon Law and the Council of Serdica*. 2nd ed. Oxford: Oxford University Press, 2002.

Hinschius, Paul. *System des katholischen Kirchenrechts mit besonderer Rücksicht auf Deutschland*. 6 vols. Berlin: I. Guttentag, 1869–97; reprinted in Graz: Akademische Druck- u. Verlagsanstalt, 1959.

Hödl, Ludwig. *Die Geschichte der scholastischen Literatur und der Theologie der Schlüsselgewalt*. BGPTM 38.4. Münster: Aschendorff, 1960.

Hoffmann, Hartmut, and Rudolf Pokorny. *Das Dekret des Bischofs Burchard von Worms: Textstufen—Frühe Verbreitung—Vorlagen*. MGH Hilfsmittel 12. Munich: MGH, 1991.

Hofmeister, Philipp. *Die heiligen Öle in der morgen- und abendländischen Kirche: Eine kirchenrechtlich-liturgische Abhandlung*. Würzburg: Augustinus-Verlag, 1948.

Holtzmann, Walther. "Die Benutzung Gratians in der päpstlichen Kanzlei im 12. Jahrhundert." *Studia Gratiana* 1 (1953): 323–49.

Horst, Uwe. *Die Kanonessammlung "Polycarpus" des Gregor von S. Grisogono: Quellen und Tendenzen*. MGH Hilfsmittel 5. Munich: MGH, 1980.

Huizing, Peter. "Doctrina decretistarum de variis speciebus excommunicationis." *Gregorianum* 33 (1952): 499–530.

Jaffé, Philip. *Regesta pontificum romanorum*. 2 vols. Leipzig: Veit, 1885–88; reprinted in Graz: Akademische Druck- u. Verlagsanstalt, 1956.

Jasper, Detlev, and Horst Fuhrmann. *Papal Letters in the Early Middle Ages*. Washington, D.C.: The Catholic University of America Press, 2001.

Johrendt, Jochen, and Harald Müller, eds. *Römisches Zentrum und kirchliche Peripherie: Das universale Papsttum als Bezugspunkt der Kirchen von den Reformpäpsten bis zu Innozenz II*. Berlin: De Gruyter, 2008.

Jong, Mayke de. "Power and Humility in Carolingian Society: The Public Penance of Louis the Pious." *Early Medieval Europe* 1 (1992): 29–52.

———. "Transformations of Penance." In *Rituals of Power*, edited by Theuws and Nelson, 184–224.

———. "What was *Public* about Public Penance? *Paenitentia Publica* and Justice in the Carolingian World." In *La Giustizia nell'alto Medioevo (Secoli IX–XI)*, Settimane di Studio del Centro Italiano di Studi sull'Alto Medioevo 44.2, 863–902. Spoleto: Centro Italiano di Studi sull'Alto Medioevo, 1997.

Kalb, Herbert. *Studien zur Summa Stephans von Tournai: Ein Beitrag zur kanonistischen Wissenschaftsgeschichte des späten 12. Jahrhunderts*. Innsbruck: Wagner, 1983.

———. "Rechtskraft und ihre Durchbrechungen im Spannungsfeld von kanonistischem und theologischem Diskurs (Rufin—Stephan von Tournai—Iohannes Faventinus)." In *Grundlagen des Rechts*, edited by Helmholz et al., 405–19.

Kennedy, V. L. "The Moment of Consecration and the Elevation of the Host." *Mediaeval Studies* 6 (1944): 121–50.

Kerff, Franz. *Der Quadripartitus: Ein Handbuch der karolingischen Kirchenreform.* Sigmaringen: J. Thorbecke, 1982.

———. "*Libri paenitentiales* und kirchliche Strafgerichtsbarkeit bis zum *Decretum Gratiani*: Ein Diskussionsvorschlag." *ZRG KA* 75 (1989): 23–57.

———. "Mittelalterliche Quellen und mittelalterliche Wirklichkeit: Zu den Konsequenzen einer jüngst erschienenen Edition für unser Bild kirchlicher Reformbemühungen." *Rheinische Vierteljahrsblätter* 51 (1987): 275–86.

Kéry, Lotte. *Canonical Collections of the Early Middle Ages (ca. 400–1140): A Bibliographical Guide to the Manuscripts and Literature*. Washington, D.C.: The Catholic University of America Press, 1999.

Klär, Karl-Josef. *Das kirchliche Bußinstitut von den Anfängen bis zum Konzil von Trient*. Frankfurt am Main: Peter Lang, 1990.

Knibbs, Eric. "The Interpolated Hispana and the Origins of Pseudo-Isidore." *ZRG KA* 99 (2013): 1–71.

Körntgen, Ludger. "Canon Law and the Practice of Penance: Burchard of Worms' Penitential." *Early Medieval Europe* 14 (2006): 103–17.

———. "Fortschreibung frühmittelalterlicher Bußpraxis: Burchards 'Liber corrector' und seine Quellen." In *Bischof Burchard*, edited by Hartmann, 199–226.

Kottje, Raymund. *Die Bussbücher Halitgars von Cambrai und des Hrabanus Maurus: Ihre Überlieferung und ihre Quellen*. Berlin: De Gruyter, 1980.

———. "Buße oder Strafe? Zur 'Iustitia' in den 'Libri Paenitentiales.'" In *La giustizia nell'alto medioevo (Secoli V–VIII)*, Settimane di Studio del Centro Italiano di Studi sull'Alto Medioevo 42.1, 443–68. Spoleto: Centro Italiano di Studi sull'Alto Medioevo, 1995.

———. "Busspraxis und Bussritus." In *Segni e riti nella chiesa altomedievale occidentale*, Settimane di Studio del Centro Italiano di Studi sull'Alto Medioevo 33.1, 369–95. Spoleto: Centro Italiano di Studi sull'Alto Medioevo, 1987.

Kretzschmar, Robert. *Alger von Luttichs Traktat "De misericordia et iustitia": Ein kanonistischer Konkordanzversuch aus der Zeit des Investiturstreits; Untersuchungen und Edition*. Quellen und Forschungen zum Recht im Mittelalter 2. Sigmaringen: J. Thorbecke, 1985.

Kuttner, Stephan. "The Father of the Science of Canon Law." *The Jurist* 1 (1941): 2–19.

———. *Gratian and the Schools of Law, 1140–1234*. Variorum Collected Studies Series CS185. 2nd ed. London: Variorum, 1994.

———. *Harmony from Dissonance: An Interpretation of Medieval Canon Law*. Latrobe, Pa.: Archabbey Press, 1960. Reprinted in Kuttner, *History of Ideas and Doctrines of Canon Law*, no. I.

———. *History of Ideas and Doctrines of Canon Law*. Variorum Collected Studies Series CS113. 2nd ed. London: Variorum, 1993.

———, ed. *Proceedings of the Fourth International Congress of Medieval Canon Law*. MIC.C 5. Vatican City: BAV, 1976.

———. *Repertorium der Kanonistik (1140–1234): Prodromus corporis glossarum*. Studi e testi 71. Vatican City: BAV, 1937.

———. "Zur Frage der theologischen Vorlagen Gratians." *ZRG KA* 23 (1934): 243–68. Reprinted in Kuttner, *Gratian and the Schools of Law*, no. III.

Kuttner, Stephan, and Kenneth Pennington, eds. *Proceedings of the Sixth International Congress of Medieval Canon Law.* MIC.C 7. Vatican City: BAV, 1985.

Kuttner, Stephan, and J. Joseph Ryan, eds. *Proceedings of the Second International Congress of Medieval Canon Law.* MIC.C 3. Vatican City: BAV, 1965.

Landau, Peter. "Ehetrennung als Strafe." *ZRG KA* 81 (1995): 148–88.

———. *Die Entstehung des kanonischen Infamiebegriffs von Gratian bis zur Glossa ordinaria.* Cologne: Böhlau, 1966.

———. "Erweiterte Fassungen der Kanonessammlung des Anselm von Lucca aus dem 12. Jahrhundert." In *Sant'Anselmo,* edited by Golinelli, 323–38. Reprinted in Landau, *Kanones und Dekretalen,* 81*–95*, with retractations at 473*.

———. "Gratian and the *Decretum Gratiani.*" In *The History of Medieval Canon Law in the Classical Period,* edited by Hartmann and Pennington, 22–54.

———. "Gratian und die Sententiae Magistri A." In *Aus Archiven und Bibliotheken,* edited by Mordek, 311–26. Reprinted in Landau, *Kanones und Dekretalen,* 161*–76*, with retractations at 474*–75*.

———. *Grundlagen und Geschichte des evangelischen Kirchenrechts und des Staatskirchenrechts.* Tübingen: Mohr Siebeck, 2008.

———. *Kanones und Dekretalen: Beiträge zur Geschichte der Quellen des kanonischen Rechts.* Goldbach: Keip, 1997.

———. "Neue Forschungen zu vorgratianischen Kanonessammlungen und den Quellen des gratianischen Dekrets." *Ius Commune* 11 (1984): 1–29. Reprinted in Landau, *Kanones und Dekretalen,* 177*–205*, with retractations at 475*–77*.

———. "Patristische Texte in den beiden Rezensionen des *Decretum Gratiani.*" *BMCL* 23 (1999): 77–84.

———. "Quellen und Bedeutung des gratianischen Dekrets." *Studia et Documenta Historiae et Iuris* 52 (1986): 218–35. Reprinted in Landau, *Kanones und Dekretalen,* 207*–24*, with retractations at 477*–79*.

———. "Die Rezension C der Sammlung des Anselm von Lucca." *BMCL* 16 (1986): 17–54. Reprinted in Landau, *Kanones und Dekretalen,* 43*–80*, with retractations at 472*.

———. "Traditionen des Kirchenasyls." In *Asyl am heiligen Ort,* edited by Barwig and Bauer, 47–61.

———. "Das Verbot der Wiederholung einer Kirchweihe in der Geschichte des kanonischen Rechts: Ein Beitrag zur Entwicklung des Sakramentenrechts." In *Studia in Honorem eminentissimi Cardinalis Alphonsi M. Stickler,* edited by Castillo Lara, 225–40.

———. "Wandel und Kontinuität im kanonischen Recht bei Gratian." In *Sozialer Wandel im Mittelalter,* edited by Miethke and Schreiner, 215–33.

Landgraf, Artur Michael. *Dogmengeschichte der Frühscholastik.* 4 vols. in 8 parts. Regensburg: Friedrich Pustet, 1952–56.

———. "Die frühscholastische Streitfrage vom Wiederaufleben der Sünden." *Zeitschrift für katholische Theologie* 61 (1937): 509–94.

———. "Grundlagen für ein Verständnis der Busslehre der Früh- und Hochscholastik." *Zeitschrift für katholische Theologie* 51 (1927): 161–93.

———. "Sünde und Trennung von der Kirche in der Frühscholastik." *Scholastik* 5 (1930): 210–47.

———. "Die Vererbung der Sünden der Eltern auf die Kinder nach der Lehre des 12. Jahrhunderts." *Gregorianum* 21 (1940): 203–47.

———. "Werke aus dem Bereich der Summa Sententiarum und Anselms von Laon." *Divus Thomas* 14 (1936): 209–16.

Lange, Hermann. *Römisches Recht im Mittelalter*. 2 vols. Munich: C. H. Beck, 1997.

Larrainzar, Carlos. "El borrador de la 'Concordia' de Graciano: Sankt Gallen, Stiftsbibliothek MS 673 (= Sg)." *Ius Ecclesiae* 11 (1999): 593–666.

———. "Datos sobre la antigüedad del manuscrito Sg: Su redacción de C.27 q.2." In *"Panta rei,"* edited by Condorelli, 3:205–37.

———. "La formación del Decreto de Graciano por etapas." *ZRG KA* 87 (2001): 67–83.

———. "Métodos para el análisis de la formación literaria del Decretum Gratiani: 'etapas' y 'esquemas' de redacción." In *Proceedings of the Thirteenth International Congress of Medieval Canon Law*, edited by Erdö and Szuromi, 85–116.

———. "Notas sobre las introducciones *In prima parte agitur* y *Hoc opus inscribitur*." In *Medieval Church Law*, edited by Müller and Sommar, 134–53.

———. "El resumen de C.37 del *Decretum Gratiani*." In *Mélanges en l'honneur d'Anne Lefebvre-Teillard*, edited by d'Alteroche et al., 639–64.

Larson, Atria A. "Early Stages of Gratian's *Decretum* and the Second Lateran Council." *BMCL* 27 (2007): 21–56.

———. "The Evolution of Gratian's *Tractatus de penitentia*." *BMCL* 26 (2004–5): 59–123.

———. "The Influence of the School of Laon on Gratian: The Usage of the *Glossa ordinaria* and the Anselmian *Sententiae* in *De penitentia* (*Decretum* C.33 Q.3)." *Mediaeval Studies* 72 (2010): 197–244.

———. *Master of Penance: Gratian and the Development of Penitential Thought and Law in the Twelfth Century*. Washington, D.C.: The Catholic University of America Press, 2014.

Lea, Charles Henry. *A History of Auricular Confession and Indulgences in the Latin Church*. 3 vols. Philadelphia: Lea Bros., 1896.

Lefebvre, Charles. *Dictionnaire de droit canonique*, s.v. "Pouvoirs de l'église." Paris: Letouzey, 1935–65.

Lefèvre, Yves. "Le *De conditione angelica et humana* et les *Sententie Anselmi*." *AHDLMA* 34 (1959): 249–75.

Legendre, Pierre. *La pénétration du droit romain dans le droit canonique classique de Gratien à Innocent IV, 1140–1254*. Paris: Jouve, 1964.

Leinz, Anton. *Die Simonie: Eine kanonistische Studie*. Freiburg im Breisgau: Herder, 1902.

Lenherr, Titus. *Die Exkommunikations- und Depositionsgewalt der Häretiker bei Gratian und den Dekretisten bis zur Glossa ordinaria des Johannes Teutonicus*. St. Ottilien: EOS Verlag, 1987.

———. "Die 'Glossa ordinaria' zur Bibel als Quelle von Gratians Dekret: Ein (neuer) Anfang." *BMCL* 24 (2000): 97–129.

———. "Ist die Handschrift 673 der St. Galler Stiftsbibliothek (Sg) der Entwurf zu Gratians *Dekret*?: Versuch einer Antwort aus Beobachtungen an D. 31 und D. 32." http://www.t-j-l.de/Sg-Entw.PDF.

———. "Langsame Annäherung an Gratians Exemplar der 'Moralia in Iob.'" In *Proceedings of the Thirteenth International Congress of Medieval Canon Law*, edited by Erdö and Szuromi, 311–26.

———. "*Reos sanguinis* [*non*] *defendat ecclesia*: Gratian mit einem kurzem Blick erhascht." In *Medieval Church Law*, edited by Müller and Sommar, 71–94.

———. "Die vier Fassungen von C. 3 q. 1 d.p.c. 6 im Decretum Gratiani: Zugleich ein Einblick in die neueste Diskussion um das Werden von Gratians Dekret." *AKKR* 169 (2000): 353–81.

———. "Zur Redaktionsgeschichte von C.23 q.5 in der '1. Rezension' von Gratians Dekret: The Making of a Quaestio." *BMCL* 26 (2004–6): 31–58.

León, Enrique de, and Nicolás Álvarez de las Asturias, eds. *La cultura giuridico-canonica medioevale: Premesse per un dialogo ecumenico*. Milan: Giuffrè, 2003.

Liebs, Detlef. "Roman Vulgar Law in Late Antiquity." In *Aspects of Law in Late Antiquity*, edited by Sirks, 35–53.

Linehan, Peter, ed. *Life, Law, and Letters: Historical Studies in Honour of Antonio García y García*. Studia Gratiana 29. Rome: Libr. Ateneo Salesiano, 1998.

Litewski, Wieslaw. "Les textes procéduraux du droit de Justinien dans le Décret de Gratien." *Studia Gratiana* 9 (1966): 67–109.

Lottin, Odon. *Psychologie et morale aux XIIe et XIIIe siècles* 5: *L'école d'Anselme de Laon et de Guillaume de Champeaux*. Gembloux: Duculot, 1959.

Lubac, Henri de. *Medieval Exegesis*. Translated by Mark Sebanc. 3 vols. Grand Rapids, Mich.: Eerdmans, 1998–2009.

Luca, Luigi de. "L'accettazione popolare della legge canonica nel pensiero di Graziano e dei suoi interpreti." *Studia Gratiana* 3 (1955): 193–276.

Luck, Georg. *Arcana Mundi: Magic and the Occult in the Greek and Roman Worlds; A Collection of Ancient Texts*. 2nd ed. Baltimore, Md.: Johns Hopkins University Press, 2006.

Luscombe, D. E. *The School of Peter Abelard: The Influence of Abelard's Thought in the Early Scholastic Period*. Cambridge: Cambridge University Press, 1969.

Luscombe, David, and Jonathan Riley-Smith, eds. *The New Cambridge Medieval History* 4.2: *c. 1024–c.1198*. Cambridge: Cambridge University Press, 2004.

Lynch, Joseph H. *Simoniacal Entry into Religious Life from 1000 to 1260: A Social, Economic, and Legal Study*. Columbus: Ohio State University Press, 1976.

———. "Spiritual Kinship and Sexual Prohibitions in Early Medieval Europe." In *Proceedings of the Sixth International Congress of Medieval Canon Law*, edited by Kuttner and Pennington, 271–88.

Maas, Pauline. *The Liber sententiarum magistri A.: Its Place amidst the Sentence Collections of the First Half of the Twelfth Century*. Nijmegen: Centrum voor Middeleeuwse Studies, Katholieke Universiteit Nijmegen, 1997.

Macy, Gary. *Theologies of the Eucharist in the Early Scholastic Period: A Study of the Salvific Function of the Sacrament According to Theologians, c. 1080–c. 1220*. Oxford: Oxford University Press, 1984.

Marchetto, Agostino. "Diritto di appello a Roma nelle Decretali Pseudo-Isidoriane." In *Scientia veritatis*, edited by Münsch and Zotzt, 191–206.

———. *Episcopato e Primato pontificio nelle decretali pseudo isidoriane: Ricerca storico-giuridica*. Rome: Pontificia Università Lateranense, 1971.

Matecki, Bernd. *Der Traktat In primis hominibus: Eine theologie- und kirchenrechtsgeschichtliche Untersuchung zu einem Ehetext der Schule von Laon aus dem 12. Jahrhundert*. Adnotationes in Ius Canonicum 20. Frankfurt am Main: Peter Lang, 2001.

May, Georg. "Die Infamie im Decretum Gratiani." *AKKR* 129 (1960): 389–408.

Mayo, Janet. *A History of Ecclesiastical Dress*. New York: Holmes and Meier, 1984.

Mazza, Enrico. *La liturgia della penitenza nella storia: Le grandi tappe*. Bologna: EDB, 2013.

Mazzanti, Giuseppe. "Graziano e Rolando Bandinelli." *Studi di storia del diritto* 2 (1999): 79–103.

McKitterick, Rosamond. *The Frankish Church and the Carolingian Reforms, 789–985*. London: Royal Historical Society, 1977.

———, ed. *The New Cambridge Medieval History* 2: *c. 700–c. 900*. Cambridge: Cambridge University Press, 1995.

Meens, Rob. "The Frequency and Nature of Early Medieval Penance." In *Handling Sin*, edited by Biller and Minnis, 35–61.

———. "Penitentials and the Practice of Penance in the Tenth and Eleventh Centuries." *Early Medieval Europe* 14 (2006): 7–21.

Méhu, Didier, ed. "*Historiae* et *imagines* de la consécration de l'église au moyen âge." In *Mises en scène*, edited by Méhu, 15–48.

———. *Mises en scène et mémoires de la consécration de l'église dans l'occident médiéval*. Collection d'Études Médiévales de Nice 7. Turnhout: Brepols, 2007.

Meier-Welcker, Hans. "Die Simonie im frühen Mittelalter." *Zeitschrift für Kirchengeschichte* 64 (1952–53): 61–93.

Melnikas, Anthony. *The Corpus of the Miniatures in the Manuscripts of Decretum Gratiani*. 3 vols. Studia Gratiana 16–18. Vatican City: Studia Gratiana, 1973–75.

Mews, Constant J. *Abelard and His Legacy*. Aldershot: Ashgate, 2001.

———. "The Council of Sens (1141): Abelard, Bernard, and the Fear of Social Upheaval." *Speculum* 77 (2002): 342–82.

———. "The List of Heresies Imputed to Peter Abelard." *Revue Bénédictine* 95 (1985): 73–110. Reprinted in Mews, *Abelard and His Legacy*, no. IV.

Meyer, Christoph H. F. *Die Distinktionstechnik in der Kanonistik des 12. Jahrhunderts: Ein Beitrag zur Wissenschaftsgeschichte des Hochmittelalters*. Leuven: Leuven University Press, 2000.

Michel, Albert. *Dictionnaire de théologie catholique*, s.v. "Reviviscence des péchés." Paris: Letouzey et Ané, 1908–50.

Miethke, Jürgen, and Klaus Schreiner, eds. *Sozialer Wandel im Mittelalter: Wahrnehmungsformen, Erklärungsmuster, Regelungsmechanismen*. Sigmaringen: J. Thorbecke, 1994.

Mirbt, Carl. *Die Publizistik im Zeitalter Gregors VII*. Leipzig: Hinrichs, 1894.

Montclos, Jean de. *Lanfranc et Bérenger: La controverse eucharistique au XIe siècle*. Leuven: Spicilegium Sacrum Lovaniense, 1971.

Mordek, Hubert, ed. *Aus Archiven und Bibliotheken: Festschrift für Raymund Kottje zum 65. Geburtstag*. Frankfurt am Main: Peter Lang, 1992.

Motta, Giuseppe. "I codici canonistici di Polirone." In *Sant'Anselmo*, edited by Golinelli, 349–74.

———. "I rapporti tra la Collezione canonica di S. Maria Novella e quella in Cinque Libri: Firenze, Bibl. Naz. Conventi Soppressi MS A.4.269 e Bibl. Vaticana, Vat. lat. 1348." *BMCL* 7 (1977): 89–94.

Müller, Wolfgang P., and Mary E. Sommar. *Medieval Church Law and the Origins of the Western Legal Tradition: A Tribute to Kenneth Pennington*. Washington, D.C.: The Catholic University of America Press, 2006.

Munier, Charles. *Les sources patristiques du droit de l'église du VIIIe au XIIIe siècle*. Mulhouse: Salvator, 1957.

Münsch, Oliver, and Thomas Zotz, eds. *Scientia veritatis: Festschrift für Hubert Mordek zum 65. Geburtstag*. Ostfildern: Thorbecke, 2004.

Murauer, Rainer. "Geistliche Gerichtsbarkeit und Rezeption des neuen Rechts im Erzbistum Salzburg im 12. Jahrhundert." In *Römisches Zentrum und kirchliche Peripherie*, edited by Johrendt and Müller, 259–84.

Murray, Alexander. "Confession Before 1215." *Transactions of the Royal Historical Society*, sixth series 3 (1993): 51–81.

Mussen, Anthony, ed. *Boundaries of the Law: Geography, Gender, and Jurisdiction in Medieval and Early Modern Europe*. Aldershot: Ashgate, 2005.

Nardi, Paolo. "Fonti canoniche in una sentenza senese del 1150." In *Life, Law, and Letters*, edited by Linehan, 661–70.

Naz, Raoul. *Dictionnaire de droit canonique*, s.v. "Ordre en droit occidental." Paris: Letouzey, 1935–65.

Nielsen, Lauge Olaf. *Theology and Philosophy in the Twelfth Century: A Study of Gilbert Porreta's Thinking and the Theological Exposition of the Doctrine of the Incarnation During the Period 1130–1180*. Leiden: Brill, 1982.

Noonan, John T. "Gratian Slept Here: The Changing Identity of the Father of the Systematic Study of Canon Law." *Traditio* 35 (1979): 145–72.

Ohst, Martin. *Pflichtbeichte: Untersuchungen zum Bußwesen im Hohen und Späten Mittelalter*. Tübingen: J. C. B. Mohr, 1995.

Pasztór, Edith. "Lotta per le investiture e 'ius belli': La posizione di Anselmo di Lucca." In *Sant'Anselmo*, edited by Golinelli, 405–21.

Patzelt, Erna, ed. *Die karolingische Renaissance*. Graz: Akademische Druck- u. Verlagsanstalt, 1965.

Paxton, Frederick S. "Gratian's Thirteenth Case and the Composition of the *Decretum*." In *Proceedings of the Eleventh International Congress of Medieval Canon Law*, edited by Bellomo and Condorelli, 119–30.

Payer, Pierre J. "The Humanism of the Penitentials and the Continuity of the Penitential Tradition." *Mediaeval Studies* 46 (1984): 340–65.

Pennington, Kenneth. "La Causa 19, Graziano, e lo Ius commune." In *La cultura giuridico-canonica medioevale*, edited by de León and Álvarez de las Asturias, 211–32.

———. "Decretal Collections 1190–1234." In *The History of Medieval Canon Law in the Classical Period*, edited by Hartmann and Pennington, 293–317.

———. "The Decretalists 1190–1234." In *The History of Medieval Canon Law in the Classical Period*, edited by Hartmann and Pennington, 211–45.

———. "Gratian, Causa 19, and the Birth of Canonical Jurisprudence." In *"Panta rei,"* edited by Condorelli, 4:339–55.

Pennington, Kenneth, Stanley Chodorow, and Keith H. Kendall, eds. *Proceedings of the Tenth International Congress of Medieval Canon Law*. MIC.C 11. Vatican City: BAV, 2001.

Peters, Edward. *The Magician, the Witch, and the Law*. Philadelphia: University of Pennsylvania Press, 1978.

Poschmann, Bernhard. *Die abendländische Kirchenbuße im Ausgang des christlichen Altertums*. Munich: J. Kösel and F. Pustet, 1928.

———. *Die abendländische Kirchenbuße im frühen Mittelalter*. Breslau: Müller and Seiffert, 1930.

———. *Handbuch der Dogmengeschichte* 4.3: *Buße und letzte Ölung*. Freiburg: Herder, 1951.

———. *Paenitentia secunda: Die kirchliche Buße im ältesten Christentum bis Cyprian und Origenes; Eine dogmengeschichtliche Untersuchung*. Bonn: P. Hanstein, 1940.

Price, Richard. "Informal Penance in Early Medieval Christendom." In *Retribution, Repentance, and Reconciliation*, edited by Cooper and Gregory, 29–38.

Radding, Charles M., and Francis Newton. *Theology, Rhetoric, and Politics in the Eucharistic Controversy, 1078–1079: Alberic of Monte Cassino against Berengar of Tours*. New York: Columbia University Press, 2003.

Rambaud, Jacqueline. "L'étude des manuscrits du Décret de Gratien conservés en France." *Studia Gratiana* 1 (1953): 119–45.

———. "Le legs de l'ancien droit: Gratien." In *L'âge classique, 1140–1378: Sources et théories du droit*, edited by le Bras et al., 3–129.

Rapp, Claudia. "Spiritual Guarantors at Penance, Baptism, and Ordination in the Late Antique East." In *A New History of Penance*, edited by Firey, 121–48.

Reinhardt, Heinrich J. F. *Die Ehelehre der Schule des Anselm von Laon: Eine theologie- und kirchenrechtsgeschichtliche Untersuchung zu den Ehetexten der frühen Pariser Schule des 12. Jahrhunderts*. BGPTM n.F. 14. Münster: Aschendorff, 1974.

Reynolds, Philip Lyndon. *Marriage in the Western Church: The Christianization of Marriage During the Patristic and Early Medieval Periods*. Leiden: Brill, 1994.

Reynolds, Roger E. *Clerical Orders in the Early Middle Ages: Duties and Ordination*. Variorum Collected Studies Series CS670. Aldershot: Ashgate, 1999.

———. *Clerics in the Early Middle Ages: Hierarchy and Image*. Variorum Collected Studies Series CS669. Aldershot: Ashgate, 1999.

———. *Law and Liturgy in the Latin Church, 5th–12th Centuries*. Variorum Collected Studies Series CS457. Aldershot: Variorum, 1994.

———. "The Organisation, Law, and Liturgy of the Western Church, 700–900." In *The New Cambridge Medieval History* 2, edited by McKitterick, 587–621.

———. "Patristic 'Presbyterianism' in the Early Medieval Theology of Sacred

Orders." *Mediaeval Studies* 45 (1983): 311–42. Reprinted in Reynolds, *Clerics in the Early Middle Ages*, no. V.

———. "The Pseudo-Hieronymian 'De septem ordinibus ecclesiae': Notes on Its Origins, Abridgments, and Use in Early Medieval Canonical Collections." *Revue Bénédictine* 80 (1970): 238–52. Reprinted in Reynolds, *Clerical Orders in the Early Middle Ages*, no. I.

———. "The South-Italian Canon Law *Collection in Five Books* and Its Derivatives: New Evidence on Its Origins, Diffusion, and Use." *Mediaeval Studies* 52 (1990): 278–95. Reprinted in Reynolds, *Law and Liturgy*, no. XIV.

Riché, Pierre, and Guy Lobrichon, eds. *La moyen âge et la Bible*. Paris: Beauchesne, 1984.

Rider, Catherine. "Between Theology and Popular Practice: Medieval Canonists on Magic and Impotence." In *Boundaries of the Law*, edited by Mussen, 53–66.

———. *Magic and Impotence in the Middle Ages*. Oxford: Oxford University Press, 2006.

Rittgers, Ronald K. *The Reformation of the Keys: Confession, Conscience, and Authority in Sixteenth-Century Germany*. Cambridge, Mass.: Harvard University Press, 2004.

Rivera Damas, Arturo. *Pensamiento político de Hostiensis: Estudio jurídico—histórico sobre las relaciones entre el Sacerdocio y el Imperio en los escritos de Enrique de Susa*. Zurich: Pas-Verlag, 1964.

Rives, J. B. "Magic in Roman Law: The Reconstruction of a Crime." *Classical Antiquity* 22 (2003): 313–39.

Rolker, Christof. *Canon Law and the Letters of Ivo of Chartres*. Cambridge: Cambridge University Press, 2010.

———. "The Earliest Work of Ivo of Chartres: The Case of Ivo's Eucharist Florilegium and the Canon Law Collections Attributed to Him." *ZRG KA* 124 (2007): 109–27.

Rosemann, Philipp W. *Peter Lombard*. Oxford: Oxford University Press, 2004.

Russell, Jeffrey Burton. *Witchcraft in the Middle Ages*. Ithaca, N.Y.: Cornell University Press, 1972.

Russo, François. "Pénitence et excommunication: Étude historique sur les rapports entre la théologie et le droit canonique dans le domaine pénitentiel du IXe au XIIIe siècle." *Recherches de science religieuse* 33 (1946): 257–79 and 431–51.

Ryan, John Joseph. *The Separation of "Ordo" and "Iurisdictio" in Its Structural-Doctrinal Development and Ecclesiological Significance: A Dogmatic-Historical Contribution towards the Renewal of Canon Law*. PhD diss., Universität Münster, 1972.

Rybolt, John E. "Biblical Hermeneutics of Magister Gratian: An Investigation of Scripture and Canon Law in the Twelfth Century." PhD diss., DePaul University, 1978.

Ryder, R. A. *Simony: An Historical Synopsis and Commentary*. Washington, D.C.: The Catholic University of America Press, 1931.

Salmon, Pierre. *Étude sur les insignes du pontife dans le rit romain: Histoire et liturgie*. Rome: Officium Libri Catholici, 1955.

Saltet, Louis. *Les réordinations: Étude sur le sacrement de l'ordre*. Paris: V. Lecoffre, 1907.

Saranyana, Josep-Ignasi, and Eloy Tejero, eds. *Hispania Christiana: Estudios en honor del Prof. Dr. José Orlandis Rovira en su septuagesimo aniversario*. Pamplona: Ediciones Universidad de Navarra, 1988.

Schiepek, Hubert. *Der Sonntag und kirchlich gebotene Feiertage nach kirchlichem und weltlichem Recht*. Adnotationes in Ius Canonicum 27. Frankfurt am Main: Peter Lang, 2003.

Schoenig, Steven A. "The Papacy and the Use and Understanding of the Pallium from the Carolingians to the Early Twelfth Century." PhD diss., Columbia University, 2009.

Siebold, Martin. *Das Asylrecht der römischen Kirche mit besonderer Berücksichtigung seiner Entwicklung auf germanischen Boden*. Münster: Helios-Verlag, 1930.

Sirks, A. I. B., ed. *Aspects of Law in Late Antiquity: Dedicated to A.M. Honoré on the Occasion of the Sixtieth Year of His Teaching in Oxford*. Oxford: All Souls College, 2008.

Smalley, Beryl. *The Study of the Bible in the Middle Ages*. 3rd rev. ed. Oxford: Blackwell, 1983.

Smith, Lesley. *The "Glossa ordinaria": The Making of a Medieval Biblical Commentary*. Leiden: Brill, 2009.

Sohm, Rudolph. *Das altkatholische Kirchenrecht und das Dekret Gratians*. Munich: Duncker and Humblot, 1918.

Somerville, Robert. *Pope Urban II's Council of Piacenza*. Oxford: Oxford University Press, 2011.

Somerville, Robert, and Bruce C. Brasington, eds. and trans. *Prefaces to Canon Law Books in Latin Christianity: Selected Translations, 500–1245*. New Haven, Conn.: Yale University Press, 1998.

Sommar, Mary E. "Gratian's Causa VII and the Multiple Recension Theories." *BMCL* 24 (2000–2001): 78–96.

Southern, R. W. *Scholastic Humanism and the Unification of Europe*. 2 vols. Oxford: Blackwell, 1995–2001.

Stegmüller, Friedrich. "*Sententiae Berolinenses*: Eine neugefundene Sentenzensammlung aus der Schule des Anselm von Laon." *RTAM* 11 (1939): 33–61.

Stickler, Alfons M. *Historia iuris canonici latini* 1: *Historia fontium*. Turin: Libraria Pontif. Athenaei Salesiani, 1950.

Stroll, Mary. *The Jewish Pope: Ideology and Politics in the Papal Schism of 1130*. Leiden: Brill, 1987.

Stutz, Ulrich. Review of Sohm, *Das altkatholische Kirchenrecht*. *ZRG KA* 8 (1918): 238–46.

Tarín, Luis Pablo. "An secularibus litteris oporteat eos esse eruditos? El texto de D.37 en las etapas antiguas del Decreto de Graciano." In *La cultura giuridico-canonica medioevale*, edited by de León and Álvarez de las Asturias, 469–511.

———. *Graciano de Bolonia y la literatura latina: La distinción treinta y siete del Decreto*. Madrid: Fundación Pastor, 2008.

Tatarczuk, Vincent. *Infamy of Law: A Historical Synopsis and Commentary*. Washington, D.C.: The Catholic University of America Press, 1954.

Teetaert, Amédée. *La confession aux laïques dans l'église latine depuis le VIIIe jusqu'au XIVe siècle: Étude de théologie positive*. Paris: J. Gabalda, 1926.

Tejero, Eloy. "'Ratio' y jerarquía de fuentes canónicas en la Caesaraugustana." In *Hispania Christiana*, edited by Saranyana and Tejero, 303–22.

Thaner, Friedrich. *Abälard und das canonische Recht: Die Persönlichkeit in der Eheschliessung; Zwei Festreden*. Graz: Leuschner and Lubensky, 1900.

Theuws, Frans, and Janet L. Nelson, eds. *Rituals of Power: From Late Antiquity to the Early Middle Ages*. Leiden: Brill, 2000.

Tierney, Brian. *Origins of Papal Infallibility 1150–1350: A Study on the Concepts of Infallibility, Sovereignty and Tradition in the Middle Ages*. Leiden: Brill, 1972.

Uhalde, Kevin. "Juridical Administration in the Church and Pastoral Care in Late Antiquity." In *A New History of Penance*, edited by Firey, 97–120.

Van den Eynde, Damien. "Les définitions des sacrements pendant la première période de la théologie scolastique (1050–1235)." *Antonianum* 24 (1949): 183–228 and 439–88.

Van Elswijk, H. C. *Gilbert Porreta: Sa vie, son oeuvre, sa pensée*. Leiden: Spicilegium Sacrum Lovaniense, 1966.

Van Engen, John. "Observations on 'De consecratione.'" In *Proceedings of the Sixth International Congress of Medieval Canon Law*, edited by Kuttner and Pennington, 309–20.

Van Hove, Alphonse. *Commentarium Lovaniense in codicem iuris canonici* 1: *Prolegomena: Editio altera auctior et emendatior*. Rome: H. Dessain, 1945.

Vetulani, Adam. "Encore un mot sur le droit romain dans le *Décret* de Gratien." *Apollinarius* 21 (1948): 129–34. Reprinted in Vetulani, *Sur Gratien et les décrétales*, no. IV.

———. "Gratien et le droit romain." *Revue historique de droit français et étranger*, ser. 4, 24/25 (1946/1947): 11–48. Reprinted in Vetulani, *Sur Gratien et les décrétales*, no. III.

———. *Sur Gratien et les décrétales*. Edited by Wacław Uruszczak. Variorum Collected Studies Series CS308. Aldershot: Variorum, 1990.

Viejo-Ximénez, José. "El derecho romano 'nuevo' en el Decreto de Graciano." *ZRG KA* 88 (2002): 1–19.

———. "Les étapes de l'incorporation des textes romains dans le Décret de Gratien." *RDC* 51 (2001): 251–60.

———. "La ricezione del diritto romano nel diritto canonico." In *La cultura giuridico-canonica medioevale*, edited by de León and Álvarez de las Asturias, 157–209.

———. "La versión original de C.29 del Decreto de Graciano." *Ius ecclesiae* 11 (1998): 149–85.

Vogel, Cyrille. *La discipline pénitentielle en Gaule: Des origines à la fin du VIIe siècle*. Paris: Letouzey et Ané, 1952.

———. *Introduction aux sources de l'histoire du culte chrétien au moyen âge*. Rev. ed. Spoleto: Centro italiano di studi sull'alto Medioevo, 1975.

———. *Les "Libri paenitentiales."* Typologie des Sources du Moyen Âge Occidental 27. Turnhout: Brepols, 1985.

———. *Le pécheur et la pénitence au Moyen Âge*. Paris: Éditions du Cerf, 1969.

———. *Le pécheur et la pénitence dans l'église ancienne*. Paris: Éditions du Cerf, 1966.

———. "La reforme cultuelle sous Pépin le Bréf et sous Charlemagne (deuxième moitié du VIIIe siècle et premier quart du IXe siècle)." In *Die karolingische Renaissance*, edited by Patzelt, 173–242.

Vogt, Helle, and Mia Münster-Swendsen, eds. *Law and Learning in the Middle Ages: Proceedings of the Second Carlsberg Academy Conference on Medieval Legal History 2005*. Copenhagen: DJØF, 2006.

Vorgrimmler, Herbert. *Handbuch der Dogmengeschichte* 4.3: *Buße und Krankensalbung*. Freiburg: Herder, 1978.

Wagner, Karen Teresa. "*De vera et falsa penitentia*: An Edition and Study." PhD diss., University of Toronto, 1995.

Wasserschleben, Friedrich Wilhelm. *Die Bußordnungen der abendländischen Kirche*. Halle, 1851.

Weber, N. A. *A History of Simony in the Christian Church to 814*. Baltimore, Md.: J. H. Furst, 1909.

Wei, John C. "The *Collectio sancte Genoveve* and Peter Abaelard's *Sic et non*." *ZRG KA* 94 (2008): 21–37.

———. "The 'Extravagantes' in the Decretist *Summa 'Reverentia sacrorum canonum.'*" *BMCL* 29 (2011–12): 169–82.

———. "Gratian and the School of Laon." *Traditio* 64 (2009): 279–322.

———. "The Later Development of Gratian's *Decretum*." In *Proceedings of the Fourteenth International Congress of Medieval Canon Law* (forthcoming).

———. "Law and Religion in Gratian's *Decretum*." PhD diss., Yale University, 2008.

———. "Penitential Theology in Gratian's *Decretum*: Critique and Criticism of the Treatise *Baptizato homine*." *ZRG KA* 95 (2008): 78–100.

———. "A Reconsideration of St. Gall, Stiftsbibliothek 673 (Sg) in Light of the Sources of Distinctions 5–7 of the *De penitentia*." *BMCL* 27 (2007): 141–80.

———. "The Sentence Collection *Deus non habet initium uel terminum* and Its Reworking, *Deus itaque summe atque ineffabiliter bonus*." *Mediaeval Studies* 73 (2011): 1–118.

———. "A Twelfth-Century Treatise on Charity: The Tract 'Vt autem hoc euidenter' of the Sentence Collection *Deus itaque summe atque ineffabiliter bonus*." *Mediaeval Studies* 74 (2012): 1–50.

Weigand, Rudolf. "Causa 25 des Dekrets und die Arbeitsweise Gratians." In *Grundlagen des Rechts*, edited by Helmholz et al., 277–90.

———. "Die Dekretabbreviatio 'Quoniam egestas' und ihre Glossen." In *Fides et ius*, edited by Aymans, 249–65.

———. "The Development of the *Glossa ordinaria* to the *Decretum*." In *The History of Medieval Canon Law in the Classical Period*, edited by Hartmann and Pennington, 55–97.

———. "Frühe Kanonisten und ihre Karriere in der Kirche." *ZRG KA* 76 (1990): 135–55.

———. *Die Glossen zum Dekret Gratians: Studien zu den frühen Glossen und Glos-*

senkompositionen. Studia Gratiana 25–26. Rome: Libreria Ateneo Salesiano, 1991.

———. *Die Naturrechtslehre der Legisten und Dekretisten von Irnerius bis Accursius und von Gratian bis Johannes Teutonicus*. Münchener theologische Studien, 3. Kanonistische Abteilung 26. Munich: Hueber, 1967.

———. "Versuch einer neuen, differenzierten Liste der Paleae und Dubletten im Dekret Gratians." *BMCL* 23 (1999): 114–28.

Weisweiler, Heinrich. "Die Arbeitsweise der sogenannten *Sententiae Anselmi*: Ein Beitrag zum Entstehen der systematischen Werke der Theologie." *Scholastik* 34 (1959): 190–232.

———. *Das Schrifttum der Schule Anselms von Laon und Wilhelms von Champeaux in deutschen Bibliotheken*. BGPTM 33.1–2. Münster i. W.: Aschendorff, 1936.

Weitzel, Joseph. *Begriff und Erscheinungsformen der Simonie bei Gratian und den Dekretisten*. Munich: M. Hueber, 1967.

Werckmeister, Jean. "Les deux versions du *De matrimonio* de Gratien." *RDC* 48 (1998): 301–16.

———. "Le manuscrit 673 de Saint-Gall: Un Décret de Gratien primitif?" *RDC* 60 (2010): 155–70.

———. "The Reception of the Church Fathers in Canon Law." In *The Reception of the Church Fathers in the West* 1, edited by Backus, 51–81.

Wielockx, Robert. "La sentence *de caritate* et la discussion scolastique sur l'amour." *Ephemerides Theologicae Lovanienses* 58 (1982): 50–86, 334–56 and 59 (1983): 26–45.

Winroth, Anders. "Critical Notes on the Text of Gratian's *Decretum* 1." https://sites.google.com/a/yale.edu/decretumgratiani/critical-notes-1.

———. "Critical Notes on the Text of Gratian's *Decretum* 2." https://sites.google.com/a/yale.edu/decretumgratiani/home/critical-notes-2.

———. "Innocent II, Gratian, and Abbé Migne." *BMCL* 28 (2008): 145–51.

———. "The Making of Gratian's *Decretum*." PhD diss., Columbia University, 1996.

———. *The Making of Gratian's Decretum*. Cambridge: Cambridge University Press, 2000.

———. "Neither Slave Nor Free: Theology and Law in Gratian's Thoughts on the Definition of Marriage." In *Medieval Church Law*, edited by Müller and Sommar, 153–71.

———. "Recent Work on the Making of Gratian's *Decretum*." *BMCL* 26 (2004–6): 1–29.

———. "Roman Law in Gratian and the *Panormia*." In *Bishops, Texts and the Use of Canon Law Around 1100*, edited by Brasington and Cushing, 183–90.

———. "The Teaching of Law in the Twelfth Century." In *Law and Learning in the Middle Ages*, edited by Vogt and Münster-Swendsen, 41–55.

———. "Where Gratian Slept: The Life and Death of the Father of Canon Law." *ZRG KA* 130 (2013): 105–28.

Winroth, Anders, and John C. Wei, eds. *The Cambridge History of Medieval Canon Law* (forthcoming).

Wojtyła, Karol. "Le traité 'De penitencia' de Gratien dans l'abrégé de Gdansk." *Studia Gratiana* 7 (1959): 357–90.

Wolter, Udo. "Die 'consuetudo' im kanonischen Recht bis zum Ende des 13. Jahrhunderts." In *Gewohnheitsrecht und Rechtsgewohnheiten im Mittelalter*, edited by Dilcher et al., 87–116.

Yarz, Fernando. *El Obispo en la organización eclesiástica de las Decretales pseudo-isidorianas*. Pamplona: Universidad de Navarra, 1985.

Zechiel-Eckes, Klaus. "Auf Pseudoisidors Spur, oder: Versuch einen dichten Schleier zu lüften." In *Fortschritt durch Fälschungen?*, edited by Hartmann and Schmitz, 1–28.

———. "Ein Blick in Pseudoisidors Werkstatt: Studien zum Entstehungsprozeß der Falschen Dekretalen mit einem exemplarischen editorischen Anhang." *Francia* 28 (2001): 37–90.

———. "Verecundus oder Pseudoisidor? Zur Genese der Excerptiones de gestis Chalcedonensis concilii." *Deutsches Archiv* 56 (2000): 413–46.

Zeliauskas, Josephus. *De excommunicatione vitiata apud glossatores (1140–1350)*. Zurich: Pas-Verlag, 1967.

Zirkel, Adam. *"Executio potestatis": Zur Lehre Gratians von der geistlichen Gewalt*. Münchener theologische Studien, 3. Kanonistische Abteilung 33. St. Ottilien: Eos Verlag, 1975.

Index of Citations to the *Decretum Gratiani*

General Index

Also in the Studies in Medieval and Early Modern Canon Law series

Kenneth Pennington, General Editor

Liberty and Law: The Idea of Permissive Natural Law, 1100–1800
Brian Tierney

Gratian and the Development of Penitential Thought and Law in the Twelfth Century
Atria A. Larson

Marriage on Trial: Late Medieval German Couples at the Papal Court
Ludwig Schmugge
Translated by Atria A. Larson

Medieval Public Justice
Massimo Vallerani
Translated by Sarah Rubin Blanshei

A Sacred Kingdom: Bishops and the Rise of Frankish Kingship, 300–850
Michael Edward Moore

A Sip from the "Well of Grace": Medieval Texts from the Apostolic Penitentiary
Kirsi Salonen and Ludwig Schmugge

"A Pernicious Sort of Woman": Quasi-Religious Women and Canon Lawyers in the Later Middle Ages
Elizabeth Makowski

Canon Law and Cloistered Women: Periculoso *and Its Commentators, 1298–1545*
Elizabeth Makowski

The Common Legal Past of Europe, 1000–1800
Manlio Bellomo

Huguccio: The Life, Works, and Thought of a Twelfth-Century Jurist
Wolfgang P. Müller

The Treatise on Laws (Decretum DD. 1–20) with the Ordinary Gloss
Gratian
Translated by Augustine Thompson and J. Gordley

Lightning Source UK Ltd.
Milton Keynes UK
UKHW011946080822
407014UK00002B/476